T0369195

EIGHTEENTH CENTURY ENGLAND

History. Literature. Theatre. Architecture. Art. Music.

EIGHTEENTH CENTURY ENGLAND

History. Literature. Theatre. Architecture. Art. Music.

A CULTURAL APPROACH

Earl A. Reitan
Professor Emeritus
Illinois State University

iUniverse, Inc.
New York   Bloomington

EIGHTEENTH-CENTURY ENGLAND
History, Literature, Theatre, Architecture, Art, Music

Copyright © 2009 by Earl A. Reitan

All rights reserved. No part of this book may be used or reproduced by any means, graphic, electronic, or mechanical, including photocopying, recording, taping or by any information storage retrieval system without the written permission of the publisher except in the case of brief quotations embodied in critical articles and reviews.

iUniverse books may be ordered through booksellers or by contacting:

iUniverse
1663 Liberty Drive
Bloomington, IN 47403
www.iuniverse.com
1-800-Authors (1-800-288-4677)

Because of the dynamic nature of the Internet, any Web addresses or links contained in this book may have changed since publication and may no longer be valid. The views expressed in this work are solely those of the author and do not necessarily reflect the views of the publisher, and the publisher hereby disclaims any responsibility for them.

ISBN: 978-1-4401-2666-6 (pbk)
ISBN: 978-1-4401-2667-3 (ebk)

Printed in the United States of America

iUniverse rev. date: 2/12/2009

Cover: Christ Church, Spitalfields. Nicholas Hawksmoor

Contents

Preface xi

Ch. 1. The Background of Eighteenth-Century English Culture 1
    The States of Western Europe 1
    The Medieval Church .3
    The Renaissance and Humanism 4
    The Reformation 5
    The Explorations 8
    The Stuart Monarchy in England 9

Ch. 2. Monarchy and Conflict in Restoration England 13
    The Restoration Settlement 13
    The Royal Court and Restoration Culture 15
    The Economic and Social Foundations 18
    The Social Structure 20
    London, Westminster 22
    The Church and Dissent 24
    John Bunyan and the Puritan Message 26
    The Crisis of the Reign of Charles II 28
    A New Faith: Science and The Royal Society 30

Ch. 3. New Directions in Literature, Theatre, and the Arts 36
    John Dryden and Classicism in Literature 36
    The Quarrel Between the Ancients and the Moderns. . . 39
    The Restoration Theatre 40
    Aphra Behn 46
    Classicism and Baroque in Architecture 48
    Christopher Wren 50
    Painting 54
    Baroque Music 56
    Baroque Opera 56
    The Violin 57
    Baroque Music in England 59

Ch. 4. Politics and Ideas in the Revolutionary Age 62
    "The Glorious Revolution of 1688-89" 62
    The Reign of William and Mary 67
    Queen Anne and the War of the Spanish Succession . . . 69
    Scotland and the Act of Union. 69
    Partisan Politics in the Reign of Queen Anne 71
    The Peace and the Succession 72
    Political Journalism in the Reign of Queen Anne. 74
    The Hanoverian Succession 77
    The Rise of the Writer 80
    Addison and Steele and the Essay Journal 83
    The Female Tatler 86

Ch. 5. Philosophy, Manners, Theatre, and the Arts. 87
    John Locke: From Humanism to Empiricism 88
    Lord Shaftesbury: The Philosopher and the Gentleman . . 91
    Two Emancipated Women. 92
    The Theatre 93
    Theatre Music 98
    Architecture 100
    Painting 104
    Music 105

Ch. 6. Politics and Culture in Hanoverian England, 1714-1754 . 107
    The Whig Supremacy 108
    The Press and the Rise of Opposition 109
    Foreign Policy and the Fall of Walpole, "The '45" 112
    The Economy: Defoe's Tour 116
    Scotland 119
    Ireland 120
    Elite Society 122
    Whig Architecture 125
    The Landscaping of the Great House. 130
    Rococo. 132
    The Furnishings of the Great House 133
    Sculpture. 134
    Masters of Gentility: Chesterfield, Nash 136

Ch. 7. Religion and Philosophy 139
    The Church of England 139
    The Architecture of the Church: Gibbs. 143
    The Music of the Church 144
    Dissent, Catholics, Jews 145
    Methodism. 148
    Philosophy 151

Ch. 8. English Culture in the Literary Marketplace 154
    The Development of Print Culture. 154
    Alexander Pope. 157
    Jonathan Swift 162
    The Beggar's Opera 165
    Lady Mary Wortley Montagu 167
    The Poetry of Nature. 169
    Thomas Gray. 170
    Allan Ramsay and Scottish Folklore 171
    The Poems of Ossian 172
    The Gentleman's Magazine. 173

Ch. 9. The Pleasures of the Imagination in a Commercial Society 176
    Daniel Defoe. 176
    Women Writers and the Novel, ... 181
    Samuel Richardson 183
    Henry Fielding. 186
    Sarah Fielding 191

Ch. 10. Theatre and the Arts in Georgian England. 192
    The Theatre 192
    Painting 196
    William Hogarth. 198
    Industry and Idleness 199
    Music: Handel, Arne. 214

Ch. 11. London 219
    The City 219
    Westminster 220
    Defoe's Tour 223
    Social Problems of London 224

Philanthropy 227
The First Modern Metropolis 228

Ch. 12. English Culture at Mid-Century. 230
The Seven Years War (1756-63) 230
The Accession of King George III 233
The Writer and the Bookseller/Publisher 235
The Novel at Mid-Century. 236
Women Writers 241
Oliver Goldsmith 242
The Age of Garrick 244
Samuel Johnson 248

Ch. 13. The Culture of Knowledge in Georgian England 251
The Professions. 251
The Law 252
Medicine. 254
The Inquiring Gentleman 257
The Vision of the World 261
Cartography 264

Ch. 14. Revolution in the Empire and in the Mind 267
George III and the Politicians 267
The King and the Colonies. 270
War in the Colonies and Crisis at Home 272
"Economical Reform" and "The Influence of the Crown" 274
William Pitt the Younger. 275
The Enlightenment 276
The Enlightenment in Scotland 277
The Enlightenment and History 278
Adam Smith and the Foundation of Classical Economics 283
Edward Gibbon and the Decline of the Roman Empire . 285
The Dissemination of Enlightened Ideas 289

Ch. 15. English Institutions and Culture in an Age of Change, 1784-92 . . 290
Economic Growth 291
The Church of England 296
Dissent, Methodism, Catholicism 299
The Slave Trade 301

The Spirit of "Improvement". 303
The Law, Prisons 306
Mrs. Elizabeth Montagu and the Bluestockings 308
Scotland 309
Ireland 310

Ch. 16. A Conservative Culture at a Time of Change 311
The Debate over the French Revolution 312
The New Toryism 316
Sir William Blackstone. 316
Samuel Johnson 318
James Boswell 321
The Theatre of Richard Brinsley Sheridan 322
Classicism and "Sensibility" in Painting 326
Tradition and Innovation in Architecture 337
Robert Adam. 340
Sculpture. 343
From Baroque to Classicism in Music 343
Frances Burney 347
Horace Walpole 349

Summation 352

SUGGESTIONS FOR FURTHER READING. 355
History. 355
Intellectual and Cultural History. 358
Historical Biographies 358
English Literature 359
Literary Biographies 360
Theatre. 363
Painting, Architecture, Sculpture. 365
Music 368

INDEX OF INDIVIDUALS 371

ABOUT THE AUTHOR 385

Preface

Eighteenth-century England is often viewed as a stable plain between the golden peaks of Elizabethan-Jacobean England and the massive ranges of Romanticism and the Victorian Age. Nothing could be further from the truth. In the long eighteenth century (1660-1793), England changed from a quarrelsome island country on the periphery of European civilization to a world power. The purpose of this book is to identify and appreciate the cultural achievements of the English people in this remarkable century.

Eighteenth Century England—A Cultural Approach is an interdisciplinary introduction to major cultural developments and figures in eighteenth-century English history, philosophy, religion, literature, theatre, architecture, painting and music, with attention to the economic and social foundations of English culture. The book provides a broad background for readers with a general interest in the period, or in one or more of the specific disciplines with which the book deals.

SUGGESTIONS FOR FURTHER READING notes books that will provide additional information about the subjects included in this book. The reader who wishes to pursue further the works of a particular artist or architect is referred to the many profusely illustrated books listed. Representative works of most major composer are available on radio, television, or compact discs.

The name commonly used in the eighteenth-century for the nation was England, and that is the name that is used throughout t this book. Authors and works from Scotland or Ireland are identified as such. As much as possible, I have avoided specialized terminology specific to one discipline and have used everyday language throughout.

Eighteenth Century England—A Cultural Approach deals with culture within its historical and social context. The public sphere of eighteenth-century England was greatly enlarged by freedom—freedom of speech and the press and freedom of religion. The growing sense of English national identity was influenced by parliamentary debates, electoral politics, political publications and meetings, petitions, coffeehouse discussions, widely-circulated newspapers and periodicals, and civic and national celebrations. Much serious literature was, to some degree, political, and spoke in a public voice.

England also had a rich and diverse civil society independent of the state, the Church, and local authorities. Genteel society mingled in assembly halls, concerts, theatrical performances, and coffeehouses. The rise of a commercial society with shops, circulating libraries, tearooms, and other public gathering places for women brought women out of the shadows of domesticity into the public realm. The associations fostered by a complex civil society shaped the English sense of identity and exerted a powerful influenced on the development of all aspects of English culture.

Historical processes rarely conform to the calendar. For that reason, scholars take liberties with the word "century" and expand or contract the calendar to fit logical divisions of the material. The term "eighteenth-century" is a good example. The later seventeenth century beginning in 1660 is commonly considered part of the long eighteenth-century because many of the characteristic features of eighteenth-century English institutions and culture emerged at that time. By the end of the eighteenth century powerful new forces—the French Revolution, Industrialism, and Romanticism—had emerged, and led to a new period in English culture.

I am indebted to my colleagues at Illinois State University—Bob Duncan, Ralph Bellas, and Dick Dammers (English), John Kirk (Theatre), Doug Hartley (Art), and Herb Sanders (Music)—whose learning and inspiration led me to think that I could and should write this books.

Earl A. Reitan

Ch. 1. The Background of
Eighteenth-Century English Culture

Since Roman times, England has been part of European culture, although its island location, mix of populations, and historical development meant that England differed significantly from the peoples of the continent. Eighteenth-century England was shaped in important ways by medieval Europe, the Renaissance, the Reformation, the development of the European states, and the emergence of classicism in literature, art, architecture, and music. Those influences were received and incorporated into English culture in a distinctively English manner.

The States of Western Europe

One of the important features of early modern Europe was the development of a distinctive political form—the state. The state is the political dimension of an organized community and claims a monopoly of law and force, although these may be diffused through a variety of subordinate bodies. The western European states that emerged in the sixteenth and seventeenth centuries were dynastic states, comprised of territories ruled by one person whose authority was inherited on the basis of family claims. In the seventeenth century the most important dynasties were the Spanish Hapsburgs, the Austrian Hapsburgs, the Bourbons of France, and the Stuart rulers of the British Isles. These dynastic states were comprised of clusters of territories, sometimes widely scattered, and with different languages and laws. France came closest to geographical compactness. The Stuarts ruled three separate kingdoms—England, Scotland, and Ireland.

The authority of rulers was bolstered by widely-accepted political doctrines, which held that the ruler received his power from God (divine right), that the authority of the ruler was transmitted by inheritance (hereditary succession), and that the ultimate power in the state was vested in the ruler (royal sovereignty). The states of Europe were built by establishing the authority of kingship over the nobility, the Church, the provinces, and the towns. Sometimes it was necessary for kings to defeat the nobles in battle and destroy their private armies and castles. More often, the nobility became partners with the king, holding high offices at the Royal Court and in the army, the navy, the courts of law, and the Church. Each of these states developed a court culture that was intended to add prestige to the monarchy, inspire loyalty among the aristocracy and clergy, and impress the people and fellow monarchs. The various provinces and towns that comprised the state maintained their own popular culture, but the court culture exerted an important influence upon them.

Kings also found ways to control the earthly powers of the Church. During the turmoil of the Reformation it seemed essential to maintain uniformity of religion, and in Protestant states the religion was determined by the ruler. In Catholic countries, the political relations of the Church and the ruler were usually confirmed by an agreement (Concordat) with the Pope.

In the latter half of the seventeenth century, France under Louis XIV, who assumed personal rule in 1661 at the age of twenty-two, became the model of a strong, powerful state. The prosperity of France produced a kingly income, which Louis XIV used to conduct a far-flung foreign policy, maintain a powerful standing army, and build a splendid palace at Versailles, a few miles outside of Paris. The "Sun King" drew the great nobility into his orbit, seducing them with offices, military commands, pensions, honors, and life at the Royal Court. His chief minister, Jean-Baptiste Colbert, an advocate of the economic policy known as mercantilism, worked to extend French trade, encourage agriculture, improve transportation with roads, bridges, and canals, and establish new industries. Although he quarreled with the Pope, Louis XIV considered himself a loyal Catholic. When Louis XIV died in 1715 the political dominance of France was waning, but the French language and culture set the standard for the rest of Europe.

An exception to the monarchical states of Europe was the United Netherlands (the Dutch Republic). After a long struggle, the Dutch overthrew Spanish rule and established themselves as a loose confederation of seven provinces dominated by Holland, the largest and most prosperous province. The Dutch flourished in an atmosphere of economic freedom, open intellectual inquiry, religious toleration, and cultural diversity. They did not have a king. In time of war they chose a stadholder/captain-general to lead their armies until the emergency passed. This office was invariably held by the family of Orange, which adopted a quasi-regal lifestyle and often quarreled with the merchants of Holland, who controlled the Estates General (Parliament).

In the seventeenth century, the Dutch were the principal commercial and maritime power of Europe. They developed flourishing industries and a prosperous agriculture. Their wealthy burghers built splendid civic buildings and solid houses, often connected to the shop or warehouse. They decorated the walls of their homes with dignified portraits and exquisite landscapes. They produced a major artist in Rembrandt von Rijn.

The Medieval Church

European culture grew out of the medieval Church, which had originated within the Roman Empire and continued the heritage of Christianity and the Latin culture of ancient Rome. The Bishop of Rome (the Pope), as successor to St. Peter, was recognized as head of the Church. The Church was hierarchical (episcopal), in that power descended from the Pope to the archbishops to the bishops and finally to the parish priests. The language of the Church was Latin. The medieval cathedral was a magnificent architectural achievement, and was ornamented with stained glass windows and statues of the saints. Sculptured memorial tombs were part of the cathedral or the parish church. Devotional paintings of Jesus, Mary, and the apostles brought the message of the Bible to illiterate worshippers. Choral music was an important part of worship. Medieval music was based on polyphony, which means an inter-weaving of distinct musical parts in such a way as to produce a pleasing sound.

An important part of the Church was the monasteries, where men and women who had abandoned the life of the world, served God through disciplined living, prayer, charity, and scholarship. By the later Middle Ages the monasteries were declining as a cultural factor, but they had played an important cultural role by preserving the learning of antiquity. Every bishop maintained a school, some of which developed into universities that trained scholars for careers in Theology, Civil Law, Canon Law (Church Law), and Medicine. The students studied the Latin authors of ancient Rome and Latin translations of Greek works. Jewish scholars in Spain provided Latin translations of important Arabic works in mathematics, geography, science, and medicine. The medieval universities combined the teachings of the Church and the secular knowledge of the Greeks and the Romans in a synthesis commonly called "the scholastic philosophy." In his Divine Comedy, the Italian poet, Dante, follows the Roman poet Virgil, representing Reason, through Hell and Purgatory, but he needs Beatrice, representing the revealed truth of God as found in the Bible to guide him through Heaven.

The Renaissance and Humanism

In the later Middle Ages, a great outpouring of creativity known as the Renaissance took place in the wealthy cities of Italy. Architecture, sculpture, painting and music broke free from the Church and were turned to secular purposes to glorify the city or wealthy civic leaders. The art of the Renaissance spread to other parts of Europe, but for three centuries Italy was the tutor of Europe in the arts.

The intellectual movement called humanism developed in Italy and spread throughout Europe. The humanist scholars of the Renaissance were literary figures who were concerned to develop a pure Latin style based on the works of the best Roman writers. Humanist studies took place in the universities as part of the study of grammar and rhetoric, but many humanists were not on university faculties. They were civil servants, lawyers, administrators of large estates, and engaged in other secular employments. The distinguished humanist, Niccolo Machiavelli, was a civil servant of the Republic of Florence, where he gained the experience of politics that contributed to his classic work, The Prince.

Humanists believed that the study of ancient literature would have a transforming effect on European culture. As they delved more deeply into the culture of antiquity, they learned Greek and their interests extended to Greek philosophy, politics, ethics and science. The surge of interest in the secular culture of antiquity also influenced the arts, as sculptors and architects gave increased attention to the remaining works of ancient Greece and Rome.

Christianity received new inspiration from Christian humanism, a movement that advocated study of the Bible in the original languages, Hebrew and Greek. Christian humanists, like the Dutch scholar, Erasmus of Rotterdam, advocated reasonable, non-dogmatic reform of the Church based on the New Testament and the teachings of the early Christians. The historic perspective of humanism brought out the gulf between the Church and the message of the New Testament. Attention was particularly directed to the Renaissance Popes, who lived in pomp and engaged in power politics with other states.

The Reformation

The Christian humanist movement was shaken by the religious turmoil of the Reformation. In 1517 Martin Luther, a German monk who was a Doctor of Theology and Professor of Bible at Wittenberg University, used the Bible to challenge the authority of the Pope and some of the key doctrines of the Church. When the movement that he unleashed caught fire, Luther called upon the princes of Germany to reform the Church in their domains. Most of the rulers of north German states, plus the kings of Denmark and Sweden, established Lutheranism as the state religion. Luther translated the Bible into German, and Lutheran churches used the language of the people in worship in place of the Latin Mass. Luther included music in the worship service and wrote hymns for congregational singing, including "A Mighty Fortress is our God" based on Psalm 46.

John Calvin, a Frenchman who lived in Geneva, Switzerland, refined the teachings of Luther. Calvin extended Luther's doctrine of "justification by faith" to the doctrine of predestination, which held that some people were chosen by God to be saved and the rest were not. He advocated a Presbyterian form of church government (rule by ministers and elders) in place of the episcopal system of Lutheranism and Catholicism. Calvinist worship was concentrated on the Bible, the sermon, and the hymn. Calvinist churches were austere, and the sculptures of the past were destroyed. Choirs and organs were banned. Calvinist hymns consisted of rhymed versions of the psalms, sung in unison and without accompaniment. Calvinism took root in Scotland and the Netherlands, and became a cause of religious tension in England.

The Catholic Church responded to the Protestant challenge with the Counter Reformation (or Catholic Reformation) as defined in the Council of Trent (1545-63), which strengthened the powers of the Papacy and further defined the doctrines of the Catholic Church. The Church vigorously defended its strongholds in Italy, southern Germany, and the Spanish and Austrian empires. Catholic scholars were thoroughly trained in the humanist education and used it to publish great volumes of medieval documents to explain and defend the claims of the Church.

The French Crown remained loyal to the Pope and Catholicism, but Calvinists (Huguenots) were an influential minority in France. The Dutch were mainly Protestant and the state Church was Calvinist. Since the Dutch Republic had a large Catholic population, religious toleration was essential, which was also extended to Jews, many of whom fled there from persecutions in Spain.

In England, King Henry VIII (1509-47), with the support of Parliament, swept aside the authority of the Pope and was declared "Supreme Head" of the Church of England. He preserved most of the Catholic doctrines and forms of worship and government of the Church by archbishops and bishops. Christian humanist reformers, like Archbishop Thomas Cranmer, struggled to push the Church of England in a Protestant direction. Edward VI (1547-53), the king's only son, succeeded his father when he was nine. He was under the guidance of a Council controlled by Protestants and was personally a zealous Protestant. Led by Archbishop Cranmer, the Church of England adopted Protestantism. The Bible was published in English and Protestant worship was introduced in The Book of Common Prayer. Edward VI was sickly and died at age fifteen without marrying. He was succeeded by his staunchly Catholic elder sister, Mary Tudor (1553-58), who returned the Church of England to Catholicism and obedience to the Pope. Her reign was marred by persecution of Protestants, including burning Cranmer at the stake. She died without an heir and was succeeded by her younger sister, Elizabeth.

Under Queen Elizabeth (1558-1603), the authority of the Pope was rejected, and the Queen became the "Supreme Governor of the Church." The Church of England returned to Protestant doctrines as stated in The Thirty-Nine Articles, and Protestant worship in The Book of Common Prayer. Many of the practices of Catholicism were preserved. The church buildings were adapted to Protestant worship. Music, using choirs and organs, continued to be used in the cathedrals and in some large parish churches. Sometimes a large choral work, called an anthem, was performed in honor of some special day or event. The moderate, middle-way of Queen Elizabeth was intended to reduce religious disputes and strengthen English national unity, and for a while it did.

Christian humanism was strong in England, where humanist studies dominated the schools. In the grammar schools and the two universities, almost all the time was spent studying ancient languages and works, which were seen as the foundation of secular knowledge as the Bible was the fount of religious knowledge. The greatest accomplishment of Christian humanism in England was the translation of the Bible from the original languages, culminating in the magnificent King James Bible of 1611.

England had a powerful literary tradition rooted in the works of Chaucer and Spenser. Poetry was written primarily for the Royal Court or the great houses of the aristocracy. Poetry took many forms—tales of chivalry and courtly love; clever, highly-polished poems about bucolic joys; and innumerable sonnets, mainly about love. London had a vital theatre with plays by Christopher Marlowe, William Shakespeare, Ben Jonson, and other talented contemporaries. Theatre companies sought royal patronage but depended largely on the patronage of the elite and the support of the public. Shakespeare had a typical grammar school education, and the influence of humanism is seen in his use of a five-act structure drawn from the plays of the Roman dramatists. Many of his plots and characters are derived from the works of antiquity or the Italian Renaissance.

In the reign of Queen Elizabeth a reform movement called Puritanism arose in the Church of England. Many of the Puritans favored Calvinist doctrines and a Presbyterian form of church government. As such, they became a threat to the authority of the Crown and the bishops. They claimed that the Church of England had been insufficiently reformed and too many Catholic practices remained. They objected to statues of the Virgin Mary and the saints and the practice of bowing to the altar. They criticized the use of organs and elaborate choral works in worship, which they said appealed to the senses and obscured the words. They advocated congregational hymn singing using rhymed psalms.

The Explorations

The states of Europe, especially those that bordered on the Atlantic, were intimately involved in the explorations that opened the world to Europeans. It is no coincidence that Christopher Columbus sailed in 1492, the year that King Ferdinand and Queen Isabella completed the reconquest of Spain from the Moors. The conquests of Cortez (Mexico) and Pizarro (Peru) brought spectacular wealth to Spain and financed the far-flung foreign policy and wars that eventually ruined that great country. The Spanish also occupied the larger islands of the West Indies. Even before Columbus sailed, the Portuguese were exploring the Atlantic coast of Africa, and Vasco da Gama sailed around the Cape of Good Hope to India. Ferdinand Magellan, a Portuguese sea captain sailing for Spain, worked his way through the Straits of Magellan at the tip of South America and crossed the vast Pacific. He was killed in the Philippines, but one of his ships returned to Spain, having circumnavigated the world.

King Henry VII (1485-1509) of England saw the importance of the Spanish and Portuguese discoveries, and sent John Cabot (Giovanni Caboto), an Italian, on two voyages to the coast of North America. Then English exploration stalled. Involvements in European wars and the crisis of the Reformation delayed further efforts for more than half a century. Under Queen Elizabeth the English established the Muscovy Company to trade with Russia, the Eastland Company to trade in the Baltic area, the Levant Co. to trade in the Middle East, and the East India Company to trade in India.

In the early seventeenth century the English established colonies along the Atlantic coast of North America. The Dutch established a colony at the strategic spot now known as New York, and the French began to settle along the St. Lawrence River. The fishing fleets of Europe exploited the rich fisheries of the Grand Banks. All three countries occupied some of the smaller islands in the West Indies. By mid-century, they had become threatening rivals of the Spanish and Portuguese empires.

The Stuart Monarchy in England

When Queen Elizabeth died without direct heirs, she was succeeded by James I (1603-1625), the first of the Stuart kings of England, thus bringing England and Scotland under the same monarch. In Scotland, James had considerable success in establishing his authority over the nobles, although the Calvinist Church of Scotland remained stubbornly independent. James adopted the political doctrines typical of the continental monarchies—divine right, hereditary succession, and royal sovereignty.

James had struggled with the Calvinist Church of Scotland and looked forward to the well-ordered episcopal government of the Church of England. In his first year James met with a group of Puritan clergymen, who presented a series of complaints about the Church of England. James made it clear that he would defend the episcopal form of church government. "No bishop, no king" he said. At the Hampton Court Conference he agreed to a request for a new translation of the Bible, which became the King James Bible (1611).

In England, James I found a strong, stable country with long-established institutions—Parliament and the Courts of Common Law—that claimed an independent share in the government of the kingdom. Parliament consisted of two houses. The House of Lords was comprised of the hereditary nobility (peers) and the higher clergy (archbishops, bishops). The House of Commons was elected from the shires (counties) and boroughs (incorporated towns). Leaders of Parliament, especially in the House of Commons, claimed that they had rights and privileges that the king could not infringe. James' attempt to join England and Scotland into one kingdom failed.

Charles I (1625-1649) held the political ideas of his father, but he was less realistic and adaptable in applying them to the special circumstances of England. When the House of Commons attempted to use "the power of the purse" to limit the royal prerogative, Charles I responded by using his right to dismiss them. For eleven years (1629-1640) Charles I ruled without calling Parliament, until an uprising in Scotland forced him to raise an army and call on Parliament to finance a war that went badly.

In the reign of Charles I, religion became a highly divisive issue. As Supreme Governor of the Church of England, Charles was devoted to its doctrines, worship, and its episcopal form of Church government. Increasingly the Church of England came under attack by Puritans. The doctrines of the Church as expressed in the Thirty-Nine Articles were not seriously challenged. Some Puritans criticized The Book of Common Prayer and wanted to reform the worship of the Church along Calvinist lines. Some wanted a presbyterian form of Church government, as in Scotland; and a few were Separatists (independent congregations) who wanted nothing to do with any established Church. William Laud, Archbishop of Canterbury, made strong efforts to root our Puritanism in the clergy, which intensified the Puritan reaction against the Church. By 1640 Puritan views had gained widespread acceptance, especially in London and other commercial towns.

Despite the insistence of the Church that all clergy adhere to its doctrines as stated in The Thirty-Nine Articles, some laymen and clergy were attracted to latitudinarianism, which sought to avoid the religious controversies of the time by urging tolerance in matters of doctrine and ceremonies that were not essential to the Christian faith. Lord Herbert of Cherbury was an aristocratic searcher for Truth. He studied at Oxford, served the Crown as a soldier and diplomat, and traveled extensively. He identifies religious Truth as the principles that all religions share rather than those that divide them. He published his conclusions in a Latin treatise, On Truth, in Distinction from Revelation, Probability, Possibility, and Error (1624), which was dedicated to the human race. Knowledge, he states, should not be based on philosophic conjectures or divine revelation, but must be based on the rational faculties inherent in mankind. The work is notable for his five fundamental principles of religion, which he claims are not derived from divine revelation or from human reason, but must be true because they are held by all peoples and religions. These are God exists; God ought to be worshipped; the essentials of religion are virtue and piety; evil acts can be forgiven by repentance; there are rewards and punishments here and hereafter.

Political and religious opposition to Charles I tended to merge. When the king met Parliament in 1640, he encountered a House of Commons that was determined to limit the royal prerogative. In 1642 Charles I was forced to agree to legislation that denied any power in the Crown to impose taxation without consent of Parliament and abolished the royal prerogative courts, leaving the Courts of Common Law supreme. The king also faced a strong group of Puritans in the House of Commons.

Seeing his power in state and Church slipping, Charles I left London and set up his capital at Oxford. He called upon his supporters to form an army to preserve the role and powers of kingship and the principles and worship of the Church of England. The parliamentary cause was supported by London, where Puritanism was strong, and in the east of England. Parliament raised its own army and took over the navy and made an alliance with the Scots. Throughout the country Englishmen were forced to take sides.

The result was two civil wars (1642-1646, 1648) in which Charles I was defeated. In 1649, a remnant of the House of Commons led by radical Puritans condemned Charles I to death. Charles redeemed his many failures by dying bravely, and the death of the king ended the hope of the revolutionaries that their new regime would achieve popular acceptance. Queen Henrietta Maria and her children fled to France, where they lived with other exiles. The heir to the throne, Prince Charles, tried to make a comeback in Scotland in 1650 and was crowned King of Scotland. The next year he invaded the west of England with an army of Scots, but was defeated at Worcester by a Puritan army led by Oliver Cromwell. After a series of near escapes, Prince Charles returned to exile in France.

By that time power in England had been seized by the Puritans. They were determined to abolish monarchy and episcopacy and establish a Puritan republic. They first established the Commonwealth (1649-53), which was followed by the Protectorate (1653-58) under their great military leader, Oliver Cromwell, who received the title Lord Protector. The Puritans were determined to make England a "godly" nation by imposing restrictions on the lives and recreations of the people, including strict observance of the Sabbath. The excesses of radical Puritans created deep resentments. When Cromwell died in 1658 most of the English people were tired of turmoil and Puritan rule.

As the English sought to restore political and religious stability, they turned to their legitimate ruling family and their traditional institutions. One of Cromwell's generals, Gen. George Monk, who was stationed in Scotland, marched on London with his troops and seized control. He assembled all living members of the Parliament elected in 1640, the last elected under Charles I. They called an election for a new Parliament and then dissolved themselves. The newly elected Parliament was identified as a Convention, since it had not been called by a king.

In April, 1660, Prince Charles paved the way for his return by issuing the Declaration of Breda, which offered a general pardon, liberty of conscience, just settlement of claims to land, payment of arrears to the army, and restoration of the Church of England—all to be decided by Parliament. The Declaration eased the fears felt by those who had fought against the king or who had gained power and property during the Civil Wars.

The Convention met at the end of April, and declared "according to the ancient and fundamental laws of this kingdom the government is and ought to be by king, lords, and commons." Charles II was proclaimed king, and later that month he landed with his entourage at Dover. The new king was received in triumph, and cheering crowds followed him from Dover to London. He quipped that if he had known he was so popular he would not have stayed so long abroad. It seemed that the English people had turned their backs on their turbulent past.

Not entirely. England marched to a different drummer than the monarchical states of the continent. The English were determined to develop a polity that provided security for life and property under a "mixed government," with power shared between the Crown, the House of Lords, and the House of Commons. When they restored the Stuart monarchy they moved toward the future by first returning to their past.

Ch. 2. Monarchy and
Conflict in Restoration England

The Restoration of Charles II in 1660 resolved some of the problems that had led to the Civil Wars, but many issues remained. Charles II and his brother, James, Duke of York (James II) were personally committed to the continental principles of divine right, royal sovereignty, and hereditary succession. These principles clashed with the claims of Parliament to a role in English government, especially in respect of taxation and the succession to the throne. The conflict between the Church of England and the Puritans (Dissenters) continued to simmer, although at the Restoration the Church of England seemed to have gained total victory. The determination of Charles and James to carry out a pro-French, pro-Catholic foreign policy ran counter to the interests and instincts of the English people and added to the growth of public discontent.

The later seventeenth century was a time of great intellectual and cultural ferment. Science transformed the concept of matter and the solar system and posed a challenge to traditional religious views. The Restoration and the Scientific Revolution set England in directions that led to great achievements, but the new and the old did not exist comfortably together.

The Restoration Settlement

When Charles II was crowned in Westminster Abbey, the Convention was waiting for him. The king confirmed their previous actions and converted the Convention into the Convention Parliament. This

13

Parliament passed the main legislation that defined the Restoration. Charles II's principal adviser, Sir Edward Hyde, was created Earl of Clarendon, and took a leading role in shaping the settlement. The previous powers of the monarchy were not fully restored, for the restrictions made in 1640-42 remained in place. The independent powers of the Crown to tax disappeared and the prerogative courts were not revived. The House of Lords was restored as before, and proposals to reform the system for electing the House of Commons were shelved.

Considering the bitterness of the previous twenty years, the Restoration Settlement was surprisingly moderate. Despite cries for revenge, the Act of Indemnity and Oblivion drew a veil over the conflicts of the Civil War period. All but a few of the revolutionary leaders were pardoned. Thirteen persons were condemned to death for their participation in the execution of Charles I. The bones of Cromwell were dug up, hung on the gallows at Tyburn, and cast into an unmarked grave. Cromwell's army was cut back to a few regiments and the rest of the soldiers were paid off and discharged.

When the work of the Convention Parliament was finished, the king still possessed the major powers of government—the power to conduct foreign policy, appoint office-holders and judges, collect and disburse the revenue, command the army and navy, nominate and promote archbishops and bishops, and appoint the lords-lieutenant and justices of the peace who governed the shires. He could call Parliament into session or dismiss it at his pleasure, and he could hold elections for the House of Commons when he pleased or not at all.

The establishment of religion was the most important issue left unsettled by the Convention Parliament. Clarendon wished to bring the nation together in religion, and for that reason he favored a broad Church of England ("comprehension") that would be acceptable to the Presbyterians, who had cooperated with the Restoration. The leadership of the Church of England, however, was inflexible. A conference intended to bring Anglicans and Presbyterians together failed to achieve an agreement, and the strict Anglicans eventually prevailed within the Church. The Presbyterians were strong in London, and the failure to reach a satisfactory agreement soon turned that great city against the restored regime.

The House of Commons elected in 1661 (the Cavalier Parliament) was strongly Royalist and Anglican. Ignoring the wishes of the King and Clarendon, the Cavalier Parliament passed legislation, misnamed "The Clarendon Code." The Corporation Act (1661) was intended to drive Puritans out of municipal governments (corporations) by requiring officials to take communion in the Church of England. A revised edition of The Book of Common Prayer (1662) restored the worship and practices of the Church without concessions to the Puritans. The Act of Uniformity (1662) required all clergy to adhere to the Book of Common Prayer and all schoolmasters to receive a license from the bishop. Almost 2,000 Puritan clergymen refused to conform to the requirements of this legislation and were ejected from their churches. When some Puritans continued to meet with their ejected ministers outside the Church, further legislation (the Conventicle Act) was passed in 1664 that prohibited all private religious meetings. The Five Mile Act (1665) prohibited an ejected clergyman from coming within five miles of any incorporated town. Many Puritans refused to conform and became the second-class citizens known as Dissenters. Despite the desire of Charles II to give toleration to Catholics, they continued to live under the severe restrictions and penalties imposed in the reign of Queen Elizabeth.

The breakdown of royal government in 1642 and the political and religious controversies of the Civil War had led to extensive publication of books, pamphlets, tracts, broadsides and other kinds of printed material. The Licensing Act (1662) established censorship of books to prevent the spread of radical political or religious ideas. All published books had to be registered with the Stationers Company, a guild of London booksellers, who did not wish to incur the wrath of the Crown by publishing controversial books. The number of master printers was limited to twenty.

The Royal Court and Restoration Culture

Charles II offended many of his subjects by bringing the French concept of a Royal Court to England. The contrast between the high ideals of monarchy proclaimed by the royalists and the Church and the disorder and low moral tone of the court was striking. Charles surrounded himself with men and women who were talented and amusing, but irreligious and self-indulgent. Whitehall Palace swarmed with ambitious nobles and impecunious adventurers, male and female. Charles treated his queen, Catherine of Braganza, a Portuguese princess, with respect, but she was personally uninteresting, and her failure to bear an heir made her a cipher at court. Instead, Charles II, more or less discretely, maintained a series of attractive mistresses, whose offspring entered into the aristocracy of England. Emancipation from the shackles of Puritan morality led to its opposite—libertinism, which means a dissolute person freed of all moral restraints. The court of Charles II was notorious for such people, and the libertine was a common figure in Restoration novels and plays.

The lifestyle of King Charles II stood in sharp contrast to the moral standards of most English men and women. Unlike his prim and proper father, the king showed disdain for the ceremonies and rituals that gave dignity to the monarchy. He offended some by bringing in a band of twenty-four violinists to provide music in the French-Italian style for dining and dancing. He loved the theatre, an institution anathema to Puritans, and at times partook incognito of the low life of London.

The court of Charles II contributed to another break with traditional culture by encouraging women to ignore the straitjacket of conventional female behavior and assert their individuality. One of the most remarkable Restoration women was Lady Margaret Cavendish, the forceful and eccentric Duchess of Newcastle. She came from a royalist family, and met and married her husband while they were in exile with the family of Charles I. She wrote about this period in a biography of her husband, The Life of William Cavendish (1667). At the Restoration they returned to England, where Lady Margaret continued her writing. In her Orations of Divers Sorts (2nd. ed., 1668) she discusses whether female subordination to men is the result of inherent inequality or lack of opportunity. Observations Upon Experimental Philosophy (1666) grew out of her interest in science. On one occasion she was invited to attend a meeting of the Royal Society and observe scientific demonstrations by Robert Boyle and Robert Hooke. She wrote plays that were published but not performed, which would be beneath the dignity of a duchess. Plays Never Before Printed (1668) included The Convent of Pleasure, where the typical Restoration rake is rejected in favor of a sincere lover. She wrote light-hearted, fanciful poems that were published in collections of her poetry.

Although he conformed to the Church of England, Charles II personally favored Catholicism. On his deathbed he received the last rites from a Catholic priest. His Queen and his brother, James, Duke of York, were Catholic, and the attitude of the king encouraged Catholicism at court. Parliament and the nation were ardently anti-Catholic, a sentiment strengthened by Louis XIV, who persecuted Protestants and conducted a foreign policy that was viewed as the latest embodiment of popery and universal monarchy.

Charles II lacked an essential ingredient of continental courts—an elegant palace. Rambling Whitehall Palace was more than a century old. St. James's Palace, another Tudor palace, was old and dowdy, although it had an elegant interior. Hampton Court Palace, along the Thames west of London, had been built in the reign of Henry VIII and was a favorite of Queen Elizabeth. Farther west along the river was Windsor Castle, an ancient stone structure where Charles II installed lavish state apartments decorated with murals that praised symbolically the powers of monarchy. King Charles' Block (1664-70) at Greenwich was a companion to Inigo Jones' Queen's House. It was England's first baroque building. Plans for further building in that area were abandoned.

Charles, who feared the anti-monarchical and puritanical views of most Londoners, planned to emulate Louis XIV's Palace of Versailles, a few miles outside of Paris, by building a modern palace at Winchester, west of London. The new palace would take the court and aristocracy away from London into the heartland of royalist support. Christopher Wren, England's premier architect, prepared a plan for a splendid domed palace with a giant portico. The palace would be linked to Winchester Cathedral by a street lined with fine townhouses. Early in his reign Charles lacked the money to undertake the project. His finances improved near the end of his reign, and he began building it. At his death it remained unfinished and was converted into a barracks.

From the beginning of the reign, Charles' brother, James, Duke of York, served as lord high admiral. The Duke was interested in the navy, especially as a means of colonial expansion. He sent a fleet that captured New Amsterdam (New York) in 1664, which led to the Second Dutch War (1665-67). After several brutal battles at sea, the English fleet was tied up at the Chatham dockyard due to lack of money to prepare it for sea. The Dutch boldly sailed up the Thames estuary and captured the fleet, destroying some vessels and towing the largest and newest back to Holland. It was the worst defeat ever inflicted on the English navy.

The real manager of the navy was Samuel Pepys (pr. Peeps), who began his progress up the administrative ladder in 1660 in the office of clerk of the acts to the navy board. Pepys came from a middle-class family with aristocratic connections, and received a Cambridge education. His cousin was an influential figure in the return of Charles II to England, and Pepys was on the boat that brought Charles to Dover. In the navy office, Pepys became aware of the mismanagement of the navy, and he devoted his career to improving the efficiency of the fleet. Pepys' career showed the opportunities available to a competent, hardworking administrator in a government controlled by an indolent king and irresponsible courtiers.

Pepys is best known for his remarkable diary (1660-69), which was written in his own cryptic shorthand, apparently as a means of reliving his thoughts and actions on a day-by-day basis. There is no indication that he thought it would ever be published. The diary provides valuable insights into the government of Charles II and the society of Restoration England. Pepys gives vivid accounts of the plague, the Fire of London, his problems with his family, servants, and young wife, and his romantic escapades. He was a frequent playgoer, although his Puritan conscience made his feel guilty about it. His accounts of music at the Royal Court, the Chapel Royal, and in the theatres are an important historical source. He tells of his collection of fine books. Finally, he writes about himself with remarkable frankness and comes across as a human being full of energy and love of life. The diary was published in part in the nineteenth century, and is now available in a complete scholarly edition.

The Economic and Social Foundations

In 1696 Gregory King, a treasury official, published a work entitled <u>Natural and Political Observations upon the State and Condition of England</u>. As an employee of the treasury, King had access to tax records and other sources of information that were the basis for his book. Using the year 1688 as his base, King attempted to determine the population and wealth of the country. He calculated a population of 5 1/2 million and a national income of approximately £34 1/2 million.

King's estimates showed that 21,586 aristocrats, higher clergy, and gentlemen had the income needed to participate fully in the refinements of an advanced civilization. Another 35,000 had incomes that would support the lifestyle of a gentleman. Approximately 450,000 self-supporting farmers, shopkeepers, artisans, and military and naval officers (almost all of them literate) would be able to participate to a limited extent. The dark side of the story was King's estimate that half the population of 5,500,500 was comprised of common sailors and soldiers, urban and rural laborers, and 849,000 vagrants, who were a net loss to the country.

"The Agricultural Revolution," as it is sometimes called, began in the later seventeenth century and made possible "The Industrial Revolution" that followed a century later. English agriculture was mainly devoted to production of wheat (for bread), barley (for beer) and oats (for horses). In parts of the country with access to urban centers via river or road, fruits and vegetables were important. England's cool, moist climate produced pastures that were ideal for cattle and sheep, the sources of milk, butter, cheese, and meat for human consumption and wool for the textile industry. In the later seventeenth century productivity of animals was improved by sowing pastures with clover and growing turnips for cattle feed. Throughout the thousands of villages of seventeenth-century England, cottage industries supplemented income from agriculture.

Landlords and farmers recognized that improvements could not be made until the narrow strips of medieval open field agriculture were consolidated into compact fields of 10-15 acres surrounded by stone walls or high, thorny hedges. This process (enclosures) had gone on piecemeal for centuries, but by the later seventeenth century the advantages were clearly seen and the process of enclosure gained momentum. Advances in agriculture required capital for improved farm buildings and for drainage of fields, which wealthy landlords were able to provide..

Economic growth took many forms. Rural England also produced textiles and other goods for public consumption and export. Towns manufactured products that were marketed throughout the country and in foreign lands. England was a commercial country with extensive imports, exports, and re-exports, all of which produced revenue for the Crown and growing wealth for merchants and bankers. The English people were busy people, whose industriousness was the economic foundation of English culture.

The Social Structure

At the top of the social structure of England were the aristocracy and gentry, both members of the landlord class. The aristocracy was identified by hereditary titles and normally they held extensive landed estates. Known collectively as the peerage, they sat in the House of Lords and figured prominently at court and in high government offices. They had important local influence too, but the estates of the greatest aristocratic families were scattered throughout the kingdom and their interests were likely to focus more on national concerns.

The aristocracy used legal devices to assure transmission of the bulk of their estates to one heir, usually the eldest son (primogeniture), and used marriages to bring additional resources into the family. The powers of the great families increased as smaller holdings were consolidated into large landed estates. To signify their influence in the region where they lived, they built imposing country mansions. For many of the aristocracy a remunerative office under the Crown was essential to the life-style that they were expected to maintain. When James II began bestowing the best offices on Catholics, the aristocracy turned against him.

The gentry were landlords with moderate estates who did not possess titles of nobility. They dominated the House of Commons and, as Justices of the Peace, the government of the shires. Under James I and Charles I they had been the heart of resistance to the royal authority in government and religion. During the civil wars, however, the gentry were appalled by the rise of nobodies to national and local prominence and by the excesses of some of the Puritan clergy and their zealous followers. In the Restoration period the gentry were strong supporters of the King and the Church of England as safeguards of social order. Under James II they were forced to choose between the two.

England was dotted with the substantial country houses of the gentry. Coleshill House, Berkshire, was typical. At the front, a flight of stone steps led up to the first floor, which was raised several feet above ground level, with a half basement for the kitchen etc. underneath. From the first floor a grand staircase led to a second floor with a parlor or reception room. On the first floor, under the reception room, was the dining room. Each of the four corners on both floors had bedrooms or rooms for special purposes, such as a library or music room. The roof was capped by a balustrade and cupola.

In the later seventeenth century, the gentry suffered a relative loss of importance. Many of the gentry experienced economic problems. Unusually cold weather brought a period of bad crops. The gentry, who did not have the prospect of public office to buoy their incomes, grumbled about taxes and poor rates, declining rents, and the fiscal mismanagement of the Crown. Their country houses decayed and many of them lacked the knowledge or capital to improve the productivity of their lands. They were dismayed by the emergence of wealthy professionals or businessmen, who bought lands and sought to enter the social elite of the county.

The aristocracy and gentry were by no means closed castes. The influence of the aristocracy was extended through the middle ranges of English society by the principle that younger sons were commoners and had to make their way in the world. Younger sons brought confidence, education, and contacts derived from an aristocratic upbringing. There is some truth in the remark that English history is the story of younger sons. The tide flowed the other way too—commoners successful in government, the law, the military, or business could rise in the social scale. The first step was to buy a landed estate and join the ranks of the gentry. The king could create new peers, but usually several generations of landed wealth, education, and high office were required for a family to move from gentry status into the peerage.

Sons of aristocrats went to school and university with sons of successful business and professional men, and developed friendships that might be of great political or personal importance. Daughters also contributed to interlocking the upper ranks of English society, for the younger daughter of a peer might marry into the gentry or mercantile wealth, while the daughter of a wealthy merchant might marry into the gentry, bringing with her fresh genes and a much-needed dowry (actually a portion). In short, the aristocracy and gentry could, with some justification, claim to speak for the people of England—or, at least, those whose opinions mattered.

London, Westminster

The growth of trade, seapower, colonies, and a money economy was especially important to London, which was the major commercial and cultural center of England. With its population of more than 500,000, London was larger than any other European city. London had grown well beyond its walls, which were torn down piecemeal, although the gatehouses remained. London was the center of coastwise and overseas trade, the banking firms that provide financial services, providers of sailcloth, ropes, barrels, etc, and freight haulers who carried the goods to their next destination. London was also the home of thousands of artisans and their apprentices who manufactured a wide variety of goods. Despite congestion, destitution, crime, plague, and fire, "the great wen" continued to grow.

London was a proud city with rights of self-government going back to the Middle Ages. The city was governed by its Mayor and Council, and sent four Members to the House of Commons. London politics were marked by conflict between the wealthy merchants and guild masters and the "middling people" who pursued their trades and crafts. Puritanism was strong in London, and Dissenters continued to be influential. Londoners resented the pro-French policies of Charles II and the Catholicism of his brother, which ran counter to their patriotic and Protestant sensibilities.

In the 1660s London was struck by twin disasters—the plague (1665) and the Great Fire (1666). The bubonic plague was called the Black Death when it first appeared in Europe in the fourteenth century. The disease was transmitted by a louse carried by the black rat. Ever since the fourteenth century, the plague had been endemic in Europe, breaking out whenever natural resistance declined. The plague of 1665 was the last violent outbreak, although scattered instances appeared for the next century. The cause of its decline in Europe seems to be that the larger, stronger Norway rat (which did not carry the louse) established itself in towns and drove out the black rat.

The population of London was crowded into wooden houses

and tenements, many of them going back to the later Middle Ages. When fire broke out in 1666 they burned like tinder. The Great Fire began in a baker's shop near St. Paul's Cathedral. It burned for five days and destroyed two-thirds of the city, including St. Paul's, the medieval Guildhall, and the Royal Exchange. Proposals to introduce a more orderly street plan were rejected, due to the legal complications of property rights and the desire of Londoners to return to normal life as soon as possible. The attractiveness and solidity of London were much improved by a Building Code that required building with brick and stone. Christopher Wren designed forty-seven of the eighty-six burned out churches, whose spires rose like tall masts over the city. The view that the Fire destroyed the plague appears to be unfounded.

London was a new kind of metropolis, spreading without planning beyond its walls. Large numbers of rootless young people were drawn to London from the towns and villages of England, where their prospects were poor. Often they found that prospects in London were not much better. Apprentices and casual workers roamed the streets, where they found shopgirls and housemaids with time off, or prostitutes and pickpockets plying their trades. Local authorities contended in vain against the tide of humanity, irreligion, and destitution that confronted them, and in the urban sprawl outside the walls they gave up in despair.

Around the bend of the Thames was Westminster, site of a former monastery, which in the later Middle Ages had become the seat of the government. Crumbling old Whitehall Palace housed the Royal Court until it burned in 1698. Parliament met in the buildings of the former abbey, and the Courts of Law were held in ancient Westminster Hall. Westminster Abbey church was the center of ceremonial functions as well as regular worship. Nearby was St. James's Park, where long-striding Charles II took walks followed by his dogs and panting courtiers.

Westminster was not an incorporated town but a collection of parishes governed by the justices of the peace for the county of Middlesex, who were noted for their venality. Connecting London and Westminster was the Strand, a busy street lined with shops and aristocratic town houses. Covent Garden, north of the Strand, once a distinguished residential piazza, had become a center of nightlife, including the two theatres. London and Westminster were a ribbon of urban development along the Thames, unconfined by walls or natural obstacles. There was only one bridge, London Bridge, which was covered with houses and shops. It burned with the rest of the city in the Fire and was rebuilt.

Although London was the dominant English city, provincial towns prospered in the second half of the seventeenth century. By 1660 most of them had outgrown their medieval walls, which fell into disrepair or were torn down. Bristol was the second seaport of England, important for trade with Ireland and the colonies. Farther north, Liverpool began to get a share of the Atlantic trade. On the east coast, Newcastle was the outlet for the growing coal trade with London. Hull was a major port for trade with Scandinavia, the Baltic area, and the Netherlands. York was a cathedral town, and served as the social center for a large area of the north. Leeds was at the heart of the Yorkshire woolen industry and famous for its cloth market. Sheffield was important for metal goods; Nottingham had a variety of manufactures, including hosiery and lace; Norwich prospered on the basis of the woolen industry and the rich agriculture of East Anglia; Gloucester and Exeter were cathedral/market towns for the west and southwest respectively.

The Church and Dissent

The Restoration settlement established the Church of England as the national church and the only legal place of worship. It also created Dissent (Presbyterians, Congregationalists, Baptists, and Quakers) as a permanent part of English life. Dissent began with the ejections of the Puritan ministers from their parishes in 1662 and the formation of Dissenting congregations outside the Church. Local authorities often looked the other way when Dissenters met for "lectures" or worshipped at their modest chapels in violation of the Conventicle Act. Some towns had large populations of Dissenters, among them prominent citizens, who maintained their religious cohesion and had considerable local influence. Much to the dismay of the Anglican clergy, Dissenters sometimes qualified for local office under the Corporation Act by taking communion once a year in the Church of England ("occasional conformity") while continuing to attend their Dissenting chapels on the other Sundays. Dissenters were not excluded from voting, and they were an important political factor in many towns, especially London.

Anglicans and Dissenters did not differ much in their understand-

24

ing of the fundamentals of Christian doctrine. Both agreed that salvation was a gift of God based on Christ's sufferings and death. The Church left more room for freedom of the will, while most Dissenters held firmly to Calvin's doctrine of predestination. The Church placed greater emphasis on participation in the sacraments, while Dissenters emphasized Scripture reading and preaching.

After the Restoration, the latitudinarian perspective of Lord Herbert of Cherbury was continued by John Tillotson, a clergyman of Church of England who became Dean of Canterbury cathedral. His objective was to heal the rift that that had divided England in the reign of Charles I. Tillotson came from a strong Puritan background and always maintained good relations with Dissenters. He rejected Calvinism and advocated a moderate, reasonable, reconciling approach to religious disputes. Although he supported the authority of the king as necessary to public order, he was outspoken against Catholicism, which was actively promoted at court. He published his ideas in the form of sermons that were notable for their clear and direct language without the flourishes common earlier in the century. He stressed the compatibility of Reason and revealed religion, and held that good conduct was as important in Christianity as forgiveness of sin.

Tillotson was a close friend of one of the most remarkable churchmen of the time, Gilbert Burnet, a voluble Scot. Burnet's career in the Church began in Scotland, where he was active in the affairs of the Church of Scotland and professor of divinity at the University of Glasgow. In 1674 he resigned his professorship and settled in London. He established a reputation as one of the best preachers in London and drew large audiences to his sermons. He became friendly with prominent latitudinarians and the Whig leaders of the political opposition. His History of the Reformation of the Church of England (1679) was a vigorous defense of the Church.

Catholicism was influential at court and in some great aristocratic families, but most Catholics lived in the north and west of England, where the Catholic gentry protected priests and preserved the faith of their fathers in their homes and among their tenants. The major concern of Catholics was the legislation passed during the reign of Queen Elizabeth, which imposed stiff fines for refusal to attend the parish church on Sundays and holy days. Catholics coped by paying their fines, if the could afford them, or taking precautions not to antagonize the public or attract the attention of the justices of the peace.

In the long run, the major threat to the Church of England was religious indifference, which characterized many of the leaders of Restoration society, including the king, and spread to other social classes. An age of secularism was dawning, fostered by the personal conduct of the man whom the Church regarded as its leader and protector—King Charles II.

John Bunyan and the Puritan Message

The continuity of Puritanism into the new age was made abundantly clear in the works of John Bunyan. As a youth from a humble background, Bunyan's formal education was minimal. He served in Cromwell's New Model Army, which was a hotbed of radical political and religious ideas. After he left the army, Bunyan became a lay preacher for a congregation of Baptists, and at the Restoration he was imprisoned for twelve years for unlicensed preaching. Bunyan's absorbing interest was the saving of souls, including his own. He went through a period of religious turmoil before he resolved his spiritual issues, a process that he describes vividly in Grace Abounding to the Chief of Sinners (1666).

While in prison, Bunyan used the time to write books intended to strengthen the religious fervor of godly people who, like himself, were driven underground and deprived of their churches and preachers. Bunyan's masterpiece is The Pilgrim's Progress from This World to That Which is to Come (1678), an allegorical tale of the Christian soul's passage through life to salvation. The characters are not empty symbols— Bunyan presents them as flesh and blood human beings, and their adventures are genuinely exciting. The hero, Christian, has read in the Bible that his city is doomed to destruction. Warned by Evangelist (the Gospels), a preacher of Christian truth, Christian prepares to flee from the City of Destruction (Earth) to the Celestial City (Heaven). He tries to persuade his family and neighbors to come with him, but they think he is ill or mad and refuse to leave their homes. Christian's flight is made difficult by the heavy burden (sin) that he carries on his back, and by hazards such as the Slough of Despond (despair). Mr. Worldly Wiseman urges him to seek relief from his burden by living up to the

Law (religious rules) in the city of Morality. At this point, Evangelist steps in and persuades Christian that he has been led astray.

Christian arrives at the Wicket Gate, where Good Will tells him that if he knocks at the gate it will be opened unto him. He knocks and is met by Interpreter, who informs him that he will be justified (lose his burden of sin) by faith, not by good works. He is shown a frightening picture of the Day of Judgment. He is informed that the Straight and Narrow Road will take him to his destination. When he reaches the Cross of Calvary and the Open Sepulchre his burden of sin falls away.

As he continues his journey, Christian is invited into a house where he meets four virgins named Discretion, Prudence, Piety, and Charity. They send him along his way armed with the sword and shield of the Christian faith. He passes through the Valley of Humiliation and uses his weapons to vanquish a fierce devil. Next he passes through the Valley of the Shadow of Death, but is able to ward off devils from Hell by reciting verses from the Psalms. After passing by two elderly giants, Pope and Pagan. Christian joins a friend named Faithful. Evangelist warns them about Vanity Fair, a business community where all the vanities of the world are displayed in order to lure travelers away from the Straight and Narrow Road. Christian and Faithful are arrested because they refuse to buy any of the products of the town. Faithful is burned at the stake but Christian escapes from the prison. He is joined by Hopeful, a resident of Vanity Fair who was impressed by the noble death of Faithful. As they approach the City of Zion, they have to cross the River of Death. As he wades into the river, Christian becomes frightened and begins to sink. He is helped by Hopeful and arrives safely on the other side. Shining angels escort them to the gates of the Celestial City (Heaven). On his trip, Christian discovers the sad fact that those who challenge or threaten him are not just the openly hostile forces of evil, but ordinary, law-abiding people who consider themselves Christians.

In a sequel (1684), Bunyan introduces Christian's wife, Christiana, and other female characters, who also make their way to the Celestial City. They represent the important role that women play in the community of Christians. In this work, Bunyan emphasizes the value of marriage and the Christian family. The Life and Death of Mr. Badman

(1680) is a critique of Restoration society. In <u>The Pilgrim's Progress</u> the Puritan cause was transmuted into great literature.

The Crisis of the Reign of Charles II

The crisis that arose in the later years of the reign of Charles II had been building for a long time. It focused on the pro-French, pro-Catholic proclivities of the king and his brother, James, Duke of York. In England Catholics were seen as loyal to foreign powers—the Pope, France, or Spain. Charles II had no legitimate offspring (he had many illegitimate children). Upon his death, the succession would pass to James, Duke of York, who was a Catholic and married to a Catholic, circumstances unacceptable to the English people in those days when religion and government were intertwined. James had two daughters, Mary and Anne, born to a previous marriage, who, by order of Charles II, had been raised as Protestants. They offered the prospect of an eventual Protestant succession.

In 1678 the succession to the throne became an issue when Titus Oates, a renegade Anglican priest, came forward with "the Popish Plot"—a far-fetched tale of a Catholic plot to murder Charles II, place the Duke of York on the throne, establish Catholicism in England, and murder prominent opponents of the Duke. Eventually inconsistencies in Oates' story, which became increasingly elaborate as he told and retold it, led to his conviction for perjury, but not before he had created a panic that contributed to a movement to exclude the Duke of York from the throne.

The anti-Catholic hysteria provided a golden opportunity for the Earl of Shaftesbury, who led an opposition that was important in the development of political parties. Shaftesbury's political base was London, where Dissenters were strong and the people were historically anti-court. His main themes were the fear of popery and arbitrary monarchy, and the prospect that the Duke of York would succeed to the Crown. His most dedicated followers were organized in the Green Ribbon Club, which turned out his London supporters to public protests as needed.

When Parliament met in October 1680, the Exclusion Bill was introduced into the House of Commons. It would exclude the Duke of York from the succession to the throne. It was rejected by the House of Lords with the king seated on his throne observing the proceedings. Shaftesbury organized massive anti-Catholic processions that gathered outside the House of Commons to support the Bill. Finally Charles II cracked down. He called Parliament to meet at Oxford, where Shaftesbury could not assemble intimidating crowds. The street to the meeting place was lined with troops. When the Exclusion Bill was again brought forward, Charles dissolved the Parliament and the Exclusion Bill was no more. He did not call Parliament again.

With the dissolution of the Oxford Parliament, Charles II began exercising stronger personal leadership. James, Duke of York, urged the king to assert his royal powers to the fullest and establish strong monarchy in England. "Things were come to such a head," he told Charles, "that the monarchy must be either more absolute or quite abolished." Observers remarked that the Duke had become the dominant force at court. His Catholicism became increasingly evident, and fears grew that he intended to establish Catholicism in England. Shaftesbury was accused of treason and imprisoned, but a London grand jury, packed with Exclusionists, rejected the charges. Crowds gathered in the streets of London and other towns, cheering Shaftesbury and denouncing popery and the Duke. Shaftesbury began planning a rebellion, but when that fell through he fled to the Netherlands with his secretary, John Locke, and died a few months later. With Parliament out of the picture, London became the heart of resistance to the court.

By 1683 Charles II seemed to have matters well in hand. Better management in the treasury, a subsidy from Louis XIV, and improving trade brought fiscal stability and Charles had no need to call Parliament. He revived his plans for a new royal palace at Winchester, and considerable progress was made in building it. Work resumed on the state apartments at Windsor Castle. When Charles died in 1685 he left to his brother James a strong monarchy, a full treasury, a humbled Parliament, and a subservient Church.

One result of the Exclusion Bill controversy was the emergence of two political parties, although their roots were deeper and broader than the succession of James. Fundamentally, their differences were cultural and to some extent they reflected rural and urban values. The Whigs advocated limitation of royal power and toleration for Dissenters. They looked to Parliament to achieve their goals. The Whigs were led by

Shaftesbury and other prominent aristocrats, but found their main strength in London and other towns and among Dissenters. Although a few wealthy Londoners were attached to the court, the majority supported the Whigs as part of their civic patriotism and love of freedom. The powerful Dissenting community of London added their religious discontents to the mix.

The supporters of hereditary succession, who were called Tories, rallied behind Charles II and opposed the Exclusion Bill, although many of them mistrusted the Duke of York. The Tories favored a strong king and preservation of the privileges of the Church of England. Toryism was strong among the country gentry, who supported the Crown and the Church as bastions of "law and order." As justices of the peace in their shires, they made life difficult for Dissenters and Catholics. They remembered the rule of Cromwell and the Puritans, and they feared that a disputed succession would bring a revival of civil and religious conflict.

The Church, fearful of another rebellion, advocated passive obedience to established authority. Thomas Spratt, Bishop of Rochester and author of <u>History of the Royal Society of London</u>, stated that passive obedience was required, even under an idolatrous ruler. It was the duty of the Church, he proclaimed, "always to keep itself in due submission to the Civil Magistrate." He was proud that the Church of England "never resist'd Authority, nor engag'd in Rebellion." James II's two daughters, Mary and Anne, who were Protestants, became the hope of the Tories and the Church for a Protestant monarchy.

A New Faith: Science and The Royal Society

In the later seventeenth century, the reliance of the scholastic philosophers on logic (deduction), the humanist reliance on the ancient classics, and the Reformation emphasis on the Bible were challenged by a new way of understanding the world based on Reason and observation. Francis Bacon, James I's lord chancellor, had advocated an approach to knowledge that proceeded from the bottom up, beginning with specific information derived from sense impressions and moving from many particular instances to reliable generalizations (induction). In his <u>Novum Organum</u> (1620), Bacon envisaged "a new instauration of learning" based on observation and experiment, a philosophical approach called empiricism. Bacon's empiricism was also pragmatic, in that he was concerned with the practical uses of sound knowledge. He enunciated a key principle in his statement, "Knowledge is power."

Bacon's New Atlantis (1626) tells the story of sailors who are shipwrecked on an unknown island in the south Atlantic. They are met by the governor who tells them they are on an island dedicated to science. Their scientists collect books from all over the world, from which they attempt to derive general principles. They also undertake experiments that are exacted to lead to useful conclusions. They have a memorial to the great discoverers and inventors. As traditional ideas of politics, morality, and religion were challenged, Bacon laid the philosophical foundations of a new faith—science.

In the reign of Charles II, the new scientific ideas were promoted by a small group of scholars and learned gentlemen who were organized in the Royal Society. Their motto—nullius in verba (on the word of no one)—stated their determination to free themselves from ancient authorities and establish a system of knowledge based on verifiable facts. King Charles II was a member as were many leading men in government, business, and scholarship, among them Samuel Pepys. There was increasing acceptance of Bacon's view that organized scientific efforts would increase mankind's understanding of Nature and reveal practical applications that could be used in everyday affairs. From time to time the Society published the papers presented by the members in a series entitled Philosophical Transactions.

Robert Boyle stood at the transition from medieval alchemy to modern chemistry. In The Sceptical Chymist (1661) he rejects the ancient idea that matter is comprised of four substances—air, fire, earth, and water. Boyle outlines a theory in which the properties of matter are attributed to the motions of atoms. He also proposed a definition of an element. He developed an air pump that enabled him to conduct experiments with air pressure, vacuums, and gases. In A Free Enquiry into the Vulgarly Received Notion of Nature (1686), he outlines what is now called "the scientific method." In the spirit of the Royal Society, he insists on the importance of well-designed experiments that are carefully recorded in detail (including false starts) and can be replicated by other scientists.

The scientific method of Boyle was advanced by Robert Hooke, a pupil of Boyle, who was a skilled maker of scientific instruments. In 1662 Hooke was appointed curator of the Royal Society. He made a microscope that enabled him to see bacteria. His <u>Micrographia</u> (1665) was illustrated with careful drawings of the cellular structure of plants. His accurate barometer led him to the conclusion that a fall in atmospheric pressure heralds the approach of a storm. Along with Christopher Wren, he was appointed surveyor of London to make plans for rebuilding the city after the Fire.

John Flamsteed was appointed astronomer royal by Charles II, and Christopher Wren built the Royal Observatory (1676), which is located on a hill above Greenwich Palace. Flamsteed's purpose was to chart the stars for navigation, both commercial and naval. Based on years of observations, Flamsteed's <u>British Celestial Record</u> (1725) was published posthumously and helped make Greenwich the dividing line between the eastern and western hemispheres.

Edmond Halley was an active officer of the Royal Society and eventually became its secretary. He succeeded Flamsteed as astronomer royal. His contributions were varied—charting the stars in the southern hemisphere, mapping the trade winds and ocean currents, and noting variations in the earth's magnetism. He is best known for his discovery of the periodic return (every 76 years) of the comet that bears his name.

Thomas Sydenham, a physician, exemplified the empirical approach in medicine. Sydenham's education at Oxford was interrupted by the Civil Wars, when he and members of his family fought with the parliamentary army and supported the rule of Cromwell. He received the degree of Bachelor of Medicine but not the M. D. degree. Probably he studied medicine in France at the famous medical school at Montpelier. Sydenham settled in London and became a close friend of Robert Boyle, who sometimes visited patients with him.

Sydenham was influenced by the empiricism of Bacon. He challenged the medical works of the Greek writer, Galen, which were the foundation of medical education in the universities. Sydenham was a disciple of the Greek physician, Hippocrates, who advocated careful observation of the patient, identified the environment as an important cause of disease, and emphasized diet and exercise in the maintenance of health. Sydenham gave special attention to the blood as the carrier of life to all parts of the body. He remarked that "physic is not to be learned by going to Universities" and "one had as good send a man to Oxford to learn shoemaking as practicing physic."

Sydenham's first medical publication was translated as <u>Method of Curing Fevers based on Original Observations</u> (1666). In this work he argues that fever results from the efforts of the body to get rid of morbid particles, and the proper treatment is to support nature in this effort rather than use the common practice of bloodletting. His mature judgments were published in <u>Observationes Medicae</u> (1676). Sydenham's reputation was based on clinical observations and his ability to make fine distinctions between different diseases. In this way he was a founder of disease classification. He was an early advocate of cinchona bark (quinine) against agues (intermittent fevers). He believed in a Supreme Creator who had established a rational natural order and diseases were aberrations that could be cured by working in harmony with Nature.

The most striking achievement of the age was in Astronomy. More than a century earlier Nicholas Copernicus, a Pole, had published a book with the hypothesis that the sun was the center of the universe (the heliocentric theory), that the earth and other planets circled the sun, and that day and night were caused by the rotation of the earth. Johannes Kepler, a German, demonstrated that the orbits of the planet were ellipses around the sun. Galileo Galilei, an Italian, showed that celestial (heavenly) matter and terrestrial (earthly) matter were the same. But it was the Englishman, Sir Isaac Newton, who developed the mathematics and physics needed to explain the Copernican system and demonstrate its unity and simplicity.

Newton's <u>Philosophiae Naturalis Principia Mathematica</u> (1687), commonly called the <u>Principia</u>, is the foundation document of modern physics. Newton showed that mathematics is the best means for expressing the laws that govern the physical universe. His work is based on three fundamental axioms. The first states the principle of inertia—that an object at rest will remain at rest until moved by some sufficient force, and a body in motion will remain in motion in a straight line at a constant velocity until changed by the application of some sufficient force. The second axiom deals with the calculation of the force (mass) need to move bodies at rest or in motion. The third axiom states that to every action there is an equal and opposite reaction. For example, if you step from a boat onto a dock, the equal and opposition reaction will push the boat farther out into the water. Newton was an empiricist, and states that his axioms were intended to explain observable phenomena.

He also explains the principle of gravitation—bodies attract each other in proportion to their mass and distance apart. He demonstrates that the moon and planets are held in their orbits by a balance between the tendency of a rotating body to move inward and inertia, which would keep them moving in a straight line. Using the principle of universal gravitation, he explains the moon's effects upon the tides. Newton's <u>Principia</u> provided the physical explanation of the Copernican concept of the heliocentric universe and the mathematical language in which to express it.

Newton believed that one great principle—which he calls the Supreme Being—had created and set in motion a perfect, unchanging universe governed by the laws of motion. This concept was the basis of Deism, which affirms the existence of a Supreme Being but insists that it is not a personal God concerned with the affairs of men. Nevertheless, Newton retained his interest in revealed religion and spent many years studying the teachings of the Bible concerning the end of the world. He was an active member of the Royal Society and held the political office of Master of the Mint. Samuel Pepys, as President of the Royal Society, was instrumental in publishing his great book.

The ideas of the Royal Society created another source of cultural tension, for they ran counter to tradional views of science and religion that were rooted in the past. Thomas Sprat, a rising cleric and later Bishop of Rochester, was chosen to explain the Society's purposes and accomplishments and defend the Society against charges that experimental science, by taking God out of the equation, undermined the Christian faith. Sprat was not a scientist; he was chosen due to his clear and economical style of preaching and writing. He supported the Society's campaign to reform the English language by eliminating ornamentation and rhetorical flourishes. He saw no conflict between science and "sound, sober, intelligible Doctrines in plain, practicable, rational Precepts."

Sprat's <u>History of the Royal Society of London</u> (1667) is very much in the spirit of Bacon. He avoids theoretical formulations (words) on the grounds that experimental science deals with "things" (facts). Science, he writes, will produce practical results that will increase England's wealth and power. God, he adds, has chosen the English people to unlock the secrets of the material world rather than pursue spiritual insights. He presents Christ as a scientist on the basis of the useful good works he performed in healing the sick and restoring eyesight to the blind. Sprat insists that experimental science is compatible with the humanist study of texts and the scholastic learning of the universities. Practical science, he says, will insulate the mind against "the spiritual distractions, of which our Country has long been the Theater."

Ch. 3. New Directions in Literature, Theatre, and the Arts

French culture, at that time the model for Europe, was promoted at the court of Charles II and had important influences in England. French classicism turned English literature and theatre in directions that were distinctly different from the great works of the Elizabethan age. The influences of Renaissance Italy and seventeenth-century France were important in English painting, architecture, and music. A few exceptional women asserted themselves in print and on the stage as important players in the cultural mix. By the turn of the century, foreign influences had been absorbed and a distinctive English culture had emerged.

John Dryden and Classicism in Literature

The Restoration brought an important cultural break with the past in the form of classicism (sometimes called neoclassicism) as defined in France during the reign of Louis XIV, the "Sun King." Essentially, classicism means adherence to a set of ideals and rules based on the works of the Greeks and Romans, as opposed to freedom of individual expression. In his L'Art Poétique (1674), Nicholas Boileau-Despréau, a French poet and critic, defined classicism in poetry as clarity, economy, vigor of expression, and metric regularity. He lay down standards of language and structure for the principal forms of classical poetry—the elegy, ode, epigram, satire, tragedy, comedy and epic. The objective of the poet was to display "wit"—perceptive insights into human character or emotions, pithily expressed.

Classicism in England emphasized clarity of expression, pleasing proportions, and harmony of parts. The polished Latin writers of Augustan Rome, especially Virgil, Horace, and Ovid, were models for the classical style in literature. Emulation of those writers, it was believed, would purify English poetry and drama from the irregularities and excesses of the past. Good prose was defined as the clear, straightforward language of a cultivated gentleman, without elaborate imagery or far-fetched conceits. The Royal Society appointed a committee "for improving the English language," which rejected "all amplifications, digressions, and swellings of style; to return back to the primitive purity and shortness, . . . bringing all things as near the Mathematical plainness as they can."

The leading literary figure of the Restoration period, John Dryden, was the master of classicism in literature and drama. Dryden came from an educated Puritan family, and imbibed the language of the King James Bible at his father's knee. He was introduced to the Greek and Roman classics at Westminster School. As a young man, he lived through the civil wars and looked to the Protectorate of Cromwell to bring order to a distracted land. When Charles II was restored, Dryden supported the monarchy as a source of political and religious stability. "To his Sacred Majesty" (1661) celebrates the coronation of the king..

Dryden's first successful poem, Annus Mirabilis (1667) defends Charles II against Puritan charges that the plague and Fire of London were God's punishment of a sinful king and court. Dryden was in the country when these events took place, so he had no personal knowledge or experience of them. No matter. The poem is an imaginative literary work, not journalism. He casts his poem in the form of an epic poem, in which specific persons and events are referred to via allusions. Charles II is presented as a noble monarch bravely confronting troubles inflicted on his country. By transferring his apologia to the fantasy world of an epic, Dryden is able to let his imagination run free. In 1668 Dryden was rewarded by appointment as poet laureate, which carried with it a stipend that gave him financial independence.

In Religio Laici (1672), Dryden presents a learned layman's view of the religious disputes of the time. He advocates a moderate Anglicanism in contrast to the rationalism of the latitudinarians, the "enthusiasm" (religious emotionalism) of the Puritans, and the authoritarianism of Catholicism. The poem includes a thoughtful weighing of the merits of Catholicism as a personal faith versus its authoritarian claims and objectionable political principles. Much of the poem is devoted to the latitudinarians, whose reliance on Reason, he charges, corrodes all forms of religious faith. Possibly Dryden saw rationalism as the main challenge of the future; very likely he had wrestled with it himself.

Dryden was much affected by the political and religious furor unleashed by "the Popish Plot" and the Exclusion Bill, which he feared might encourage a revival of Puritan zealotry and an attempt to restore the Puritan Commonwealth. In <u>Absalom and Achitophel</u> (1681), a long poem written in heroic couplets, he transposes the partisan turmoil of the time to the Old Testament account of the revolt of the foolish Absalom (the Duke of Monmouth) against King David (Charles II), his wise and benevolent father. The revolt is stirred up by the unprincipled courtier, Achitophel (Shaftesbury), who is determined "to ruin or to rule the State." Achitophel organizes malcontent Jews (Whigs), and sends Absalom on tour throughout Israel (England) claiming falsely that a plot exists to convert Israel to the Egyptian (Catholic) religion. Finally King David decides that he has been too lenient and cracks down on the Sanhedrin (Parliament). Heaven shows its approval as "peals of thunder shook the firmament." The Old Testament story of Absalom was, of course, well-known to the public, and the Biblical analogy lent force to Dryden's argument.

Under James II Dryden accepted Catholicism. He expressed his religious views in the allegorical poem, <u>The Hind and the Panther</u> (1687). The hind, a gentle female deer (the Catholic Church) debates religious issue with the gleaming but treacherous panther (the Church of England). Protestant sects are represented by wolves, bears, and other dangerous animals. The poem represents the conclusion of Dryden's quest for certainty, but it aroused charges of opportunism that were difficult to refute. Dryden held to his Catholic faith after "the Glorious Revolution," which cost him his post and income as poet laureate.

Music was important to Dryden, and in home entertainments he was a creditable performer on several instruments. His <u>Song for St. Cecilia's Day</u> (1687) is an expression of his love of music. <u>Alexander's</u>

Feast, or, The Power of Musique (1697) was highly praised by contemporaries. After the Revolution of 1688-89 Dryden supported himself by masterful translations of the classics, which further advanced the classical standards that he had done so much to establish.

Dryden was a philosophical poet, who used carefully controlled language in subtle patterns of rhyme and meter to discuss the political and religious issues of the time. As a writer Dryden was a self-conscious professional, seeking to establish critical principles of good literature as well as to exemplify them in his own works. His The Art of Poetry (1682) was an English version of Boileau's principles.

The Quarrel Between the Ancients and the Moderns

The emergence of new ideas in philosophy and science and new standards for literature provoked a cultural reaction that took the form of "the quarrel between the ancients and moderns." The dispute was launched by the French writer, Charles Perrault, who challenged Boileau by claiming that modern writers had exceeded the achievements of the ancients. The dispute raged in France until stopped by Louis XIV. Perrault also wrote a collection of folk tales that included Cinderella, Little Red Riding Hood, and Sleeping Beauty. His stories were published in England under the title Mother Goose Tales (1697).

Sir William Temple, a retired diplomat, brought the controversy to England. He published An Essay upon Ancient and Modern Learning (1690) in which he claims that the achievements of the ancient world were based on a true view of Nature, while modern equivalents are pale imitations of the works of their great predecessors. Temple was answered by William Wotton in Reflections upon Ancient and Modern Learning (1694). Wotton argues that in literature and the arts the ancients could be equaled but not surpassed, but in geography, science, and other subjects where knowledge is cumulative, the modern world far exceeded its ancient foundations.

Temple's secretary, Jonathan Swift, expressed his view of the matter in "The Battle of the Books," is a satirical essay in which the ancient and modern books in a library get into a fight. They do considerable damage to each other but neither wins. The "quarrel between the ancients and the moderns" quickly blew over, but the existence of the question demonstrated a growing awareness of a gulf between ancient and modern times and hinted at the idea of progress.

The Restoration Theatre

The theatre was restored after the Puritan interlude and assumed great importance in the life of the court and fashionable society. Charles II issued letters patent to Thomas Killegrew and Sir William Davenant to establish two theatres. A theatre was also licensed to present plays at Smock Alley, Dublin. Killegrew was a Royalist courtier and play-wright who had gone into exile during the inter-regnum, and returned to England with Charles II in 1660. Davenant was a playwright who wrote several successful plays in the 1630s that are a bridge between the Shakespearean drama and the Restoration. Davenant went into exile with Queen Henrietta Maria. During the inter-regnum he returned to London and became a theatrical promoter despite the opposition of the Puritans to the theatre. He managed to put on a series of musical plays, including The Siege of Rhodes (1656, 1658), that passed Crom-well's censor by claiming they were entertainments, not plays.

The patents of Charles II gave the holders a monopoly of theatrical productions. Killegrew's company of actors was known as the King's Men, and inherited many of the plays of Shakespeare and Ben Jonson. His theatre began performing old plays, but soon he recruited new playwrights, among them John Dryden. He also produced some of his own plays, and was the first to use actresses on the stage. Davenant's company was patronized by James, Duke of York, and was called the Duke's Men. He was able to obtain a fair share of the old plays claimed by Killigrew, and he also produced his own plays, including adapta-tions of Shakespeare. Davenant had a great asset in Thomas Betterton, the finest actor of the time.

At first each company had to adapt existing buildings to serve as theatres, but soon they built their own. Theatres were small, with one or two galleries surrounding a central pit with wooden benches. Plays were given great flexibility by the use of moveable flats to show scenes in a variety of locations—indoors or out, London or elsewhere. Dav-enant died in 1668 while Charles II was in his theatre watching one of his plays, but his family continued producing plays.

Many plays were written by courtiers who sought the patronage of the king, his mistresses, or prominent figures at court. Audiences were surprised to find women performing women's roles, in contrast to the Shakespearean theatre where these roles were played by men and boys. This innovation was generally accepted, although the proper middle class, who saw the theatre as no place for respectable people, cited actresses as one example of its immorality. When they were offstage, the actresses associated freely behind the scenes with male theatre-goers.

The audience was comprised primarily of a coterie of courtiers and the elite of London, but the theatres also attracted law students from the Inns of Court and fashionable young men-about-town. Women also attended the theatre, the upper class in the boxes that surrounded the stage on three sides, and the others on benches on the ground floor ("the pit"). The two theatres were small and the audiences often were disorderly. Prostitutes plied their trade in the corridors, and girls selling oranges and walnuts engaged in banter with the customers. One such girl, Nell Gwyn, who became a successful actress, caught the eye of Charles II and became his mistress. The respectable middle class found the theatre no place for decent people, and worried about the evil influence of plays on their offspring.

In accord with court culture, Restoration theatre adopted the alien doctrines of classicism from France. English playwrights were impressed by the French effort to refine and polish French language and literature, which made the rambling form and luxuriant speech of Shakespearean drama seem excessive. Tragedies dealt with great persons torn by a conflict between duty and passion. The comedy of humors (personal traits) competed with the comedy of wit (clever dialogue). The theatres presented adaptations of plays by Shakespeare and Ben Jonson, translations from French, Italian, and Latin plays, and works by contemporary English playwrights. The masque, with its scenery, singing, and dancing, was an important part of the theatrical season.

In 1665 John Dryden turned to the theatre as a better source of income than poetry. He developed the heroic drama, in which great people deliver lofty speeches in a grand manner. Dryden's tragedies deal with issues such as love, ambition, duty, fate, and free will. His heroic play, The Conquest of Granada (1670) was set at the decisive battle between the Spanish and the Moors in 1491. The complex plot concerns Moorish lovers in the midst of a crucial battle against the Spanish.

All for Love, or, The World Well Lost (1678) is commonly regarded as Dryden's best play. Set in Egypt in the first century BC, the play is not an adaptation of Shakespeare's Antony and Cleopatra. Dryden's plot is simplified and takes place in one day, as required by the French neoclassical principle of unity of time, place, and action. The number of scenes and actors is greatly reduced. To add dignity to the play, Dryden uses blank verse for the dialogue.

The play mainly concerns Mark Antony, a defeated hero, who faces a future based on unattractive choices. After his defeat by Octavius, adopted son of Julius Caesar, Antony flees to Egypt, where he is besieged in Alexandria by the army of Octavius. He is bound to Cleopatra, Queen of Egypt, by ties of love, but these prove to be frail. One of his generals offers him an opportunity to abandon Cleopatra and seek safety in Syria. His wife, the sister of Octavius, offers him the opportunity to return to Rome if he abandons Cleopatra and is reconciled with her powerful brother. Cleopatra insists that, as her lover, Antony must stay in Egypt and share her fate. While Antony tries to decide where his true loyalties lie, Cleopatra commits suicide. Antony sees the Egyptian fleet join with the Romans and believes that Cleopatra has treacherously allied with Octavius. He falls on his sword and the tragedy of the fallen hero is complete.

Dryden's heroic tragedies received a powerful counter-blow in The Rehearsal (1671) by George Villiers, Duke of Buckingham, a prominent politician and courtier. The Rehearsal is a hilarious satire of the pompous language and sentiments of the heroic tragedy, especially as found in the plays of Dryden. It was performed almost three hundred times in the next century, long after heroic drama had disappeared from the stage. Throughout the eighteenth century the lead role was taken by the best actors, including Colley Cibber and David Garrick.

Dryden's comedies were "comedies of wit," with characters that are cynical and self-centered and use flattery and deception to achieve their goals. The theme is invariably the battle of the sexes, and the plays include parts for strong, articulate women who can hold their own in the struggle. The main characters and plot usually are supplemented by a cast of eccentrics—a country bumpkin, pedantic scholar, superstitious servant, or a pompous fop. Comic incidents and witty repartee come thick and fast. Restoration comedy laughed at hypocrisy and eccentricity, and found fun in love, marriage, seduction, and clever tricks.

Dryden's <u>Marriage à-la-Mode</u> (1671) is one of the best examples of Restoration comedy. The play takes place in Sicily, and combines a courtly plot with a romantic plot. The courtly plot concerns King Polydamas, a usurper, who interviews a fisherman who has raised a boy, Leonidas, who he claims is Polydamas' long-lost son. The fisherman also has a daughter, Palmyra, whom he says is his own. In a surprising reversal, Palmyra turns out to be King Polydamas' daughter. She loves Leonidas, who, as a commoner, cannot marry her. The courtly plot is resolved when Leonidas is revealed to be the son of the true king, who had lost his throne to Polydamas. Leonidas claims the Crown, King Polydamas is forgiven for his usurpation, and Leonidas and Palymyra are married.

A secondary plot deals with the theme of love outside of marriage. Restoration morality regarded marriage as the logical outcome of love. However, many marriages were arranged by the parents with an eye toward property and inheritances, with the expectation that love would appear later. The hedonistic courtiers of Charles II argued that marital love wears off quickly, and for that reason extramarital affairs are to be expected. In <u>Marriage à-la-Mode</u>, this view is exemplified by two young libertines, one married and one betrothed. They are both in love with another woman, but the men discover that the women they intend to seduce are the wife or fiancée of the other. It is equally disconcerting when they find that the two women seem interested in being seduced. When the play ends, the two couples agree to respect each other's marital commitments, but the desire for variety that led them to the intended seductions remains.

Thomas Shadwell, playwright and Whig activist, was a successful writer of Restoration comedies. Some of his plays were adaptations of plays by Molière, the French master of the comedy of humors. <u>The Virtuoso</u> (1676) was a satire on the Royal Society and experimental science in general. Shadwell shows Robert Hooke, secretary of the society, learning to swim on dry ground by reading the instructions in a book. <u>The Tempest, or, The Enchanted Island,</u> (1674), an adaptation of Shakespeare's play with singing, dancing, and elaborate costumes and scenery, was a popular and financial success. The music and the drama were more fully integrated in Shadwell's <u>Psyche</u> (1675), for which he also wrote the score. These musical plays were highly successful commercially, and were precursors of English opera.

As a Whig, Shadwell was a member of Shaftesbury's Green Ribbon Club and wrote Whig propaganda during the disputes over "the Popish Plot" and the Exclusion Bill. His <u>The History of Timon of Athens</u> (1678) transformed Shakespeare's play from the story of a bitter misanthrope into a movement to overthrow the tyrants of Athens and restore democracy amid cries of "Liberty." <u>Teague O'Divelly, the Irish Priest</u> (1681) was an anti-Catholic play written during the panic of "the Popish Plot." Shadwell criticized Dryden's comedy of wit as amoral. He was attacked by Dryden in <u>Absalom and Achitophel</u> as a self-important mediocrity. Dryden's poem, <u>Macflecknoe</u> (16282), is a mock-epic about a kingdom ruled by Shadwell, whose dullness and mediocrity are shared by other inhabitants of his kingdom. Shadwell supported the accession of William and Mary, and replaced Dryden as poet laureate in 1689.

William Wycherley is notable for his comedies. He was handsome, dashing, and witty—the prototype of the Restoration rake. His romantic relationship with the Duchess of Cleveland, one of the king's mistresses, gave him the influence he needed to get his plays performed. Wycherley's masterpiece, <u>The Country Wife</u> (1675), contrasts the veneer of propriety demanded by society with the amorality beneath the surface. Horner, who has a reputation as a seducer, spreads the rumor that he has become impotent. Consequently, husbands make no effort to protect their wives from his attentions, and Horner takes the opportunity to pursue his career of seduction. One of Horner's friends, Pinchwife, has married a simple, unsophisticated young woman from the country. Pinchwife knows well the temptations of the town, and for that reason he keeps his wife locked in the house. The comedy has four strands—Horner's attempts to seduce the country wife, her determination to enjoy the attractions of society, Pinchwife's surly efforts to protect her virtue, and the brilliant sexual banter of the other characters. <u>The Country Wife</u> was popular in the eighteenth century and has been revived occasionally in the twentieth.

Wycherley followed <u>The Country Wife</u> with another success, <u>The</u>

Plain Dealer (1676). The hero of the play is Capt. Manly, who is honest and straightforward with everyone. The Captain's determination to act as a plain dealer is frustrated by deceptions that arise in relationships with others. His problems are resolved when Manly discovers that Fidelia, his faithful page, is really a wealthy heiress whose love for him led her to disguise herself as a boy to be near him. After The Plain Dealer, Wycherley wrote no more plays.

Thomas Otway was a failed actor who became an outstanding playwright. The History and Fall of Caius Marius (1679) adapts the plot of Romeo and Juliet to the civil clashes of the Roman Republic, an obvious reference to the partisan conflicts of "the Popish Plot." The play that made Otway famous was The Orphan (1680), a lurid tragedy in which two brothers are in love with the same woman. When the elder brother marries the girl, the younger brother sneaks in to the bride's bedroom, not knowing that she is married, and rapes her. When he realizes that he has committed incest by lying with his brother's wife, he commits suicide. The play continued to be performed throughout the eighteenth century.

Otway's most popular play was Venice Preserv'd, or A Plot Revealed (1682). Otway had a remarkable ability to stir the emotions and arouse sympathy at a time when tragedies were formal and artificial. The play deals with treason, intrigues, and betrayals in a scene of civil discord, echoing the tensions created by Shaftesbury and the Exclusion Bill. The central character (Jaffier) and his young wife (Belvidera) become involved in a plot to overthrow the government of Venice. Jaffier's motivation is not heroic—it is resentment of Belvidera's father, a wealthy senator who opposed their marriage and refuses to help them financially. Another conspirator, Pierre, a friend of Jaffier, seems to be a heroic figure as he calls for liberty and honest government, but his motivation is anger at a senator who has stolen his mistress. Jaffier heedlessly gives Belvidera to the leader, Renault, as a hostage to guarantee his sincerity. Renault, another of the ignoble plotters, attempts to rape Belvidera and is driven off by her screams. Jaffier confides to Belvedera that the conspirators plan to take over the city and assassinate the senators, including her father. Belvidera is shocked and persuades Jaffier to inform the Venetian Senate of the plot in exchange for a promise of amnesty. The senators are informed and the plotters are seized and imprisoned.

Despite the promise of amnesty, the prisoners are executed. To spare his friend, Pierre, from an ignoble death, Jaffier stabs him and then himself. Belvidera, in a famous "mad scene" goes insane and dies.

Venice Preserv'd is a "pathetic tragedy," designed to stir the emotions of the audience. Venice—the corrupted state—sets the theme of the play, for the senators and conspirators alike are far from heroic. This melodramatic play was admired for its powerful, bombastic language and a plot that allows for a variety of interpretations. The role of Belvidera was played by Elizabeth Barry, the greatest tragic actress of her time, who was noted for her ability to "move the passions." Belvidera became one of great eighteenth-century roles for actresses. The more lurid parts of the play, including the rape scene, were usually cut to avoid offending middle-class proprieties.

Aphra Behn

Aphra Behn was the first English woman to earn her living as a writer. Her family background is obscure, but she is described as very beautiful. She spoke French fluently and possibly read Latin. She may have lived for a short time in Surinam, an English colony in northeastern South America (ceded to the Dutch in 1667), and seems to have served as a royalist spy on a mission to Antwerp. She married a German merchant named Behn but soon was widowed. She had many influential friends at court and among writers. As a woman adrift in the world, she supported herself by writing—"I write for bread," she said, when complaints were made that her plays were too "bawdy." She wrote nineteen plays, most of them racy comedies that seemed all the more daring since they came from the pen of a woman.

Her first play, The Forc'ed Marriage; or, The Jealous Bridegroom (1670), takes up a theme that appears in many of her plays—the evils that occur when women are compelled to marry for estates or money instead of marrying for love. The Rover; or, The Banish'd Cavaliers (1677), a comedy of intrigue and seduction set among a regiment of royalist soldiers in Italy, was her most successful play. Her heroines are liberated from traditional restraints, and she criticizes women who accept their dependent status passively. She was a staunch royalist, and as the Exclusion Bill crisis emerged her plays became more political. The

Roundheads; or, The Good Old Cause (1682) ridicules the Puritans and advocates monarchy and hereditary succession.

Behn also played an important role in the origins of the novel. She adapted French novels of amorous intrigue and turned them into romantic stories of love and adventure. Love Letters between a Nobleman and his Sister (3 vols.,1684-87) is a cluster of love stories told in letters, one of the earliest examples of the epistolary novel. The several parts total over 1,000 pages and went through seven editions in the next century. Actually, it is a roman a clef, based on the scandalous relationship of a Whig nobleman with his sister-in-law, and was written by Behn to damage the reputation of the Whigs.

The best of Behn's prose fiction is Oroonoko, or The Royal Slave, A True History (1678). Oroonoko is a handsome, well-educated African prince who falls in love with and marries the beautiful and modest Imoinda. When the king learns that Oroonoko and Imoinda are married, he sells Imoinda into slavery and tells Oroonoko that Imoinda is dead. On a visit to an English merchant ship, Oroonoko and his friends are seized and sent as slaves to a sugar plantation in Surinam. Oroonoko's master is so impressed by his noble slave that he gives him important responsibilities. Oroonoko hears of a beautiful slave girl and goes to see her. He discovers that she is Imoinda and they are reunited.

Oroonoko, seeking freedom for himself, his wife, and their unborn son, urges the slaves to assert their humanity and rise up against their masters. The revolt fails, and the governor's evil deputy, Byam, promises Oroonoko that if he surrenders there will be no punishment. When Oroonoko complies, he is severely whipped and released to the custody of his master, who receives him kindly. He fears that Imoinda will be ravished by Byam, and with her loving consent, he cuts off her head. When he is found grieving by the body of his dead wife, Oroonoko is executed by dismemberment.

The narrator of this lurid story, identified as an English gentlewoman, claims to have learned the story first-hand, and includes abundant detail to give the story an air of authenticity. Romantic love is shown as a powerful driving force, and Behn's characteristic theme—that marriage should be for love—is proclaimed. The English were fascinated by the New World, and detailed information is included about plants and animals. The Indians of Surinam are depicted as living in a golden age of primitive simplicity. Africans are presented sympathetically and the evils of slavery are exposed. Behn's Toryism is seen when she attributes Byam's misrule to the absence of a strong royal governor to exercise the necessary authority of the Crown. In 1694, Thomas Southerne converted Oroonoko into a touching play that was performed throughout the eighteenth century and called attention to the evils of slavery. Southerne's play, The Fatal Marriage, or, The Innocent Adultery (1694) was also based on a novel by Behn. Both plays continued to be performed throughout the eighteenth-century, the latter in a revised form as Isabella, or, the Fatal Marriage.

Classicism and Baroque in Architecture

In seventeenth century Europe painting, architecture, and sculpture were dominated by a style called baroque. Baroque art was flamboyant, and communicated ideas through emotions and the senses rather than through the spoken word, as in Protestantism. Baroque architecture developed in Rome in the seventeenth century to display the pomp and power of the Papacy and the Church. To some extent baroque was stimulated by the new spiritual energy generated by the Counter Reformation.

Baroque architecture is complex, lavish, and theatrical, and uses size and mass to convey a sense of power, wealth and magnificence. Large ceiling frescos and a prominent dome characterized the style. Baroque architecture spread from Italy to Spain, Austria, the Spanish Netherlands (modern Belgium), and southern Germany. The leading baroque architect and sculptor was Gianlorenzo Bernini, whose major works were executed in Rome under the patronage of the Papacy. Bernini was important in reshaping St. Peter's in Rome by adding a dramatic façade and the great piazza—scene of large gatherings to the present day. He added to the interior a striking canopy over the presumed burial spot of St. Peter. He ornamented Rome with spectacular tombs, statues, and fountains. His influence extended throughout the Catholic countries of Europe.

Baroque architecture was challenged by classicism, which emphasizes clear, simple, well-defined principles that give clarity and unity to the structure. Classical architecture contrasts with baroque in that it is small and restrained, and emphasizes horizontal lines. Classicism was compatible with the Protestant emphasis on simplicity and plainness, whereas baroque was associated with Catholicism. In the eighteenth century High Baroque became an international style that included many classical features.

The style of Bernini was not popular in France, where French classicism prevailed over baroque. The challenge facing French architects was to combine the principles of classicism with a baroque display of power and magnificence. A characteristic feature of French classicism was a building with an elaborate façade on the central structure with two wings that enclosed a formal garden, thus making the garden an integral part of the structure.

Louis le Vau was the dominant architect in the early years of Louis XIV. Assisted by Claude Perrault, he designed the east façade and the the south wing of the Louvre, the royal palace in Paris—now a great art museum. As architect to the king Le Vau was responsible for the rebuilding of the central block of the Palace of Versailles, giving the old chateau a new façade and opening the back to a formal garden. Jules Hardouin Mansart added the north and south wings which included the famous Hall of Mirrors. The work was finished in 1679. Mansart did not invent the mansard roof, although he refined it. French architecture had an important influence in England, especially on the architecture of Christopher Wren.

English architects were not without classical models of their own. Inigo Jones brought a pure classicism in architecture to England. In 1615 Jones became surveyor of the king's works for James I, an appointment that was continued by Charles I. He was influenced by the study of the ancient classics, including the treatise, De Architectura, a handbook for architects by the Roman architect, Vitruvius. Jones made two visits to Italy, where he studied examples of ancient architecture and the architecture of Andrea Palladio, a sixteenth-century Italian architect who used a clean-lined, classical style. Jones rejected the ornate magnificence of baroque. He planned many ambitious projects that would have made London a model of classical architecture had they been carried out. The masque, a play based on a classical theme that featured music, dancing, and elaborate scenery was a popular form of courtly entertainment. Parts were taken by members of the royal family or courtiers. Jones designed at least 25 of them.

Jones used a classical style for the Queen's House at Greenwich, downriver from London, which was intended for James I's queen. When she died the work languished, but Jones finished the project for Queen Henrietta Maria, Charles I's queen. Jones' best known work is the tasteful Banqueting Hall in Westminster, which he built for Charles I. The Banqueting Hall was intended to be an elegant setting for royal ceremonies. The building is a two-story rectangular hall proportioned as a double cube. Outside, each story is defined by a row of columns in classical style. Inside, the two stories are separated by a colonnaded balcony. In contrast, the flat ceiling was painted in lush baroque style by the Flemish painter, Peter Paul Rubens.

Jones drew up ambitious plans for a large new royal palace to replace Whitehall Palace, which was a century old and showing the effects of time. Had it been built, it would have rivaled the Louvre in Paris, and would have symbolized the kind of royal power to which the Stuarts aspired. Ironically, this ambitious and costly plan was developed just as the monarchy of King Charles I was collapsing into bankruptcy and civil war.

In the 1630s Jones was employed by a private developer to design Covent Garden Piazza, which was located north of the Strand, the street that connects the City of London with Westminster. Covent Garden was similar to the Place des Vosges in Paris, with upscale urban residences, shopping arcades, and colonnaded walks around a rectangular open space. At the west end Jones built St. Paul's Church in classical style with a large columned portico as found in a Greek temple. St. Paul's, Covernt Garden was the first new Protestant church built in England, and it demonstrated the suitability of classical restraint for Protestant worship. Jones was also involved in rebuilding St. Paul's Cathedral, which had become decrepit. The tower was strengthened and the west front was extended by building a large portico of ten Corinthian columns.

Christopher Wren

Architecture in England was distinguished by the work of Christopher Wren, who successfully bridged the cultural gap between the baroque style and English classicism. His father was the rector of a rural parish, and he received a good education at Westminster School.

The Wren family remained royalist and Anglican throughout the Civil Wars. In 1649 Wren went to Oxford, where he studied mathematics and science, and early in life he met many of the prominent scientists of the time. In 1657 he became Professor of Astronomy at Gresham College in London, an institution that offered career-oriented instruction in applied mathematics and science. In his inaugural address, he praises "the new philosophy" which has freed the sciences from the limitations of the past. He was one of the original members of the Royal Society, and the next year he became Professor of Astronomy at Oxford.

Wren's skills in mathematics, science, and engineering, combined with his good sense in design, made him an architect capable of handling a wide variety of buildings and using many different styles. Wren believed that the basic structure of a building should be geometrical, but softened by baroque decorations that invoked familiar images. He read extensively in Italian and French books on architecture, and in 1665 he visited Paris for nine months. There he met French architects and engineers and observed the French synthesis of classicism and baroque for large buildings. French architecture had an important influence on Wren. He did not continue on to Italy, the center of baroque architecture, and never went abroad again.

Wren's first project after his return from France was the Sheldonian Theatre in Oxford, an unusual structure intended for degree-granting ceremonies and other academic gatherings. Lacking clear precedents, Wren adopted the D-shaped design of ancient Roman theatres. The Sheldonian is comprised of tiers of seats that enable everyone to see and hear. An attic immediately above the seating consists mostly of windows to provide light. With a 70 foot span, a conventional roof would have required pillar that would obscure the view. Wren's solution was a light shallow roof with a cupola on top that was supported by a wooden floor laid on a grid of wooden trusses. The Sheldonian was a creative solution to an unusual need, and exhibits some of the features of the architecture that Wren had seen in Paris. Wren also designed the elegant library at Trinity College, Cambridge (1676-84), adopting a classical style in the tradition of Inigo Jones.

Wren showed his talent for architecture and city planning while working with the authorities of London in rebuilding the City after the Fire. Jones and Robert Hooke quickly produced a radical street plan that would have created straight streets and broad avenues and swept away the tangle of medieval streets and alleys. The people wanted to begin rebuilding immediately, and the plan was not adopted, although some changes were made. In 1669 Wren was appointed surveyor of the king's works, which included a house at Scotland Yard and a position of authority in the process of rebuilding London. He was involved in drafting the London Building Acts (1667, 1670), which laid down regulations for buildings to make them safer and more attractive, including prohibition of wooden construction. Wren's <u>Monument</u>, built at the spot where the Fire was said to have begun, is a fluted Doric column with narrow stairs inside that can be climbed to an observation deck.

A decision was made to build fifty parish churches to replace the eighty-six that had been destroyed in the Fire. A tax on imports of coal was imposed to pay for them. Wren was administrator of the project under a commission that was established for that purpose. He had a hand in the design and construction of forty-seven new churches. He did not attempt to rebuild the churches in their original form, for they were Catholic churches that had been adapted to Protestant uses at the Reformation. Wren redesigned them as Protestant churches with the emphasis, not on the altar and the sacraments, but as "auditory churches" for reading of Scripture, congregational singing of the Psalter (rhymed psalms), and the sermon. The lectern, pulpit, and a modest altar were at the front of a wide nave with galleries, where all could see and hear the preacher and participate in the worship service. Windows of clear glass filled the church with daylight. The exteriors of Wren's churches were often quite plain, jammed as they were among other buildings. He made up for that with dramatic bell towers or steeples that rose like spikes on the low London skyline. Typically, the new churches were built of red brick with stone trim. A stained-glass window overlooked the altar. The interiors of some churches were richly ornamented, for Anglicanism did not favor Calvinist austerity. Most of the churches were completed by 1690.

A typical Wren church is St. James's, Piccadilly, located just off one of London's busiest streets. St. James's is built of red brick with white stone trim and a three-stage tower with a clock on the middle stage topped by a tall, slim steeple. The ceiling is a barrel vault supported by Greek classical columns of white stone. The nave is wide and shallow to allow all to see and hear. Capacious galleries supported by square columns extend over the side seats. At the back is an organ loft. A carved marble font stands at the front on one side, and behind the modest Protestant altar is a wooden screen with floral woodcarvings by Grinling Gibbons. At the other side are a carved wooden lectern and a tall, imposing pulpit carved with Biblical figures by Gibbons. A six-part cluster of stained glass windows at the east end, a clerestory with large arched windows over the galleries, and smaller arched windows on each side admit light. The church probably will seat 500 people comfortably.

Grinling Gibbons was an outstanding practitioner of the art of woodcarving. Born in Holland of English parents, he learned his craft in Holland and much of his work was influenced by Dutch still-life painting. He settled in London about 1671, and gained distinction as a carver of wood mantelpieces and other decorations for country houses. He was introduced to Charles II, who admired his work and commissioned him to do woodcarvings for the Chapel Royal and the renovation of the state apartments at Windsor Castle. He also did woodcarvings at Whitehall Palace and for King William III at Hampton Court Palace. His specialty was naturalistic carvings of foliage, fruit, and flowers, a fine example of which can be seen at St. James's, Piccadilly. His most ambitious project for Wren was his oak carvings for St. Paul's cathedral.

As surveyor of the king's works, Wren designed <u>Chelsea Hospital</u> (1674-6), a refuge for disabled soldiers founded by Charles II. The design is plain but serviceable, and with modern facilities it continues to be used for the red-coated Chelsea pensioners. After "the Glorious Revolution of 1688-89" he made important additions to Greenwich with the Queen Mary Block ((1699 ff.) and the King William Block (1698 ff.), the Painted Hall and the chapel, both surmounted by impressive domes. Under Queen the Greenwich complex was converted into the Royal Naval Hospital.

Wren's great achievement was St. Paul's Cathedral. The old St. Paul's had been destroyed in the Fire. A replacement on a magnificent scale was seen as essential to the dignity of the Church of England and the civic pride of the Londoners. In contrast to Wren's parish churches, the cathedral clergy wished to keep the medieval form of a cathedral, with a raised choir at the east end and a long narrow nave. The crucial feature of Wren's plan was a large dome, a kind of construction unknown in England. The central space under the dome has transepts on each side that give the cathedral a cruciform shape. The massive west end dominates the exterior. Two towers and a columned portico with a pediment provide an impressive entrance. The style of St. Paul's is often called English baroque, a term that implies a fusion of baroque and traditional styles. St. Paul's imposing dome and towers and its rich, magnificent interior embody the majesty and emotional power of the baroque.

Construction moved gradually from east to west. Each contractor was responsible for the construction of a section, from top to bottom, until the section was completed and building the next section could begin. Wren made many changes in the plan as the work proceeded, which he kept secret to avoid constant bickering. As the work dragged on, the City and Parliament became impatient, and Parliament suspended half Wren's salary until the choir was completed. In 1697 the choir was finished and the first services were held. By 1700 the body of the cathedral was finished and the supports of the dome were visible. In 1711, when Wren was almost eighty, Parliament declared St. Paul's finished and paid the arrears of his salary. After he died, he was buried in St. Paul's. His epitaph read "Si monumentum requires, circumspice. (If you seek his monument, look around you.)

Painting

The center of seventeenth-century art was Italy, and the influence of Italian artists spread throughout Europe. The spirit of the baroque was evident in the rich imagination and emotional appeal of baroque art. Baroque painting was used to ornament palaces and churches with works based on the ancient mythology or the Bible or lives of the saints. The paramount baroque painter, was a Fleming, Peter Paul Rubens of Antwerp, whose altar paintings dramatized events in the life of Jesus and glorified the sacrament of Holy Communion. Rubens was also a secular painter whose lush landscapes and voluptuous nudes were used to decorate palaces throughout Europe.. The walls and ceilings of great buildings provided opportunities to Rubens to express on a large scale the imagination and exuberance of the baroque.

Painting in England was devoted mainly to portraits, where Sir Anthony Van Dyck was the outstanding figure. In his early years Van Dyck worked in the studio of Rubens. He first came to England in 1620 as court painter for James I, but the next year he left for six years in Italy, where he painted many of his greatest portraits and works of religious art. When he returned to Antwerp, he established a studio and painted altarpieces and portraits.

Van Dyck moved to England in 1632 and was employed by King Charles I and his courtiers as a painter of portraits. His first major works, Charles I and Queen Henrietta Maria with their two Eldest Children, Charles, Prince of Wales, and Mary, Princess Royal (1632) and Charles I on Horseback with M. de St. Antoine (1633) set the standard for portraiture in England. Working in a Protestant country, Van Dyck abandoned the religious spirit of much of his previous art and concentrated on producing attractive pictures. His full-length portraits were much in demand by the aristocracy. Van Dyck gave a firm and lasting direction to portraiture in England, and his graceful poses were used in portraits throughout the eighteenth century.

The importance of portraits increased in the courtly, aristocratic society of Restoration England. Charles I had brought Van Dyck to England to paint portraits of himself, his family, and his courtiers. The Court of Charles II needed a foreign painter of similar distinction. The man who filled the bill was Peter Lely, son of a Flemish soldier, who studied art in Holland and first came to England in 1641. During the Commonwealth and Protectorate Lely thrived doing portraits of Puritans, including Cromwell. At the Restoration Charles II appointed Lely as his court painter. He established a shop where he turned out large numbers of portraits and copies with the aid of assistants. He was able to live in a grand style and assemble a valuable collection of Italian art, which substituted for his lack of study in Italy.

Lely's portraits are invariably flattering, with a certain sameness of appearance that makes them easily recognizable and led a contemporary to remark: "Lilly's Pictures was all Brothers & sisters." Nevertheless, at times he could be more than just a successful society painter, and some of his male portraits show strong character. His portraits or copies of them hang in all the best country houses of England, and his influence on portrait painting in England was very great.

Baroque Music

In the seventeenth century the dominant musical style was the baroque, which developed in Italy and spread throughout Europe. The medieval foundation of baroque music was polyphony, which consists of an interweaving of melodic lines. Polyphony began in the early Middle Ages as simple plainsong used for chanting the text of the mass. In the Renaissance the plainsong text of the mass was placed in the tenor part and secular tunes were added above or below it to give the music variety, which was criticized by churchmen as irreverent. As the voices intersected, chords were formed, which musicians recognized as pleasing. Giovanni Pierluigi da Palestrina a Renaissance composer of masses for the Papacy, was the master of a polyphonic style that maintained a constant flow of polyphony that was also richly harmonic and genuinely religious

Baroque music was a transition from Renaissance polyphony to music based on melody and chords. Fundamental to much baroque music was <u>basso continuo</u> (figured bass), in which the bass shown in the bass clef as one line of notes with numerals to indicate the harmony. The melody was written in the treble clef. The continuo was usually played on an organ or a harpsichord, a keyboard instrument with strings that were plucked. The keyboard player ornamented the continuo (melody or bass) with arpeggios, dissonances, rapid runs, trills and grace notes. In the opera or the theatre the keyboard player normally served as the conductor and played the continuo.

Baroque Opera

Baroque music was intended to please the intellect and move the emotions of the listener. The most important form of baroque music in Italy was opera, which communicated the sense of drama that was vital to baroque. Every town of any size had its own opera, and Italian opera singers spread all over Europe. The outstanding composer of operas was Alessandro Scarlatti, who established many of the characteristics of the Italian baroque opera. He composed almost 100 operas and many oratorios and cantatas.

The heroic or tragic opera (<u>opera seria</u>) dealt with great persons at a time of crisis. <u>Opera seria</u> began with an orchestra overture of three movements—a fast movement of rapid scales and runs, a chordal slow movement, and a fast movement in triple meter. The drama developed through arias, duets, or trios linked by recitative, sung dialogue similar to speech with light accompaniment on the harpsichord. A scene or act often ended with a virtuoso aria sung by one of the stars or a passionate love duet by the leading couple followed by a dramatic exit accompanied by applause.

The star singers were castrati, male singers who had been castrated so their voice did not change. The castrati had high, powerful soprano voices and played the heroic male lead. In the eighteenth century the <u>prima donna,</u> a star female singer appeared. The high drama of the opera was offset by comic operas (<u>opera buffa</u>), which dealt with ordinary people with local accents and plots based on everyday life. The main singer was usually a baritone or bass (<u>basso buffo</u>), who was at the center of the action.

The cantata arose in Italy and spread throughout Europe. It resembled opera in that it had an overture, arias, choruses and recitative but it did not include acting. Secular cantatas concerned with love and featuring pleasant melodies developed in Italy for Lent, when performances of opera were prohibited. The sacred cantata sung by a choir and soloists with organ continuo was an important part of worship in Lutheran and Catholic churches. In Germany, Johann Sebastian Bach wrote many cantatas, some using a familiar hymn as the text.

<u>The Violin</u>

Baroque music was revolutionized by the emergence of the violin and related stringed instruments (viola, cello, string bass), which were perfected in Italy in the seventeenth century. The violin communicated a warm tone not found in the organ and a smooth flow of sound not found in the harpsichord. Much violin music was also suitable for the flute. When combined in an orchestra or small group, the stringed instruments gave a rich sound that lent itself to display of virtuosity or expression of feeling.

Violin music was written in many forms. The sonata began as the instrumental equivalent of the cantata, but late-seventeenth century it was refined as music for a solo instrument in several movements. Most commonly the sonata was written for violin or flute with continuo. Sonatas were written for church use (sonata da chiesa) or as secular chamber music. Often a cello was added to form a trio sonata, which gave a richer sound. The. suite was a collection of pieces performed by a small group of string players.

In the early eighteenth century, violin playing was stimulated by Arcangelo Corelli, a violinist and composer in Rome. Corelli was the founder of violin playing in respect of fingering, bowing, and a lyrical tone. His main compositions were published in six collections of violin music, primarily violin sonatas, trio sonatas, and concertos. His compositions were straightforward and balanced, and communicate a baroque dignity congenial to his times. His influence was spread through Europe by his many pupils. About 1700 a boom began in music publication, and the influence of Corelli was spread throughout Europe by publication and his many pupils. Corelli's works continued to be regarded as "classic" long after his style had become passé.

The virtuoso performer found his medium in the concerto, a work for soloist and string orchestra that was intended to enable a soloist to display his virtuosity. Corelli established the form of the concerto as fast-slow-fast with the soloist and the orchestra alternating. The master of the concerto was Antonio Vivaldi, a fiery Venetian violinist. In 1711 Vivaldi's L'estro Armonica, a collection of twelve concertos for one or two violins and orchestra, was published in Amsterdam and widely circulated throughout Europe. More concertos followed, including the popular "the Four Seasons." Vivaldi's concertos pushed the violin far beyond its previous technical boundaries. He was enormously productive, and his works also include a wide range of operas and choral works. Vivaldi's bold and imaginative works had a powerful influence on eighteenth-century music.

Vivaldi's concertos consist of fast-slow-fast movements. The soloist and orchestra perform as a team. In a typical movement, the orchestra ("tutti") begins with a main theme followed by a solo passage, which is followed by a return (ritornello) to the main theme or variations of it played by the full orchestra. Vivaldi established the concerto in a form that was widely accepted. Another form of concerto was the concerto grosso, in which the soloist was replaced by a small group of instrumentalists known as the concertino. The concerto grosso initially was popularized by Corelli. Bach's <u>Brandenburg Concertos</u> (1722) are the best-known examples of the concerto grosso.

Classical discipline and order characterized French music. At the Court of Louis XIV, Jean-Baptiste Lully established a string orchestra that was notable for its precision. His many operas reflect French classicism in that they are dignified and orderly with careful correlation of the music and the words. François Couperin, an organist and musician at the Court of Louis XIV, developed the harpsichord as a solo instrument. His music displays the French qualities of his time—restraint and naturalness. Most of his harpsichord pieces were in dance forms, to which he could impart a high degree of intensity. His ornamentations were written out rather than being left to improvisation by the performer. His compositions were popular in England and influenced his contemporary, Henry Purcell.

<u>Baroque Music in England</u>

As in other aspects of English culture, music in the later seventeenth century was dominated by the French influence. Charles II brought the French musical style to England. At the Restoration he was accompanied by a band of twenty-four violins. Horns, oboes, flutes, and trumpets were added for musical odes and other kinds of formal court music. The function of the court musicians was to provide music for court ceremonies, the Chapel Royal, dining, dancing, and theatricals. The violins played at Charles II's coronation in Westminster Abbey, which led Pepys to comment, "instead of the ancient, grave, and solemn wind musique accompanying the organ, was introduced a concert of twenty-four violins, between every pause, after the French fantastical light way, better suiting a tavern, or playhouse, than a church."

Apart from Charles IIs band of twenty-four violins, the violin was not common in England in the seventeenth century. In 1674 John Evelyn, author and diarist, heard Nicola Matteis, an Italian violinist perform in London. Evelyn was amazed. In his diary Evelyn wrote "certainly never mortal man Exceeded on that Instrument." Matteis, he wrote, "seem'd to be so <u>spiritato'd</u> and plaied such ravishing things on a ground (bass) as astonished us all." Matteis settled in London, where he performed concerts and took students. He published a collection of 120 violin pieces in 1676 and another 70 pieces in 1678. He also published works for his students. He and his son, who had the same name, can be designated as the founders of violin playing in England.

Interest in music was seen in the rise of public concerts for mixed audiences, often featuring a foreign-born performer. A society to sponsor concerts was established in London in 1672. Music was important in the Restoration theatre, but as a diversion or interlude. Some plays with music were called operas, but these were not true opera, for the music was not an integral part of the drama. In the theatre witty, clever words were dominant, and the potential for the development of English opera was choked off by the Englishman's delight in the spoken word.

Restoration England boasted a composer of the first rank—Henry Purcell. Like Mozart, Purcell was the precocious son of a musician, for his father was head of the choristers at Westminster Abbey. The son joined the singers at the Chapel Royal as a choirboy when he was nine, and when his voice changed he was given a Court appointment as composer for the violins. Although most of his compositions were choral, Purcell was an excellent violinist, and, in this office he wrote Sonnatas in III Parts (1683) for that instrument, 22 trio sonatas for two violins and bass viol and eight suites for harpsichord..In 1679 he became organist at Westminster Abbey, a post that he held for the rest of his life. In 1682 he was appointed organist and composer of sacred music at the Chapel Royal,.

Purcell wrote many long, full-voiced anthems with string accompaniments, including a series of choral odes to celebrate the feast of St. Cecilia, patron saint of music. One of his best anthems is My Heart is Inditing (1685), written for the coronation of King James II. Purcell appears to have had Catholic sympathies, and the reign of James II was one of his most productive periods. After "the Glorious Revolution" Purcell kept his position as organist at Westminster Abbey and his court positions, but his suspected Catholicism led to a reduction in his production of sacred music, and he turned almost exclusively to secular music. The famous, "Hail, bright Cecilia" (1692) takes 45 minutes to perform and contains brilliant solo and choral singing. Purcell composed six birthday odes for Queen Mary. Probably his greatest work is the music for the funeral of Queen Mary (1694), a spectacular occasion set off by Purcell's powerful yet poignant music. The same music was performed later in the year at his own funeral.

After 1689 court music declined, and Henry Purcell was primarily a composer for the theatre. He wrote much fine theatre music in the form of overtures, incidental instrumental music, serenades, drinking songs, and dances. He also wrote orchestral suites to accompany plays.

In his four semi-operas (masques), the narrative is little more than a framework for elaborate portrayals of ceremonies, rituals or magical events. His opera, Dido and Aeneas (1689) was performed privately and was not seen in public in his lifetime. He collaborated with Dryden in King Arthur (1691), a Restoration style masque that was a theatrical success. The plot concerns the efforts of King Arthur to rescue his fiancée, who has been abducted by the evil Saxon king. The major earthly characters do not sing; the supernatural characters do.,

Purcell composed before the baroque sonata, cantata, and concerto were fully formulated, and hence his music harks back to earlier music. His florid vocal ornamentation exhibits a Renaissance exuberance, while the logical structure of his works shows the influence of French classicism. In his many sacred anthems he combines solos and choruses in a manner that is dramatic and almost operatic. Like Wren, Purcell was able to draw upon a variety of styles and fit them together into a satisfying whole.

Ch. 4. Politics and Ideas in the Revolutionary Age

The historical process usually moves slowly and gradually, but sometimes a timely event advances it rapidly. The flight of King James II and the intrusion of William of Orange into English politics opened opportunities for rapid change. The English called these memorable events "The Glorious Revolution of 1688-89." The long wars against Louis XIV of France made it necessary for Crown and Parliament to meet annually and learn to work together. Triennial elections involved a broad segment of the population in politics. Freedom of the press and the advance of literacy opened the way to public discussion of political issues. Partisanship was intensified by war and religious dissensions. When Queen Anne died in 1714, the institutions of "the mixed and balanced constitution "of the eighteenth century were in place, and the political, religious, and cultural life of the British Isles had been profoundly changed. The accession of the Hanoverian king, George I, stabilized the new political system that had emerged under King William and Queen Anne. The rise of commercial publication and increasing literacy spawned a cluster of brilliant writers who were important players in the political process.

"The Glorious Revolution of 1688-89"

When Charles II died in 1685, he was succeeded by his brother as James II. In the euphoria of a new reign, Parliament voted James revenue for life large enough that he did not need to call Parliament again. Three years later, James was out on his ear. What happened?

James II brought many of his troubles upon himself. He made no secret of his determination to rule with a strong hand. He assembled a standing army that he stationed near London. He intimidated judges, and he interfered with the rights of incorporated towns and the universities. James was a convert to Catholicism. With the zeal of a convert he used the royal power in every possible way to advance his religion. His Catholic faith was openly avowed; he surrounded himself with Catholic courtiers and priests; he appointed Catholics to posts in the army and in the universities. He made clear his determination to use the royal authority to remove the legal restrictions on Catholics.

In April, 1688, James issued a <u>Declaration of Indulgence</u> suspending the laws against Catholics and Dissenters. To show his determination, James ordered the <u>Declaration</u> to be read aloud in all churches. When seven bishops, including Archbishop William Sancroft refused to read the <u>Declaration</u> in their cathedral churches, James prosecuted them. The seven bishops were acquitted by a London jury, which was followed by public rejoicing.

The opponents of James II, who now included the Church of England, knew that their time had come. They sent a message to William of Orange inviting him to intervene to protect their "religion, liberties, and properties." They assured him that "nineteen parts of twenty" desired a change. William was quick to accept this opportune invitation. Much as we might respect James II's loyalty to his religion, we must realize that in 1688 religion was not a private matter—especially the religion of kings.

Fortuitous events often have an important influence on the historical process, and such was the case in 1688. James II's first wife, the mother of the princesses Mary and Anne, died in 1671, and James married again—Mary Beatrice of Modena, an Italian and a pious Catholic. Mary Beatrice had many pregnancies, but either the pregnancy miscarried or the child died at a young age. In June 1688 a son was born who would take precedence over Mary and Anne and would undoubtedly be raised a Catholic. The English people faced the prospect of an indefinite succession of Catholic rulers. In Holland, William of Orange saw Mary's claim to the English throne vanishing.

The birth of a son to James and his queen seemed so opportune that many could not or would not believe it. The story was spread that the infant was smuggled into the queen's bed in a warming pan while she pretended to be giving birth. No one today believes that story, but people will believe what they want to believe. The story eased the consciences of many who had previously proclaimed their devotion to the principles of divine right and hereditary succession. William had to act immediately or abandon his hopes for the English throne. After agonizing delays, William prepared to sail for England, only to be delayed further by unfavorable winds. Eventually "the Protestant wind" blew from the east and wafted William to England and his destiny.

On November 5, 1688, Guy Fawkes Day, William of Orange, stadholder of the Dutch Republic, landed in the southwest of England near Plymouth. He came with a Dutch army of 15,000 men. His action was an armed invasion of the island—the first since William the Conqueror in 1066—but it was a friendly invasion. William declared that he had come at the request of English leaders to defend English liberties from the usurpations of King James II and to secure the election of a free Parliament.

Soon the aristocracy and landed gentry of England rallied to his side. As William and his army moved slowly toward London, King James found himself virtually friendless. His eldest daughter, Princess Mary, was in Holland awaiting news of her husband. The king's younger daughter, Princess Anne, slipped out of the palace one night and took refuge with supporters of William. John Churchill, commander of the king's army, left his post with many of his officers and joined the rebels. The London mob turned ugly and James II sent his wife and infant son to France for safety. James called a meeting of prominent noblemen who advised him to come to terms with the Prince of Orange. By this time James II had lost his grip on himself as well as his kingdom. Shortly thereafter he followed his wife and son into exile, appearing at the court of King Louis XIV on Christmas Day, 1688.

Confidently, William moved into London with his army and occupied the royal palaces. His wife, Mary, soon joined him. With the approval of those members of Parliament who were in London at the time, William took over administration of the government and collection of the revenue. Writs were issued for a meeting of Parliament as William had promised, although that body, since a king was not present, was called a Convention. As usual, the election was determined primarily by local influence; it did not become a national referendum on William or James. The public remained calm, but a flurry of pamphlets proposed changes more radical than getting rid of an unpopular king.

The Convention met in January 1689, and after preparing a <u>Declaration of Rights</u> offered the Crown to William and Mary, with William exercising the royal power. The <u>Declaration</u> was deliberately non-controversial. It complained that King James II had ruled in violation of the law and stated the principle that the king was under the law. It confirmed certain rights that Parliament had attempted to establish over the previous century—parliamentary control of taxation and the army, free elections, and frequent meetings. The <u>Declaration</u> specified a few rights of individuals—the right of petition, bearing arms "as allowed by law, "and fair trials with reasonable bail, fines, and punishments. A new <u>Coronation Oath</u> required the king and queen to govern according to law, maintain justice with mercy, and support the Church of England. There was nothing in the <u>Declaration</u> that threatened the existing structure of government or the power of the political and social elite. The <u>Declaration</u> was as un-revolutionary as it was possible to make it. "The Glorious Revolution of 1688-89" was over. Or was it?

William seized his opportunity, but in 1688-89 the opportunity appeared as the result of a remarkable expression of the national will. William was the leader of "the Glorious Revolution" but in a low-key way the English people were the heroes. When a few prominent politicians of both parties came forward to join William, others followed. The London mob rioted enough to help send James on his way, but in general good order was maintained. The elections for the Convention varied little from previous elections, and the efforts of partisans and extremists to arouse strong feelings had little result. Collectively the nation held its breath, hoped for the best and was determined to avoid civil war.

The Convention wanted a change of ruler without introducing substantive and controversial issues. They carried out a revolution in the seventeenth-century meaning of that term—a change of persons at the top. As the implications of the Revolution unfolded, changes took place that was revolutionary in the modern sense—triennial elections, freedom of the press, and parliamentary control of the cost of the civil government and the military forces. The events of 1688-89 were not the Revolution but the prelude to revolution.

When we consider "the Glorious Revolution," we must remember that there was a larger community than that represented in the Convention. The king of England was also king of Scotland, but otherwise Scotland was a separate country. The Revolution in Scotland was out of William's control. William agreed to the <u>Claim of Right</u> (1689), which reviewed the principles of Scottish law and declared James II deposed due to his violations of the law. William and Mary were declared King and Queen of Scotland. Scottish leaders also used the opportunity to strengthen their independence both in government and in the Church of Scotland. Although loyalty to James II and Catholicism lingered in the Highlands, William and Mary were proclaimed joint rulers. A modest show of force was all that was needed to establish that point. In North America the English colonists used the opportunity to get rid of unpopular governors and restore the independence of their assemblies.

In Ireland circumstances led to a revolution more drastic than in any of William III's other kingdoms. In March 1689 James II attempted a comeback and landed in Ireland with a French army and a supply of French weapons. The Irish Catholics rallied to his support while the Protestant minority held on desperately. William III was determined not to allow Louis XIV, his mortal enemy, to establish a base in his back yard. The next year William landed in Ireland with his faithful Dutch troops, and on July 1 he defeated James II at the Battle of Boyne, an event still celebrated with parades and orange banners by the Protestants of Northern Ireland. James II returned to France, where he lived out the rest of his life. The Protestant minority in Ireland took advantage of the opportunity to establish a grip on power that they held for more than two centuries. Irish Catholics were stripped of any political role and were kept in a subordinate status by a network of laws that resembled Jim Crow in their thoroughness and complexity.

The accession of William and Mary involved England in a long period of war with Louis XIV of France. Louis attacked in the Rhineland in the autumn of 1688, which gave William of Orange his opportunity to land in England. As King of England, William III was able to form a powerful coalition of England, the Austrian Hapsburg Empire, and the Dutch Republic to resist the aggressions of the French king. Spain and the Duchy of Savoy in northern Italy joined later. In American history this war is called King William's War. The allies were able to stop the French. In the Peace of Ryswick (1697) Louis XIV gained nothing.

In 1700 the King of Spain died and left the entire Spanish inheritance to the grandson of Louis XIV. Acquiescence in this step would destroy the European balance of power and threaten England and the Dutch Republic. William established another European alliance to resist the overweening ambitions of Louis XIV. In 1701, as French troops were occupying the Spanish territories in the name of the Philip V, the war of the Spanish Succession broke out. In 1702 William III died due to a fall from his horse. He was succeeded by Mary's younger sister, Queen Anne.

The Reign of William and Mary

Under William and Mary and Queen Anne, the role of the Royal Court as a cultural center declined. The continental concept of a court had been brought to England by Charles II, whose court was a center of entertainment and political intrigue, but by the end of his reign the cultural role of the court had declined. The court of James II was dominated by the intense Catholicism of the king and his wife. James' major cultural expenditure was a magnificent Catholic Chapel for Queen Mary Beatrice. When James tried to reduce the cost of the Chapel Royal, Princess Anne, who was a devout Anglican, insisted on preserving orchestral music in the Chapel and supported the composer, Henry Purcell.

William III was not interested in court life, but Queen Mary was very sociable. When William was absent on the continent, as he was much of the time, she maintained the usual court functions, which helped establish the new monarchs among the aristocracy. After her death in 1694, the court became a setting only for routine functions. Queen Anne enjoyed court life and music, but her health limited what she could do. In any case, the center of cultural life had become the great houses of the aristocracy and the thriving publishing and entertainment world of London.

William III and Mary were interested in strengthening the Church

, and John Tillotson, who regarded the Revolution as a miraculous rescue from popery and tyranny, became archbishop of Canterbury. As a latitudinarian, Tillotson supported the Toleration Act of 1689, but he was disappointed when he proposed a policy of mutual concessions (comprehension) intended to bring some Dissenters back into Church. Neither the Anglicans nor the Dissenters wanted it. Tillotson worked closely with Queen Mary in the task of religious revival. He instructed his bishops to insist that the clergy set a good moral example, hold divine services regularly, administer communion frequently, and provide pastoral care for their parishioners.

Tillotson's friend, Gilbert Burnet, a devoted Whig, was close to William and Mary. As the crisis concerning James II intensified, Burnet moved to the Dutch Republic, where he became an adviser to William of Orange on Church matters. As William's chaplain, Burnet came to England in 1688 in the same boat that brought William. He became Bishop of Salisbury, where he was active in promoting Whig and latitudinarian views, despite the resistance of most of his parish clergy. His Exposition of the 39 Articles of the Church of England (1698) was a major statement of latitudinarianianism. Bishop Burnet's History of His Own Time, published after his death, is one of the great English memoirs. Burnet began by writing an autobiography and transformed it into a gripping narrative with well-defined characters who interact with each other as they deal with personality conflicts and great issues.

Thomas Bray, an Anglican clergyman, was active in the effort to revitalize the Church of England. He solicited support to establish parish libraries for religious instruction in England and the colonies. With the support of the Bishop of London, he founded the Society for Promoting Christian Knowledge (SPCK), which printed religious books and pamphlets that were distributed by supporters in their parishes. The SPCK also encouraged the founding of charity schools and promoted missionary efforts in the colonies. At the urging of the bishop of London, who had a vague authority over the Church of England in the colonies, Bray founded the Society for the Propagation of the Gospel in Foreign Parts (SPG), to strengthen the work of the Church in America and engage in missionary activities among the Indians.

Queen Anne and the War of the Spanish Succession

When Queen Anne succeeded William III, the War of the Spanish Succession was already in progress. The Bourbon monarchs of France and Spain had the advantage of being in possession of the Spanish territories; their strategy was to hold what they had. It was up to the Allies to dislodge them. The objective of the Allies was to end French control of Spain and the Spanish colonies, including the valuable slave trade (the asiento) to the New World.

Queen Anne relied heavily on John Churchill, Duke of Marlborough, the greatest military commander of the age and a skilled diplomat. Marlborough concentrated his efforts in the Low Countries in an attempt to defeat the forces of Louis XIV in battle. He won a series of victories, but France under Louis XIV was too strong to be defeated. Marlborough's greatest victory, the Battle of Blenheim (1704), took place in south Germany. When Louis XIV sent an army to attack Vienna, the Austrian capital, Marlborough marched his forces up the Rhine valley and defeated the French at the village of Blenheim. England opened a second front in Spain to place the second son of the Austrian Emperor on the throne, but it failed. By 1710 much of the English public was ready for peace, but Marlborough hoped that one more battle would yield complete victory.

Queen Anne identified politically with the Tories and the Church of England, but she learned that she needed the support of the Whigs and their mercantile friends to finance the war. In 1705 the Whigs gained control of the government, and their skill in electioneering and managing the patronage enabled them to obtain a complaisant House of Commons. They worked closely with Robert Harley, the non-partisan speaker of the House of Commons, who joined the government as secretary of state. Harley objected to the partisanship of the Whigs— "the Crown must not be a party," he said—but he worked with the Whigs to prosecute the war.

Scotland and the Act of Union

The Scots were largely passive observers of "the Glorious Revolution." Although they felt strong loyalties to the Stuarts, there was some consolation in knowing that William III was a Calvinist. A Scottish

Convention that met in Edinburgh in March 1689 proclaimed William and Mary the rightful rulers of Scotland. The necessities of the War of the Spanish Succession brought about an action that James I and others had proposed—the political and economic union of England and Scotland. To the Scots the advantages of the proposed union were economic. The backward economy of Scotland was hard hit by English restrictions on imports of Scottish cattle, textiles, and grain. Equally important to Scotland was access to trade with the English colonies.

Robert Harley was an important member of the commission that negotiated the terms of union. After much political maneuvering and many political payoffs, the Act of Union was passed in 1707. The Act provided for a common succession to the crowns of England and Scotland. The English and Scottish Parliaments were combined into one Parliament of Great Britain meeting at Westminster. The Scots were given 45 members in the House of Commons and 16 elected peers in the House of Lords. The Act for Securing the Church (1706), which guaranteed that the Church of Scotland would continue as a Presbyterian polity, satisfied the Church, and thereafter clerical resistance to the Act of Union was minimal. The administrative structures and legal systems of the two countries remained separate. Both economies were fully merged, including access of the Scots to the colonies, thus creating the largest free-trade area in existence at that time. The benefits of the Act of Union came slowly to Scotland, but the Scots were now full participants in the life of a nation whose civilization was entering into a period of remarkable growth and achievement.

The Act of Union did not go into effect without resistance. Many Scots, known as Jacobites, remained loyal to James Francis Edward, son of James II, and they resented the loss of their independent Parliament. Jacobitism also found support among elements of the Tory Party in England. In 1708 James Edward prepared to invade Scotland to assert his claim to the Crown of Scotland, but the attempt never got off the ground. Had James succeeded in reaching Scotland, a substantial uprising in his favor doubtless would have taken place. It is possible that English Jacobites might have given him considerable assistance. With English troops engaged in the Low Countries and Spain, the challenge to the Whig ministry could have been serious.

Partisan Politics in the Reign of Queen Anne

During the reign of Queen Anne, partisan politics rose to a high level of intensity. Apart from the war, the most divisive issue was the privileges of the Church of England. From the beginning of the reign, the Tories had attempted to pass the Occasional Conformity Bill, which would prevent Dissenters from qualifying for local offices by taking communion once a year in their parish church while continuing to attend their chapels on other Sundays. The Tories had consistently been blocked by the Whigs, who depended upon the Dissenting vote in the boroughs. In 1708, when the Whigs abused their influence in the government, Harley resigned and intrigued with Queen Anne and the Tories to counter-balance the Whigs.

The Whigs dug their own grave by a spectacular impeachment of the Rev. Henry Sacheverell, a popular Tory preacher. In 1709 Sacheverell delivered a violent sermon at St. Paul's on the theme, "The Church in Danger." Sacheverell was impeached in the House of Commons, where a zealous young Whig named Robert Walpole was one of the managers of the impeachment. The Whigs discovered that they had misjudged the mood of the country. Resentment of the Whig government was rising, and the anxieties of the Anglican clergy were communicated to a public disturbed by the political and social changes fostered by the war. Sacheverell became a public hero for his passionate defiance of the Whigs. Riots broke out in London that had to be suppressed by troops, and expressions of support for Sacheverell poured in from all parts of the country. In the House of Lords, Sacheverell was convicted in a close vote, but his support among the people was so strong that he was given only token punishment, after which he made a triumphal tour of the country. Queen Anne felt deep resentment that she had been put in a position that cast doubt on her loyalty to the Church.

Underlying the conflict of Whig and Tory lay deep differences between those who identified with the new England that was emerging in the early eighteenth century and those who were struggling to preserve the values and social relationships of the past. The new England exercised an active role in European diplomacy and war, maintained a large army as well as a powerful fleet, and governed a far-flung empire. In this new age political power went to politicians who gained the support of the Crown and used "the influence of the Crown" and party loyalties to manage the House of Commons.

An important element in the new England was the "money power" of bankers, ship-owners, merchants, and contractors, whose support was essential to any government. The new England was tolerant of religious differences. The new England was proud of its achievements, optimistic about the future, impressed by the potential of Reason and science, and increasingly interested in the larger world beyond its shores. Although they were a minority in the nation, the Whigs welcomed these developments and assumed that they were the best qualified to assume the role of leadership in this dynamic new age. They mingled with the bankers, merchants, and professional men whose importance was increasing.

The Tory base was in the old England—an England of manor houses, parish churches, cathedral and market towns, and rustic villages. The economic base of the old England was agriculture and handicraft industries; its social relationships were based upon tradition, deference, and inherited status. This old England was strongly represented in the House of Commons, where its instincts were antithetical to political leadership and party discipline. The old England preserved the humanistic traditions of the Renaissance and the theological formulations of the Reformation. Tory England was inclined to stress tradition and authority as checks upon pride and sinfulness; it was dubious about the claims made for Reason and science and the prospects for "improvement."

Tories tended to reject the new directions that England was taking. They disliked extended diplomacy and war and a large standing army. They deplored the swollen expenditures of the Crown, which created a dependence on bankers and businessmen. They reluctantly accepted toleration of Dissenters and the Act of Union with Scotland. The new England and the old were the social and religious foundations of the division between Whig and Tory.

The Peace and the Succession

As partisanship intensified, Robert Harley opened private contacts with Queen Anne. He also established contact with the Tories, who saw in him a leader who could bring them back into power and pass the

Occasional Conformity Bill. In 1710 the mask was thrown off when Queen Anne dismissed the Whigs and appointed Harley as lord treasurer to lead a government that was supported primarily by the Tories. The most important step was to dissolve Parliament and determine the future of the new government on the hustings. The election of 1711 was one of the most decisive in the eighteenth century, as the Tories won a majority in the House of Commons. Harley continued as lord treasurer and was raised to the peerage as the Earl of Oxford. Henry St. John, secretary of state, a strongly partisan Tory, became Viscount Bolingbroke. Oxford tried to moderate the partisanship of his Tory majority, but he was now in the House of Lords and could not control the Tories in the House of Commons.

By that time, the Queen and the country were tired of the war, which dragged on indecisively at unprecedented expense. As secretary of state, Bolingbroke began secret negotiations with France for peace. Marlborough was dismissed from his commands and narrowly escaped impeachment. The Church was gratified by passage of the Occasional Conformity Act against the violent opposition of Whigs and Dissenters. Jonathan Swift, a clergyman of the Church of Ireland, came to the defense of the Church in An Argument Against Abolishing Christianity (1711) and The Sentiments of a Church of England Man (1711). In 1714 the Tories passed the Schism Act, which required schools for Dissenters to be licensed by the bishop and the teacher to take communion in the Church of England once a year..

Louis XIV was desperate for peace, for in addition to defeats on the battlefield France was approaching bankruptcy, trade and industry had collapsed, and famine stalked the land. "The Sun King" would accept peace on reasonable terms, but he would not turn on his grandson and drive him from the Spanish throne. Pressed by his Tory majority, Oxford decided to make peace on the best terms he could get, for the war was now the main reason for the polarization of English politics, which he had always deplored. Queen Anne was eager to bring an end to the bloodshed and expense. Bolingbroke made it clear to the French that England was prepared to accept a settlement that would secure England's interests even if it meant abandoning her allies. When the terms of the peace were revealed, an intense partisan conflict erupted. The House of Commons approved the terms but the Whig-dominated

House of Lords balked. At that point Queen Anne settled the matter by creating twelve Tory peers, and the Lords gave in.

Political Journalism in the Reign of Queen Anne

The war of the Spanish Succession and the peace dominated English public affairs, but politics were also stirred by disputes concerning the succession to the throne and the role of Dissenters in English society. These issues were fought out between the Whig and Tory parties. Partisanship was aggravated by triennial elections and a free press, which made public opinion an important factor in the political process.

Political journalism was raised to a high art. The Whigs found a spokesman in Capt. Richard Steele, an officer in the army and man about town. Steele began his career as a political writer with The Christian Hero (1701), a tract that praised William III. Steele left the army and associated with the Whig politicians who gained power in 1705. He was a member of the Kit Cat club, founded by the publisher, Jacob Tonson, which also included Joseph Addison, William Congreve, Robert Walpole, then a rising Whig politician, and the Duke of Marlborough. The Whigs provided for Steele by making him editor of the Gazette, a government publication that contained announcements and bits of news gleaned from diplomatic dispatches, hand-written newsletters, reports by ship-captains, etc.

Bolingbroke's peace proposals unleashed a furious pamphlet war. Oxford used Jonathan Swift to support the peace treaty among the Tory gentlemen and churchmen. Swift became editor of a Tory weekly, The Examiner (1710-11), in which he savagely attacked the Whigs and the Duke of Marlborough. In this role, Swift was involved with Oxford, Bolingbroke, and other key members of the Tory government. His pamphlet, The Conduct of the Allies (1711), was intended to persuade the country gentlemen in the House of Commons of the need for peace. In this pamphlet, Swift charges that Marlborough and the Whigs prolonged the war for their own glory and personal enrichment, and the Allies were exploiting England for dynastic, territorial, or financial gain. In true Tory language, Swift excoriates the financiers and war contractors who grew wealthy at the expense of the landed interest. The pamphlet ran to six editions, a total of 11,000 copies. In The Public Spirit of the Whigs (1714), Swift attacks the Whig leaders and writers for inciting fears that the Tories threatened the Protestant succession to the throne.

Capt. Steele returned fire. His essay journals, The Guardian (1713) and The Englishman (1713-14), were the principal voice of the Whigs. In his pamphlet, The Crisis (1714), Steele declares that the Tory ministry of Oxford and Bolingbroke threatened the Protestant succession to the throne. Steele, who had been elected to Parliament, was charged with seditious libel and expelled from the House of Commons. His friend and colleague, Joseph Addison, joined the fray with his play, Cato (1713), which was based on the life of the Roman statesman. In the play, Addison calls upon Englishmen to unite in support of their country. The play was a hit that attracted sold-out audiences. Both parties claimed that the play supported their policies, but in tone Cato leans toward the Whigs.

Swift and Steele did not know that Oxford had another spokesman who promoted his policies from the perspective of the literate shopkeeper, craftsman, or farmer. Daniel Defoe came from a modest Puritan family in London and lived through the persecution of Dissenters under Charles II, from which he developed a powerful commitment to freedom of religion and the press. He supported William III in his poem, The True Born Englishman (1701), an enormously popular work. In his satirical The Shortest Way with Dissenters (1702), he opposes the Occasional Conformity Bill and satirizes the bigotry and intolerance of the Tories and the Church. He was charged with seditious libel, fined, sentenced to three days in the pillory, and imprisoned until Robert Harley came to his rescue.

When he left prison, Defoe was bankrupt and his prospects as a businessman were ruined. He broke new ground with his A Review of the State of the British Nation (1704-13), a periodical that combined items of general interest with news and comment about politics, foreign affairs, war, and the economy. Defoe's Review usually contained one essay written by Defoe plus shorter pieces. It was intended for middle-class merchants and shopkeepers and was widely read in coffeehouses. Defoe's readers aspired to the respect given to gentlemen, even if they lacked the necessary financial resources, formal education, and cultivated manners. Defoe assured them that they were as good as anyone. In Defoe's view, civilization follows trade, which gives the merchant a role beyond that of accumulating wealth. He describes with pride how trade had raised families to the status of gentlemen and eventually to statesmen.

Harley, then speaker of the House of Commons, established a secret connection with Defoe, who used the <u>Review</u> to promote Harley's policies. Defoe traveled extensively for Harley, including a trip to Scotland to promote the Act of Union. When the Tories came to office, Oxford (Harley) used Defoe to appeal to the business community to support his policy of peace. Swift and Defoe appealed to different constituencies and came from distinct social classes. It was said that Swift, a gentleman, entered Oxford's house through the front door and Defoe through the back.

The Peace of Utrecht (1713) was a landmark in English foreign relations. For the first time, England emerged as a major factor in the European balance of power. Philip V was recognized as King of Spain with the provision that the Crowns of France and Spain could never be joined. France was required to banish James Edward, son of James II, and repudiate any support for his cause. England received Gibraltar and Minorca, which were needed to control the Mediterrean and check the French Mediterranean fleet.

Commercial and colonial considerations were important. Acquisition of Newfoundland and Acadia (renamed Nova Scotia) gave England strategic bases on the grand banks fisheries and near the mouth of the St. Lawrence River. England gained limited trade privileges in the Spanish Empire, an objective of English merchants since the days of Queen Elizabeth. The Asiento Treaty gave the Royal African Company the monopoly of the slave trade to the Spanish colonies for thirty years.

Bolingbroke also negotiated a commercial treaty with France that would reduce barriers to trade and perhaps mitigate the rivalries that had contributed to two major wars. The proposed treaty aroused a cry of protest from the English woolen industry and from English artisans and craftsmen who felt threatened by French goods of superior quality. The proposals failed and smuggling continued to be the main channel for trade between England and France for almost three quarters of a century.

As the health of Queen Anne declined, another controversial issue was the succession to the throne. Queen Anne's last child died in 1700, and the Queen was dying without direct heirs. In the Act of Settlement (1701) Parliament had declared that the Crown would pass to Sophia, Electress of Hanover, granddaughter of James I, who was the closest Protestant relative of Queen Anne. Sophia died in 1714, a few weeks before Queen Anne, who was determined to outlive her. Her claim passed to her son, George, Elector of Hanover, a medium-sized state in north Germany.

The Hanoverian Succession

In 1714 Queen Anne died, and the Elector George was proclaimed king as King George I. His son, George Augustus, became Prince of Wales and heir to the throne. When George I arrived in London, it was clear that he would give political office to the Whigs, for in his view the Tory ministry of Oxford and Bolingbroke had betrayed the great Duke of Marlborough and the cause for which he had fought. The king appointed Whigs to the major offices, and they in turn purged the subordinate offices of Tories. Joseph Addison rose to the peak of his ambition by serving briefly as Secretary of State, and Richard Steele was rewarded for his services by receiving a patent to operate a theatre at Covent Garden. The Tories were deprived of their leaders—Oxford was imprisoned and impeached, but eventually the impeachment was dropped. Bolingbroke was in France plotting a Stuart restoration.

George I was a mature man and an experienced ruler when he became king in 1714. He had commanded the Hanoverian forces under the Duke of Marlborough in the War of the Spanish Succession. As Elector of Hanover, he was concerned at various times by rivalry with neighboring Prussia, potential threats from the rising power of Russia, and territorial controversies growing out of the declining empire of Sweden. As king, he purged the army of Tory officers and paid close attention to promotions, training, and discipline. He was less directly involved with the navy. He left the complex issues and personal rivalries that characterized English politics to his ministers.

In 1694, George divorced his wife on charges of adultery and shut her up in a castle for the rest of her life. They had one son, George Augustus, who eventually became King George II, Their daughter married the King of Prussia. For female companionship, George I brought with him his mistress and step-sister, whom politicians recognized as useful intermediaries in reaching the king. A good deal of public discontent fell on his Hanoverian friends and courtiers, who were accused of lining their pockets through corrupt exploitation of their influence at court As a Lutheran, George I had no difficulty conforming to the Church of England. He turned Church patronage over to his Whig ministers, which contributed to their influence in Parliament and elections.

George I spoke English haltingly, and at court he spoke French or German. When he opened the annual session of Parliament with the speech from the throne, he read the first sentence and then gave the text to the Lord Chancellor, who read the rest for him. In Cabinet meetings the king spoke French, which most of the members understood. He disliked pomp and ceremony and devoted himself to business, interrupted by annual visits to his beloved electorate. His English subjects resented a foreign-born ruler who seemed to prefer Hanover and its interests to his new kingdom.

Without a queen, the Royal Court was not the social center it had been in the reigns of Charles I and Charles II. The Prince and Princess of Wales were socially active, and George I made a serious effort to match them. Court life was drastically reconfigured in conformity with the courts of the north German states. The king held the usual receptions, balls, card parties, and the like. From time to time, George I attended the theatre, partly to display himself to the public. Probably he understood the dialogue of the play, and he enjoyed the entertainments that followed it.. He showed a clear preference for the devotedly Whig theatre of Sir Richard Steele at Drury Lane. He brought with him from Hanover a love of music, especially opera.

The main threat to George I and the Whigs came from James Francis Edward Stuart, the "warming pan baby" whose birth had set off "the Glorious Revolution." James Edward had grown up in France with a sense of mission to restore the Stuart dynasty and to promote the interests of Catholicism. Over the years, dissident English politicians had intrigued with James Edward, but his dour personality and staunch Catholicism made it unlikely that he would be an acceptable alternative to the Hanoverians. With Bolingbroke at his side, however, he might possibly draw Tory support. In Scotland loyalty to the Stuart name continued, especially in the Highlands, where opposition to the Act of Union was strong. In 1715 James Edward was proclaimed king, and the Highland clans turned out in large numbers to await his arrival.

The plan was for him to land on the coast of Scotland, rally the Scots behind him, and march on England, where Tory malcontents and "Jacobites" would rise to his support. Characteristically, James Edward had difficulty getting his expedition organized. In Scotland, close to 15,000 men, including 18 peers, joined the uprising. Several thousand English Jacobites, many of them Catholics from the Northwest, rose in support.

The leader of the Scottish Jacobites was John Erskine, Earl of Mar, and the scion of an old but impoverished Scottish noble family, with close ties to the Stuarts. His active involvement in the negotiations for the Act of Union (1707) brought him to the attention of English politicians, especially Robert Harley, and led to political offices that eased his financial problems considerably. He became leader of the Scottish contingent in the House of Lords and of Scottish Jacobites in the House of Commons. With the accession of George I, Mar's Tory connections meant that he was excluded from public office, which he needed for personal and financial reasons. To repair his fortunes, he became involved in the Jacobite plot to restore the Stuarts to the throne.

In September, 1715 Mar assumed leadership of the Scottish uprising. His army of Highlanders won an indecisive battle at Sheriffmuir (Nov., 1715), but government forces, aided by Dutch troops, were able to stop any further advance and regained the initiative in Scotland. A Jacobite rising in northwestern England was quickly suppressed. By the time James III arrived in Scotland in December, "the '15" was over. James, accompanied by Mar, returned to Paris. Mar's efforts to obtain a pardon and return to Scotland were rejected by the Whig government, and discredited him at the court of James Edward. He died in Rome in 1768, disgraced and impoverished.

Jacobitism continued strong in Scotland and was an active factor in English politics, where it fused with Toryism. The threat of Jacobitism provided opportunities for foreign enemies to make trouble. In 1717 the government uncovered a Jacobite invasion plot backed by Sweden, and two years later a Spanish invasion plot was scattered by a storm.

Bolingbroke eventually was permitted to return to England, but his political career was over.

Steps were taken to strengthen the powers of the Whig government. George I appointed the Whigs to office and in 1715 an election was held, the last under the Triennial Act. The Whigs managed the election of 1715 so effectively that they gained control of the House of Commons, although the majority of the population still favored the Tories. Riots in London led to the Riot Act (1715), which authorized the mayor to read the Act to a mob that threatened to disturb public order and command them to leave within one hour. If they did not, force would be used to disperse them. In 1717, with another election approaching, the Whigs passed the Septennial Act, which required an election no later than every seven years. The Act gave the Whig majority in the House of Commons an additional four years and reduced considerably the political agitation that had contributed to political instability. The practice developed of letting a Parliament run for approximately six years before calling an election.

The Tories were cast into the political wilderness. Toryism remained strong among the clergy and the country gentlemen. The Tories developed a "Country" agenda that attacked Whig misuse of the "influence" of the Crown, which they claimed had corrupted the House of Commons and threatened the liberties of the people. Some Tories were Jacobites, who gathered from time to time to drink toasts to "the king over the water."

The Rise of the Writer

One of the major developments of the eighteenth-century was the rise of the professional writer, which was made possible by the growth of the publishing industry and the emergence of a broad market for printed material. In the sixteenth and early seventeenth centuries, authors of imaginative literature were supported primarily by a patron, positions in government or the Church, or an independent income. Poetry was written to be read aloud or circulated in manuscript. Print was not a means of earning income but another way to bring the writer to the attention of those who might support his work.

The theatre provided one means by which a writer could earn a living with his pen, as Shakespeare had demonstrated, but his profits came from his position as a partner in his theatrical company and not from the publication of his plays, which were published after his death. Through his prose writings Milton learned the value of print in reaching readers and obtained the political post of Latin Secretary to Cromwell, which ended with the Restoration. Milton received modest remuneration for his great epic poems, written and published during the Restoration era, but he could not have survived without some independent income.

The Revolution of 1688-89 and its aftermath made England a country in which a broad public was involved in the discussion of politics, religion, and social problems. There was a remarkable increase in literacy, so that ordinary businessmen, shopkeepers, artisans, farmers and yeomen were able to read and be informed about public affairs. Female literacy throughout the country has been estimated as 25 percent and double that in London. Women of all social classes learned to read, write, and express their thoughts through letters and literary compositions. England was becoming wealthier and more people had the time, money, and inclination to purchase printed material. Writers and publishers hastened to exploit the opportunities offered by the new reading public, and the quantity and quality of printed matter increased remarkably. It was still difficult for a writer to make a living at his trade, and even the most talented writers required some other form of financial support. The time when professional writers could earn a good living from their pen was approaching, but had not yet arrived.

The <u>Declaration of Rights</u> said nothing about freedom of the press. When the Licensing Act expired in 1695, the Whig government did not renew it, which opened the floodgates to a mass of publication, much of it concerned with current political and religious issues. The Stationers' Company's monopoly of publication was increasingly ignored. Authors and booksellers were still subject to prosecution for libel, including seditious libel (publication intended to defame the government), but a prosecution for libel required a jury, and London juries were inclined to support freedom of speech and the press.

The bookseller/publisher was the key figure in the explosion of print. Booksellers published books and other printed material for sale in their shops. Their publications—if they pleased the public—were sold in other bookshops throughout the country. The premier publisher of the early eighteenth century was Jacob Tonson. He came from a family of bookseller/publishers, and in 1678 he established his own firm. In 1686 he became a member of the Stationers' Company. Tonson, a Whig, established his position as the most prestigious English publisher with a splendid edition of Milton's Paradise Lost, which had to wait for publication until 1688, when the political climate changed in favor of a Puritan poet.

Tonson's relationship with John Dryden was important to both of them. He published the works of Dryden, beginning with Absalom and Achitophel (1681), and joined with Dryden to publish a series of translations of the ancient classics. Dryden's most ambitious project was a translation of Virgil's Aeneid plus other works, which was published by Tonson in magnificent volumes with over 100 engraved illustrations. The project was financed by more than 500 subscribers. Dryden's translations of other ancient classics followed. They were published in well-made volumes that graced a gentleman's library and added distinction to the works themselves.

Tonson regarded Shakespeare, like Milton, as a major figure in the English literary heritage. He hired Nicholas Rowe, a minor politician and dramatist, to prepare a corrected edition of the Bard's plays. He paid Joseph Addison £107, an unheard of sum at that time, for publication rights to his popular play, Cato. He also published the works of Aphra Behn. His series of Miscellaneous Poems gave young poets, like Alexander Pope, opportunities to publish their works. He was a devoted Whig, although he did not personally engage in politics. He established a club called the Kit Cat Club, which drew its name from the owner of the tavern where they met and his mutton pies known as kit-cats.

John Dryden was perhaps England's first professional man of letters. He supported himself by a combination of places and pensions, writing for the theatre, and money paid by booksellers for the right to publish works that would be commercially successful. With the Revolution of 1688-89 Dryden lost his post as poet laureate, leaving him in serious financial difficulties. His survival as a literary man was due to his association with Jacob Tonson.

Addison and Steele and the Essay Journal

The first essay journal was John Dunton's <u>Athenian Mercury</u>, which began in 1691. It was based on answers to questions on a variety of topics, some of them far-fetched. Many similar essay journals sprang up to provide items of interest or entertainment to readers, but Addison and Steele brought the essay journal to its peak of perfection. For the next fifty years, the essay journal was the dominant form of periodical publication.

In 1709, while serving as a pamphleteer for the Whigs, Capt. Steele established <u>The Tatler</u>, an essay journal that came out three times a week. The journal contained essays purportedly from several distinct individuals. Some of the best essays were by Steele himself and were headed "From My Apartment." Jonathan Swift contributed many essay until their political differences led him to withdraw. Joseph Addison contributed about fifty, plus others written cooperatively with Steele. The main concern of <u>The Tatler</u> was the development of taste and decorum.

Joseph Addison, a scholarly Oxford graduate, had early attracted the attention of the Whigs. Under William III, they provided him with a stipend to travel on the continent and prepare for a diplomatic career. When he returned to England in 1704, the Tories were in office. Addison renewed his contacts with the Whig leaders and his schoolboy friend, Capt. Steele. His long narrative poem, <u>The Campaign</u> (1704), praised the victory of the Duke of Marlborough at the Battle of Blenheim and established his literary reputation. In 1705 the Whigs came into office and Addison pursued a diplomatic career, serving as an under-secretary of state and as secretary to the viceroy of Ireland, where he met Jonathan Swift. In 1710, when the Whigs were replaced by the Tories, the political situation turned against Addison and Steele. Steele terminated <u>The Tatler</u> and joined with Addison, to publish <u>The Spectator</u> (1711-12, 1714), which was a periodical similar to <u>The Tatler</u> but more thoughtful. Although presumably non-political, perceptive readers noticed that it was slightly Whiggish in tone.

<u>The Spectator</u> was the most successful of all essay journals. Each issue consisted of one long essay or a collection of letters to the editor. <u>The Spectator</u> was published six days a week in small type on one sheet of paper. The issues (numbers) were approximately 2,500 words

in length. The letters to the editor were used to discuss a variety of social issues, such as a young woman's complaint about men who stare at young ladies in church. The articles were attributed to "Mr. Spectator." Average circulation was about 3,000 copies per number, but each copy might be read by 6-10 people in coffeehouses or other public places. The Spectator was interrupted in 1713 due to an increase in the taxes on paper. Eventually The Spectator ran to 555 issues. In 1714 Addison revived it briefly, but without Steele. The Spectator was republished in volumes that were more profitable than the subscriptions.

Addison and Steele stated that their purpose was "to enliven morality with wit, and temper wit with morality." Addison and Steele shared responsibility, but Addison was dominant and wrote some of the most noteworthy essays. Steele was practical and down-to-earth—he comments on interesting or unnoticed aspects of everyday life. Addison was more philosophical. As a Whig, Addison was sympathetic to business, and one of his most famous pieces (No. 69) tells of his delight in visiting the Royal Exchange, where the products of all nations were displayed, confirming England's superiority as a center of world trade. Literary criticism was a major interest of Mr. Spectator, who presented essays on tragedy, poetry, comedy, and wit, plus essays on standards of Taste. Addison made a major contribution to literary criticism in his twelve essays entitled "The Pleasures of the Imagination." His eighteen essays on Paradise Lost raised Milton's work out of the partisan conflicts of Anglican and Puritan and made him a major figure in English literature. He also commented on the natural truths of old ballads, like "Chevy Chase," and the falsity (as he saw it) of Italian opera.

The central figures of the Spectator are the members of "the Club," a cross-section of English gentlemen. Sir Roger de Coverley is an elderly representative of the landed gentry. He is presented as good-hearted but old fashioned, and a typical country Tory. The de Coverley essays (No. 106-131) give a varied picture of country life. They were especially popular and were frequently republished. Sir Andrew Freeport, the successful merchant, is a man of solid good sense, and thus a Whig. Capt. Sentry is a brave soldier who gave up the military life because it had become too political. The clergyman is noted for his integrity and devotion to his calling. The lightweights in the group are the Critic, who is supposedly studying law but is more interested in books and plays, and Will Honeycomb, a man-about-town mainly concerned with amusing himself. They are all gentlemen—financially independent and with common intellectual and cultural interests—and able to spend considerable time enjoying the social life of London.

Addison and Steele were influential in shaping the eighteenth-century concept of politeness, which meant more than refined manners. It meant a generous conviviality, ability to mix and converse easily with other people in social situations, and concern for other people's feelings. Refined taste in dress and language and absence of socially disagreeable habits or mannerisms were part of the ideal of politeness. Addison expects that a gentleman will be politically informed and active, but he urges a politics based on moderation and patriotism rather than the bitter partisanship of his time. He makes it clear (No. 341) that his purpose is to moderate conflicts based on partisan or religious differences. Although the members of "the Club" represent different interests and political views, they are seen as able to get along with each other, discuss their differences with moderation and good humor, and remain friends.

In his political thought Addison expresses eloquently the characteristic Whig ideas of the time. He was proud of his country and its achievements. Much of the success of England was, in Addison's view, a result of the liberty that Englishmen enjoyed. With the memory of the excesses of the Civil Wars in mind, Addison opposes the religious "enthusiasm" (God within) of the Puritans, which he regards as abandonment of man's most distinctive quality—his rationality and sense of reality. He feels similar repugnance for Roman Catholicism, which he identifies with another abandonment of rationality—"superstition."

Addison's concept of God is based primarily on his delight in the beauties of Nature, which he regards as the mind of God "writ large." "The creation is a perpetual feast to the mind of a good man," he writes, "everything he sees cheers and delights him. Providence has imprinted so many smiles on nature, that it is impossible for a mind which is not sunk in more gross and sensual delights, to take a survey of them without several secret sensations of pleasure . . . and raises such a rational admiration in the soul, as is little inferior to devotion."

The Female Tatler

Capt. Steele's Tatler was matched by The Female Tatler (1709 ff.), which appeared three times a week. The first 52 issues were written by Thomas Baker, an attorney and minor dramatist. Tunbridge Walks, or, The Yeoman of Kent (1703) was his most successful play and was frequently performed during the first half of the century. The authorship of The Female Tatler was attributed to "Mrs. Crackenthorpe, a Lady that knows everything." Women's issues predominated.

Bernard Mandeville, a physician-philosopher of Dutch origin, better known as a contrarian philosopher, succeeded Baker as principal writer of the Female Tatler. Mandeville, in the guise of a society of ladies, wrote 32 issues between November, 1709 and March, 1710. He continued to emphasize the capacities of women and their lack of opportunities to use them to the fullest. He expresses his contrarian views in The Virgin Unmask'd (1709), a dialogue between a maiden aunt and her young niece that demonstrates the disadvantages to women of marriage and childbearing.

Ch. 5. Philosophy, Manners, Theatre, and the Arts

The Revolutionary era was a period of philosophical and cultural creativity. John Locke continued the revolution in thought that began with the Royal Society and the Scientific Revolution of the later seventeenth century. Locke challenged the humanist emphasis on the authorities of the past with a philosophy of empiricism. He based his concept of knowledge on sense impressions that the mind organizes into general ideas. As part of his re-examination of knowledge, Locke challenged the divine right doctrines of government...

The philosophy of Locke's pupil, the Third Earl of Shaftesbury, explored the implications of Locke's philosophy for religion. Shaftesbury was an advocate of a refinement of manners and "Taste "that set standards for a cultivated gentleman or lady. Mary Astell and Celia Fiennes made their own definition of the life of a lady.

A burst of creativity in the theatre took Restoration drama to a new level by introducing new themes and a greater range of characters. Increasing prosperity enabled noblemen and gentlemen to build larger houses and stock them with works of art brought back from Italy. Although England led the continent in constitutional government, religious toleration, and science, the tide flowed the other way in the fine arts. The story of eighteenth-century architecture, painting, and music is one of English responses to continental influences.

John Locke: From Humanism to Empiricism

John Locke was the key figure in the transition from Christian humanism to empiricism. Locke served Charles II's nemesis, Lord Shaftesbury, as physician and tutor of his grandson, and lived in his house for eight years. For a time he was secretary to the council of trade and plantations, where he became interested in the affairs of the colony of Carolina and the Royal African Company. Locke was a quiet scholar, not a politician, but his relationship with Shaftesbury doubtless sharpened his understanding of the fundamental principles of the Whigs. While living with Shaftesbury, Locke wrote his Two Treatises of Civil Government and Essay Concerning Toleration, which were not published until later. He followed Shaftesbury into exile in Holland, and returned to England in 1689 on the same boat that brought Queen Mary. He was rewarded with a position on the board of excise, which gave him a middle-class salary and considerable freedom to prepare his manuscripts for publication. Later he was appointed to the board of trade, which paid a better salary but also took up more of his time.

Locke's most important philosophical work was his An Essay Concerning Human Understanding (1690), which was written during his exile in Holland and published when he returned to England. In this work, Locke expounds most fully his doctrine of empiricism. His purpose, he says, is to establish the origins and limits of human knowledge. The mind initially, he writes, "is like white Paper, void of all Characters." Sense impressions, he says, are the basis of all knowledge. As the mind reflects upon the sense impressions it has received, it organizes them into perceptions or ideas, such as white, yellow, cold, sweet etc. By observing the functioning of their minds, people formulate their ideas of thinking, doubting, and believing. Simple ideas are organized by the mind into ideas that are more complex, such as space, duration, number, and cause and effect. The mind connects and compares ideas ("the association of ideas"), and thus our ideas grow. This process, Locke says, is ordinarily called thinking.

Locke concedes that empirically based knowledge is only probable, not absolute. The test of the validity of knowledge is Reason, which should be applied in a common sense manner, recognizing the limitations of the mind. "I suppose it may be of use to prevail with the busy mind of man," he writes, "to be more cautious in meddling with things exceeding its comprehension; to stop when it is at the utmost extent of its tether; and to sit down in a quiet ignorance of those things which, upon examination, are found to be beyond the reach of our capacities."

Locke is best known for his <u>Two Treatises of Government</u> (1690), published anonymously. They were seen as a justification of the Revolution of 1688-89, although actually they were written as a response to events surrounding "the Popish Plot" and the trial of Lord Shaftesbury. Locke rejects the "top-down" philosophy of divine right and the sovereignty of kings. He adopts a "bottom-up" approach to government. He bases the state and its powers upon the will of the people, who can take back the powers they have delegated to rulers if they are abused or the rights of the people are violated.

Locke's <u>First Treatise</u> refutes divine right, royal sovereignty, and hereditary succession. His <u>Second Treatise</u> is subtitled <u>An Essay Concerning the True Original, Extent, and End of Civil Government.</u> Locke bases his argument on the rationality of mankind. He states that even before governments were formed, people were reasonable creatures, for they could grasp the natural laws that enjoin concern for the welfare and rights of others. He posits a state of nature in which each individual governs himself, but the state of nature is not anarchy. "The state of nature has a law of nature to govern it," Locke writes, "which obliges every one, and reason, which is that law, teaches all mankind, who will but consult it, that being all equal and independent, no one ought to harm another in his life, health, liberty or possessions." Slavery, he adds, is so opposed to natural law "that it is hardly to be conceived that an Englishman, much less a gentleman, should plead for it."

Locke recognizes that some form of government is necessary, and justifies government on the basis of a political contract between the people and their rulers. Governments were formed by men, he states, not to take away rights, but to strengthen social relationships and make rights more secure. Locke identifies the crucial rights as the right to life, liberty, and property—rights that government can infringe only with the consent of the governed. The functions of government, he writes, are to make laws to protect and regulate property and protect the people from injury by foreign countries. He predicates an executive power that is constantly in being and is responsible for carrying out the laws. The legislative power meets periodically to vote taxes (i.e., take away property for the public benefit) and pass such laws as might be needed. The legislative body is the supreme power but it cannot be arbitrary, and must act according to established laws that are interpreted by recognized judges. Locke's principle that the ultimate power lies in the people became the foundation of modern democracies.

Locke also posits a social contract, in which the members of a group join together in a community and willingly subject themselves to the will of the community, as long as their natural rights are not violated. Individual consent is confirmed when an individual comes of age and takes an oath of allegiance. In the last analysis, he concludes, the will of the people should be supreme and be expressed through election of representatives or by resort to revolution, if necessary. Locke's theory of government was a minority view in eighteenth-century England, but it became important in the American colonies at the time of the American Revolution and was the philosophical basis of The Declaration of Independence (1776).

Locke was a forceful advocate of religious toleration. In his Letters on Toleration (1690-92), he argues that the Church should be a free and voluntary society, since religious belief depends on sincerity and cannot be forced. He accepts the existence of an established Church, but he holds that the civil government should not support its organization, doctrines, or forms of worship. Locke's exceptions to toleration include the Roman Catholic Church, which calls upon its followers to overthrow Protestant rulers and is a persecuting Church, and atheists because they have no reason to live up to "promises, covenants and oaths, which are the bonds of human society."

In The Reasonableness of Christianity (1695), Locke defines the essentials of the Christian faith in order to clear away the dogmatic interpretations that had been added to Christianity over time. These are simple—Christ is the Messiah; He revealed a moral law to replace the formal prescriptions of the Old Testament; His life demonstrates what God wants of men; and God's expectations are reasonable. Locke does not affirm or deny other Christian doctrines, such as the resurrection, but he insists that the simple principles that he has derived from the Biblical accounts of Christ's life and teachings are sufficient for salvation. Faith can never conflict with Reason, he says, because our assent to matters of faith grows out of our conviction that they are reasonable. For example, belief in life after death has no basis in Reason but can be accepted as not unreasonable.

One of the most important consequences of Locke's theory of knowledge was his concept of the Self. The Christian concept of the soul was that it was a spiritual substance that came from God and entered into a material body, bringing with it aspirations toward the divine except as corrupted by sin. Locke's concern is with the Self, not the soul. He points out that each individual is conscious of himself or herself as a thinking being with a distinctive body of ideas and traits. He states that the mind goes through a process of personality growth by interaction with the environment, especially with other people. In this way the mind develops the ideas and characteristics that form each individual Self. People are aware of the distinctive Selves of other people, too. Locke's concept of the Self encourages subjectivity, i.e., the exploration of oneself, which was important in the development of eighteenth-century poetry and the novel.

The notion of a developing Self made Locke an important influence on eighteenth-century ideas of childhood and education. He applies his ideas in his Thoughts on Education (1693), where he questions the authoritarian approach of the grammar school, which attempts to form the minds of children by stuffing them with classical learning and disciplining them by application of the principle "Spare the rod and spoil the child." Locke favors education that gives the child the opportunity to grow through well-designed experiences that foster learning and self-control.

Lord Shaftesbury: The Philosopher and the Gentleman

The social ideal of the eighteenth century was that of the gentleman. The third Earl of Shaftesbury, grandson of the Charles II's nemesis, defined a gentleman as a man of leisure, morality, and culture. Shaftesbury, who was to some extent educated by John Locke, spent three years on the Grand Tour, studying art in Germany, Italy, and France. He served briefly in the House of Commons before taking his seat in the House of Lords. He cultivated the life of a gentleman and wrote for gentlemen and ladies. He identified the characteristics of a gentleman as a good education and manners, a commitment to public service, an appreciation of the finer things of life, and a desire to contribute to his fellow man. He took for granted that the lifestyle of a gentleman required a suffient independent income. His major works were collected in his <u>Characteristics of Men, Manners, Opinions and Times</u> (3 vols., 1711, 1713), which was widely influential throughout the eighteenth century.

Shaftesbury was known primarily as a moral philosopher. He viewed God as a benevolent and merciful Providence, whose rationality is seen in his creation. He was an advocate of the "philanthropic" view of mankind, which holds that people are essentially good and are born with a capacity for moral conduct and wholesome social relationships. People have a natural capacity to understand and enjoy Goodness, Beauty, and Truth, Shaftesbury writes, but these capacities have to be cultivated through education and discussion to achieve the mature judgment that he calls "Taste."

Taste was defined by Shaftesbury as informed and sensitive reactions to works of literature and art of undoubted merit—poetry, plays, paintings, architecture, and operas and other creative musical works. To Shaftesbury, Taste is an important element in living a good life, for the effort to understand Beauty through art contributes to a life that is beautiful: "The Taste of Beauty," Shaftesbury writes, "and the Relish of what is decent, just, and amiable, perfects the Character of the GENTLEMAN and the PHILOSOPHER."

Two Emancipated Women

While Shaftesbury defined the standards of a gentleman, a few women challenged the conventional expectations for genteel women. Mary Astell was educated at home by her uncle, a learned clergyman. He died when she was thirteen, and after that she educated herself by extensive reading in history, politics, religion, and philosophy. The early death of her father left her without money for a dowry. She accepted her condition as a spinster and became a writer. She located in Chelsea, then a suburb of London, where she was befriended by a group of aristocratic women who appreciated her contributions to their discussions of intellectual subjects. She gained public attention through her works on the condition of women. In <u>A Serious Proposal to the Ladies for the Advancement of Their True and Greater Interest. By a Lover of Her</u>

Sex (1694) she urges greater educational opportunities for women. In 1700 she published Some Reflections upon Marriage. She points out that marriage is in many ways disadvantageous to women. She complains that women are expected to be decorative appendages of their husbands rather than fully-developed human beings. She criticizes men who marry for power, wealth, prestige, or only on the basis of physical attraction. Marriage should be a partnership, she writes, not a condition of inferiority for women. She revealed her pro-royalist views in An Impartial Inquiry into the Causes of Rebellion and Civil War in this Country (1703). In her last published work, The Christian Religion as Profess'd by a Daughter of the Church of England (1709) she continued her campaign for women's education. With the support of wealthy patrons, including Lady Mary Wortley Montagu, the learned daughter of the Duke of Kingston, she and her friends opened a school for girls in Chelsea, a suburb of London.

Celia Fiennes (pr. Fines) was the daughter of an army colonel who was the younger son of an aristocratic family. She never married and refused to accept the established social standards for an unmarried woman. She traveled extensively on horseback with one or two servants. Travel was difficult, especially for a single woman, due to lack of good roads and inns. In 1698 she carried out her "Great Journey," which took her across England from Newcastle-on-Tyne on the east coast to Cornwall, the farthest point in the southwest. Eventually she visited every county in England. Like her contemporary, Daniel Defoe, she expresses pride in the progressive spirit that was rising in England. She points out things that are new—busy towns, new country homes, improved roads and signposts, and new manufacturing, mining, and drainage projects. She also discovered how wild and unimproved much of England was. She kept extensive diaries in which she recorded her observations and later worked up into a memoir for her family. As a woman of upper-class status, she did not write for publication. Her diaries were published in 1888 as Through England on a Side Saddle.

The Theatre

With the accession of William III and Mary, the theatre lost the royal patronage it had possessed under Charles II, and the two patent theatres fell into disorder. William and Mary supported the efforts of the bishops to reform the Church and public morality, and did not attend plays that might be morally offensive. In 1698 Jeremy Collier, a clergyman, published A Short View of the Immorality and Profaneness of the English Stage. The pamphlet was a hard-hitting attack on Restoration comedy and an important expression of the movement for respectability and godliness. "The business of the theatre," Collier wrote, "is to "recommend virtue" by presenting exemplars of virtue for emulation by the audience.

Sir John Vanbrugh was the first of a generation of playwrights who brought new vigor to the theatre. He was the grandson of a Flemish merchant who had settled in England. His early life included a variety of experiences, including a voyage to India with the East India Company. He studied art in France for two years. While visiting France he incautiously praised King William III and spent several years in French prisons as a spy. His family managed to get him exchanged for a Jacobite spy and he returned to London. Lacking a settled career, he became a playwright and later a self-taught architect. In 1696 his bawdy comedy, The Relapse; or, Virtue in Danger opened at the Theatre Royal, Drury Lane and was a great success. His career as a playwright was launched.

Vanbrugh's play, The Provok'd Wife (1697), was one of the most popular comedies throughout the eighteenth century. The play was built around the talents of Elizabeth Barry, the outstanding dramatic actress of the time. Barry was paired with Thomas Betterton, who played the abusive husband, Sir John Brute, a crude, vulgar lout. Sir John roars around the stage, casting curses and epithets left and right, and in one scene he puts on his wife's clothes to evade the law. Lady Brute gets even by taking a lover, her worthy, faithful suitor, Ned Constant. By showing a bad marriage, made for monetary reasons, the play communicates its message that marriage should be based on love and respect.

William Congreve came from a prominent Anglo-Irish family and attended Trinity College, Dublin, where he met Jonathan Swift. He came to London as a law student, but instead he followed the usual life of a young gentleman about town until he discovered his talent for comedy. Encouraged by Dryden, Congreve wrote two of the best Restoration-style comedies, Love for Love (1695) and The Way of the World (1700). Elizabeth Barry performed in all of Congreve's plays, but the delightful Anne Bracegirdle was his favorite actress and he wrote his plays for her. She played Angelica in <u>Love for Love</u> and Millimant in <u>The Way of the World</u>. Power, sex, and money were the main themes of Restoration comedy, and they often concerned marriages and inheritances. Essentially Congreve was a Restoration playwright in the more prim and proper age of William and Mary. After 1700 the taste for Restoration comedy declined, and Congreve's career with it.

Congreve's <u>Love for Love</u> is a typical Restoration comedy but with a different message. As the title suggests, mutual love and respect must be part of marriage. Valentine, a handsome young libertine who has been disinherited by his father, seeks to restore his fortune by marrying Angelica, a beautiful young heiress with a considerable fortune of her own. The play is well-stocked with comic characters who engage in intrigues and tricks. Angelica tests Valentine by pretending coldness toward him that she does not feel. He tries to win her pity by feigning madness. At the end, Angelica abandons her aloof pose and confesses that she always loved Valentine. "Here's my hand;" she says to him, "my heart was always yours, and struggled very hard to make this utmost trial of your virtue." Valentine, repentant that he had tried to win his bride by deceit, responds with a passionate declaration of his undying love.

<u>The Way of the World</u> deals with the games people play in the marriage market, but eventually conflict is resolved by mutual respect and concessions. Mirabell, a reformed rake, is sincerely in love with Millimant, an independent-minded young woman who is not eager to surrender her freedom to the bonds of marriage. She lets Mirabell know that she wants to be courted, not be an object of negotiation. If she marries, she wants to be treated as an equal and not be trivialized with pet names or public kissing. She wants to lie abed in the morning as long as she wishes; to write and receive letters or make visits and receive visitors without prying questions; to be excused from making conversation with people she does not like just because they are his friends or relations; come to dinner or not as she pleases; and her husband must not approach her tea table uninvited, or enter her room without knocking. "These articles subscribed," Millimant concludes, . . . "I may by degrees dwindle into a wife." Mirabell replies with a few requirements of his own, such as limiting her tea table to simple foods

and drinks, not painting her face, and not squeezing her body into a corset to obtain a slim waist. With these good-natured concessions, they agree to marry. The complicated tricks and relationships of the other members of the cast are an important part of the play.

In his popular play, The Constant Couple, or, A trip to the Jubilee (1699) George Farquhar, another Irishman, abandoned Restoration wit for good-natured humor. The Jubilee, as it was usually called, was a huge hit. It ran for 53 nights, a record that was not exceeded until the fabulous success of The Beggar's Opera. The play was performed more than 400 times in the eighteenth century. For several years Farquhar served in the army as a recruiting officer, which provided experience for another of his hit plays, The Recruiting Officer (1706), which was performed 512 times in the eighteenth century.

Farquhar's best known play, The Beaux' Stratagem, was also written in 1706, the last year of his life. The play concerns two impoverished younger sons, Aimwell and Archer. They go to the Midlands town of Litchfield, where Aimwell hopes to marry Dorinda, an heiress. She is the sister of Squire Sullen, a drunken lout. Aimwell poses as his elder brother and Archer as his servant. When Aimwell goes to church to observe the heiress, Dorinda notices him and is immediately attracted. Mrs. Sullen, who is friendly with Dorinda, also notices the handsome stranger. Aimwell pretends to be ill and is brought into the Sullen house, where he and Dorinda quickly fall in love. Mrs. Sullen, who is unhappy in her marriage, falls in love with Archer and begins an affair.

At the inn, a highwayman named Gibbet, with whom the innkeeper is allied, decides to rob the Sullen house. Archer, who has sneaked into Mrs. Sullen's bedroom, confronts Gibbet and the other robbers. Aimwell comes to his assistance, and they drive the robbers away. The complex plot is resolved when Sir Charles Freeman, brother of Mrs. Sullen, arrives at the inn after spending several years abroad. He is outraged that his sister has married the brutish Sullen and negotiates her freedom, leaving her able to respond to her love for Archer. Aimwell learns that his elder brother has died, and he is now Lord Aimwell and able to marry Dorinda. The comedy of the play arises, not only from the complex plot, but from the relationships among Farquhar's colorful characters.

Farquhar also has a cause to advocate—the dissolution of an un-happy marriage. While the Restoration accepted love affairs outside of marriage, they also threatened the husband with ridicule as a cuckold. Sullen states to his wife; "If you can contrive of being a whore without making me a cuckold, do it and welcome." Farquhar puts happiness ahead of the common morality.

The changing spirit of the post-Revolutionary period was also seen in tragedy, where the grand heroic tragedies of the Restoration were re-placed by melodramatic plays that would stir the emotions. The leader in this type of drama was Nicholas Rowe, an amiable lawyer turned playwright. He was a zealous Whig, and for two years was under-sec-retary of state for Scotland. At the accession of George I he was ap-pointed poet laureate, and other political plums came his way later.

Rowe's first play, The Ambitious Stepmother (1700) was written in blank verse, and was revived from time to time throughout the century. His political play, Tamerlane (1701), lacked dramatic power, but it praised William III and was annually performed to celebrate the Revolution. Rowe took tragedy in a new direction with his "she-plays," which deal with women in distress. The Fair Penitent (1703) was an early example of the domestic tragedy, and was described by Rowe as "a melancholy tale about private woes." One of the characters, a handsome man named Lothario, is a seducer of women who seduces the female lead. The name Lothario has since been applied to any un-principled lover. Jane Shore (1714) and Lady Jane Grey (1715) were written in Shakespearean language and attempted to evoke sympathy by depicting the problems of badly-treated women.

Rowe was more successful as a scholar. He prepared a much-ad-mired translation of Pharsalia, an account of the civil war between Pompey and Caesar written by the Roman poet, Lucan. He prepared the first modern edition of the plays of Shakespeare, published in six volumes in 1709 by Jacob Tonson. Rowe modernized the spelling and punctuation, and made a few judicious modifications of the original printed text. He introduced his edition with the first full account of Shakespeare's life. Rowe was not a major talent, but he was a popular figure in the world of literature and theatre, and a friend of Pope, Ad-dison, Steele, Swift, and Congreve.

Susannah Centlivre, like Aphra Behn, discovered that the freewheeling life of the theatre offered opportunities not available to a young woman of no family or fortune. Theatre managers realized that attractive actresses were often more successful than men in filling a theatre. Centlivre ran away from an unhappy home with a troupe of traveling actors. Her beauty and talent opened doors for her in the London theatre, and she began a career as an actress. Frequently she played "breeches roles," in which an actress plays the part of a young man wearing tight-fitting breeches that showed off her figure, otherwise hidden under a long dress. She wrote sixteen plays and became part of a theatrical circle that included Rowe, Vanbrugh, Farquhar, and Richard Steele. Her play about gambling, The Gamester (1705), was her first big success. The Busybody (1709) had a thirteen-night run, remarkable for the time, and was performed 450 times during the eighteenth century. Many of her plays were published, some of them several times.

Centlivre was a strong Whig, and her plays often include a stubborn, narrow-minded Tory father who stands in the way of the happiness of the hero and heroine. Her plays urge women to take control of their lives. In A Wonder: A Woman Keeps a Secret (1714), which she dedicated to George I. She writes: "The Custom of our Country inslaves us from our Very Cradles, first to our Parents, next to our Husbands; and when Heaven is so kind as to rid us of both these, our Brothers still usurp Authority and expect a blind Obedience from us; so that Maids, Wives, or Widows, we are little better than Slaves to the Tyrant Man." Eventually she married one of the cooks in the royal household and settled down to respectable married life.

Theatre Music

Although the spoken plays have gained the most attention, a large part of eighteenth-century theatre was musical productions. John Eccles succeeded Purcell as the most successful composer of theatre music. In 1685 he became the house composer at Drury Lane and composed music for at least fifteen plays starring the popular actress, Anne Bracegirdle, who would sing only songs by Eccles. In 1695 Eccles joined Bracegirdle, Elizabeth Barry, and Thomas Betterton in seceding from Drury Lane and establishing their own theatre at Lincoln's Inn Fields. Eccles provided songs for plays, masques, and an early opera, Rinaldo and Armida (1698). Eccles composed the music for William

Congreve's masque,, The Judgment of Paris (1701)..In 1700 he became master of music for King William with an attractive salary. He continued in that office under Queen Anne and King George I. In that role he composed music for New Year, birthdays, St. Cecilia's Day, and notable events.

Eccles noted the increasing popularity of Italia opera, which was first brought to England by Thomas Clayton, a court violinist under William and Mary. Clayton traveled to Italy and brought back a libretto entitled Arsinoe, Queen of Cyprus (1705). Clayton wrote some of the arias and others probably were adapted from Italian sources. The libretto was in English and the opera was a commercial success. One reason for the popularity of the opera was a stunning new singer, Catherine Tofts, who had first come to public attention in a series of concerts the previous year. Her sweet, silvery voice (Cibber's words) and youthful freshness made her the first English prima donna. Two years later, Clayton presented another opera, Rosamond (1707), using an English language libretto written by Addison, who had criticized Italian opera as artificial and unsuitable for Englishmen. Although Tofts again took the title role, the opera was a commercial failure.

The next year Tofts sang several operatic roles but experienced a nervous breakdown and never sang in England again. She traveled to Venice and married Joseph Smith, a wealthy merchant who later became the English consul there. Tofts continued to sing in private concerts, and lived out her life in Venice.

In 1705 Congreve and Vanbrugh joined to build a new theatre in the Haymarket with the intention of putting on operas, beginning with Congreve's opera, Semele. John Eccles, who was chosen to write the music, recognized the attraction of Italian opera, and he adopted the Italian style, including replacement of spoken dialogue with plain (dry) recitative. Semele might have set a new trend, but it was not performed at the time, although Congreve's libretto was later used by Handel.

Eccles stood at the end of Restoration theatre music. In 1710 Eccles retired from the theatre and spent his time angling. Many of his songs for the theatre were published separately or in collections, and remained popular throughout the eighteenth century.

Architecture

The desire to display taste and refinement was seen in architecture, where the aristocracy were the major patrons. It was expected that an aristocrat would live in a grand country mansion (known today as a "stately home"). After the Restoration many of the aristocracy expanded their rural residences or built new and grander ones. The stately home was the physical embodiment of a way of life that combined political power, landed wealth, elegant living, and social prestige. Grand rural mansions displayed the importance of the leaders of English landed society and the continuity of their families. With the usual English eclecticism, architects used a variety of styles and fused architecture, painting, sculpture, and landscaping into an imposing and coherent work of art.

Three of the greatest stately homes of England were built in the early eighteenth century. The characteristics of many later stately homes are found in the classical exterior of Chatsworth (1686) and its richly decorated interior, with ceilings painted by the outstanding practitioners of the art and a great collection of pictures and sculpture. Chatsworth is set in a magnificent park, landscaped in mid-eighteenth century by Lancelot ("Capability") Brown", the leading exponent of the English natural garden.

The second of the great country houses of the period is Castle Howard (1699-1724) in Yorkshire. At that time architecture was still open to the gifted amateur. As a result of his Whig connections, the project was offered to Sir John Vanbrugh, who had a bold, theatrical imagination. For technical expertise, Vanbrugh turned to Nicholas Hawksmoor, an assistant to Wren, who was experienced in draftsmanship, detailing, and negotiating prices with contractors.

At Castle Howard (1701-12), Vanbrugh sought to achieve massiveness and magnificence in the English baroque style. The exterior has dramatic curving wings and a central dome. The interior is dominated by a vast stone hall leading to broad staircases that give a theatrical effect. Vanbrugh foreshadowed a new trend in English landscape architecture by setting Castle Howard in a spacious park with broad vistas dotted with Roman temples, arches, bridges and an Egyptian obelisk and pyramid. Set in this splendid park, Castle Howard is one of the most imposing stately homes of England.

After the Battle of Blenheim, Queen Anne persuaded Parliament to grant the royal manor of Woodstock to the Duke of Marlborough and vote an appropriation to build a great house for him at public expense. Vanbrugh's Whig friends obtained for him the most prized architectural commission of all—Blenheim Palace. Untrammeled by limitations of size or cost, Vanbrugh planned the greatest of all English great houses. He considered Blenheim Palace, not as a family residence, but as a national monument, which, he wrote, should have "the qualitys proper to such a monument, vizt. Beauty, Magnificence and Duration."

Blenheim Palace (1705-25) was intended to rival the Louvre and Louis XIV's palace at Versailles. Again Vanbrugh worked with Hawksmoor in preparing the plans. Vanbrugh found himself engaged in constant quarrels with Sarah, Duchess of Marlborough, about the design and with the treasury about costs. The exterior of Blenheim Palace features a massive columned portico at the entrance, three-story turrets on each corner, and a vast courtyard formed by dramatic wings linked to the main building by colonnades. The interior is dominated by the Great Hall with a ceiling painted by Sir James Thornhill depicting the Battle of Blenheim. Vanbrugh also did the landscaping. The trees were planted to illustrate the order of battle at Blenheim.

The election of 1711 produced a Tory House of Commons, which had no desire to glorify the Duke of Marlborough. Work on Blenheim Palace stopped and Vanbrugh lost his position as architect and comptroller of the queen's works. With the accession of George I and the triumph of the Whigs, construction on Blenheim Palace was resumed. Once again Vanbrugh had to deal with the Duchess, whose tenacious opposition to him compelled him to turn the project over to Hawksmoor, who worked well with the Duchess to complete the design and construction. When Blenheim Palace was completed, Vanbrugh was not permitted to enter the grounds to view the finished product.

Vanbrugh continued to work as an architect, designing several fine country homes and completing Wren's work at Greenwich Naval Hospital. Vanbrugh brought to English architecture a theatrical flair that may have grown out of his experience as a playwright. His powerful, dramatic style made Castle Howard and Blenheim Palace notable examples of the English baroque.

Nicholas Hawksmoor was heir to the English baroque style of Wren and Vanbrugh. About 1680 Wren employed Hawksmoor, a lad of eighteen, as his personal assistant, and taught him the principles of architecture. Hawksmoor lived in Wren's household at Scotland Yard, and was increasingly involved in the buildings that Wren supervised, including Chelsea Hospital, the new churches for London, Hampton Court Palace, and the drawings for St. Paul's Cathedral. Wren seems to have given him extensive responsibilities at the Royal Naval Hospital at Greenwich. By 1689 Hawksmoor was a well-trained architect. He became clerk of the works at Kensington Palace and began taking private commissions.

Hawksmoor did not have the opportunity to travel or study abroad, but he was an avid reader about antiquity and classical architecture. With both Wren and Vanbrugh his role was to provide expertise in matters of detail, but he did much more than that and contributed architecturally to the designs. When they gained power in 1710, the Tories diverted the money for Blenheim to a plan to build fifty churches in the under churched new areas of London and Westminster. Hawksmoor was appointed one of two surveyors (1711-33) to supervise the project, and was commissioned to build six of the churches himself. Wren had proposed modest churches built of brick, which would be the quickest and least expensive to build, but the triumphant Tory Party provided funds to build churches of considerable size and grandeur. Each church was required to be built of stone and have a prominent tower. Many of them had an impressive portico and a steeple atop the tower. With the accession of the Whigs in 1714, support for the project, which was associated with the High Church Tories, lapsed, and only sixteen of the intended fifty churches were built.

One of Hawksmoor's most impressive churches is Christ Church, Spitalfields (1723-1729), built to show the authority of the Church in an area inhabited (at that time) by Calvinist Huguenot immigrants. The front is dominated by a large columned portico in the style of a classical temple with a small arched pediment. The three-stage tower with a clock is pierced by a tall narrow arched window and topped by a slim steeple. The church is built of white Portland stone. The nave has a flat decorated ceiling with barrel vaults over the sides. The interior combines massive white stone columns with dark wood side panels and galleries. Clear glass windows on the sides and small clerestory windows above the galleries admit light. The impressive east end is enclosed by white columns topped by a magnificent carved walnut organ case that originally contained the largest organ in Europe. At the east end is a cluster of three large stained glass windows.

Christ Church, Spitalfields

Hawksmoor also did important work for Oxford and Cambridge Universities, which were expanding as gentleman's sons included a stint at a university, usually without taking a degree, as part of their personal development. The flamboyance of baroque did not suit the restraint and simplicity of English taste, and after Vanbrugh and Hawksmoor English baroque faded, except as the architecture of the Church.

The accession of George I in 1714 and the triumph of the Whigs brought important changes in architecture. The aged Wren was dismissed from his office as surveyor of the king's works. Hawkesmoor's connection with Vanbrugh saved him from the vindictiveness of the Whigs and enabled him to continue building churches. He was a capable and diligent architect who had served a long apprenticeship by working as second fiddle to Wren and Vanbrugh. He stood at the end of an age, carrying on the style of the giants of English baroque architecture.

Painting

The successor to Lely as the premier portrait painter of the age was Sir Godfrey Kneller, a German who studied in Holland and Italy before coming to London in 1675. Kneller did portraits of Charles II, James II, and prominent courtiers. William and Mary made him the principal painter to the Crown, and in 1692 he was knighted. His William III on Horseback (1701) depicts the king as the Protestant hero surrounded by allusions to the return of the Golden Age.

Kneller's popularity was such that crowned heads of Europe came to London to have him paint their portraits. Like Lely, he developed a factory system, quickly sketching the subject in chalk, which he transferred to canvas in oils, leaving the rest to his assistants. His portraits have more individuality than those of Lely, and are characterized by a dignified manner and informal dress. He did a series of forty half-length, life-size portraits of the members of the Kit-Cat Club, a group of Whig politicians and writers. He also painted a portrait of Peter the Great of Russia, who visited England at that time. A form of painting popularized by Kneller was the conversation piece, which shows an informal group of people who are socially connected, often a family. His prices were comparatively high, but his wealthy clientele was willing to pay them and he accumulated a fortune. Kneller associated freely with leading political and literary figures, built a fine country house for himself, became a justice of the peace for Middlesex, and at his death in 1732 a monument to him was erected in Westminster Abbey.

In the eighteenth century, the prevailing taste held that the most prestigious and important form of art was history painting—works of grandeur that depict a familiar story based on events from Greek or Roman history and mythology or from the Bible. The one English history painter comparable to his European counterparts was Sir James Thornhill, a master of history painting in the Italian baroque style. Thornhill's earliest work was a room at Chatsworth, where he covered the walls with figures from the history of the early Roman Republic. He also painted the ceiling in the Great Hall of Blenheim Palace and later the salon at Canons, the great house of the Duke of Chandos.

Thornhill's major project was to decorate the ceilings of the Painted Hall at the Royal Naval Hospital, Greenwich. His murals in full baroque style glorify the Protestant succession from William and Mary to

George I. A large mural shows William and Mary in Heaven surrounded by allegorical figures representing England's maritime and commercial strength. Other paintings honor Queen Anne and the House of Hanover. Thornhill worked on this project, off and on, for the rest of his career.

Thornhill's work at the Royal Naval Hospital brought him the contract to decorate the interior of the dome at St. Paul's, the largest and most prestigious project open to a history painter. Thornhill responded with eight scenes from the life of St. Paul painted on the cupola and the drum. He also decorated the chapel at Hampton Court Palace. His many other projects included illustrations for the Oxford Bible and for Jacob Tonson's editions of the works of Milton and Addison. In 1718 Thornhill was appointed sergeant painter to King George I in recognition of his distinguished work. He was knighted and spent his remaining years as a country squire and a Member of Parliament.

Music

Johann Christophe Pepusch was a German musician who settled in London about 1704 and began a distinguished musical career. Between 1705 and 1718 he published five sets of six violin sonatas and two of trio sonatas. He was active in popularizing the concerto in England. He was an advocate of Corelli's approach to violin playing, and in 1732 he published a revised version of Corelli's sonatas and concertos.

The cantata came slowly to England, but by 1710 large numbers of cantatas by English or Italian composers was being published. The best English cantatas were composed by Pepusch, who published <u>Six English Cantatas</u> (1720) that were intended to show that the English language was suitable for an Italian form of music. He published another set in the 1720s. Pepusch used the Italian form of recitative, arias, ensembles, and choruses. Accompaniment was provided by a harpsichord or organ continuo and sometimes stringed instruments were added. Later in the eighteenth century large scale cantatas accompanied by an orchestra were popular in the pleasure gardens of London.

Pepusch was a major figure in the musical world of London. He was composer and music director (1716-32) for John Rich's theatre in Lincoln's Inn Fields, a theatre that thrived by offering pantomimes— light entertainment consisting of a variety of skits and acts for which

Pepusch wrote the music. As such, he composed the music for John Gay's The Beggar's Opera. He also served with Handel as music director for the Duke of Chandos' personal orchestra at Canons. In 1710 Pepusch founded the Academy of Ancient Music, which performed and published madrigals, folk songs, and early Church music. For these efforts he received a Doctor of Music degree from Oxford University.

Growing interest in the violin and related stringed instruments is seen the career of Francesco Geminiani, a pupil of Corelli, who came to London in 1714 as a concert violinist and teacher of the violin. In 1716 Geminiani published a popular collection of sonatas for the violin and harpsichord. In 1726 he published a collection of concertos. He organized a subscription series of twenty concerts for the 1731 season. His principal influence was as a teacher of the violin. His The Art of Playing the Violin (1751) was a publishing success, and contributed to the growing popularity of the violin in England. He spent the rest of his life alternating between Paris, Dublin, and London.

England was not without homegrown violinists. Members of the Valentine family were musicians in the Midlands for more than a century. Robert Valentine went to Rome about 1708 to study the violin. From there he moved to Naples, where, as Roberto Valentino, he was one of a cluster of string players known as the Neapolitan school. Probably due to ill health, Valentine returned to England in 1731, where his XII Solos for the Violin, with a Thorough Bass (1731) were published. Joseph Gibbs, an organist in East Anglia, published Eight Sonatas for the Violin with a Thorough Bass for the Harpsichord (1746) and later a collection of string quartets.

Ch. 6. Politics and Culture in Hanoverian England, 1714-1754

Under George I (1714-27) and George II (1727-60) England changed from the most turbulent country in Europe to one of the most stable. The issues that had disturbed the Stuart reigns declined. The dynastic question was settled with the peaceful accession of King George I. Crown and Parliament had learned to work together, and the theoretical supremacy of Parliament was modified by a compromise generally described as a "mixed and balanced constitution" with "checks and balances."

Strong executive leadership developed by giving the major offices of government to Peers or Members of the House of Commons. Periodic elections and an active press guaranteed that a strong government could not become a tyranny. The emergence of Sir Robert Walpole showed that the system might produce an "over mighty" leader, and the fall of Walpole demonstrated that Parliament and the people were indeed sovereign.

A variety of other factors contributed to internal stability. The wars of the age of Louis XIV came to an end and Europe settled into a fitful peace. The existence of a large national debt meant that a substantial class of investors had an important stake in the stability of the regime. Economic growth in England, Scotland, and Ireland contributed to social stability. Religious contentions subsided—the Church of England maintained its privileged position, and the Dissenters came to terms with a society that gave them an assured, if subordinate, place. New developments in architecture and landscaping displayed the wealth and assurance of the Whig aristocracy. Classicism in architecture stimulated a great age in sculpture.

The Whig Supremacy

Once the Whigs had established themselves in power, factional disputes broke out. The ultimate survivor was Sir Robert Walpole, a highly partisan Whig, who demonstrated his value to the Whig government by his capable handling of the South Sea Bubble of 1720-21. In the Peace of Utrecht, Britain had gained the <u>asiento</u>, the monopoly of the slave trade to the Spanish colonies in the New World and the right to send one merchant ship per year. The South Sea Company was organized to take advantage of the high expectations aroused by these opportunities for trade. The Company raised capital by an issue of stock (shares), and to grease the wheels generous grants of stock were made to political leaders, among them the king, his mistresses, and prominent Hanoverian courtiers. The price of the stock rose quickly. As the price of its stock rose, the Company issued more stock. The mania induced by South Sea stock encouraged formation of other companies that also sold their stock at inflated prices. When the South Sea Bubble burst in 1721, those who held stocks were ruined.

The government was blamed for the disaster and a political crisis developed, which was all the more threatening to the Whigs since an election was required in 1722. Walpole became first lord of the treasury, and it was he who rescued the court, the ministry, and the Company from their folly. He deflected angry cries for investigations and punishments, and obtained help from the money-men of London to reorganize the South Sea Company. Walpole had prevented a political crisis that could have overthrown the Whigs and threatened the Hanoverian dynasty.

By that time Walpole had won the confidence of King George I. Backed by "the influence of the Crown," he established the political dominance of the Whig Party. The crucial test of dynastic and political stability came in 1727, when King George I died suddenly and his son succeeded him as King George II. George II was a talkative, peppery man who was well versed on foreign courts, marriages, and treaties, and played an active role in the formulation of foreign policy. His sharp tongue let his ministers know the importance of consulting him on all important matters. Advised by Queen Caroline, who understood Walpole's political skills, he continued Walpole as first lord of the treasury.

Queen Caroline (Caroline of Ansbach) lost her mother at age thirteen and grew up in Berlin at the cultivated Court of the King of Prussia. She was well educated and developed a high level of personal charm. In 1705 George Augustus of Hanover, son of the Elector, visited his sister at the Court of Prussia. He was immediately struck by Caroline's character and good looks, and shortly thereafter they were married. When the Elector of Hanover became King George I, George Augustus and Caroline moved to England and became Prince and Princess of Wales. In contrast to George I, the Prince and Princess were socially very active. They maintained a separate court that attracted leading political and cultural figures and aroused the resentment of George I.

Caroline recognized the political ability of Walpole, and for the rest of her life she worked closely with him, especially in managing her husband. She had wide intellectual and theological interests, and added a library to St. James's Palace to house her large collection of books. She was much interested in the new "natural" style of landscaping, and actively supervised the landscaping of Kensington Gardens. She displayed her interest in English philosophy by installing in Richmond Park portrait busts of five "English Worthies," including Locke and Newton. She died in 1737 after a painful illness. George II attended her bedside and proclaimed his devotion to her. When she suggested that he might marry again, he replied: "No, no. I will only have mistresses."

The Press and the Rise of Opposition

Under George II, Walpole dominated the government to such an extent that some accused him of being a "prime minister," as in European courts. He was well aware of the importance of public opinion and was active in using and controlling the press. The <u>Daily Courant</u>, a Whig newspaper established in 1702, continued to be supported by the treasury, and some of the leading Whig politicians and churchmen contributed to its columns. As the Court Whigs consolidated their power, John Trenchard and Thomas Gordon, Country Whigs, founded the <u>London Journal</u> to express their disappointment that the Whig leaders were more interested in the sweets of office than achieving Whig ideals. They published 144 essays (1720-23) under the name Cato, in reference to the Roman statesman, Cato the Younger, who defended the Roman Republic against Caesar. Many of the letters were directed against Walpole; their main themes were freedom of speech and religion. They were published as Essays on Liberty, Civil and Religious (1725), commonly known as Cato's Letters. In the years before the American Revolution, Cato's Letters was popular in the American colonies and can be regarded as one of the foundation stones of American republicanism.

When Trenchard died in 1723 Walpole purchased the London Journal and turned it into the principal voice of his government. In 1735 the various government papers were combined into the Daily Gazetteer. Walpole subsidized the Gazetteer through the treasury and used the post office to distribute copies throughout the country. He attempted to restrict the press by taxation, interference with distribution of hostile publications, and occasional trials for seditious libel.

Under the circumstances, the rise of a powerful opposition was a remarkable accomplishment. Leadership within Parliament came from two Whigs who resented Walpole's domineering ways—Lord Carteret, a brilliant and individualistic peer with a wide knowledge of foreign affairs, and Sir William Pulteney, one of the most effective speakers in the House of Commons. They charged that Walpole ruled by using "the influence of the Crown" to corrupt Parliament and elections. William Pitt the Elder, a fiery orator and strong imperialist, entered Parliament in 1735 and immediately became a violent opponent of Walpole. Pitt accused Walpole of "appeasement" of the Spanish, who abused British sailors in the Caribbean. He sharply criticized the Duke of Newcastle, principal secretary of state (and indirectly, King George II) for a foreign policy designed to protect Hanover rather than advance British interests.

With the growth of opposition to Walpole, political journalism revived. Recognizing the decisive weight that the ministry carried in Parliament and in elections, the only recourse of the Opposition was to appeal to public opinion. The mastermind of the Opposition was Lord Bolingbroke, the former Tory leader, who was permitted to return to England from exile in France but was excluded from taking his seat in the House of Lords. The major voice of the Opposition was the Craftsman, a weekly journal combining news and comment, which was founded by Bolingbroke and Pulteney in 1726. The Craftsman raised political journalism to a high level of intelligence, bitterness, and tenacity. It was a huge success and attained a circulation of 8,000 copies per week, which was phenomenal for the time. Bolingbroke contributed approximately 100 articles. His articles in 1730 were the basis of his <u>Remarks on the History of England</u> (1730). In an obvious reference to Walpole, his book emphasizes weak kings and evil advisers who are resisted by brave Members of Parliament. His articles in 1733-34 were collected to form his book, <u>A Dissertation upon Parties</u> (1735), in which he calls upon men of both parties to join in a formed opposition to the Walpole regime.

Bolingbroke had intellectual interests, and much of his time out of office was spent in study and writing. His works on philosophical and religious subjects were critical of historic Christianity. He expresses a kind of Deism that accepts the existence of a divine creator who had removed himself from the world, which proceeds on its course according to inherent natural laws. Although his criticisms of Christianity were denounced by the Church, he continued to support the idea of an established Church as a contribution to public order and morality.

Bolingbroke was primarily a political writer. His stated purpose was to bridge the political and religious disputes that had bedeviled the reign of Queen Anne. He argued that the old issues were dead and had been replaced by new issues, especially Walpole's use of "the influence of the crown" to concentrate power in one man and trample on the "mixed and balanced constitution." Bolingbroke's <u>The Idea of a Patriot King</u> (written 1739, published 1749), which seems to have been directed toward Frederick, Prince of Wales, calls for a king who will rise above partisan politics and use the royal power for the benefit of the nation. His ideal was to establish a Tory Utopia with a wise and patriotic ruler, a Parliament of landed aristocrats and country gentlemen, a faithful Church, and a loyal people going about their appointed tasks. He cited the example of Queen Elizabeth, who "united the great body of the people in her and their common interest (and) inflamed them with one national spirit." It was an ideal far removed from the new forces that were transforming eighteenth-century England.

A new player appeared in the political scene in 1737 when Frederick Lewis, Prince of Wales, eldest son of King George II and Queen Caroline joined the Opposition. Frederick was born in Hanover in

1707 and remained there as the representative of the Hanoverian dynasty when George I became King and his parents moved to London as Prince and Princess of Wales. They showed no interest in Frederick, and there is reason to believe they gladly would have left him in Hanover indefinitely.

When George, Prince of Wales became King George II in 1727, the claims of Frederick could not be ignored. He was 22 years of age when he came to England and joined the royal family as Prince of Wales. He received a financial provision from the Civil List and settled down as a cultivated English gentleman. He bought a town house in London and a country estate at Kew, which he landscaped with the advice of a Scottish courtier, the Earl of Bute. He was a patron of the opera, collected paintings, played the cello, bred and raced horses, and sponsored a cricket side (team). In1736 he married a German princess, Augusta of Saxe-Gotha. Throughout their married life they maintained a close personal relationship, and Augusta gave birth to seven children, including the future George III.

Relations with his parents had always been strained, and in 1737 Frederick was excluded from the Royal Court. He joined the Opposition and prepared elaborate plans for the day when he would succeed to the throne, which never came. He died in 1751 of a sudden illness. The Princess Augusta and her children led a secluded life until the death of King George II and accession of King George III in 1760. Frederick bequeathed to his son his wide cultural interests and his plans to rule as "a patriot king."

Foreign Policy and the Fall of Walpole, "The '45"

The great success of the Opposition was the fall of Walpole in 1742. In foreign policy Walpole's major concern was to avoid a costly foreign war, for he remembered the partisanship and contentions aroused by the War of the Spanish Succession. He feared that war abroad would lead to tumult at home, including a possible Jacobite attempt to restore the Stuarts. War meant great expense, higher taxes, and accumulation of debt, which would destroy his successful efforts to bring stability to the public finances. Walpole attempted to continue the Whig policy of good relations with France, but relations with France declined as

France began to reassert itself as a factor in the European balance of power and as a colonial rival.

Ultimately Walpole's downfall was the result of failure in foreign policy and war. His foreign policy problems began with Spain, where relations continued to be aggravated by disputes concerning Gibraltar, Minorca, and Spanish efforts to exclude English traders from their colonies in the West Indies. English ships that were engaged in legal trade (or smuggling) were often stopped by the Spanish coast guards, searched, and sometimes plundered. Whipped up by the press and Opposition politicians, a powerful public reaction took place, as national pride and pugnacity were joined with hatred for Spain going back to the days of Queen Elizabeth. These sentiments were reinforced by greed, for Spain was viewed as a declining power whose empire was ripe for the picking. Carteret and Pulteney led the attack in Parliament, joined by the dynamic William Pitt, who first gained public acclaim by his attacks on Walpole's passivity toward Spain.

In March 1738. A group of London merchants gathered to prepare a petition against "Spanish depredations." The case of Capt. Robert Jenkins, whose ear had been cut off by a Spanish guarda costa in 1731, was revived. The House of Commons held hearings on these complaints, and Capt. Jenkins was called upon to testify. Whether or not he actually appeared is questionable, but the press published an account of his stirring words as he displayed his withered ear, which he carried with him, packed in cotton, in a little box. The case of Jenkins' ear caught the attention of the public, and became an emblem of Spanish cruelty and disdain for international law.

In 1739 Walpole was pushed into a declaration of war against Spain—a war known to history as the War of Jenkins' Ear. A bold attack from the sea captured Porto Bello, a Spanish port on the Atlantic coast of Panama. In 1740 the ministry prepared an expedition that was sent to the West Indies to attack Cartagena, Santiago de Cuba, and Panama. The Duke of Newcastle did not know how to organize such an expedition, coordination between the army and navy was non-existent, and the men died like flies from tropical diseases and bad food and water. In the previous two decades the Spanish had vigorously fortified the key points of their empire and had improved their colonial administration and military forces. The British entered the war inspired by the raids of Sir Francis Drake. They found to their amazement that the Spanish could fight. In 1742 the expedition was recalled and the fiasco was subsumed in a greater war. Commodore George Anson, was sent around the tip of South America to attack the Spanish colonies on the Pacific coast, with the prospect of capturing the treasure that was shipped each year from Panama to the Philippines.

In the meantime Walpole faced a foreign policy crisis when the War of the Austrian Succession (1740-1748) broke out in central Europe. In October 1740 the Emperor of Austria died and a challenge arose immediately to the succession of his daughter, Maria Theresa. Frederick II, the new King of Prussia, attacked and over-ran the Austrian province of Silesia, which bordered his domains and was of great economic value. Maria Theresa's plight took a turn for the worse in 1741 when France joined the fray. One French army invaded the Austrian lands while another entered the Rhineland and threatened Hanover. Parliament voted a generous subsidy for Maria Theresa to support "the liberties and balance of power in Europe." Maria Theresa became a heroine in Britain as the public rallied to her cause.

As if foreign problems were not enough, Walpole faced an election in 1741. The court interest and the o\Opposition both fought hard, but the election returns were inconclusive. The crucial test came later in 1741 when Parliament met and the first votes were taken in the House of Commons. In the votes on disputed elections (the surest test of parliamentary alignments) Walpole found his support crumbling. The decisive factor was that Walpole was losing favor with the independent Members. Although he still had the support of King George II, Walpole chose to resign, realizing that he needed the support of the House of Commons as well.

The immediate concern of King George II was the War of the Austrian Succession, which threatened Hanover. Britain's continental ally, Maria Theresa of Austria, was struggling to hold her diverse territories against assaults from Prussia, France, and Spain. In 1743 George II personally led a British-Hanoverian army at the battle of Dettingen, the last time that an English king commanded troops in battle. The king led his troops into a French trap, but the impulsiveness of the French cavalry and the steady musket volleys of the redcoats won the victory. The Duke of Newcastle and his brother, Henry Pelham, who had held office under Walpole, returned to office. They followed a moderate policy to reconcile the various Whig factions, and with the fall of Walpole partisanship declined.

In the meantime, Commodore Anson's expedition to South America miraculously succeeded. Four of his six leaky ships survived the storms of the South Atlantic and rounded Cape Horn. With his men decimated by scurvy, Anson sailed along the west coast of South America, where he captured a rich Spanish ship and plundered a town. Since the Spanish were alerted, his only route home was to cross the vast Pacific. He reached China where he had to scuttle all but one of his remaining ships. After meeting with Chinese authorities, Anson sailed to the vicinity of the Philippines, where he captured the Manila galleon, the Spanish ship that brought gold, silver, and other valuable items from Panama to the Philippines. Having emulated the exploits of Sir Francis Drake, Anson and his remaining ship arrived back in England in 1744 with a treasure worth £600,000. He and his men received a hero's welcome.

In July 1745 another crisis arose when "Bonnie Prince Charlie," son of James Edward, landed in Scotland to assert the Stuart claim to the throne. Many (although not all) of the Highlanders rose in his support, but the Lowlanders were unenthusiastic. Prince Charles was crowned in Edinburgh and his army of Highlanders won a startling victory over a hastily organized British force at Prestonpans, near Edinburgh. Seizing his opportunity, the Prince invaded England, and advanced into the Midlands. He hoped that English Tories and Jacobites would join him in overthrowing George II and the supremacy of the Whigs. He was mistaken.

The unexpected success of "the Young Pretender," as he was called, brought consternation in England. Most of the British Army was in the Netherlands, and fear of a French invasion in support of the Prince and the Jacobites was rampant. The militia was hastily embodied to defend the coasts. Depositors rushed to withdraw their money from the Bank of England, which bought time by paying in sixpences. A sense of excitement prevailed as the nation rallied behind its leaders. Thomas Arne's patriotic song, "God Save the King," was sung every night in Drury Lane Theatre until the crisis had passed.

The Duke of Cumberland, commander of the British troops in

the Netherlands, hurried home with part of his army, and additional soldiers were recruited. Faced with overwhelming opposition, Prince Charles began a retreat and his army of ragged Highlanders began to fall apart. Cumberland pursued them northward into Scotland, where he defeated the Scots at the brutal Battle of Culloden (1746). Cumberland's troops penetrated deep into the Highlands, burning homes and crops. He earned the nickname "The Butcher" with what he called "a little bloodletting." After various adventures, Prince Charles escaped to France and eventually settled in Rome, where he died in 1788.

"The '45" completed what the Act of Union had begun. The leadership of the Highland chiefs was destroyed. The Highlanders were disarmed, wearing the kilt and tartan were forbidden, roads and forts were built, schools were established, and the process began by which the Highlands were integrated into the British community.

The War of the Austrian Succession became a stalemate. Under Gov. William Shirley, the men of Massachusetts captured the great French fortress of Louisbourg on Cape Breton Island. In 1748 the Peace of Aix la Chapelle was signed, in which all parties agreed to return to their pre-war territorial and colonial status. The colony of Massachusetts was disappointed when Louisbourg was returned to France at the peace settlement.

Henry Pelham, as chancellor of the exchequer, was able to return England to a stable budget and begin reducing the cost of the national debt. When Pelham died in 1754, George II said, "Now I shall have no more peace."

The Economy: Defoe's Tour

In the reigns of George I and II, the British economy was in a pre-industrial stage, but many of the prerequisites for industrial growth were beginning to appear. A land rich in human and material resources needed time and encouragement to make the best use of them, and time was what the Hanoverian settlement provided. A stable government that protected individual liberty and property, and a parliamentary system that gave paramount influence to the possessors of wealth, offered the stability needed to encourage investments that could bear fruit only over a long period of time. The Bank of England was the lynch-pin of a system of banking and credit that enabled entrepreneurs to mobilize capital for potentially productive enterprises. The navy, merchant marine, and colonial empire contributed to an expanding trade, which provided outlets for manufactures and yielded profits that could be invested at home. A mode of thinking that emphasized rational analysis and the application of knowledge to practical uses contributed to economic development. An intelligent and resourceful people turned their attention from political and religious controversy to the more mundane business of creating, accumulating, and consuming wealth.

The changing face of Britain was delineated by Daniel Defoe. A lifetime of observation and writing was crowded into his <u>A Tour Thro' the Whole Island of Great Britain</u> (3 vols., 1724-26). Defoe's <u>Tour</u> is rooted in a fiction. His <u>Tour</u> is not an account of an actual journey made for that purpose, but the distillation of a lifetime of travel, observation, and collecting information. Defoe lived at a time when roads were improved and travel was growing rapidly. His <u>Tour</u> was written as a guide for travelers, and as such, with revisions, it continued in print until near the end of the century. While the <u>Tour</u> directs the attention of the traveler to interesting sights, it does more than that—it points out those aspects of British life in which the traveler <u>should</u> be interested, especially economic activities and the lives of ordinary people. Throughout, the <u>Tour</u> is infused with Defoe's essential message—his pride in his country, his enthusiasm for "improvement," his delight in humanity and its variegated activities, his impatience with that which was narrow, rigid, and ignorant, and his ever-flowing optimism. Defoe's <u>Tour</u> showed his countrymen the Britain that Defoe wanted them to see, and it continues to shape our view of pre-industrial Britain.

Leaving London, Defoe gives an idyllic view of the Thames valley, seen as an attractive setting for the works of man, from Hampton Court Palace and Richmond Lodge to the fine country seats of gentlemen (many of them of City origin) to the homes and villages of ordinary people, surrounded by gardens, walks, and fertile fields. The busy Thames serves as the main artery, linking these varied people and activities to the great metropolis that dominates their lives.

In his <u>Tour</u> Defoe gives some attention to the activities of the aristocracy, including fine stately homes and gardens, their collections of pictures, and the amusements of gentlemen and ladies at Tunbridge

Wells. He describes with pride the ivy-towered world of learning at Oxford and the massive splendor of Blenheim Palace. But his major interest is ordinary people involved with the world of work. In the east of England he observes the turkey growers of Suffolk and the woolen textile industry of Norfolk. He notes the castle, cathedral, and ancient walls of Norwich, but he is most impressed by the industriousness of the people. In the west of England he finds a shift in agriculture from sheep-raising to tillage. Previous reliance on the woolen textile industry has been eased by new kinds of agricultural income, primarily from malting barley, cheese, and bacon for the London market. He approves the practice of putting moveable sheep-folds upon meadows and fallow fields to fertilize the land with the sheep's droppings, and he recommends this practice to farmers in other parts of England.

Defoe's delight in economic growth was especially stimulated by Yorkshire. Formerly thinly populated and backward, the West Riding of Yorkshire was in the early stages of the process that would eventually become the Industrial Revolution. The city of York was an attraction, with its magnificent cathedral and well-preserved walls. But Defoe was especially interested in the woolen cloth industry, centered on Halifax and Leeds. He was amazed at the complexity of the industry—the elaborate division of labor, the many separate skills involved, the utilization of the terrain and the surface water, the industriousness of the people, and the elaborate system for financing, transporting, and marketing the cloth. Farther west, Liverpool was a rapidly growing port, serving as an outlet for the region and taking advantage of its access to Ireland and the American colonies. At Manchester Defoe found "the greatest mere village in England." Lacking the municipal institutions of an incorporated town, Manchester was already a thriving urban community, and its cotton textile industry had a future that Defoe could not possibly have imagined.

In the parts of his Tour dealing with Scotland, Defoe describes a land with which he had strong associations. Defoe had been sent by Harley to Scotland to promote the Act of Union and to report on its politics and people. In his Tour Defoe is eager to make English readers more aware of a nation about which they knew little, and to persuade them of the value of the Union. He describes Edinburgh as an ancient capital with a dignity all its own. With his keen sense for the future,

Defoe points out the potential for expansion across the lough (a narrow lake), where the "new town" was built at the end of the century. Glasgow was totally different from Edinburgh. Its interests were commercial while Edinburgh was the political, legal, administrative, and cultural center of Scotland. Defoe notes that Glasgow had benefited more from the Union than any other part of Scotland, and with his usual alertness to business potential he points out the possibilities for future growth of Scottish manufactures to export to the colonies through Glasgow.

As a frequent traveler, Defoe was acutely conscious of the condition of the roads. The movement for turnpikes (toll roads) was gathering momentum when he wrote, and he includes a long section in his <u>Tour</u> encouraging this development. He recognizes the importance of good roads for travel, the mail, transportation of manufactured goods and agricultural products, and the strengthening of national unity. To Defoe turnpikes were examples of enterprise, investment, economic growth, and a general spirit of "improvement." As such, they embodied the values that he had expounded in a lifetime of writing and nowhere more effectively than in his <u>Tour Thro' the Whole Island of Great Britain</u>.

<u>Scotland</u>

To the north was Scotland, which was politically and economically incorporated with England by the Act of Union (1707), but in other respects was a separate nation, with its own established Church, legal system, and traditions. The secretaries of state in London exercised power over Scottish domestic affairs through an official called the lord advocate, who controlled the Scottish legal and administrative structure. The Scottish members of the British Parliament were mainly subservient to the Crown and the ministry, for politics to them was primarily a source of patronage and privileges.

The Act of Union was at first unpopular in Scotland, but under the Union Scotland began to grow in population and wealth. Lowland Scots found a good market for its cattle in England. The quality of Scottish cattle was improved by the introduction of turnips for fodder and by better pastures based on clover and grasses. Potatoes were introduced, which became a valuable addition to the diet. The Scottish woolen cloth industry was injured by English competition, but the linen industry grew. The most important economic effect of the Union was access to trade with the empire. Glasgow merchants thrived on the growing trade in colonial sugar and tobacco, and a ship-building industry developed. Outgoing vessels needed cargoes, which encouraged the growth of Scottish industries. In his <u>Tour</u>, Defoe noted the close relationship between Scotland and the American colonies.

Edinburgh continued as the principal city, although it had lost its Parliament. Nevertheless, Edinburgh remained an important sub-capital for the Scottish administration, the courts of law, and the Church of Scotland. Edinburgh was a center of printing and publishing, and its shops and craftsmen made a variety of high-quality consumer goods. It was the social center of Scotland. Despite the disapproval of the earnest Presbyterians of the Church of Scotland, a theatre was built in 1746. The University of Edinburgh added to the prestige and cultural life of the city.

Ireland

Ireland was Britain's largest and most important dependency. In mid-century the population of Ireland (3 million) was almost half that of England and Wales and greater than the combined population of the North American colonies (2 million). Dublin, with a population of 100,000 was the second largest city in the British Isles and one of the largest cities in Europe. Irish trade was roughly equal to that of all thirteen North American colonies. Although the British market was in most respects closed to Irish products (apart from a large smuggling industry), Ireland was a major exporter to Europe of meat, cheese, wool, linen, and hides. Irish provisions became especially important to the British army and navy in time of war.

The political system of eighteenth-century Ireland was designed to maintain the Protestant ascendancy. The King of England was also King of Ireland, with the right to fill all offices in state and Church. The Crown exercised its authority through the viceroy (lord lieutenant), usually a prominent English aristocrat, who maintained an elegant court in Dublin Castle. The Irish Parliament was constituted on the British model of Lords and Commons, but legislatively it was subordinate to the British Parliament. The Irish revenue was almost entirely hereditary in the Crown, and consequently the Irish Parliament had no significant "power of the purse". The Irish Parliament usually met every two years and sessions were brief, which further reduced its influence.

The people of Ireland were divided politically, socially, and by religion. The Anglo-Irish ruling class was English in language and culture. They were centered in Dublin, but held large estates scattered throughout the island. They held the political offices and controlled the Irish Parliament, Church, army, and local government. They were educated in good grammar schools and at Trinity College, Dublin, and provided the professional people. The Anglo-Irish identified with England, and kept in close touch with British ideas, books, and fashions. Many of the most able and ambitious young men went to England to pursue careers. The Church of Ireland was the Irish equivalent of the Church of England. It served the Anglo-Irish, but not well. A few dedicated and distinguished clergymen, such as Jonathan Swift, mitigate the severity of this charge. Most of the bishops and many of the clergy were English. To English clergymen, appointment to a living in Ireland was an exile mitigated only by the mail, books, and periodic visits to England.

The Scots-Irish were archiepiscopal immigrants from Scotland who began settling in Ireland in the reign of James I. They were excluded by religious tests from holding office under the Crown, sitting in Parliament, or serving in a profession, although these restrictions were mitigated by Acts of Indemnity. The Scots-Irish had the right to vote, and the Irish Toleration Act of 1719 gave them the same freedom of worship possessed by Dissenters in England. Most of the Scots-Irish were farmers or artisans, and were settled predominantly in the northern counties of Ireland (Ulster). The Catholic Irish were approximately 75 percent of the population. They were primarily peasant farmers tilling small patches of land, paying rents to their landlords, and living at a subsistence level. Legislation passed by the Irish Parliament was designed to keep Catholics poor, uneducated, and politically powerless.

While the Irish Protestants used their political power to hold down the Catholics, they also became increasingly resentful of British control of Irish affairs. British politicians used Irish offices and pensions to provide incomes for their family and friends, and Ireland maintained a large standing army to back up the British army. From time to time the British Parliament used its legislative supremacy to restrict the Irish economy for the benefit of British producers. Confined unwillingly to Ireland, Jonathan Swift was not only an active administrator in his ecclesiastical duties but he was also an Irish patriot. He became a national hero through his five Drapier's Letters (1724), which expressed Irish outrage at a particularly obnoxious piece of Walpolean corruption. In A Modest Proposal for Preventing the Children of Poor People from being a Burthen to their Parents, or the country, and for Making the Beneficial to the Publick (1729) Swift savagely attacked the policies that brought misery to Ireland, suggesting satirically that the surplus children of Ireland could profitably be sold and eaten. There are times when the vanity, perversity, and destructiveness of mankind drive a reasonable, humane individual to exasperation mingled with rage. At such moments one can most fully appreciate the acid pen of Jonathan Swift.

By the 1740s, many of the political and social tensions in Ireland had diminished. Despite restrictions, a Catholic middle class of landowners and merchants was beginning to emerge. Ireland had a shortage of skilled labor, and those Catholic Irish with needed skills were often permitted to ply their trade. Catholic priests learned to serve their flocks under the Protestant ascendancy. Supported by voluntary contributions from the faithful, a network of bishops and priests developed, including rural "mass houses." Some Protestants began to think that it was possible to get along with the Catholics without constant suspicion and hostility.

Elite Society

Under George I and II the Royal Court was not the social center it had been under Henry VIII, Queen Elizabeth, or the Stuarts. George I was a bluff soldier who did not have a Queen and was not comfortable in English society. George II and Queen Caroline (especially the latter) had considerable personal charm and delighted in social life, but after the death of Queen Caroline the role of the court as a center of elite society languished. The royal palaces were unimpressive, and the first two Georges spent little to improve their appearance. St. James's Palace in Westminster fell far short of European standards, but after Whitehall Palace burned in 1698 it became the principal royal residence. Kensington Palace (purchased and expanded by William III) was an agreeable residence, since it was close to Westminster and it still had the advantage of country air. Hampton Court Palace, which William III enlarged, was the favorite country residence of the royal family. Farther west along the Thames was Windsor Castle, a mighty stone pile with a large park. Charles II had installed magnificent state apartments, but the first two Georges made little use of it. The royal palaces were not well maintained and compared unfavorably in appearance, elegance, and comfort with palaces on the continent and the finest of the stately homes of England.

The political situation also reduced the attractiveness of the monarchy. The dependence of George I and II upon Walpole and his narrow circle discouraged many of the most talented men and women from coming to court. Appearances at court functions were still important politically and socially, but the lively people were found elsewhere—in the stately homes or elegant London townhouses of the aristocracy, the opera, the theatre, or at Bath. When monarchy possessed power, as under Queen Elizabeth, or when it became a symbol of nationhood, as under Queen Victoria, it had the cachet to attract. The first two Georges were foreign-born kings dependent upon uninspiring politicians. The mystique of monarchy was absent.

The aristocracy captured the social role that the monarchy had lost. The word "peerage" refers to those persons with a right to sit in the House of Lords, either by inheritance or by royal creation. There were five ranks in the peerage—duke, marquis, earl, viscount, and baron. The title passed from father to eldest son, or if there was not a son, to the closest male relative. It was usual to make legal arrangements by which the heir inherited most of the property. All English peers were eligible to sit in the House of Lords; the Scottish peers elected 16 representative peers; Irish peers sat in the Irish House of Lords. The king could create new peers but the Hanoverian monarchs were sparing in the use of this power, and the House of Lords remained at about 180 peers and bishops.

The aristocracy was politically the dominant class—they held the great court offices and most Cabinet members were peers. From their vantage point in the House of Lords, the peers shared in legislation (taxation and expenditure were the exclusive privilege of the House of Commons) and exercised extensive influence over the Members of the

House of Commons. They controlled elections in many boroughs, and they carried great weight in the government of the shires. Their stately homes, surrounded by magnificent parks, dominated the countryside. Although they were an aristocracy of birth, the peerage was not a closed caste. The king conferred new peerages on successful politicians, military officers, lawyers, and others who had gained distinction. The peers freshened their purses and genes by marrying their heirs to the daughters of wealthy commoners. Since the peerage was inherited by the eldest son, their younger sons were commoners. As such, they diffused themselves through society, becoming politicians, civil servants, clergymen, judges, lawyers, physicians, officers in the army or navy, colonial officials, merchants, ship-captains, gamblers, scoundrels, or black sheep.

The heir to a peerage and the landed estate that went with it, customarily spent a year or two at Oxford or Cambridge, but usually did not take a degree. At the university, the young heir would mingle with his social equals and also with able young commoners preparing for a career. Sometimes friendships were established that continued into adult life. Since it would be desirable for a young aristocrat to know something of the Common Law, a year or two at the Inns of Court were also seen as advantageous. Legal instruction at the Inns of Court was haphazard, at best, and many young aristocrats used the Inns as an opportunity to experience the social and cultural delights of London. The Grand Tour of France and Italy was the culmination of the young heir's education. He usually was accompanied by a tutor, and the tour might include a period of study at a university, meetings with prominent continental statesmen, an introduction to the politics and economy of the country, and visits to the historical and artistic marvels of Italy.

The main emphasis of the Grand Tour was the art and architecture of antiquity. Joseph Addison in <u>Remarks upon Several Parts of Antiquity</u> (1705) describes Italy as a monument to the achievements of the ancient world. Another major interest was the art, sculpture, and architecture of the Italian Renaissance. For some, the Grand Tour was a powerful introduction to the languages, history, art and architecture of a glorious past that set standards that the English should emulate. In all too many cases, the young man enjoyed the experience of travel in foreign lands but learned little of substance.

Whig Architecture

Architecturally, the Whigs promoted classicism as an alternative to baroque, which they identified with the Tories and the Church. Classicism was infused into the mentality of the leadership class by education, which was devoted almost entirely to studying the ancient classics. Classical themes and references were integral to journalism, oratory, poetry, and theatre, and were part of the everyday vocabulary of educated people.

The Whig aristocracy used architecture and the arts to display their power and wealth. The Whig architectural style was classical, as defined in the works and publications of Andrea Palladio, a sixteenth-century Venetian architect. The essential features of Palladianism were formality, symmetry, uncluttered architectural lines, a linear profile, and carefully balanced proportions. The architecture of Inigo Jones a century earlier facilitated the assimilation of Palladian principles in England. Furthermore, Palladian architecture was regarded as compatible with constitutional government and Protestantism as opposed to the ornate baroque style of Italy and Spain, which was identified with Catholicism and despotism.

A highly influential work on the principles of Palladio was Vitruvius Britannicus (3 vols., 1715-25) by Colen Campbell, a Scot who had recently arrived in London. The book was planned by a group of booksellers as a collection of prints of the most important buildings, public and private, in England. They called upon Campbell to write the introduction and the notes to each plate. On the cover Campbell is cited as the author. The introduction to the first volume damns the excesses of the Italian baroque, and is a powerful statement of patriotic pride in English architecture. Palladio and Inigo Jones are cited as models of classical harmony and simplicity. Each of the first two volumes has 100 engraved plates of plans and elevations of well-known houses built during the previous two centuries. Campbell promoted the Palladian cause by including engraved plates that showed works by Palladio and Inigo Jones and some of his own Palladian designs. The second volume (1717) and third volume (1725) attracted a large number of subscribers, mainly aristocrats. The work had enormous influence on English architecture. It also made publication of architectural designs an important topic for publishers and architects.

Campbell was a major figure in the Palladian movement. His first major house was Wanstead in Essex (1714-20), a suburb of London. Wanstead (1714-20) was intended to rival Castle Howard and other great houses. Typically, it had a row of stone steps leading to a portico that was the entrance to the main floor. The design was horizontal, with uniform rows of rectangular windows on the main floor and square windows on the floor above. Campbell also designed Houghton, the great country house of Sir Robert Walpole (1722-ff.) in Norfolk and Stourhead in Wiltshire for Henry Hoare, a wealthy London banker. In 1729 he published an account of the architectural principles of Palladio in The Five Orders of Architecture.

The most important advocate of Palladianism was Lord Burlington, a great Whig landlord with extensive estates and thousands of tenants in Middlesex, Yorkshire, and Ireland. In 1714-15 he took the Grand Tour to France and Italy, where his main interests were art and music. When he returned, he actively devoted himself to the role of a connoisseur. He became a patron of John Gay and Alexander Pope and gave lavish support to music and the arts. He was attracted to architecture by Colen Campbell's Vitruvius Britannicus. He employed Campbell to remodel Burlington House, his London townhouse on Piccadilly. Burlington came of age in 1715 and immediately became a powerful figure at court and among the Whigs. In 1718 he used his influence to dismiss Wren, Hawksmoor, and others of that school from the office of works and install his own protégés. Sir John Thornhill was deprived of the commission to decorate the state apartments at Kensington Palace. As he became more deeply involved in architecture, Burlington realized that he needed to return to Italy. On his second trip (1719) he studied the architecture of Palladio and architecture became his main interest.

Burlington saw himself as a proponent of the "national taste" in architecture, which he believed should be based on austere Greek and Roman principles of classicism. In the 1720s he began making his own designs. His Palladian villa at Chiswick displayed his Palladian approach to architecture. In addition to the example set by his own designs, he undertook an extensive program of publication. The first was The Designs of Inigo Jones, with some Additional Designs (1727). One of Burlington's associates published The Four Books of Architecture of Andrea Palladio (1738). These and other works spread Palladianism to the great Whig aristocrats, who had the money to build Palladian mansions that proclaimed their wealth and power.

While Burlington was in Italy, he met William Kent, who was studying painting in Rome. They returned to England together, and for the rest of his life Kent lived at Burlington House. Kent's first project was the decoration of Burlington House. Burlington used his political influence to gain for Kent the commission to decorate the state apartments at Kensington Palace, which established Kent's reputation as a creative decorator in the Italianate mode. In 1735, Kent was appointed deputy surveyor in the office of works. In this office, he designed the King's Mews (stables) at Charing Cross, the Treasury Building, and the Horse Guards Building, where the offices of the army and a contingent of cavalry were located.

Burlington was also an enthusiast for music. He supported the opera and was a director of the Royal Academy of Music. From 1712-1715, Burlington House was the residence of Handel. Burlington brought three Italian string players back from Rome to perform in musical gatherings at Burlington House and Chiswick. They also gave concerts and played in the orchestra of Handel's operas.

The life of an aristocratic woman had many constraints, but offered freedom to assert individuality that lesser women lacked. Unusual behavior was tolerated and often admired. Lady Burlington was one of many aristocratic women whose social position enabled them to develop their own talents and interests. She was heiress to a great estate that provided additional financial support for Lord Burlington's architecture and their active social life. William Kent taught her to make pen and ink sketches, in which she excelled, especially in caricatures. She was a friend of Alexander Pope, who visited Burlington House occasionally. She shared her husband's interest in music and theatre, and maintained a close friendship with David Garrick, the actor and theatre manager. For eight years she was one of Queen Caroline's ladies of the bedchamber. When opportunity arose, she also rode to the hounds.

The major influence of Palladianism was seen in the great stately homes of the aristocracy. The typical Palladian house had a columned porch at the entrance, which was surmounted by a triangular pediment. An imposing set of steps led to the potico (porch), which opened into a spacious reception room for receiving guests, entertaining, and display of art works. Symmetrical wings on both sides provided additional space to display works of art and sculpture. The attic provided space for storage and quarters for the servants. The roof might be enhanced by a dome or cupola. The austerity of Palladian exteriors was balanced by considerable freedom in decoration of interiors. Palladian architecture did not leave large spaces for murals, but left many smaller spaces for pictures that were hung on the walls. Kent's main influence as a decorator was to emphasize the use of architectural features, such as doors, windows, cornices, fireplaces and decorative plasterwork for decoration.

Robert Walpole, with the vast personal resources gained from his offices as first lord of the treasury, chose Colen Campbell to build Houghton, one of the great country houses of England. The exterior appearance is severely Palladian, but that is offset by the interiors, which were designed by Kent and are of the utmost richness and splendor. Kent also designed the furniture, which owed much to his ten years in Italy. He made mahogany fashionable, with an elegant mahogany staircase, mahogany paneling, and gilt mahogany chairs with Genoese silk upholstery. Walpole amassed a great collection of Renaissance art, which after his death was sold to the Empress Catherine the Great of Russia and now constitutes the core of the collection at the Hermitage, the great art gallery in St. Petersburg.

Perhaps the most perfect Palladian mansion is Holkham Hall in Norfolk, which was built for Thomas Coke, Earl of Leicester, a friend of Burlington. Coke spent five years on the Grand Tour, studying art and architecture and purchasing large quantities of paintings, sculptures, books, manuscripts and coins. When he returned to England, he inherited his estate and built Holkham Hall as a stately home to dignify his family and display his rich collection of paintings and sculpture. He was politically close to Walpole, a neighbor, from whom he received a sinecure office of £1,000 per year as postmaster-general. He suffered heavy losses in the South Sea Bubble, which delayed construction of the house. When he died in 1759, his wife completed the construction.

Holkham Hall is characterized by a severely Palladian brick exterior, with a columned Greek portico at the main entrance. Otherwise,

2

the windows are few and plain. Four symmetrical wings are located at the corners. At each corner are stubby capped towers with a large window. The portico leads into an elegantly ornamented vestibule followed by a high-ceiling marbled hall. Parallel to the marble hall is the statue gallery where Burlington's collection of sculpture was displayed. William Kent designed a magnificent interior that offsets the severity of the exterior. The house is set in a spacious park landscaped by Kent. Kent designed the furniture in an ornate Italianate style, which immediately became fashionable.

Burlington and Campbell also established the vogue for the Palladian villa or country retreat. Burlington designed Chiswick House, a small house just west of London, for this purpose. Chiswick has a flight of stone steps leading to a six-columned portico that opens into a central pavilion covered by a dome. It was intended to be a place of relaxation and contemplation—a place to display Burlington's art collection and enjoy musical performances. Chiswick was not intended to be a residence, which was provided by a nearby Jacobean house joined to the villa by a link building. It was surrounded by an Italian-style garden with a variety of Mediterranean plants. Such villas became fashionable and soon began sprouting all over England.

Pattern books adapted to the resources and skills of local builders spread Palladianism throughout England. William Halfpenny's <u>Practical Architecture</u> (1724) showed how Palladian principles could be applied to modest homes. In this way the tasteful classicism of the great aristocracy filtered down to public buildings, country homes of the gentry, and comfortable middle class homes throughout the British Isles and America.

The Palladians were not without rivals. James Brydges, Duke of Chandos, accumulated a vast fortune as paymaster of the forces under the Duke of Marlborough. He used much of it to build Canons, the most imposing and costly stately home in England at that time. Brydges came from a genteel family, was well-educated, and held a variety of cultural interests. When he decided to build a great house, he rejected the dominant Palladianism of Burlington and his school and called in Vanbrugh, who was devoted to the English baroque style. The core of the house had a magnificent marble staircase and a richly-appointed chapel designed by James Gibbs, a protégé of Wren and Hawksmoor.

Long wings extended on each side of the core building. The most costly materials were used, and the best mural painters (English and Italian) were called in to decorate the walls. Handel composed eleven magnificent anthems for the parish church, which Chandos rebuilt and decorated. Canons was torn down in 1741, but manuscripts remain to describe it.

Chandos also built several townhouses in London. He had no political ambitions, but participated in a variety of business and philanthropic enterprises. He was much interested in music and attended meetings of the Society of Gentlemen Performers of Music. He kept an orchestra and choir that were directed by Dr. Pepusch.

The Landscaping of the Great House

The Palladian ideal conceived of the great house or country villa in a rural setting, and thus landscaping became an important part of architecture. The aristocracy and gentry of England retained their roots in the country and found their principal satisfactions in country life. This predilection was reinforced by the works of Roman and Renaissance writers who idealized the countryside as a refuge from the busy life of the city. In his <u>Characteristics of Men, Manners, Opinions and Times</u> (1711), Shaftesbury refers to the picturesque setting of the villa of the Roman writer, Pliny the Younger. He sees the country as conducive to the development of virtuous living. Alexander Pope adopted the idea of the Roman garden for his country home at Twickenham. A garden in Italian style surrounded Lord Burlington's rural retreat at Chiswick.

William Kent gave material expression to these ideas when he created the English garden as the setting for a stately home or villa. Kent took up landscaping as an adjunct to architecture and eventually made it his major interest. His objective was to break the domination of formal gardens by using the beauties of Nature as they already existed; "nature abhors a straight line," he declared. He was influenced by Vanbrugh's gardens at Castle Howard, with their temples, arches, and Roman bridge. Kent did not hesitate to improve on Nature by building lakes and bridges, planting trees, laying out paths, and building artificial ruins.

Kent's most influential project was Stowe in Buckinghamshire, the country seat of Richard Temple, Viscount Cobham, a prominent Whig opponent of Walpole. The original plan for the gardens was laid out by Sir John Vanbrugh and later modified by Kent. Kent also designed several buildings, among them the temples of Ancient Virtue and British Worthies. Stowe Gardens features carefully contrived vistas of glades and meadows dotted with classical temples and sculptures. The Whig ruling class identified themselves with the stern leaders of the Roman Republic—the Temple of Ancient Virtue displays statues of Greek and Roman heroes. Nearby is the satirical Temple of Modern Virtue, a ruin with a headless statue identified with Walpole. The Temple of Liberty glorifies prominent persons in English history, including King Alfred, Shakespeare, Milton, and Newton. In recognition of the Anglo-Saxon past, held by the Whigs to be the foundation of English liberty, the distinguished sculptor, Michael Rysbrack, did a series of seven statues of Anglo-Saxon deities. The Temple of Concord and Victory celebrates famous battles, most of them English victories over the French. Kent undertook similar projects at other great houses and established a style of landscaping that dominated the century.

Stourhead Gardens was laid out by Colen Campbell. It is filled with buildings and statues representing ancient gods and goddesses—a Pantheon, a Temple of the Sun, and a Temple of Flora. The Pantheon houses a full size marble statue of Hercules by Rysbrack. Stourhead also includes a Druid cell, Turkish tent, Chinese bridge and alcove, and a Gothic church. In this manner the great Whig families identified their power and wealth with the cultures of the past and the greatness of the present.

The successor to Kent as the most distinguished of Georgian landscape gardeners was Lancelot, "Capability" Brown, a man of humble Northumberland origins with an amazing instinct for the distinctive features of land, water, and sky. In 1741 he began working at Stowe and learned the art of landscaping under the direction of Kent and James Gibbs. He soon demonstrated his own capabilities and was put in charge of some 40 employees. His work at Stowe included supervision of the building of the Cobham monument, the Greek Temple, the Queen's Temple, alterations to the lakes, the excavation of the Grecian Valley, redesigning paths to give attractive vistas, and extensive planting of trees.

In 1751 Brown went into business for himself and earned his nickname by telling potential clients that their property had "capabilities of improvement." In the 1760s he had more than forty large contracts for landscaped gardens. Sometimes he prepared a plan for buildings and landscaping which the owner of the estate carried out with his own labor. Or he would provide a foreman to supervise the execution of the plan. At his peak, Brown employed more than 20 foremen for his projects. His foremen were skilled workmen who also did business on their own. The most expensive arrangement was for Brown to supervise the work personally. He also worked as an architect, turning out well-designed houses in a conventional Palladian style.

The purpose of landscaping was always to set off a great house, and Brown left his mark on many of the great houses of England. His method was to accentuate the natural contours of the land, using broad sloping lawns, a serpentine lake with a classical bridge, clumps of trees carefully arranged to provide broad vistas, and artificial temples and ruins. Typically, Brown's designs include a shelter belt of trees encircling the fields and gardens, trees to screen the stables and other outbuildings, and a long winding drive that offers glimpses of the house through the trees. He liked to use a variety of plantings—the arboretum, the flower garden, the wilderness, and the quarry garden. Sometimes he planted formal gardens along a winding path. He was interested in the entire estate, including the fields and hunting grounds. Although most of his commissions were small, some of the estates that he landscaped were immense. In 1764 "Capability" Brown became the master gardener at Hampton Court Palace. By the time of his death in 1783, complaints were being raised of the "dullness" and stereotyping of his landscapes.

Rococo

In the early eighteenth century a new artistic style known as rococo became dominant on the continent. Rococo began in France and spread to Germany, Austria, and Spain. Rococo was an alternative to the magnificence of baroque and the austerity of classicism. The new style emphasized grace, lightness, curved lines, elaborate ornamentation, and delicate colors. The most prominent French painter in the style was Jean-Antoine Watteau, whose <u>fêtes</u> <u>galantes</u> were small paintings of well-dressed people gathered in some secluded spot where they engage in conversation or making music. His most famous work is Departure for Cythera (1717), which depicts happy people leaving on a journey to an idyllic island that was the center for worship of Aphrodite, goddess of love.

Rococo was not popular in England to the extent it was on the continent, probably due to a Puritanical distaste for frivolity. In England, the influence of rococo was seen primarily in the decorative arts. Huguenot engravers and silversmiths brought rococo to England and popularized it. Rococo was characterized by elaborate ornamentation such as scrolls, animals, and clusters of flowers. Italian stucco swirled in a variety of shapes was a preferred form of decoration for ceilings..A fashionable interest in China popularized Chinese decorative motifs (chinoiserie). Lord Chesterfield, a Francophile, maintained classical principles in building his house but added a variety of rococo decorative touches. He described his painted ballroom as a la française.

The Furnishings of the Great House

The houses of the aristocracy and gentry also required suitable furnishings. Mahogany was the most popular wood for furniture. Walpole used mahogany for the staircase and paneling at Houghton, and exempted Jamaican mahogany from import duty to help the colony and make mahogany more affordable in England. Mahogany was popular with cabinetmakers because it was stable and responsive to carving. Kent designed heavy mahogany furniture that was in keeping with the dignity of the Palladian house. Walnut declined in popularity, but furniture was still made from native woods such as oak and beech. Many who went to Italy on the Grand Tour wanted marble-topped tables.

In the 1740s, the rising generation adopted a more relaxed lifestyle and preferred lighter, more ornate interior decoration and furniture. Thomas Chippendale's furniture and his book, Gentleman and Cabinet Makers Directory (1754) disseminated his graceful style widely in England and America. The first edition referred to "furniture in the Gothic, Chinese, and Modern taste." Chippendale often provided furniture for the houses of Robert Adam. In England, the playful style of rococo was most popular in porcelain, at first imported from France and Saxony. Porcelain requires a fine, white clay and high craftsmanship to bring it to perfection in statuettes and other ornamental items.

In the 1740s porcelain made in England began to equal its continental rivals. Chelsea and Worcester were the leading centers of porcelain production. Statuettes of historic figures were popular. On the continent, Chelsea toys were the favorite English porcelains.

When Louis XIV expelled the Huguenots from France (1685), more than a hundred Huguenot goldsmiths fled to England. They adopted the simplicity of the Queen Anne style and carried it forward into Georgian silverware. Sometimes highly ornamented, Georgian silver never lost its basic simplicity of design. Throughout the eighteenth-century Huguenot silversmiths dominated the trade.

Sculpture

The major art form supporting Palladian architecture was sculpture, and in the Georgian period sculpture flourished in England to a degree previously unknown. The Grand Tour introduced the aristocracy to the sculpture of the ancient world and Renaissance Italy. They purchased large quantities of sculpture (some genuine, some not), which they shipped to England to ornament their stately homes. As part of their identification with the Romans, the Whig aristocrats commissioned sculptured portrait busts and memorial tombs; sometimes the subject was depicted wearing a toga. The tombs and monuments of Westminster Abbey were an important venue for sculptured memorials of important political and literary figures. Addison pointed out that a cluster of literary figures was buried in "the Poet's Corner" without suitable memorials, and Pope was involved in putting up monuments to Shakespeare, Milton, Dryden, Kneller, John Gay and others.

John Michael Rysbrack, born and trained in Flanders, was the outstanding sculptor in the classical style. He was twenty-six when he arrived in England in 1720. He brought with him a classical style characterized by heroic figures in Greek or Roman dress and static poses. He excelled in sculptured monuments and portraits. Lord Burlington became his patron and chose him to do statues of Palladio and Inigo Jones for Chiswick House and a bas relief of a Roman marriage for Kensington Palace. Thereafter, commissions flowed in, as the Whig aristocracy sought to immortalize themselves and their accomplishments in stone. Examples of Rysbrack's memorial sculptures are a large bronze equestrian statue of King William III for the city of Bristol, and a monument to the Duke of Marlborough at Blenheim Palace. Westminster Abbey was the location for his splendid memorials to James, Earl Stanhope, Whig leader at the accession of George I, and Sir Isaac Newton.

Rysbrack was instrumental in establishing the vogue among the nobility for portrait busts. He did them in two forms—in contemporary dress and in Roman toga. His portrait bust of Daniel Finch, Earl of Nottingham (1723) is severely classical. His bust of Sir Hans Sloane (1737), a distinguished physician, botanist, and collector of books, manuscripts, coins etc. is in contemporary dress. Pride in English history and culture was displayed in Rysbrack's portrait busts of Shakespeare, Milton, and Pope, and in seven statues of Anglo-Saxon deities at Stowe Gardens. Queen Caroline saw the statue of William III before it was shipped to Bristol, and immediately ordered a series of portrait busts of English kings and queens for the new library that William Kent was building for her at St. James's Palace. Rysbrack was a leader in doing sculptured portraits of children. He presented to the Children's Hospital a marble relief entitled <u>Charity Children Engaged in Navigation and Husbandry</u>.

The rococo spirit is seen in the sculpture of a lively Frenchman, Louis François Roubiliac, whose statues exhibit an easy informality and warm humanity. Roubiliac was able to capture a sense of life, movement, and personality in his subjects. French by birth and training, in 1730 he moved to London, where he worked with several English sculptors. Within a few years he was receiving his own commissions. Roubiliac's reputation was made by the famous statue of Handel for Vauxhall Gardens (1738), which shows the great composer in a relaxed pose, playing a lyre, wearing an informal cap and with one shoe off.

At first Roubiliac did not compete with Rysbrack in making sculptured monuments. His main activity was portrait sculptures of professional men, writers, and musicians. His portrait busts of Pope, Hogarth, and Lord Chesterfield also displayed his perceptive sense of personal character. His objective was to move the portrait bust from a mere accurate likeness to a medium for artistic expression and depiction of personal character.

By 1750 Roubiliac had begun receiving commissions for large monuments in marble. The first was an imposing monument to the second

Duke of Argyll in Westminster Abbey (1749), with dramatic figures of History and Eloquence. His gift for portraying grief was fully displayed in his monument to Lady Elizabeth Nightingale (1761). Her desperate husband attempts to ward off Death with one arm while supporting his wife with the other. Roubiliac also began producing full-length portrait statues. One of his finest was his portrait of Lord President, Duncan Forbes of Scotland (1752), who gestures as he enunciates some point of law from his chair. Another was the statue of Shakespeare he did for David Garrick, actor and promoter of Shakespeare's plays. One of his finest is his monument to Handel (1761) in Westminster Abbey. The composer is shown in the process of inspired composition, taking from an angel the melody, "I Know that my Redeemer Liveth" from The Messiah.

Rysbrack responded in some degree to Roubiliac's popularity by introducing more individuality and humanity into his works. Roubiliac used Rysbrack's stricter classical mode when it suited him or his patron. Together Rysbrack and Roubiliac made sculpture an important means of communicating the ideals and values of the English aristocracy.

Masters of Gentility: Chesterfield, Nash

Two men are notable for defining the characteristics and social role of a gentleman. One was Lord Chesterfield, who attained some importance as a politician, diplomat, pamphleteer, and viceroy of Ireland. He was educated at Cambridge, where he became a fine classical scholar. An extended visit to France gave him the polished manners of the French court. In the House of Lords he was a superb orator, but his political career languished because he disliked the heavy-handed methods of Sir Robert Walpole. His periodical, Common Sense (1737-43) attacked the administration of Walpole and contributed to his downfall. After the fall of Walpole, Chesterfield engaged in several diplomatic missions and served briefly as secretary of state.

Chesterfield abandoned politics in 1748 because he disliked the preoccupation of politicians with mundane matters of patronage and elections. Thereafter he wrote for intellectual periodicals, carried on an extensive correspondence, and devoted himself to his elegant townhouse in London and his extensive library. He was a frequent contributor to The World (1753-5), a periodical of informed opinion on many topics. He is known primarily for his <u>Letters to his Son</u> (1774), in which he conveyes the detached, cultivated, cynical outlook of a gentleman of high rank with wide experience of the world. <u>Letters to his Son</u> was criticized by his contemporaries and subsequent generations for their emphasis on the importance of presenting an elegant appearance to the world while acting on the basis of a cynical view of the selfishness and gullibility of mankind. Despite the charge of hypocrisy, Chesterfield encourages his son to develop genuine merit, although he recognizes that merits will have little effect if they are not presented with a glossy finish. Samuel Johnson commented that the letters "teach the morals of a whore and the manners of a dancing master." Johnson admitted that, apart from Chesterfield's cynical morality, the letters present in an elegant form the true essentials of a cultivated gentleman.

Bath, in the west of England, became a center of genteel society during the winter social season. The hot springs had made it a favorite of the Romans, and in the eighteenth-century Bath became a city of distinguished Palladian architecture. At the center of the city was Bath Abbey, an early sixteenth-century church with splendid fan vaulting. Nearby was the elegant eighteenth-century Pump Room, where people assembled every morning to drink the waters, which were thought to be health-giving. Others immersed themselves in a pool of steaming water clad in voluminous garments.

Bath contains some of England's most distinguished Palladian architecture. John Wood, architect and builder, gave Bath a distinctly Palladian look. His work began with the two parades, where society met during morning walks. Wood was instrumental in the design of the Circus, a circular terrace of Palladian townhouses around an open space with a pump in the center. His son completed the Circus and linked it to the Royal Crescent, a spectacular semi-circular terrace of townhouses overlooking a lake. A new Guildhall, begun in 1776, has a magnificent Banqueting Hall. Farther up the slope are the Upper Assembly Rooms, where society met for cards, dancing, and conversation. In 1768 a licensed theatre opened.

Beau Nash transformed Bath into a center of polite society and refined entertainment. Nash was educated as a gentleman and for a time served as an army officer. He was the self-appointed master of ceremonies at Bath. He realized that Bath could be a success as a social center only if it were a place where gentlemen and their families could come without being offended by vulgarity and immorality or threatened by crime.

As master of ceremonies at Bath, Nash controlled admission to the social life of Bath to exclude unwelcome participants. He provided a variety of precisely scheduled activities. He rigorously enforced his standards of social decorum—dueling was prohibited; a strict code of dress and manners was imposed; adventurers, card sharks, and ladies of ill repute were excluded (although they turned up anyway); and daily attendance at worship was expected. He introduced a spirit of informality, breaking down the formal manners and class distinctions typical of genteel society. Persons who refused to adhere to Nash's rules were excluded from the social gatherings and various entertainments of Bath. Tailors, dressmakers, milliners, cabinetmakers, and purveyors of other goods and services set up shops to provide for the needs of an affluent clientele. When he died in 1761, Nash became the subject of a fascinating biography, The Life of Richard Nash (1762) by Oliver Goldsmith.

Bath replicated, on a smaller scale, the London social season. A theatre drew actors from the Theatre Royal in nearby Bristol. Public concerts were frequent, and Handel visited Bath to perform his works. The principal musical figure was William Herschel, a musical promoter and conductor, who gained fame as an astronomer.

The elegant world of Bath was open to all who could meet its requirements in money, manners, dress, and style of life. Bath thrived as a place where the gentlemen and ladies of England, with their sons and daughters, could meet others of appropriate social standing, enjoy common recreations, arrange marriages, recuperate from illness, and talk politics. Bath typified the assurance and stability of a ruling class that felt secure enough to accept, at least at Bath, men and women on the basis of their attributes rather than their ancestry. The remarkably open society of Bath best embodied the unique blend of stability and mobility that characterized the society of eighteenth-century England.

Ch. 7. Religion and Philosophy

The changes in philosophy and religion that grew out of "the Glorious Revolution" were as revolutionary as the changes that took place in government. Reason became the test of Truth. Many Churchmen and Dissenters, whose beliefs rested on faith, were compelled to respond to rationalism. David Hume, a Scottish philosopher, carried the arguments of Locke to their logical conclusion, which dissolved all absolutes and led to a philosophy called Skepticism.

The Church of England

In the reigns of George I and II the Church of England was struggling to retain some of its former importance as the embodiment of the religious life of the nation. After "the Glorious Revolution" the powers of the state expanded enormously, leaving the Church an unwilling dependent where formerly it had considered itself a partner in the government and discipline of the kingdom. The Toleration Act permitted Protestant rivals to exist and manage their own affairs. Dissenters were permitted to maintain their own clergy, chapels, and schools. The Test and Corporation Acts excluded them from holding office under the Crown or in municipal government. Under the Whigs, annual Acts of Indemnity removed the penalties for so doing. In 1719 the Occasional Conformity Act and Schism Act were repealed. Dissenters had the right to vote, and their votes were important in some parliamentary constituencies. Most Dissenters accepted their subordinate status, although they organized a body called the Dissenting Deputies to protect their interests.

With the Hanoverian succession and establishment of the Whig supremacy, the politicization of religion subsided and the Church and its rivals settled into an uneasy modus vivendi. In dealing with the Church, Walpole relied heavily on Edmund Gibson, bishop of London, a man of strong character and convictions. Gibson countered the Toryism of the Church by arguing that the Revolution Settlement, the Hanoverian monarchy, and the Whig dominance were the main securities for the role of the Church of England as the established church. While maintaining his political commitment to the Whigs, Gibson mollified the Tory clergy by insisting that appointments to Church offices should be tendered only to men of orthodox views. He ran afoul of many Whig politicians when he successfully opposed the efforts of the Dissenters to obtain repeal of the Test and Corporation Acts, which he and other churchmen thought would threaten the role of the Church of England as the national church. He strongly opposed Methodism.

The Quakers were a special case. They recognized no government except that of Jesus. However, as individuals they lived peaceably and obeyed the laws. They refused to take their hats off when dealing with government officials or swear an oath in court. In 1721 legislation was passed that authorized Quakers to "affirm" rather than swear. A more difficult problem was the tithes, a tax imposed on crops and village crafts to support the parish priest. Disputes concerning tithes were decided in the Church courts, usually at great expense and often for trivial amounts. Walpole, who respected the Quakers as hard-working, law-abiding people, introduced legislation to bring disputes concerning tithes before the justices of the peace. The Tithe Bill (1738) passed the House of Commons overwhelmingly, but a great clamor arose against it among the clergy. In the House of Lords, Gibson led the bishops in a vigorous opposition that defeated the Bill and ended his relationship with Walpole.

One of the most powerful defenders of the religious policies of the Whig government was the bishop of Bangor, Benjamin Hoadly, an exponent of latitudinarian views. The Hanoverian succession was still insecure, and he was worried by the association of many Tory churchmen with Jacobitism. Hoadly also criticized increasing sacerdotalism (emphasis on the sacraments) in the Church, which smacked of Roman Catholicism. In addition to his religious sympathies, he was a strong advocate of toleration of Dissenters as important supporters of the Whig government.

Hoadly challenged the Church's claim to privileges granted by the state in his inflammatory sermon entitled The Nature of the kingdom or Church of Christ (1717). Using the text, "My kingdom is not of this world," Hoadly defines the Church as a spiritual body that should not possess powers and privileges in worldly things. Thus the Church should not call upon the state to enforce religious laws that were to its advantage. Hoadly went beyond his attack on ecclesiastical power. He would greatly extend the authority of the state to regulate the Church as part of its general responsibility to order the affairs of men. Tory churchmen were outraged, and many prominent Whig clergymen were shocked by Hoadly's extreme views. The controversy raged for a decade.

Walpole and most Whigs favored the more moderate views offered by William Warburton, later Bishop of Gloucester. In a reply to Hoadly entitled The Alliance Between Church and State (1736). Warburton traces the origins of the Church to a primitive contract, similar to that postulated by Locke for the state. He justifies an established Church with political privileges on the basis of its contribution to society. Warburton supported the Walpole administration through letters to the London Journal, the government's political voice.

The principal challenge to the Church came not from theological differences but from the claims of Reason and science. Latitudinarians conceded that some of the teachings of Christianity were reasonable, or at least useful to society, and they insisted that Reason should be the test of religion, and not the reverse. In the light of Reason, the Christian doctrines of sin and salvation seemed less valid. While latitudinarians sought to simplify Christian doctrine, Deism went a step further to postulate an impersonal God who was the Creator of a rational world order that functioned by its inherent laws without divine intervention. Deists held that knowledge of God comes, not from the Bible or the Christian creeds but from Nature.

The attractions of Deism and the pragmatic and empiric limits placed on knowledge by Locke, confronted the Church with an intellectual challenge that could not be avoided. The most effective of its defenders was Bishop Joseph Butler, whose <u>The Analogy of Religion, Natural and Revealed, To the Constitution and Course of Nature</u> (1736) was his most important work. Butler does not support Christianity on the basis of the authority of the Bible or the orthodox creeds. He accepts the philosophy of Locke, which regards ideas as probable rather than indubitable. Butler argues that the doctrines of Christianity have high probability. The marvelous regularity of Nature, he writes, makes it probable that there is a Divine Creator, just as the existence of a watch makes probable the existence of a watch-maker. The fact that in Nature good conduct leads to pleasurable experiences and bad conduct to unpleasant experiences gives high probability to the existence of a moral code. The capacity of individuals for love and charitable actions gives reason to believe that Man is born with a spiritual dimension that goes beyond his own self-interest. Butler agrees that such arguments do not prove that God exists, but he believes that it was up to others to prove that God does not exist, which they could not do. If one studies Nature and Mankind closely, Butler argues, the probabilities dictate that there is a God and a moral order.

Another approach was presented by William Law in his <u>A Serious Call to a Devout and Holy Life</u> (1728). Law was expelled from Cambridge due to his refusal to accept the Revolution settlement of the Crown and Church. He emphasizes a religion of piety and feeling rather than strict adherence to the doctrines and requirements of organized religion. His work had an important influence as the doctrinal disputes of the early eighteenth century were replaced by desires for a more personal relationship with God.

Most of the clergy had no choice but to accept the wrenching changes to which the Church of England had been subjected during the previous seventy years. They followed the principles of the vicar of Bray, the subject of an anonymous poem. The vicar states that "whatever King shall Reign, I will be Vicar of Bray, Sir." He was a High Church man in the reign of Charles II and a Catholic under James. When William of Orange arrived "Old Principles I did revoke," the vicar admits. Under Anne he became a Tory and under George I he became a Whig. "But George, my Lawful King shall be," he declares, "Except the Times shou'ld alter." The poem ends where it began: "And this is Law, I will maintain/Until my Dying Day Sir,/That whatsoever King shall reign,/I will be vicar of Bray, Sir."

The Architecture of the Church: Gibbs

Despite the triumph of the Palladian style among the Whig aristocracy, the Tory architecture of the Church remained firmly wedded to the English baroque of Wren and Hawksmoor. The successor to Hawksmoor as the leading architect in the English baroque style was James Gibbs. He was born and educated in Scotland and brought up a Catholic. At eighteen he left for the continent to study architecture and remained there for eight years. He spent much of his time in Rome, where he was imbued with the classicism of the ancients and the splendor of the baroque. He returned to London in 1708. His connection with a Scottish lord, the Earl of Mar helped him get started in the practice of architecture. In 1713 the Tory government made Gibbs co-surveyor with Hawksmoor of the project to build fifty new churches in London. He was viewed by some Whigs as a crypto-Catholic, and his connections with the Earl of Mar, leader of the Scots in the uprising of 1715, put him under suspicion of Jacobitism. He remained a covert Catholic to the end of his life.

Gibbs' first commission was St. Mary-le-Strand (1714-23), which stands in the middle of the Strand with streams of traffic passing by on each side. Construction began in 1714, but was interrupted by the death of Queen Anne and the triumph of the Whigs. The semi-ciculap porch is outlined by stone columns, and the tower, with a clock, is in three stages, including a spire. The magnificent baroque altar was much criticized because the focus of the church (unlike Wren's churches) is on the Sacrament, not the Word. In the next few years Gibbs was engaged in private commissions, most of them for Tories. He carried out in baroque style an ambitious rebuilding of Canons, the seat of the Duke of Chandos. He was also involved in designing buildings for the Harley estate, owned by Sir Edward Harley, heir of Robert Harley, Earl of Oxford. Gibbs received a steady flow of commissions for country houses. In his interiors, Gibbs realized that doors, windows, and fireplaces should be used for decorative effect. His reputation was enhanced by publication of his Book of Architecture (1728) and Rules for Drawing the Several Parts of Architecture (1732).

Gibbs' best known church is St. Martin-in-the-Fields (1721-26), where he adopted an uncharacteristically classical style. The spacious columned portico is topped by a large pediment and a bold three-stage tower with a clock and a steeple. To avoid the criticisms of St. Mary-le-Strand, the interior of St. Martin's resembles Wren's unquestionably Protestant interior of St. James's Piccadilly. St. Martin is one of the best-known churches in London because it overlooks Trafalgar Square, a center of traffic, entertainment, and tourism.

As a philanthropic activity, Gibbs designed three of the proposed new buildings for St. Barthomew's Hospital, including the elegant Court Room and a staircase that features two paintings by Hogarth. In his later years, Gibbs' major work was the Radcliffe Camera (1749), a library in baroque style at staunchly Tory Oxford. The library has an octagonal base with a circular reading room and a dome on top. He did architectural work at Stowe Gardens, where he designed the Temple of Friendship (1741) and the Temple of Liberty (1747). The latter was built in the Gothic style to recognize the medieval origins of "the ancient constitution," which his patron (Lord Cobham) and other opposition Whigs held that Walpole had violated. Gibbs was a confident, gregarious man who enjoyed the friendship of many of the leading literary and artistic figures of London.

The Music of the Church

The music of the Church of England was excellent in the Chapel Royal and the cathedrals, but in many of the parish churches the level of music was low. The Book of Common Prayer includes the singing of metrical psalms, and until near the end of the eighteenth century the Church refused to use melodious hymns of the kind used by Dissenters and Methodists. Since hymnbooks were not furnished and most people did not own one, the usual practice was for the parish clerk with his pitch pipe to intone one or two lines, which would then be sung by the congregation.

In mid-century, some parish churches recruited young men to practice the psalms and lead the congregation in singing them. Some parishioners complained that they dominated the singing and used unfamiliar tunes and elaborate arrangements while the congregation listened. Organs were introduced into those parish churches that could afford them. One commentator identified an advantage in organs when he wrote, "The greatest blessing to lovers of Music in a parish church, is to have an organ in it sufficiently powerful to render the voice of the clerk, and of those who join in his out-cry, wholly inaudible."

Dissent, Catholics, Jews

The largest body of Dissenters was the Presbyterians, who also tended to be the most prosperous, but Dissent also included Baptists, Independents (Congregationalists), and Quakers. The Quakers were famous for their honesty and uprightness, and some Quakers prospered remarkably, but ordinarily they held themselves aloof from the rest of the community. The Dissenters were found primarily in the towns, where they earned their livings in small businesses and skilled crafts. They were especially influential in London, and some rose to wealth and prominence. Significant numbers of Dissenters lived quietly in rural areas.

Dissenters worked hard, lived modestly, saved their money, and valued education. Their chapels were usually modest in appearance and simple in I. Dissenting worship emphasized Scripture-reading, prayer, hymn-singing, and the sermon. Accordingly, the pulpit and lectern might be quite grand and the altar was minimized. Dissenters maintained their own schools, which offered practical subjects such as accounting, surveying, and navigation. For higher education they went to the Scottish universities or to Leyden in the Netherlands. For Dissenters, social mobility often meant loss of identity. Those who prospered, as many did, were likely to become Anglicans or see their sons and daughters marry Anglicans and be absorbed into the main stream of English life.

Despite their theological and social differences, the Dissenters were held together by their sense of a heroic past in the face of adversities. Their story was recorded in the classic history of Dissent, Daniel Neal's The History of the Puritans (4 vols., 1732-38). Neal recounts vivid narratives that tell of the travails of the Puritan clergy ejected from their parish churches and the persecutions carried out under the Act of Uniformity, Corporation Act, the Conventicle Act, and the Five Mile Act.

Theologically, Dissent split in two directions. Under the influence of the new philosophic and scientific rationalism, some Dissenters drifted into Unitarianism, which rejects the doctrine of the Trinity as incompatible with Reason and inclines to a form of "natural religion" that accepts the existence of a Supreme Being and regards Jesus as a moral teacher. Others continued in the Calvinism of their forebears and appealed to the emotions rather than Reason. They emphasized a Gospel message that Jesus was the suffering Savior whose death and resurrection brought eternal life to his followers.

Isaac Watts, a Dissenting clergyman, was, to a considerable extent, the creator of modern hymnody in the form of attractive, singable hymns. When he left grammar school, Watts, a studious young man of a Dissenting family, was offered an opportunity to attend one of the universities, but he declined because he would have to join the Church of England. Instead, he attended a Dissenting academy, and in 1699 he became assistant minister at a distinguished Congregationalist congregation in London. In 1702 he was ordained and called to serve the congregation as minister. Under his leadership, the congregation grew and built a new and larger meeting-house, but he suffered from ill-health and much of the time was unable to perform his duties.

Due to his poor health, Watts concentrated on writing poetry and hymns. Hymns and Spiritual Songs was published in 1707 and en-larged two years later. Divine Songs Attempted in Easy Language for Children (1715) and The Psalms of David Imitated in the Language of the New Testament (1719) followed. Among his psalm-based hymns are "O God our help in Ages Past," (Ps. 90), a hymn especially mean-ingful to Dissenters in the light of the persecutions they had suffered in the past and the uncertainties they faced. "Jesus shall reign wher'er the sun," was based on Psalm 72. Other favorite hymns by Watts are "When I survey the wondrous cross," and the Christmas carol, "Joy to the World!"

Watts was more than a hymnodist. He was interested in the educa-tion of children and published a catechism that was widely used. His Short View of the Whole Scripture History (1732) was intended for religious education, and Logick, or The Right use of Reason in the Enquiry after Truth (1725) dealt with a major theme of eighteenth-century thought from an evangelical point of view. His The Christian Doctrine of the Trinity (1722) refuted the Unitarian wing of Dissent, and Evangelical Discourses (1747) appealed to the traditionalists. He corresponded with evangelicals in the Church of England and John Wesley, who adopted many of Watt's hymns for the Methodist hymnbook. Watts was also in touch with leaders of the Great Awakening in New England. The first American edition of <u>Hymns and Spiritual Songs</u> was published by Benjamin Franklin in 1741. At a time when Dissent was stagnating or decaying, Watts' hymns and other works contributed to maintaining its vitality.

Catholics and Jews were not part of Dissent in that they did not have freedom of worship under the Toleration Act nor did they have political rights, but the law protected their persons and property. The severe Elizabethan restrictions on Catholics continued in force and strong anti-Catholic prejudices erupted from time to time. Most of the time the anti-Catholic laws were laxly enforced. Catholics paid a double land tax and paid the fines imposed for non-attendance at the Sunday service in the parish church.

The Jewish population was small, and some Jewish bankers and merchants were influential in London and important to the government. The career of Samson Gideon, a Jewish stockbroker, illustrates the opportunities to make a fortune in the enlarged financial markets of the 1740s and 1750s. When he began his career as a financier, Gideon had a capital of £1500, a modest stake. In 1729 he bought one of twelve licenses for Jewish brokers. At that time, his fortune was £25,000. He underwrote marine insurance and financed voyages of the East India Company. He served as broker to provide gold and silver to the East India Company, which needed specie to pay for its purchases of tea and other items in India and China.

Gideon's main importance was as financier for the Crown. As Britain became involved in the War of the Austrian Succession, Sir Robert Walpole called upon him for financial help. Gideon responded by forming a syndicate that raised £3 million to finance a government loan. He subscribed £600,000 of his own money, and much of the rest came from Jews in the Netherlands. The initial success of "Bonnie Prince Charlie" in 1745 caused a panic in the banking system and the stock market. The Bank of England bought time by paying off depositors in pennies until people calmed down. Gideon invested in discounted stocks, and was praised by the treasury for supporting public credit. He also doubled his money when the uprising failed and the stock market rose. When the War of the Austrian Succession ended in 1748, Gideon assisted Henry Pelham, chancellor of the exchequer, in reducing the interest on government debt from 4 percent to 3 percent—a huge saving.

Gideon wanted to establish himself and his family in the English upper class. He married an English woman and their children were brought up as Anglicans. He bought landed estates and a country house. After the death of Sir Robert Walpole, Gideon purchased an important collection of paintings from Houghton, Walpole's grandiose stately home. His aspirations seemed to be fulfilled in 1753, when the Duke of Newcastle's government passed legislation naturalizing Gideon and several other Jewish bankers in recognition of their services to the Crown. The "Jew Bill" of 1753 evoked an outbreak of mob violence in London that showed that anti-Semitism, anti-Catholic, and anti-foreign feeling lurked beneath the surface of eighteenth-century rationality and tolerance. Reluctantly, Newcastle repealed the Act.

Bitterly disappointed, Gideon gave up his broker's license and resigned from his synagogue, although secretly he supported it financially. After his death, his objective was achieved when his son was made a baronet, inherited his father's estate, and became a Member of Parliament. Gideon's daughter married an English viscount, bringing with her a dowry of £40,000. When he died, Gideon's estate, mainly invested in land, was worth £350,000.

Methodism

In December 1738 a fiery young preacher named George Whitefield returned to England from a mission to Georgia, and in January 1739 he launched a powerful religious revival. An ordained clergyman of the Church of England, Whitefield first sought to preach in churches, but when he was refused the pulpit in Bristol he began preaching outdoors and drew large crowds. A few months later he went on a preaching tour which led to London, leaving two of his associates, John and Charles Wesley, to continue his work in the west of England. In London Whitefield was again refused pulpits. He continued to preach outdoors, and large numbers of people attended. Later that year he returned to the American colonies, where he became a leader in the religious revival called "the Great Awakening."

More than any other person, John Wesley brought new fervor to English religious life. Son of an Anglican clergyman, he grew up in a large family where order and regularity were rigorously enforced. He studied at Oxford with his brother Charles and George Whitefield. They founded an earnest religious group whose methodical approach to godly living later gave them the name, "Methodists." John Wesley was much influenced by William Law's A Serious Call to a Devout and Holy Life (1728), which held out the possibility of Christian perfection, an objective that the young Wesley struggled to achieve. He was ordained as a clergyman of the Church of England, and in 1735 the Society for the Propagation of the Gospel in Foreign Parts sent him to the colony of Georgia to minister to the colonists and do missionary work among the Indians. James Oglethorpe and a group of humanitarians had founded the colony as a place where people imprisoned for debt could begin a new life. As governor, Oglethorpe hoped that Wesley and his friends would bring discipline and civility to the disorderly lives of the colonists. Wesley's zeal was unappreciated in the rough and ready life of the newly-founded colony and his work was a failure, made worse by complications arising from a muddled courtship.

Wesley returned to London in 1737 filled with doubts about his relationship with God and his efforts to serve Him. On the voyage to Georgia, Wesley had met a group of Moravian Brethren whose Christian faith impressed him greatly. In 1738 his contacts with the Moravians in London led to a religious experience similar to that of Martin Luther more than two centuries earlier. Thereafter salvation by faith as a gift of God became central to Wesley's message. He did not abandon his previous ideas and held that justification by faith was just the first step in a process that led to living the Christian life.

Wesley's conversion unleashed his remarkable personal energy and stamina for a lifetime of Christian endeavor. He joined his friend Whitefield in Bristol in 1739, and, like Whitefield, he took his message to unchurched people in remote locations. The emotional excesses that often accompanied his preaching led to charges of "enthusiasm" unbecoming to a clergyman of the Church of England. As he collected followers, he built a small chapel in Bristol for preaching and meetings.

When Whitefield left for the colonies, Wesley moved to London and began preaching in open spaces. Large segments of the population in that great city were ill-served by the Church and responded warmly to his message. He began establishing Methodist societies that met regularly for Bible-reading, hymn-singing, preaching, and prayer. Throughout his life Wesley remained within the Church of England and attended worship every Sunday. The societies were intended to invigorate the Church, not leave it.

Wesley was a great organizer. He traveled extensively, establishing Methodist societies throughout England. He created a centrally directed network of Methodist societies with its headquarters in London and northern headquarters at Newcastle upon Tyne. He introduced annual conferences to maintain unity of doctrine and discipline. As the societies grew, they were grouped into circuits with local leaders. Occasionally the Methodists and their meeting houses were attacked by mobs that suspected nefarious intentions and, perhaps, resented people who did not fit into the community. John's brother, Charles, was active with him in his work, and wrote many of the hymns that were published in Collection of Hymns for the Use of the People Called Methodists (1780). Among them are the Christmas carol, "Hark, the Herald Angels Sing," the Easter hymn, "Christ the Lord is Risen Today," "Love Divine, all Loves Excelling," and "Jesus Lover of my Soul." The Methodist hymnbook included some of the hymns of Isaac Watts.

Wesley rejected rigid adherence to many traditional doctrines, insisting that only the fundamentals mattered. A major bone of contention within Methodism was the Calvinist doctrine of predestination, which Wesley rejected in favor of freedom of the will. Although he accepted justification by faith as fundamental, increasingly he emphasized the importance of holy living. He wrote and published devotional material through his own press. He published A Christian Library of 50 volumes (1349-55) to serve the needs of the Methodist societies.

The bishops did not share Wesley's views and regarded the Methodist societies as disruptive to Church discipline. In time, Methodist preachers were formally ordained, although not by bishops of the Church, and began administering communion. Before Wesley's death in 1791 the Methodist movement had become virtually another Dissenting denomination enjoying the protection of the Toleration Act.

Wesley's message appealed primarily to those whom the Church of England had neglected—the urban poor, the inhabitants of new industrial towns, coalminers, provincial shopkeepers and artisans. Methodism drew many women into its ranks. Wesley sharply criticized luxury and conspicuous consumption. He urged his followers to earn money honestly, save all they could, and give all they could to the needy. Methodist morality was Puritanical and censorious, but it brought self-discipline to the lives of people who desperately needed it.

Philosophy

The philosophical and religious views of the new age were challenged by a mischievous contrarian, Bernard de Mandeville, and a Scotsman, David Hume. Mandeville was educated in philosophy and medicine at the University of Leyden and moved to London, intending to establish himself as a physician. When that did not work out, he decided to pursue a career as a writer. His major work, The Fable of the Bees, or, Private Vices, Publick Benefits (1714), is a clever, witty book intended to shock and amuse. He reverses the genteel, public-spirited views of Addison, and Steele. He presents conventional morality as a tissue of hypocrisy by which individuals conceal their self-centered natures and motivations from others and even from themselves. Mandeville argues that human vices, such as pride, greed and lust, can be highly beneficial to society by encouraging great actions, stimulating the economy, and leading to procreation. Dueling has advantages by curtailing verbal abuse. Luxury, much criticized by social commentators, should be welcomed, for it is the inevitable result of living in a flourishing, wealthy country. The wealth spreads from those who have too much to those who need more, and society as a whole benefits. Thrift makes sense only in a poor country, a fate that the English would not wish upon themselves.

A second and enlarged edition in 1723 became the talk of the town when the Tory sheriffs of London presented The Fable of the Bees to a grand jury as morally corrupting. A chorus of refutations and denunciations of Mandeville's works arose, but his powerful Whig friends protected him from prosecution. Mandeville had exposed bluntly a typical literary theme. Eighteenth-century satire rests essentially on Mandeville's distinction between the generally-accepted principles of morality and the actual conduct of individuals. Novels and plays were often based on the difficulties that a virtuous heroine faces in a Mandevillian society of seduction, deception, and depravity.

David Hume was the most profound thinker of the age. His father was a prosperous lawyer, and his family intended David to follow in his father's footsteps. After attending Edinburgh University, he tried several careers but found them unsatisfying. From his early years, Hume wanted to be a writer and support himself with his writings. He developed a style of writing using common language that was clear and persuasive and accessible to the ordinary reader. In 1734 he moved to La Flèche, France, perhaps because it was associated with the French philosopher, René Descartes. At La Flèche he completed A Treatise of Human Nature (1739), part of which was revised and expanded in Enquiry Concerning Human Understanding (1748). Another part was published as An Inquiry Concerning the Principles of Morals (1751). His Essays, Moral and Political (1741, 1742) was enjoyable reading and was his first public success. The essays dealt with political, social, and moral questions from fresh perspectives, including an unflattering portrait of Walpole. In another essay he concludes that despotism is likely to be the final result of trends in English government.

As a philosopher, Hume takes Locke's empiricism to its ultimate conclusion. Hume bases knowledge on the mind's perception of external reality (sense impressions), which will vary with each individual. For that reason, the ideas of each individual are bound to be subjective and merely probable, not certain. Philosophy, he says, "is nothing but the reflections of common life, methodized and corrected."

Hume explains the process by which the mind converts sense impressions into general ideas as one of association of like or related experiences. The importance of Hume's empiricism was to recognize ideas as mental constructs with greater or lesser degrees of probability. Hume was intrigued by the tendency of the mind to claim a higher degree of probability than its data warranted. He goes beyond Locke by identifying the empirical basis of the emotions. He argues that individuals experience the world, not only intellectually, but with the pleasure or pain that accompanies personal experiences. For example, the sense impressions that accompany eating apples normally build a pleasurable feeling, while the eating of oysters may or may not have the same effect.

When this principle is applied to love, anger, and fear we find that our emotions, like our ideas, are the result of our experiences.

In the same manner, the individual develops a capacity for relationships with other people ("sympathy") by being part of a family and a community. In this way, he adds a social dimension to Locke's concept of a developing Self. Hume's empiricism gave increased validity to the emotions, which, since they arise from the same empirical basis as ideas, can be equally valid in making judgments or as guides to conduct. In this way Hume's philosophy contributed to the rise of Romanticism.

Hume discards the divinely-revealed morality of Christianity and also demolishes Locke's concept of a universal natural law inherent in all mankind. In his Enquiry Concerning the Principles of Morals (1751), Hume bases ethics on experience—personal experiences of pleasure or pain make certain kinds of conduct desirable (i.e., moral) and other kinds of conduct undesirable (i. e., immoral). Custom and habit and other social influences are important in the development of a sense of right and wrong. Thus the web of social relationships fosters the development of a moral dimension in the Self.

The idea of justice—and the state as a means to enforce justice—Hume argues—did not derive from immutable natural laws, as Locke had stated, but evolved over time to meet immediate needs. The philosophy of Hume apparently left no reliable or predictable basis for human conduct apart from prescriptive law or social pressures. For that reason, he is sometimes called a Skeptic.

Hume shattered the "top-down" certainties of the past in matters of government, religion, and morality. In his Dialogues Concerning Natural Religion (1779), prudently published after his death, Hume ridicules deist efforts to base religion on Nature. To Hume, religious faith is a feeling based on experience, and social conditioning, which bore no relation to Reason or Science. In 1776 he died a philosopher's death, insisting that he had no need to believe in life after death.

Ch. 8. English Culture in the Literary Marketplace

The English have always savored the spoken and written word, and the crowning achievement of eighteenth-century culture is its literature. After "the Glorious Revolution," freedom of the press and an expanding market for printed material gave writers enlarged opportunities to publish their works. The collaboration of writers and booksellers in a market that depended on public favor led to publication of much that was shallow and ephemeral. Surprisingly, the literary marketplace also produced creative works that broke new ground in the literary history of England.

Alexander Pope, Jonathan Swift, John Gay, James Thomson, and Thomas Gray would have been luminaries at any time. The Gentleman's Magazine set a new direction for periodicals and gave Samuel John his start as a writer. Out of a welter of printed material emerged a literature that cast luster on the age.

The Development of Print Culture

The writer worked within in a print culture that included the author, the publisher, and the reader. The writer had to earn his living in an expanding but highly competitive market. The bookseller/publisher had to publish and sell books that would appeal to the reading public. Publication was encouraged by the Copyright Act of 1710, which gave the bookseller exclusive right to a new work for a period of 14 years and an existing work for 21 years. The initial advantages went to the bookseller/publisher, who paid the writer a lump sum for the book and took all profits resulting from publication. In due time the benefits of the Copyright Act redounded to the writer, because copyright enabled the booksellers to pay more and competition raised the demand for the most popular works. An important business arose among booksellers in selling and reselling copyrights for the purpose of reprinting popular works. The notion of paying a royalty for each copy published had not yet emerged.

The printing trade employed a great many typesetters, bookbinders, illustrators, and other craftsmen, since no technological breakthroughs were made and the slow, tedious hand press continued to be used for more than a century. Print runs were short—approximately 300-500 copies—and for that reason reprinting was common. Although splendid books were published by publishers like Jacob Tonson, much of the great mass of printed material was printed with small type on cheap paper and was poorly bound.

By the middle of the eighteenth century, literacy among the aristocracy, gentry, and professionals was almost total, and among the merchant class it was high. Many artisans and craftsmen were literate, and the influence of print was extended by listening to books read aloud while they worked. Women readers were an important element in the market for printed material, and a wide variety of books and periodicals were published with women in mind. Literacy was higher in cities, cathedral towns, and market towns, and perhaps no higher than 30 percent in rural villages. A definition of literacy is difficult—it might mean no more than ability to sign one's name or decipher simple books of popular sayings. Almost every town of any size had one or more bookshops, and larger towns had commercial lending libraries with several thousand books that could be borrowed for a small fee. Coffee houses provided newspapers for their customers, and some had small collections of books as well. A complex network of wholesalers, middlemen, bookshops, and the mail made books, periodicals, and newspapers available throughout the nation. Cheaply printed and bound booklets were sold by peddlers on city streets or along country lanes. Lists of newly published books that could be ordered were an important feature of periodicals like The Gentleman's Magazine. London was the center of publication, but an important provincial press also developed.

The most read works were the Bible and books of sermons, which in many households were read aloud as part of the daily routine. Works of history, geography, and travel were popular among serious readers, as the reading public sought to orient themselves in a world changed by the growth of trade, exploration, and colonial rivalries. Poetry dominated imaginative literature, but by mid-century novels had become an important source of entertainment. Latin and Greek works for scholars continued to be published in considerable numbers. John Newbery was an important publisher of children's books.

Unless the writer had an independent income, he was totally dependent on the bookseller. He sold his work for a lump sum, and the bookseller's copyright was enforced by the Stationers Company. Addison and Steele were gentlemen and their literary careers were made possible by holding public offices when the Whigs were in power, and other sources of income. Jonathan Swift was supported by his post as dean of St. Patrick's Cathedral, Dublin. Daniel Defoe was able to earn a living with his pen by virtue of his fertility of imagination and unremitting industry. During part of his career he was supported by Robert Harley, Earl of Oxford. After the fall of the Oxford-Bolingbroke ministry Defoe developed a new career as a novelist.

Although illustrations have been a part of books going back to the illuminated manuscripts of the Middle Ages and the woodcuts of the Reformation era, the eighteenth-century was the first time that illustrations became an important part of the print culture. Although woodcuts continued to be used, most illustrations were engraved and some were colored by hand. Engraving was done by cutting fine lines into a copper plate to make the picture and then filling the lines with ink for printing. Engraving was used to make reproductions of portraits and other works of art, anatomical diagrams, maps, and other subjects that could be bound in books or sold as separate prints by booksellers. After exhibiting a popular picture, artists often issued prints of the picture that were sold separately. Newspapers and magazines still used woodcuts, in which the lines were raised by cutting away the surrounding wood and the printing was done by inking the raised lines.

George Vertue was the paramount engraver of his time. After a period of apprenticeship, Vertue went into business for himself, engraving reproductions of portraits by Sir Godfrey Kneller. His engraved print of Kneller's portrait of George I was his first great success. He became the official engraver of the Society of Antiquaries and later engraver of almanacs for Oxford University Press. He was also active in producing engraved frontispieces for books. Vertue began publishing collections of his prints in book form—Heads of the Kings of England (1733-36) was one of them. His list of his engravings shows more than 500 prints. Vertue's reputation as an engraver was eclipsed by Hogarth and other engravers who produced original prints rather than copying existing subjects for publishers.

He began a study of the history of art in England. He collected forty volumes of notes that were published by Horace Walpole as Anecdotes of Painting in England (1762-71), a work that is a fundamental source for English art history.

Samuel Buck established a niche for himself and his brother as engravers of English towns and historical remains. Born and raised in Yorkshire, Buck's career as an engraver began with prospects (distant views) of two Yorkshire towns, Leeds and Wakefield. When these sold well, he went on to engrave prospects of ten more northern towns. He moved to London and worked with the Society of Antiquaries issuing engravings of decaying ruins, including abbeys, and castles. He also published prospects of towns throughout England and Wales. Buck was assisted by skilled engravers, some of them Huguenots, who refined the quality of his engravings. All told, Buck issued 428 engravings of ruins and 87 prospects of towns, which constitute a remarkable record of the appearance of pre-Industrial England.

Alexander Pope

Alexander Pope was an outsider in Walpole's England. His father was a successful London merchant and a Catholic, who moved his family to Windsor Forest due to the anti-Catholic spirit in London aroused by "the Popish Plot" and the reign of James II. In this sylvan retreat, Pope learned to appreciate the beauties of Nature. He experienced ill health from childhood, which stunted his growth and deprived him of the usual vigorous activities of boys. He received sporadic schooling from priests, although he was largely self-educated. As a Catholic, Pope was excluded from a career in government, the Church, or the learned professions. He was forbidden from entering London, although occasionally he visited friends incognito. His modest income made it necessary for him to bargain with booksellers to get the maximum possible return. To that extent, he was a professional writer who wrote for money.

In 1714 Pope signed a contract with Jacob Tonson to prepare a translation of The Iliad, which would compare with Dryden's translation of The Aeneid. Pope's The Iliad required six years to complete (1714-20), but when sold by subscription it yielded the poet £5,000, a modest fortune. His translation of The Odyssey netted him a similar sum. Pope was well remunerated when Tonson commissioned an edition of Shakespeare's plays. In this edition Pope took considerable liberties with the text to shape it to fit eighteenth-century standards. Two years later Lewis Theobald, a sound scholar, published Shakespeare Restored (1726), a reliable edition of Shakespeare's plays, in which he pointed out the many inaccuracies in Pope's version. Pope was the first English writer able to live comfortably off the income from his works.

Pope was a staunch Tory and friend of Bolingbroke, Swift, Gay and other Tory writers. He established himself as a major poet with Windsor-Forest (1713), a word-painting of the beauties of Nature as seen in the place where he grew up. Pope uses the forest as the setting for a wide-ranging commentary on English history and contemporary life. He was devoted to the Stuart dynasty, especially Queen Anne, whom he compares to the goddess, Diana: "Whose Care, like hers, protects the Sylvan Reign, / The Earth's fair Light, and Empress of the Main."

Pope supports the Peace of Utrecht, which had been negotiated by Bolingbroke and vigorously defended by Swift. He notes with regret that the treaty includes the asiento, the monopoly of the slave trade to the Spanish colonies, which leads him to express his disapproval of slavery. The poet looks forward to a time when the fame achieved on the banks of the Thames will overshadow the glories of the Tiber and other famous rivers of the past—when oak from Windsor Forest will travel the world in English ships and "Fair Liberty, Britannia's Goddess, rears / Her cheerful Head, and leads the golden Years." The poem concludes with a hymn to peace: "Oh stretch thy Reign, fair Peace! from Shore to Shore, / Till Conquest cease, and Slav'ry be no more:"

Windsor-Forest established Pope's reputation as a major poet, which was confirmed by The Rape of the Lock (1714), a light-hearted poem that grew out of a minor incident. At a social event, a friend of Pope, Lord Petre, playfully clipped a lock of hair from Miss Arabella Fermor, which led to a family quarrel. Pope turned this petty incident into an entertaining satire that displayed his precocity. Belinda, the pretty young heroine, is visited by Ariel, a sprite, who declares that something bad will happen to her that day and warns her against jealousy, pride, and men. Belinda and her friends take a cruise on the Thames and visit a palace where Belinda plays cards. A bevy of sprites attempt to protect Belinda from the evil designs of Lord Petre, who is determined to have a lock of her hair. Lord Petre rapes the lock with a pair of scissors, which he praises as if they were a Homeric sword. One of the ladies, Clarissa, delivers a homily about the vanity of women and the folly of men who fawn over them. A struggle ensues to regain the lock, but it ascends to Heaven and becomes a star. The poem was written mainly as jeu d'esprit and display of virtuosity, but it also serves as a commentary on the rigid conventions that protected the modesty of young women.

Pope was a philosophical poet who had to come to terms with the claims of Reason and science. He sees Reason as the means to understand Nature, a word that has several meanings. Nature could mean the outdoors—that which was not shaped or constructed by people. Newton, Boyle, and other scientists had demonstrated the great regularities inherent in Nature (the material universe). The word was also used to refer to inherent regularities applicable to people ("human nature"). Locke used Reason to define universal principles of justice and humanity that he called "natural law." Although Man cannot understand God, the existence of God, Pope writes, is evident to all mankind from the order and simplicity of Nature—the argument from design. "Lo! The poor Indian, whose untutor'd mind," Pope writes, "Sees God in clouds, or hears him in the wind."

The word "Nature" is central to the poetry of Pope, who conceives of poetry as an attractive way of expressing universal truths. Pope customarily presents his views in artfully constructed, rhymed, self-contained couplets that express a complete idea. An Essay on Criticism (1711), published when Pope was twenty-two, identifies principles of literary criticism that he claims are based on "true taste," which is derived from Nature. "First follow Nature," Pope writes, "and your judgment frame / By her just standard, which is still the same; / Unerring Nature, still divinely bright, / One clear, unchanged, and universal light, / Life, force and beauty must to all impart,/At once the source, and end, and test of Art."

Pope sees some merit in formal rules of poetry, especially as developed by the ancients, since they were derived from Nature: "Those RULES of old discover'd, not devis'd / Are Nature still, but Nature Methodized." As to critics who invoke the rules mechanically, he remarks "Fools rush in where Angels fear to tread."

In the eighteenth century, poetry was used as a persuasive method of expounding views on public issues as well as a means of expressing personal feelings. Pope expresses his philosophical and religious views in his <u>Essay on Man</u> (1733-34), a poem addressed to Bolingbroke. The foundation of the poem is the concept of "the great chain of being," which means a universe filled with a vast variety of creatures, from the lowest, simplest beings up a chain of increasing complexity, with God—the Creator—at the peak. "Vast chain of Being!" Pope writes, "which from God began, / Nature ethereal, human, angel, man / Beast, bird, fish, insect, what no eye can see / No glass can reach; from Infinite to thee / From thee to Nothing."

Man's Reason leads him to explore matters beyond his ken. The key to wisdom, Pope writes, is to know the limitations of human knowledge, especially in matters of religion. "Know then thyself, presume not God to scan; / The proper study of Mankind is Man." Man's problem is that he is "Placed on this isthmus of a middle state, / A being darkly wise, and rudely great: / With too much knowledge for the skeptic side, / With too much weakness for the Stoic's pride." Man's tragedy is that he is "Sole judge of truth, in endless error hurled: / The glory, jest, and riddle of the world!"

In the third part of the poem Pope outlines his political theory, which is based on the concept of a divine order that Man sees imperfectly and corrupts due to his own imperfections. After tracing the rise of states and the development of tyrannies, Pope hails the steps taken in England to restrain political power. The people, he writes, claimed their original rights and established "the according music of a well-mixed state" in which all could live harmoniously.

A dynamic age is likely to foster satire, in which those who find the new developments unwelcome express their discomfort by contrasting an unsatisfying present with an idealized past or an imaginary future. The age of Walpole, with its German kings, dull court life, corrupt administration, complacent Parliament, commercialized publication and entertainment, and low level of public taste made satire a major literary form. Pope was especially concerned about bad literature, which he saw as a force that corrupts all aspects of a culture. Pope believes that the poet has a duty to shape the moral principles of society, not only by pointing out faults but also by holding forth a vision of a better world.

His most important satirical work, the Dunciad (1728, extended 1729), is a satiric parody of Virgil's Aeneid. As a Tory, Pope despised the Hanoverians and remained loyal to the Stuart dynasty. The accession of a German king in 1714 and the establishment of the Whig supremacy destroyed the optimism that he had expressed in Windsor-Forest. He became a bitter satirist of the Hanoverian regime and the politicians and writers that fed off it. Pope was offended by the proliferation of works by pedantic scholars, partisan journalists, and hack novelists. Art, philosophy, and religion, he complains, have been corrupted by the dead hands of the new political and cultural leaders of society.

In imitation of the Aeneid, the Dunciad begins with a description of the abode of the goddess of Dulness (mediocrity and decadence) and the perpetrators of dull writing who gather about her. She selects one of them, Tibbald (his enemy, Lewis Theobald) to be their king. The coronation is followed by Virgilian "heroic games," but the contestants are not heroes. They are Pope's favorite targets—booksellers, critics, political hacks, writers of popular fiction (among them Daniel Defoe)—who are subjected to humiliating (sometimes scatological) treatment. Pope condemns the two theatres, which compete to reach the lowest possible level of vulgarity. In a dream, the king of Dulness is transported to Hades, where he meets past examples of Dulness. As the king awakens from his dream and begins his reign, "Universal Darkness buries all."

Pope revised and expanded The Dunciad in The Dunciad in Four Books (1743), which was in some respects a new work. Throughout his career as a poet, Pope's works had been attacked, often scurrilously, and in The Dunciad he settled old scores. Pope was outraged when Colley Cibber, comedian and theatre manager, was appointed to the post of poet laureate, which he saw as a gratuitous insult to literature and a symbol of political corruption and moral decay. Cibber replaces Theobald as King of Dulness. The plot is essentially the same as the earlier version, but much of the substance is changed to suit Pope's darker view of a new crop of dull people.

Jonathan Swift

Jonathan Swift, another outsider in Walpole's England, was the ultimate master of satire. The death of Queen Anne, the fall of the Oxford-Bolingbroke ministry, and the triumph of the Whigs destroyed Swift's hopes for preferment in England. He returned to Ireland, where he spent his remaining years as Dean of St. Patrick's Cathedral, Dublin. He became an Irish national hero with his five Drapier's Letters (1724), which expressed Irish outrage at a particularly obnoxious piece of Walpolean corruption. In A Modest Proposal for Preventing the Children of Poor People from being a Burthen to their Parents, or the Country, and for Making them Beneficial to the Publick (1729) Swift savagely attacked the policies that brought misery to Ireland, suggesting satirically that the surplus children of Ireland could profitably be sold and eaten. Swift visited England from time to time and maintained his association with Bolingbroke, Pope, and other Tory writers.

After the accession of George I, Swift intensified his attacks on the Whigs. He was totally out of sympathy with the new developments of his age—German kings, Walpole's use of corruption to maintain power, the rise of merchants and bankers to influence in the state, the vogue of rationalism and science, and the lack of respect for traditional religion, cultural values, and social relationships. Above all Swift was a Christian and a Churchman, and he was concerned about the fate of Church of England under the Whig supremacy.

Unlike the Deism of Bolingbroke, Swift advocates the historic doctrines of the Church of England, the value of an established Church, and the importance of Christian charity. He strenuously supports the political privileges of the Church of England as essential to the concept of England as a Christian community. His defense of the Church includes criticism of those who, under the influence of Reason and science, reject many of its doctrines.

Swift had expressed his view of the religious disputes of the age earlier in <u>A Tale of a Tub: To which is added an Account of a Battle Between the Ancient and Modern Books in St. James's Library; and the Mechanical Operation of the Spirit</u>, which he wrote about 1694, although the book was not published until 1704. His purpose, he says, is to ridicule "the numerous and gross corruptions in religion and learning." He has in mind pedantic scholars, egotistic critics, religious fanatics, and philosophers who undermine religious faith.

The central narrative of <u>A Tale of a Tub</u> tells about the adventures of three brothers, Peter (the Catholic Church), Jack (the Dissenters) and Martin (Church of England) as they make their way through the world. They interpret their father's will (The Bible) to suit themselves, and alter their coats (doctrines) whenever they feel like it. Martin's coat remains a little closer to the original coat than the others,' although, like Peter, he still wears ornaments with it while Jack does not. In his discussion of Jack, Swift comes down hard on Bible-spouting, fanatical Puritans, whose determination to impose their religious ideas on others resemble Peter. The discussion of religion clearly favors Martin, who represents "the middle way" of the Church of England.

The core tale is interrupted by digressions, in which Swift focuses on the main objects of his satire. In the first digression, he attacks modern critics who cater to their vanity by finding flaws in authors and their works rather than pointing out their excellences. In another digression he criticizes writers who praise their own works and disparage the works of the ancients. Modern writers who neglect established principles of style are also satirized. In the digression on madness, Swift argues that madness takes place when malign vapors rise from the lower parts of the body and poison the brain. When that happens, fancy (imagination) gains control of Reason, which may have bad effects, like wars, but also produces the great achievements of the human race.

Swift's <u>Travels into Several Remote Nations of the World, in Four Parts, by Lemuel Gulliver, First Surgeon, and then a Captain of Several Ships</u> (1726), commonly known as <u>Gulliver's Travels</u>, was a huge success when it appeared, and is justly regarded as a classic of English literature. Like <u>Alice in Wonderland</u>, it tells an interesting story with a variety of excellences lurking beneath the surface. Swift's prose style is clear and pungent with a sharp cutting edge. The work can be read as a satire on politics and society in the age of Walpole, but it probes more deeply to display human traits that are universal.

Swift rejects the "philanthropic" view of mankind, which assumes that people are essentially good. He holds the "misanthropic" view, based on Christian doctrine, which teaches that the human race is deeply flawed and that evil is inevitable, although that does not excuse the evildoer. Swift's blunt treatment of elemental bodily functions such as eating, drinking, urination, bowel movements, and body odors is his way of humbling mankind by reminding them of the animal aspects of human nature that they prefer to keep hidden. His "fierce indignation" falls hardest on those whose pride and vanity keeps them from seeing their own limitations and seeking the cleansing experience of repentance.

With the age of explorations in full swing, travel literature was a popular form of publication, and Swift adapted the format for his own purposes. Lemuel Gulliver, the central character, goes to sea as a surgeon and takes four voyages, each of which reveals aspects of himself and humanity in general that collectively shatter his confidence and self-esteem. In his first voyage Gulliver is cast ashore in the land of Lilliput, where he is twelve times larger than the people. In Lilliput Gulliver is fair-minded and magnanimous while the Lilliputians display vanity and pettiness. On his second voyage conditions are reversed. Gulliver finds himself in the land of Brobdingnag, where the people are twelve times as large as he is. Here he learns the fear and anxiety of being small and weak. In these circumstances Gulliver becomes highly defensive and seeks to enhance his own importance by a patriotic harangue about England and the states of Europe and their religions. His ego is deflated by the penetrating questions of the king. The third book takes Gulliver to places that give Swift an opportunity to satirize the philosophers and scientists of the Royal Society, whose confidence in Reason leads them to say or do ridiculous things. A magician enables him to speak with the ghosts of historical figures, which becomes a recap of "the quarrel between the ancients and the moderns." Each time Gulliver returns from a voyage, his view of human beings and himself as one of them becomes more negative.

The fourth voyage finally shatters Gulliver's self-esteem as a man and an Englishman. He lands on an island where the two main constituents of humanity are separated. Rationality and rational virtues are represented by horses (Houynhnms), and the sinful and disgusting aspects of Man are embodied in vile, ugly, stinking ape-like creatures called Yahoos. Gulliver is dismayed when the Yahoos treat him as one of their own, and he is devastated when the admirable Houynhnms, despite his efforts to win their favor, come to the same conclusion and ask him to leave.

By this time Gulliver has been put through the wringer and deprived of all the illusions and self-deceptions that sustain human personality. Forced to face what he really is, he experiences a nervous breakdown, obtains some relief from a kindly ship-captain who rescues, feeds and clothes him, and returns him to his home. He cannot bear living with people, including his wife and children, and becomes a recluse, spending several hours every day in the stable with the horses. The book ends at this point. Perhaps Gulliver will accept the world and himself as they are. Perhaps not. Swift takes Gulliver to the brink and leaves him (and the reader) there.

Swift treats himself in a similar manner in his "Verses on the Death of Dr. Swift" (1739), in which he reviews his own life with a degree of objectivity that few can match. He takes satisfaction in the role that he had played in the Oxford-Bolingbroke ministry and in his efforts to stand up for Ireland. He notes disappointments along the way. He is proud that he "exposed the fool and lashed the knave," but he insists that his satire was aimed at general human faults, not specific individuals.

The Beggar's Opera

John Gay was a popular member of "the Tory wits," which included Swift and Pope among others. Gay grew up in the West of England and received a good grammar school education. He was apprenticed to a silk mercer in London, which he disliked. He soon began writing little pieces and poems for periodicals. He was a charming young man, and in 1714, with the support of Pope, he became a member of the Scriblerus Club, which gave him access to the leading Tory writers. Gay had a knack for light-hearted parodies and satires. He wrote a number of minor poems, among them Trivia, or the Art of Walking the Streets of London (1716), a pleasant account of the delights and hazards of London life. A light comedy, Three Hours after Marriage (1717), drew packed houses for ten performances. Gay was a welcome guest in aristocratic homes but still a minor writer until the smashing success of his musical play, The Beggar's Opera (1728).

The Beggar's Opera was rejected by Colley Cibber at Drury Lane (his greatest mistake) and produced by John Rich in a small theatre at Lincoln's Inn Field's. The play was an immediate hit and may justly be regarded as the first popular musical show. A play was considered a success if it ran for five or six nights. The Beggar's Opera ran for 62 performances in its first season, and continued to be produced throughout the century. Gay wrote the words for the songs. The tunes were based on English, Scottish, and Irish folk songs, among them the ever-popular Greensleeves. The songs were arranged by Johann Christoph Pepusch, who was musical director and composer at Lincoln's Inn Fields. Pepusch was an active member of the Academy of Ancient Music and had an interest in folk songs that made him the ideal musical collaborator for Gay's show.

The play is based on the career of Jonathan Wild, a London fence who organizes bands of thieves and sells their takings. When the play begins, Peachum, the fence, states that he is as honest as politicians and lawyers. When he sang, "the Statesman, because he's so great/ Thinks his trade as honest as mine," the audience glanced up at Walpole, who was taking in the show. Sometimes Peachum resells stolen goods for thieves; sometime it is more profitable to turn them into the magistrates for the reward. Profiting from crime is his business, and hence his "duty."

Peachum's sweet daughter, Polly, is in love with MacHeath, the handsome highwayman. When Polly announces that she has married MacHeath, Peachum is appalled that his daughter has come under the influence of love. He tells her it is her "duty" to assist her parents in apprehending MacHeath. Likewise, the thieves declare that it is their "duty" to rob, and the prostitutes of Drury Lane sing that love is their "duty." In this environment of reversed morality, Peachum decides to do the best he can for Polly by betraying MacHeath to the magistrates for the reward, which will make his daughter a rich widow. Peachum, assisted by several of MacHeath's low-life girlfriends, accompanies the constables who arrest MacHeath and take him off to Newgate Prison.

Lucy Lockit, the daughter of the jailer, who also loves MacHeath, helps him escape, although she fears he will go to the arms of Polly, her rival. Instead, MacHeath returns to the lovely ladies of Drury Lane and is again betrayed to the magistrates. Lucy and Polly kneel before their fathers and plead for MacHeath's release, but both refuse. An improbable happy ending saves MacHeath from the gallows. He affirms his love for Polly, for they were "truly married."

Gay appealed to English patriotism and filled the house by turning Italian opera on its head. The Beggar's Opera is thoroughly English, not a foreign import. Instead of dealing with the affairs of great people, as in Italian opera, the characters are recognizable types from the criminal class of London. The play is sung in English, instead of Italian, and it is filled with lively tunes instead of the formal arias, recitatives, and choruses of opera. The play is a vehicle for the music, which consists of 69 songs interrupted briefly by spoken dialogue. The music of the Beggar's Opera is based on familiar folksongs, many of which were well-known to the audience. The show has colorful characters, a dashing hero, a winsome heroine, true love, and a happy ending. Complaints were made that it glorified immorality, which made it seem daring, even mildly wicked, to attend it.

The Beggar's Opera rubbed many people at court the wrong way. Gay was informed by the lord chamberlain that his sequel, Polly, would not be permitted to be performed. Gay then gambled on publishing the play without performing it, and turned a nice profit. Actually, Polly was politically innocuous and pretty conventional, but its banishment sent a disturbing message from the Walpole government. Gay died two years later and was buried in Westminster Abbey.

Lady Mary Wortley Montagu

Lady Mary Wortley Montagu, one of the most remarkable women of her time, was a friend of Pope, Swift, and their circle until politics changed her allegiances. She was the daughter of the Duke of Kingston. Encouraged by Bishop Gilbert Burnet, she read extensively in ancient and modern works, and by the age of fourteen she began writing poetry. She also established a friendship with the feminist, Mary Astell. Lady Mary was tall and strikingly beautiful until her face was disfigured by smallpox, but her charm made her an attractive woman.

In 1712 she eloped with Edward Wortley Montagu, the impoverished heir to a large estate.

The accession of George I brought political and social advancement to the Wortley Montagus. Her husband, a zealous Whig, was elected to the House of Commons and took office as one of the lords of the treasury. Lady Mary was a popular figure at the court of the Prince and Princess of Wales. In 1716, Wortley Montagu was appointed English ambassador to Turkey. The couple traveled across Europe, stopping at Hanover and Vienna, and crossed the Balkans, a fierce and dangerous place, to Constantinople. Lady Mary wrote long, vivid letters about the trip and kept copies. She was fascinated with Turkey and traveled extensively, learning about its people, customs, and culture. She gave special attention to women, and was invited to visit a harem. After two years, her husband was recalled due to a change in the Whig government and they returned to England.

Lady Mary's friendship with Pope and Swift broke up when her friend, the Princess of Wales, became Queen Caroline and Lady Mary became a defender of the Hanoverian regime. Pope was bitter toward her, possibly because she had rejected his advances. He included her in The Dunciad. Anonymously she established a periodical, The Nonsense of Common Sense (1737-38) to refute Lord Chesterfield's periodical, Common Sense, which was harshly critical of Walpole.

Lady Mary learned about inoculation for smallpox in Turkey, and had her son inoculated while they were there. She actively promoted inoculation in England. She was supported by some of the most prominent physicians and Queen Caroline, who had her own daughters inoculated. As an experiment, six Newgate convicts condemned to death were inoculated. They all survived exposure to smallpox and were pardoned.

Lady Mary's relations with her husband were distant. In 1740 she left for Italy, claiming that she was traveling for her health. She spent the next twenty years moving from place to place. During those years, she sent her daughter, Lady Bute, long lively letters on a wide variety of subjects from philosophy to fishing. She corresponded regularly with her husband but they never met again. Mortally ill, she returned to England and died in London in 1762.

Lady Mary had the talents of a major writer, but writing for publication was beneath the dignity of the daughter of a Duke. Some of her poems were pirated and published as Town Eclogues (1716). After her death, the letters she had written from Turkey were published as Letters Written during her Travels (1762). More of her poetry was published in 1768, but her letters had to wait until the twentieth century for a complete edition.

The Poetry of Nature

Before the death of Pope, the public voice of poetry was giving way to poetry of feeling based on a delight in the beauties and powers of Nature. The works of James Thomson, a Scot who came to London to pursue a career as a writer, exhibited the growing awareness of the natural world. To lend dignity to his poetry, Thomson returned to the blank verse of Shakespeare and Milton. His popular poem Winter (1726) was the first of a series of poems depicting the natural landscape. Thomson followed with Summer (1727), Spring (1728), and Autumn (1730). These poems were collected with Hymn to the Seasons to form The Seasons (1730, rev. 1744). Queen Caroline headed the list of subscribers. Samuel Richardson printed and distributed it, and William Kent did the engraved illustrations.

Instead of the stable, ordered universe of Addison and Pope, Thomson shows the natural world as an awesome phenomenon comprised of vast spaces, rugged mountains, mighty waterfalls, and mysterious processes—the heat of summer, the cold of winter, the charms of spring, and the sweet sadness of autumn—that display Nature's changing moods and colors. In this light, Nature appears as a body of vast and impersonal forces in constant movement that overwhelm mankind and invoke feelings of awe and wonder, feelings that the English called "the sublime." In "Summer" Thomson's description of tropical heat and storms includes material on the violence of the slave trade. In the majesty of Nature Thomson finds a power and beauty that provide a glimpse of the majesty of God.

In addition to The Seasons, Thomson was a political writer associated with the opposition to Walpole. In his poem, Britannia (1729), he chides Walpole for his passivity toward Spain in regard to conflicts in the West Indies. His poem Liberty (1734) reviews the long history of the struggle for personal freedom and also warns against the threat from political corruption, a typical theme of opposition writers. He gained lasting fame from the song, "Rule, Britannia!" in <u>Alfred</u> (1740), a masque written for a courtly entertainment for Frederick, Prince of Wales.Henry Carey, a composer for the theatre, is thought to have written the music. Ever since, "Rule, Britannia!" has been England's patriotic song. The opening lines "Rule, Britannia! / Britannia rules the waves / Britons never will be slaves" refer, not only to sea power but to the claims of the political opposition that the Walpole government was a threat to liberty. Thomson was also a successful playwright. His most popular play, <u>Tancred and Sigismunda</u> (1744), a sentimental melodrama, was frequently performed throughout the eighteenth century.

Edward Young was another writer who attempted to eke out a living in the world of commercial publication. He gained attention with his <u>Poem of the Last Day</u> (1713), a vivid description of Judgment Day, and had some success with a bombastic tragedy, <u>Busiris, King of Egypt</u> (1719). Young was a clergyman who became chaplain to Princess Caroline and chaplain to King George II. He was already an established author when he published <u>The Complaint: or Night-Thoughts on Life, Death, and Immortality</u> (1742-46). The nine nights were first published serially. He struck a sympathetic chord in this long, somber poem about death. The poem became enormously popular in England and on the continent. In an age of rationalism and skepticism, the poem was a welcome advocate of the Christian faith, which triumphs over death.

Thomas Gray

Thomas Grays' serene poem, <u>Elegy, Wrote in a Country Churchyard</u> (1751) was about people who live close to Nature. Gray grew up in London and attended Eton, an elite secondary school, and Cambridge. From 1739-41 he took the Grand Tour with Horace Walpole, son of the prime minister and budding connoisseur. Gray's mother retired to the quiet village of Stoke Poges, site of the famous <u>Elegy</u>, and Gray spent his summers there. His "Ode on a Distant Prospect of Eton College" (1747) expresses the sense of timelessness found in rural England—"where ignorance is bliss," Gray writes, "Tis folly to be wise."

As a poet, Gray was distinguished by his careful craftsmanship. Gray achieves a style of haunting simplicity and honesty with a touch of melancholy. The poem was immediately recognized as a masterpiece. Gray takes the reader from the city—the bustling, contentious world of politics, and commerce, and entertainment—to the quiet, peaceful, natural rhythms of rural England, where humble people live in harmony with their environment. Gray's idealization of village life is offset by recognition that the people are trapped by the limitations of their existence—poverty, ignorance, and lack of opportunities.

In lines of touching eloquence Gray gives the lives of the villagers an aura of importance and timelessness: "Far from the madding crowd's ignoble strife/ Their sober wishes never learned to stray;/ Along the cool sequestered vale of life/ They kept the noiseless tenor of their way." The poem contains another famous line: "Full many a flower is born to blush unseen/ And waste its sweetness on the desert air."

Gray did not seek the life of a writer and wrote his poems for his friends, who arranged for publication. He was shy and reclusive, and often in poor health. He spent much of his life at Cambridge living the life of a scholar and a gentleman. He had an appointment as Professor of history, but he did not teach. He declined an appointment as poet laureate. He was interested in the untutored vigor of Nordic poetry, which he saw as akin to that of the early Greeks and a contrast with the polished poetry of his time. He expressed this interest in The Bard (1757), a poem in the "barbaric" style.

Allan Ramsay and Scottish Folklore

Allan Ramsay was an Edinburgh shopkeeper. From his youth, Ramsay had been fascinated by the folklore and poetry of Scotland. He was bitterly disappointed when the Act of Union (1707) joined England and Scotland politically. He flirted with Jacobitism, but was not actively involved. He became a bookseller and wrote poetry in the Scottish language. In 1718 Ramsay published Scots Songs, which included some of his own poems. He followed this work with Fables and Tales (1722) and A Tale of Three Bonnets (1722), a satire on the Act of Union. His Tea-Table Miscellany: a Collection of Scots Songs (3 vols, 1723, 1726, 1727) made Ramsay a major figure in the Scottish revival.

Ramsay's pastoral play, The Gentle Shepherd (1724) was converted into a ballad opera and became a huge success. In the eighteenth century it was performed 101 times in London, 47 times in Scotland, and 5 times in the American colonies. He advocated establishing a theatre in Edinburgh, but that was blocked by Walpole's Licensing Act (1737), which banned stage plays outside of London. Ramsay is best known as a collector of Scottish songs and folklore and as an advocate of the Scottish cultural inheritance.

The Poems of Ossian

While some poets sought inspiration in Nature, others turned to primitive times, which were deemed more poetic than the over-refined literature of civilized society. Nordic and Celtic poetry were especially admired, in that they were outside the Greek and Roman traditions that were the basis of classicism. A striking example of the fascination with the primitive was the popularity of James Macpherson's version of the tales of Ossian, whom he identified as a Gaelic bard of the third century AD. Macpherson grew up in a remote part of Scotland that was strongly Gaelic, Jacobite, and Catholic. He attended Aberdeen University and then moved to Edinburgh, where he associated with scholars who were interested in Scottish tales and ballads. In 1760 he published Fragments of Ancient Poetry Collected in the Highlands of Scotland, which he claimed he had translated into English from early Gaelic poems. He hinted that a Gaelic epic might be found. The work aroused considerable interest, and Macpherson received financial support to travel through Scotland searching for the lost epic.

More translations of Gaelic poetry followed that Macpherson attributed to Ossian, a Gaelic poet. These poems told about a heroic figure, Fingal, and his band of warriors. They were published as Fingal, an Ancient Epic Poem (1762), Temora (1763), and The Works of Ossian (2 vols., 1765).

The reaction against artificiality in poetry was so great that the poems at first were hailed as superb examples of the greater poetic feeling of primitive peoples who live close to Nature. The Ossianic poems were challenged as forgeries by Samuel Johnson and others, which aroused a heated controversy. Modern scholars have concluded that Macpherson did collect primitive Celtic poems but used his own imagination to fill the gaps and adapt the poems to the prevailing fascination with the primitive. The Ossianic poems were enormously influential in the early stages of Romanticism in Germany and other continental countries, where they stimulated many poetic works, plays, and operas.

The Gentleman's Magazine

An important development in publication was the magazine, a monthly periodical containing articles, often abridged from other publications, bits of news and interesting events, and information about prices, exchange rates, weather, and the like. The first and most important was the Gentleman's Magazine, founded in 1731 by Edward Cave. In the eighteenth century the word "magazine" meant a storehouse, as for military supplies. The Gentleman's Magazine was presented as a storehouse of interesting reading, culled and abridged from newspapers, political journals, and other publications.

In 1732 Cave began publishing brief accounts of the parliamentary debates, which was illegal, but they became so popular that in 1738 they were expanded under the transparent fiction that they were debates in the Senate of Lilliput. The appeal of the magazine was enhanced by including illustrations, beginning with woodcuts and, as circulation increased, moving on to copperplate engravings of individuals, buildings, songs, and maps. The annual twelve issues of the magazine were indexed and were intended to be bound in volumes as a permanent record of the year.

The magazine was directed at gentlemen broadly defined, including country gentry, clergy, businessmen, and professional people, who wanted to keep up with the world of ideas but could not afford to subscribe to a wide variety of newspapers and periodicals. Many of its subscribers lived in the provinces, remote from the intellectual ferment of London. The magazine early attracted contributions from readers, which eventually dominated the magazine. It also attracted poetry, but none of the prominent poets of the day would stoop to publish in its pages. The magazine's contributors show that it was popular among women.

As periodicals flourished, they provided opportunities for writers. In 1738 Cave employed Samuel Johnson, a young man from the cathedral town of Lichfield, who had come to London to pursue a career as a writer. Johnson's father was a bookseller, and in his father's bookshop Johnson was introduced to the world of books. The lad was clumsy and near-sighted but physically strong and robust. He was an omnivorous reader, and his enormous powers of retention enabled him to stock his mind with an astonishing range of knowledge of ancient and modern writers.

The limited financial resources of his father made it impossible for Johnson to get the education that would have opened careers to him. One way or another, money was found to send him to Oxford for a year, but after that he was compelled to fend for himself. Had he received his degree, he undoubtedly would have had a successful career in the law or the Church. But he did not graduate, and thus he was compelled to use his intellectual talents in the best way he could.

Johnson first attempted keeping a school. Normally, one man maintained a school with several assistants, and the reputation of the school and its master depended upon the performance of his pupils at the university or in careers. Johnson had difficulty in getting students, and he was not personally suited to deal with boys. In 1737, age twenty-eight, he decided to leave Lichfield to try the possibilities of a career in London. He was accompanied by one of his pupils, the eighteen-year old David Garrick.

An important part of Johnson's personal development was his struggle to earn a living in Grub Street, the term applied to the world of London hack writers. He arrived in London when a great number of publishers, booksellers, and writers sought to capitalize on the opportunities afforded by the great increase of the reading public. Johnson's first success as a writer was his poem, London: A Poem in Imitation of the Third Satire of Juvenal (1738), a powerful portrait of pervasive corruption—the debasement of government under Walpole, appeasement of Spain, national decay, and the evils of the metropolis.

After several unsuccessful overtures, Johnson obtained employment at the Gentleman's Magazine. He remarked that when he first saw St. John's Gate, the location of the magazine, he "beheld it with reverence." Johnson became Cave's editorial assistant, writing special articles and short biographies as well as accounts of foreign news and the parliamentary debates. He wrote the debates out of his head, using rough notes of the speakers and topics and giving the gist of the argument in his own splendid prose. He felt guilty about passing off his creations as authentic speeches, but the debates were enormously popular.

Most speakers probably were flattered to have their ideas presented in such a correct and eloquent style. Johnson's career on the <u>Gentleman's Magazine</u> gave him a wide acquaintance with politics, journalism, and the literary world.

After the fall of Walpole in 1742 the place of politics in the magazine declined, and most of the material dealt with intellectual, cultural, and religious topics, including considerable attention to science, exploration, and social problems such as crime, poverty, and disease. When Cave died in 1754 the <u>Gentleman's Magazine</u> had spawned many competitors, and its title had given a new meaning to the word "magazine."

Elizabeth Carter, a young woman of scholarly bent, broke into the world of publishing at the <u>Gentleman's Magazine</u> through her father, who was a personal friend of Cave. Her first literary efforts were poems and epigrams, which gave her something of a reputation as a female prodigy. She became a member of Cave's circle of minor writers and a lifetime friend of Samuel Johnson. In 1738, Cave printed a small volume of her poems entitled <u>Poems on Particular Occasions</u>. Carter's major accomplishment was her translation of the works of Epictetus, the Stoic philosopher (1758), which was published by a group of booksellers. She received £1,100 for the work, which made her financially secure. In 1762 another collection of her poetry, <u>Poems on Several Occasions</u> was published. The poems were mainly addressed to women.

Ch. 9. The Pleasures of the Imagination in a Commercial Society

One of the great achievements of eighteenth-century England was the development of the novel from a long tale of adventure (often emphasizing romantic intrigues) to a literary form that offered insight into the complexities of individual personality and motivation. Women played an important role as authors, heroines, and readers of novels. The novels of Defoe, Richardson, and Fielding made the novel the premier literary form from the eighteenth-century to the present time.

Daniel Defoe

The political revolution of 1714 changed the fortunes of Daniel Defoe, whose patron, Robert Harley, Earl of Oxford, fell from power. Once again, Defoe had to depend on his pen to survive. He began with works that dealt with practical matters of everyday life. <u>The Complete English Tradesman, in Familiar Letters; Directing him in all the several Parts and the Progressions of Trade</u> (1725) was a series of 25 letters advising a young man how to conduct a business. Defoe emphasizes diligence and the importance of maintaining good credit and the re-spect of other businessmen. Pitfalls to be avoided are over-expansion, expensive living, marrying before the business is well established, and entering into an imprudent partnership. His knowledge of the London underground enabled him to write vivid accounts of criminals, among them <u>The True and Genuine Account of the Life and Actions of the</u>

Late Jonathan Wild (1725). In his tales of crime and unusual occurrences Defoe includes an abundance of specific details to give the illusion of reality.

Defoe's first great success was The Life and Strange Surprising Adventures of Robinson Crusoe of York, Mariner, who lived Eight and Twelve Years, all alone in an uninhabited Island on the coast of America near the Mouth of the Great River of Oroonoque; Having been cast on Shore by Shipwreck, wherin all the Men perished but himself. With An Account how he was at last as strangely deliver'd by Pirates. Written by Himself (1719). Defoe's hero is an English sailor, Robinson Crusoe, whose ship is wrecked on a desert island. With the tools of civilization that he salvages from his ship, Crusoe struggles to deal with life apart from other human beings. His life is one of constant fear and anxiety. By virtue of intelligence, hard work, and constant care, Crusoe thrives and achieves a civilized, albeit lonely, existence. He reads the Bible and becomes religious. Crusoe's isolation is complete until a native of the islands escapes from cannibals and is made into a servant by Crusoe, who names him Friday.

Friday represents Defoe's conception of the natural human being unaffected by civilization. As such, Friday cannot be a companion in the fullest sense, but Crusoe governs him with concern for his wellbeing. In so doing, Defoe expresses his own view of the responsibility of colonial powers to the native peoples who come under their authority. Eventually a ship appears that has been taken over by mutineers, who intend to maroon the captain on the island. Crusoe and the captain capture the ship and return to England. Robinson Crusoe was so popular that Defoe published a sequel, Farther Adventures of Robinson Crusoe (1719) and the novel spawned many imitations.

In Defoe's novels, individuals have to make their way in an alien or hostile world. The Fortunes and Misfortunes of the Famous Moll Flanders, Etc., Who was born in Newgate, and during a life of continu'd Variety for Threescore Years, besides her Childhood, was Twelve Year a Whore, five times a Wife (whereof once to her own brother), Twelve Year a Thief, Eight Year a Transported Felon in Virginia, at last grew Rich, live'd Honest and died a Penitent. Written from her own Memorandums (1722) took the novel of amorous intrigue to a new level. It is an intimate study of the life and loves of a rootless woman, who relies on her good looks, shrewdness, and quick-witted fibs to rise from the amoral underground of London to social acceptance. Born in Newgate Prison, Moll was abandoned when her mother was transported to the colonies as a felon. At first Moll was befriended by a band of gypsies, but they abandoned her and she became the responsibility of the parish. She was such a delightful child that she was taken in by the mayor and raised with his other children. The elder son in the family gets her pregnant, and the younger son marries her.

After a failed marriage, Moll marries a sea-captain who takes her to Virginia. She discovers that the sea-captain is her half-brother, which invalidates the marriage. She returns to Bath and lives with a man whose wife is demented. After this man leaves her, she marries an Irishman who tells her he has money. He turns out to be a penniless highway robber. After they break up, she marries a banker, and they have a quiet, stable marriage until he dies leaving her destitute at age forty-eight with two children.

At that point, Moll begins a life of crime, disguised as a beggar woman. She is clever and nimble, and prospers. Eventually she is apprehended, sent to Newgate Prison, and sentenced to death. She is reprieved and sentenced to transportation to America. Her former husband, the Irish highwayman, is also in prison and receives a similar sentence. Together they establish a plantation in Maryland. They work hard and prosper, and are respected throughout the colonies. At the age of seventy, they return to England and live out their days in repentance for the sins and crimes they had committed.

Defoe's characters, especially the indominatable Moll, are sharply defined, and the locations of Moll's escapades are richly detailed. Her sense of triumph at each escape from disaster is infectious. Defoe's knowledge of business appears in many references to money and contracts. Newgate Prison and the lives of the criminal class are vividly depicted. America is presented as a place where broken lives can be mended and given a fresh start. Defoe titillates his readers with a peek-a-boo approach to Moll's sexual relationships with men. The book is so vividly written and so candid about Moll's intimate thoughts, it convinces the reader that it must be a personal memoir, not a work of fiction.

Defoe recognizes the limitations that society places on the lives of women, who are dependent on fathers, husbands, brothers, or sons. Moll is determined to escape from poverty, and her good looks make marriage the best bet. But Moll wants more—she wants to be a gentlewoman with a place in society. Even when the wolf is no longer at her door, she pursues money as the only way to gain social status. The fact that Moll repents at the end makes it possible for Defoe to include intimate material and avoid the moral hazard of making Sin seem attractive.

Defoe takes up a similar theme in Roxana, the common abbreviation of The Fortunate Mistress: Or,A History of the Life and Vast Variety of Fortunes of Mademoiselle de Beleau, Afterwards called the Countess de Winselsheim, in Germany, Being the Person Known by the Name of the Lady Roxana, in the Time of King Charles II (1714). Roxana's parents were Huguenots who had fled to England to escape religious persecution. She grows up in England and becomes a beautiful young woman. At age fifteen she marries a handsome man who spends all her money and leaves her with five children. Her faithful maid, Amy, remains with her through all her ups and downs. Roxana's landlord offers to set her up as his mistress. Roxana feels guilty about this immoral arrangement but has no choice, and they live together for several years. When Roxana fails to conceive a child, Amy sleeps with the landlord and gives birth to a child that Roxana, despite a guilty conscience, passes off as hers. Her lover takes her to Paris (fully described) with a bag of valuable jewels. He is attacked and murdered by robbers, but Roxana is able to retain the jewels and keep them from his wife. In Paris she is courted by a Prince, who supports her in lavish style and showers her with valuable gifts. When the Prince's wife dies, the Prince, filled with remorse, abandons Roxana, now a wealthy woman, who has to find her way back to England.

Before sailing, Roxana engages a merchant to ship her money and jewels to England. He wants to marry her, but she enjoys the independence that money gives her and rejects him. Roxana learns that great wealth brings many anxieties with it. Defoe's account of the difficulties that Roxana faces in transporting her money from Holland to England gives a fascinating insight into international economics at that time. Back in London, Roxana sets herself up in a splendid apartment and gives lavish parties attended by fashionable people. A wealthy lord offers her a substantial income to be his mistress. She accepts and lives a modest life with him, accumulating more wealth in the process. She tires of this arrangement and the sense of shame that goes with it. She breaks it off and moves to another part of the city. Now fifty, she decides to devote herself to her children. By chance, she meets the merchant that she had known in Holland. She accepts his proposal and they marry, with the intention of living in Holland. Roxana is ashamed and embarrassed by the life she has led, and in Holland she can begin afresh.

Like Moll Flanders, Roxana struggles first for security, sacrificing her individuality by accepting dependence on men. Moll and Roxana begin life as social outcasts, which motivates them to do the things that they do. Defoe understood them, because he had been through a similar struggle himself. Roxana's life seems to offer a moral hazard, in that she prospers from bad deeds and escapes punishment. Defoe resolves that problem by making her suffer pangs of guilt and shame that turn her gold to dust.

Defoe's A Journal of the Plague Year (1722) is a novel that places its protagonist in the midst of the London plague of 1666. Defoe was six when the plague took place, and he may have had some personal recollections of the sights and sounds that took place. Doubtless he drew upon stories that he had heard from people who had lived through it. To that extent, the novel has some validity as an historical source. But Defoe does more with the plague than tell the story. He gives a searing account of the human responses to the plague, which in many respects resemble the mass psychology of people under siege. The protagonist of the novel is torn by a variety of impulses as he seeks to understand the causes and implications of the disaster. He must decide what he should do in these unique circumstances. Eventually Defoe brings God into the picture.

Defoe gave the tale of adventure an intense insight into human personality, especially under stress, and thus transforms it into the novel. He abandons the "heroic" model of earlier novels of action and adventure, and uses the novel to depict the challenges faced by ordinary people caught in extraordinary situations. His prose is clear and straightforward, without flourishes or allusions to the classics.

Defoe's novels were not directed to upper-class gentlemen of

"Taste," but to the men and women of the new middle-class reading public, an audience that Defoe understood intimately. In <u>Robinson Crusoe</u>, <u>Moll Flanders</u>, <u>Roxana</u>, <u>A Journal of the Plague Year</u> and many other works of fiction, Defoe established the characteristics that identify the modern novel as a distinct literary form.

<u>Women Writers and the Novel,</u>

Novel reading was already a favorite recreation of women. Aphra Behn brought to England the French novel of amorous intrigue, which titillated readers with fast-moving tales of adventures, intrigues, catastrophes, violence, and seductions. Delarivier Manley, the daughter of a royalist military officer, was a free spirit who led a highly irregular and controversial life. She began her literary career as a writer for the theatre. Manley's first play was a comedy called <u>The Lost Lover, or, The Jealous Husband</u> (1696). The play was not a success. A tragedy entitled <u>The Royal Mischief</u> (1696) was more successful, and Manley's prolific career as a playwright was launched. She was satirized in an anonymous play entitled <u>The Female Wits</u> (1696). Her last play, <u>Lucius, the First Christian King of Britain</u> (1717), is highly patriotic and displays her feminist principles by giving a strong role to Rosalind, the queen.

Manley's main interest, however, was politics. After an early friendship, Manley and Steele became bitter enemies, political and otherwise. Manley was personally involved in Tory politics and assisted Swift with <u>The Examiner</u>. As the Whigs consolidated their grip on power, Manley published <u>Secret Memoirs and Manners of Several Persons of Quality of both Sexes, From the New Atalantis, an Island in the Mediterranean</u> (1709). The novel tells of the scandalous behavior of the leaders of the government and society of Atalantis, who were identified as prominent Whigs in a separately published key. In 1709 Manley was accused of seditious libel and taken into custody. She was released a year later when the Tories came to power. Undaunted, she published another scandal novel, <u>Memoirs of Europe, Towards the Close of the Eighth Century, Written by Eginardus, Secretary and Favorite of Charlemagne</u> (1710), which continues her attacks on the Whigs. For this novel, she received £50 from Robert Harley. Her last novels, published as <u>The Power of Love in Seven Novels</u> (1720) were derived from Italian and French novels, and were typical of the genre in that they had racy plots and sexy scenes.

Romance novels served as an escape from the narrowly confined lives of genteel women. The queen of romance fiction was Eliza Haywood, who began as an actress and went on to become an important writer. Haywood married too young, was widowed, and found an opportunity to support herself and her two children in the theatre. She gained public notice as an actress in Henry Fielding's The Historical Register for the year 1736, an attack on the politics of Walpole that led to the Licensing Act of 1737. As a playwright, Haywood's most successful play was The Opera of Operas (1733), a musical with music by Thomas Arne and modeled on a play by Fielding.

Haywood made her living as a writer, turning out a variety of publications. She wrote political novels that included dissertations on government and politics and veiled allusions to current events. Some of her political commentary was disguised by using the form of imaginary countries. The Adventures of Eovaai (1736) tells the story of a kidnapped princess who discusses forms of government with an elderly man. Haywood tried her hand at periodicals. Her most successful was The Female Spectator, based on a group of intelligent women who discuss politics, books, plays, fashion, love, and marriage. She was an astute critic of the theatre. A Companion to the Theatre (1740) listed and commented on plays and was periodically updated and republished . She wrote and published several essay journals, which included essays on a wide variety of subjects—politics, publishing, literary criticism, and courtship and marriage.

Haywood was a major figure in the development of the novel. Along with Defoe, she discovered the huge market for fiction. She developed her skills as a novelist by translating French and Spanish romance novels, in which she was able to explore themes of female liberation and sexuality. She published about 55 prose fictions, most of them novels of the action-adventure type but with greater depths of character and motivation than her French and Spanish models. She was satirized by Pope in The Dunciad.

Her first novel, Love in Excess (1719), was a work in the French tradition of novels about amorous intrigue. In this novel, she uses a variety of women characters to explore different aspects of female sexuality. The novel differs from the French prototype in that the obstacles that the lovers face grow out of their own actions, not external circumstances. The British Recluse (1722) tells the stories of two women— one has been ruined by a seducer, and the other escapes seduction and begins a new life. Both find happiness without men. The Rash Resolve (1724) and The Force of Nature (1724) are stories of single mothers supporting their children.

Her novels center around the difficulties women face living under male domination and shackled by the role assigned to women by social conventions. She condemns the rituals of courtship, which make communication difficult and lead to bad marriages. The History of Miss Betsy Thoughtless (1751) is considered to be her most important novel. It is a novel about marriage rather than the usual novel of courtship or seduction. The novel deals with an independent-minded woman whose impulses lead her into romance and marriage. She learns the principles of morality from the bad outcomes of her reckless conduct. Haywood's novels are sprinkled with astute comments about books and plays and the influence of the print culture on personal and public conduct.

Samuel Richardson

Samuel Richardson was a successful printer and publisher whose business flourished by doing printing for the House of Commons. He printed periodicals and reference works, including The Philosophical Transactions of the Royal Society. He also printed a second edition of Defoe's Tour Thro' the Whole Island of Great Britain (1738) and an edition of Aesop's Fables with engraved illustrations (1739). Richardson was an assiduous and fluent letter writer, and began his career as a writer by publishing small pieces in the form of letters that dealt with social problems of London. His first book, The Apprentice's Vade Mecum (1733), a handbook of advice to a young apprentice, was in the form of personal letters. Knowing his talent for letter-writing, a group of publishers asked him to prepare a book of model letters on common subjects that individuals could use to improve their own correspondence. Richardson's Letters Written to and for Particular Friends, on the Most Important Occasions (1741) contained letters for baptisms, wedding, and funerals etc., and also included letters dealing with personal and moral problems.

Richardson, who held strong moral views, countered the popular novels of love, intrigue and seduction with <u>Pamela: Or Virtue Rewarded</u> (1740), which originally was published anonymously. Richardson's achievement was to reconfigure the romance into a new form—the domesic novel. Pamela is a fifteen-year old servant girl whose challenge is to protect her virtue and virginity by resisting seduction by Mr. B___, the son of her mistress, Lady B____. When her mistress dies, she is exposed to the immoral designs of Mr. B ___. Pamela writes long letters to her parents telling them of her predicament. Personal letters filled with emotional detail communicate Pamela's feelings and state of mind in an intensely intimate way. When she decides to return to her parents, Mr. B____hides in her closet and attempts to overcome her resistance by force. He is foiled when Pamela falls into a fit. Mr. B___ tricks her into going to his country estate, where she is held prisoner and abused.

Eventually Mr. B___ apologizes for his conduct, proposes marriage, and Pamela discovers that she loves him. She enjoys her status as a gentlewoman, and her virtue and charms win the support of Mr. B___'s family. Mr. B___ also provides for Pamela's parents. When Pamela learns that Mr. B___ has become involved in an affair with a countess, she overwhelms him with love and affection and he returns to the role of faithful husband.

A bare recitation of the plot fails to communicate the believability and tensions established by the exchange of letters, if the reader accepts the premise that people have time to write and read such long letters. Much of the appeal of the book lies in the sexually-charged episodes, which hold the reader in suspense for page after page but are never consummated. By basing a novel on the feelings of the individuals involved rather than a sequence of interesting events, Richardson changed the character of the novel.

<u>Pamela</u> swept genteel society off its feet with its probing of feminine emotions and sexuality, and went through five editions in the first year. The novel spawned a rash of imitations and parodies. Eliza Haywood weighed in with <u>Anti-Pamela, or Feign'd Innocence Detected</u>

(1740). An adaptation for the stage soon followed, and the vogue for Pamela spread to the continent.

Richardson followed with Clarissa, or, The History of a Young Lady, which was published serially in 1747 and 1748 and reprinted in seven volumes. He states the theme of the book as "the distresses that may attend the misconduct both of parents and children in relation to marriage." The word "distresses," as used in the eighteenth century, refers equally to personal circumstances and emotional states.

Clarissa Harlowe is a beautiful young woman with a middle-class upbringing who is torn by a bitter family quarrel concerning property that she inherited from her grandfather. She angers her family when she refuses to marry a rich man chosen by her father. She states firmly that she will never marry any man against her will. Desperate to escape her cruel and domineering family, the unsuspecting Clarissa absconds with Robert Lovelace, a rake who attempts to seduce her. Lovelace takes her to a house of ill repute where she is kept as a virtual prisoner. They fill her with drugs, and Lovelace rapes her. She escapes, but is recaptured by Lovelace and cast into debtor's prison on false charges. She is rescued by a friend of Lovelace, who attempts reconciliation with her family, but without success. Filled with shame at his evil act, Lovelace offers to marry Clarissa, but she will have nothing to do with him. Finally, Clarissa's family relents and offers to take her back, but by that time she has died a noble death—a martyr to her standards of virtue and decorous behavior.

Like Pamela, the story is told through letters, some of them incredibly long, that communicate the thoughts and feelings of Clarissa and the friends with whom she corresponds. Many of the letters include long stretches of dialogue, which gives them a theatrical quality, as each character speaks in their own distinctive voice from their own point of view. The letters interrupt the narrative flow, but actions are less important in Richardson's novels than personal feelings and moral issues.

Richardson was a moralist who defended the existing standards of female virtue and behavior. Nevertheless much of the suspense in his novels is derived from the tantalizing steps by which his heroines approach or retreat from moral dangers. Richardson finds ways to include sexual titillation without being too explicit or abandoning his moralistic stance. He exhibits a strong religious purpose—he uses Clarissa Harlowe to show the value of the Christian faith in meeting the challenges and disappointments of life. Clarissa's death was tragic in the human sense, but from the Christian perspective it was a spiritual triumph.

Richardson was upset when he discovered that many of his readers were more attracted to the rakish conduct of Lovelace than the drawn out segments devoted to the virtuous Clarissa. Thereupon, he decided to write a novel about a virtuous man to show that virtue could be interesting too. He followed Clarissa with Sir Charles Grandison (1753-54), a novel told in 182 family letters about a good man who is the reverse of Lovelace. Harriet Byron, a beautiful and virtuous country girl, comes to London to participate in the social scene. She attracts many suitors. One of them, Sir Hargrave Pollexfen, abducts her and attempts to rape her, but she is rescued by Sir Charles Grandison, who hears her screams. Sir Charles has inherited the family estate, which he manages with care. He treats others with kindness, even his father's mistress. He accepts Harriet as a member of the family and treats her as a sister. His life is complicated by two women he had met while traveling in Italy. After he has resolved the problems that they create, he returns to England and proposes to Harriet, who accepts.

In many respects, Harriet is a fortunate counterpart to Clarissa Harlowe. She helps members of the family overcome rough spots in their lives, assisted by Sir Charles, who is always kind and generous. Sir Hargrave Pollexfen dies and leaves his fortune to Harriet to compensate for his previous treatment of her. The novel, despite its enormous length, was a publishing success and went through many editions before 1800. Richardson's works were popular on the continent and were translated into many European languages.

Henry Fielding

Richardson's rival as a novelist was Henry Fielding, who came from a prominent family and was a gentleman, whereas Richardson, a printer, was not. Fielding attended Eton and the University of Leyden in Holland. His father, an army officer, was unable to provide an allowance sufficient to enable his eldest son to live as a gentleman, and Fielding had to find a way to earn a living. His cousin, Lady Mary

Wortley Montagu, encouraged him to come to London and try his hand as a writer.

In the 1730s, Fielding became the dominant playwright in London. The Beggar's Opera had shown that "irregular" comedies that did not follow the usual formulas could be successful, and that is the tack that Fielding took. In The Author's Farce (1730) the actors play puppets. The Tragedy of Tragedies, or, the Life and Death of Tom Thumb the Great (1731), featuring a small man, is a burlesque of the traditional tragedy. The play, which is set at King Arthur's Court, was a huge success, running to packed houses for forty nights. Tom Thumb was an evening of entertainment, with music, dancing, parodies and satirical skits. The play began as a brief afterpiece to be performed after a main play. When Tom Thumb was a success, it was greatly expanded and published as The Tragedy of Tragedies, an extended satire on the stale formulas of the heroic tragedy as it had developed in the late seventeenth century. Fielding despised pedantry and false learning. The published version includes a mass of pseudo-scholarship attributed to the pedant, H. Scriblerus Secundus.

In 1736 Fielding formed his own company of actors and presented The Historical Register for 1736, which satirizes and ridicules the events of the year, including taking potshots at Walpole. Fielding intensified his attack on Walpole with Pasquin: A Dramatick Satire on the Times (1736). Pasquin was Fielding's most audacious attack, and ran for more than 60 nights. Walpole had had enough, and responded with the Licensing Act for theatres (1737), which established the lord chamberlain as censor. Many people agreed that the theatres had gotten out of hand, not just for political reasons but for aesthetic and moral reasons. Lord Chesterfield, a prominent opposition Whig, argued against the Act as an infringement of freedom of expression. Colley Cibber defended the Act on the grounds that freedom in print and freedom in the theatre were different things. The Act ended Fielding's career as a political playwright and condemned the English theatre to a generation of convention and mediocrity until rescued by Garrick and Sheridan later in the century.

With a wife and child to support, Fielding had to find another way to earn a living. He gave up the theatre, studied law, and was admitted to the bar. He became a journalist and wrote anti-Walpole articles for

The Craftsman and Commonsense. He edited The Champion (1739-41) a periodical that was a leading voice in the political attacks that led to the fall of the great prime minister.

Fielding's law practice was not very successful, and he turned to the novel for additional income. Always a satirist, his purpose was to expose the shallow morality and sentimentality of Richardson. His An Apology for the Life of Mrs. Shamela Andrews (1741) was a successful parody of Pamela and set him on course to be a novelist. He followed Shamela with The History of the Adventures of Joseph Andrews, and of His Friend Mr. Abraham Adams (1742), a comic novel about the Pamela's brother, Joseph, who is a handsome footman in the household of Lady Booby, Fielding's name for Richardson's Lady B___.

Joseph, a virtuous young man, is determined to preserve his virginity for his fiancée, Fanny Goodwill. He is dismissed from his post when he resists the advances of Lady Booby. He flees from Lady Booby's London household and hits the road to Booby Hall. On his first night on the road he is attacked by robbers and beaten. A passing coach picks him up and takes him to an inn, where he is recognized by his former tutor, the good-hearted Parson Adams. They proceed together on their way to Booby Hall, taking turns riding the good Parson's horse. On the way, Parson Adams hears a young woman screaming for help. She is being attacked by a ruffian, but the spirited clergyman wades in, fists flying, and rescues her. She turns out to be Fanny Goodwill, Joseph's beloved, and joins the party. On the way they have various adventures and visit a variety of inns until they finally reach Booby Hall.

Pamela, Joseph's sister, tries to persuade Joseph not to marry Fanny, who is of a lower social class. Suddenly it is revealed that Fanny is the sister of Pamela. Furthermore, Joseph is the long-lost son of a respectable couple who had given the travelers hospitality along the way. Since he is not related by blood to Pamela and Fanny, and is of good family, the lovers are free to wed.

Unlike the sentimental novels of the time, Joseph Andrews presents a realistic picture of the attitudes, manners and customs of ordinary people. In the process, Fielding ridicules pretension and its twin, hypocrisy. The lovable Parson Adams is not just a Christian in his professional role as a parish clergyman; he is a Christian in his heart and in his deeds. As such, he puts most people who call themselves Christians to shame.

Fielding's <u>The History of the Life of the Late Mr. Jonathan Wild the Great</u> (1743) is a study of the evils that grow out of power unalloyed by morality. Although contemporaries might apply it to Walpole, the novel relates to all the great conquerors and tyrants of the world, past and present. It is not the story of Jonathan Wild, the fence, which had been previously published by Defoe and used by John Gay for <u>The Beggar's Opera</u>. Fielding's novel is a study of two men, Jonathan Wild, the embodiment of "the great man" and Mr. Heartfree, the "good" man, who is kind and generous to all, including Wild. Beginning in boyhood as a pickpocket, Jonathan Wild becomes a professional robber and confidence man. His weakness is his lust for women, which he seeks to consummate by use of force, not mutual affection. Wild exerts his "greatness' by ruining Mr. Heartfree and running off to Holland with his wife. Wild ends on the gallows, while the reunited Heartfrees enjoy a happy ending

Fielding's masterpiece, <u>The History of Tom Jones, A Foundling</u> (1749), is his rejoinder to Richardson's novels, but it is more than that—it established the comic novel as a genre in English literature. In <u>Tom Jones</u>, Fielding explores the "natural" instincts of a young man in contrast to the "artificial" moral sentiments of Richardson's heroines. He tells a rollicking tale of Tom Jones, who is thought to be the illegitimate child of Jenny Jones, a servant girl in the household of the high-minded Squire Allworthy. About the same time, Bridget, the sister of Squire Allworthy, marries a Capt. Blifil and gives birth to a son, Master Blifil. As Squire Allworthy's heir, Master Blifil is brought up in the household of Squire Allworthy with Tom. Blifil is the opposite of Tom—uptight, sanctimonious, and resentful of Squire Allworthy's fondness for Tom.

Squire Allworthy's neighbor is Squire Western, the coarse father of the beautiful Sophia. Sophia and Tom fall in love, but her marriage to a foundling without family or fortune is impossible. Despite Sophia's objections, marriage to Squire Allworthy's heir will join two adjacent estates, and arrangements are made for her to marry the obnoxious Blifil. Tom hits the road to London and gets in one scrape after another, but he is redeemed by his good nature and personal resilience. Sophia, who is confined to her room for refusing to marry Blifil, also flees, accompanied by her maid. Tom rescues a woman, Mrs. Waters, who is being raped by a soldier. He takes her to an inn. Coincidentally, Sophia and her maid stay at the same inn. When Sophia learns that Tom is there with a woman, she is understandably upset by Tom's fickleness, but she continues on to London where she stays with a family friend.

Squire Western comes to London and takes Sophia home. Squire Allworthy also comes to London looking for Tom, who has become involved in a duel and is in jail. Squire Allworthy is informed by a friend of Tom that Mrs. Waters really are Jenny Jones. Jenny tells Squire Allworthy that Tom's true mother was the squire's sister, Bridget, and Jenny had agreed to accept responsibility. Squire Allworthy also learns that Blifil has plotted to disgrace Tom in a variety of ways, and Blifil is disinherited in favor of Tom. With Tom's genteel maternity revealed and his expectation of inheriting the estate, Tom gets the hand of his true love—Sophia.

Fielding's ideal is Squire Allworthy, an embodiment of the sentimental man of benevolence and sympathy, whose wisdom and goodness proceed from a broad understanding of human nature, a warm heart, and true Christian charity. Squire Western, on the other hand, is a caricature of the vulgar, violent, hard-drinking, bullying country squire. Fielding depicts Squire Western, not as a villain but as a strong individual who is a victim of his own ignorance and impulses. Master Blifil and his tutors represent the worst kind of moralistic religiosity. Fielding admires religion when it inculcates kindness and charity to others, but he is unsparing in his criticism of a church that is just another selfish interest.

Fielding deals with the full range of social relationships. Despite differences in rank and abilities, in Tom Jones all men and women are equal because the fundamental distinction is between those who are good, generous, and kind, and those who are vain, narrow, and selfish—qualities that exist in both genders and at all levels of society. Like Tom Jones, we are all foundlings on this earth and must find our own way. Tom finally achieves happiness when he gains his true love, Sophia, whose name means "wisdom."

In his last novel, The History of Amelia (1751), Fielding returns to political and social satire, but in a darker and grimmer mood. Amelia, a virtuous and loving wife, is destroyed by the evil society that surrounds her. She must cope with the reckless improvidence of her husband and various attempts at seduction brought on by her good looks. By the time he wrote <u>Amelia</u>, Fielding had become a London magistrate. In that office, he had probed the depths of that great city, where he found a large criminal class and a corrupt system of law enforcement, much of which he attributed to the self-indulgence of a pleasure-loving society. He gives a lurid picture of the evils of the time from the perspective of Amelia, who attempts to lead a moral life in the midst of this amoral quagmire.

Sarah Fielding

Sarah Fielding, sister of Henry Fielding, also pursued a career as a novelist. She did not marry, and her writings provided her with a modest living. Her first novel, <u>The Adventures of David Simple</u> (1744), tells the story of a young man in London who is looking for a true friend and discovers the great variety of evils in that city. Eventually he finds what he seeks in marriage and the marriage of his friend. The two couples form a small community of virtuous people isolated from the world. The novel was a success, and a second edition appeared within two months. <u>The Governess; or Little Female Academy</u> (1749) was a story for girls about life in a girls' school. It remained popular for the rest of the century.

Sarah's distinguished brother was dead when <u>The Adventures of David Simple, Volume the Last</u> (1754) was published. In the second volume David is buffeted by a series of reverses that evoke the sympathies of the reader. Other novels followed, most of them concerned with the problems of single women in a man's world. Sarah had scholarly inclinations, and in 1762 she published translations of Xenophon's <u>Memoirs of Socrates</u> and <u>Defence of Socrates</u>, which remained in print for many years. Sarah Fielding accepted the limitations within which women writers had to work, but not without complaint.

Ch. 10. Theatre and the Arts in Georgian England

The culture of Georgian England was not limited to the world of print. The theatre brought a broad segment of society together to enjoy the spoken word, painted scenery, colorful costumes, and music. In contrast, the works of Hogarth offered a portrait of London life that hit home. The music of Handel stirred the heart and elevated the soul. These works were an important factor in knitting the English people into a community of shared values.

The Theatre

Georgian London had two "legitimate" theatres with royal patents that gave them a monopoly of the production of plays. The Royal Opera House offered Italian opera performed by Italian singers. In the Georgian era the theatre changed from an intimate place catering to a small courtly elite to a commercialized entertainment appealing to large audiences. The middle class began attending the theatres, and they demanded plays that were both entertaining and moral. Religious objections to the immorality and immodesty of the theatre continued. The fact that Covent Garden and Drury Lane were located in centers of crime and vice added to the association of the theatre with bad company. The most serious criticism was that the theatres had debased an art form capable of nobility of language and elevated purposes.

The key theatrical figure of the early eighteenth century was Colley Cibber, comedian and manager of the Drury Lane theatre. Cibber

made his mark as an actor/playwright at Drury Lane with his play
Love's Last Shift, or the Fool in Fashion (1696), in which he starred
as Sir Novelty Fashion, a fop who prides himself on wearing the latest styles. His version of Shakespeare's Richard III (1699) became one
of the most popular roles for actors in the eighteenth century. Cibber
became actor/manager at Drury Lane in 1704 and partner with Steele
in 1715. He wrote some twenty-five plays, many of which remained
popular throughout the century. She Wou'd and she Wou'd Not (1702)
and The Careless Husband (1704) were predecessors of "the sentimental comedy," which replaced wit and satire with tender romance. He
had another big hit with The Nonjuror (1717), a political play that
ran for eighteen nights. A nonjuror was a clergyman who refused to
take the oath supporting King William III. In the play, the nonjuror is
a Catholic priest who incites rebellion. The play was welcomed by the
Whig government, which used the fear of a Jacobite uprising to win
political support. Cibber's The Provok'd Husband (1728) responded
to the emphasis on sentiment and moral conduct. It was based on an
unfinished play by Vanbrugh and made a strong defense of fidelity in
marriage. The first production ran for 28 nights. From 1747-1776, The
Provok'd Husband was performed 189 times.

Cibber used the star system and elaborate staging to draw large audiences. He established close personal connections with the court and
the Whig leaders, which led to his appointment as poet laureate and
outraged Pope. Cibber tells the story of his own life in An Apology for
the Life of Mr. Colley Cibber, Comedian (1740), a lively and interesting book that is an important contribution to the early history of the
eighteenth-century theatre.

Richard Steele helped change the tone of the theatre with The
Conscious Lovers (1722), an "exemplary comedy" intended to provide
moral instruction for men and women. It was Steele's most successful
play, and brought in more money than any previous play. Bevil is engaged to marry Lucinda, who loves Bevil's friend, a young gentleman
named Myrtle. Lucinda objects to Bevil on the grounds that he already
keeps a mistress. The plot is resolved when Lucinda's father discovers that Bevil's mistress is really his long-lost daughter, whom Bevil
has befriended. Bevil marries his mistress and Lucinda is free to marry
Myrtle.

Steele's play set a precedent for the "sentimental comedy," in which benevolence and sympatric understanding are emphasized. The polished, witty comedies of the Restoration continued to be performed, but were suspect due to their amorality. The theatre was dominated by sentimental plays that depicted the courage of a good heart when faced with a scheming villain, ending with the triumph of true love over all obstacles.

The growth of theatre attendance was phenomenal. In a good week in the 1730s all theatres, including the Royal Opera House, could attract about 15,000 patrons. George II and Queen Caroline enjoyed opera and oratorio, and Frederick, Prince of Wales and Princess Augusta were enthusiastic theatre-goers. The aristocracy and other people of quality continued to attend. Most of the audience was drawn from prosperous business and professional men and their wives, cultivated individuals living on independent incomes, visitors to the metropolis from the provinces or abroad, and single gentlemen-about-town. Shopkeepers and artisans and their wives might enjoy an occasional night out at the theatre, and apprentices, shop assistants, and domestic servants were packed into the upper gallery. There were frequent complaints of rowdiness in the theatre and from time to time riots broke out.

Most of the plays that were performed were established plays, such as The Recruiting Officer, but the theatres offered some new plays every year, few of which found a permanent place in the repertoire. Popular actors and actresses were important in drawing an audience. The main play of the evening was normally followed by a farce and special acts, such as clowns, singers, dancers, tumblers, etc. The commedia dell'arte, a rough-and-ready form of street drama that originated in Italy, was popular. The commedia used a few familiar plots that centered on the efforts of a pair of lovers (who do not wear masks) to marry. The comedy arises from the actions and verbal interplay of a stereotyped cast of characters who wear masks—Harlequin (the clever servant), Columbine (the pretty housemaid), the Doctor (the elderly pedant), Pagliacci (the clown), Il Capitano (the boastful, cowardly soldier), and Pantalone (an avaricious old man with an attractive young wife or daughter). Music was an essential element in Georgian theatre, either in the main performance or in the afterpieces that followed the play.

One of the few successful Georgian tragedies was George Lillo's The London Merchant (1731), a powerful melodrama that capitalizes on the growing sense of self-worth of the merchant class by presenting a merchant as an example of virtue. For many years, merchants sent their apprentices to see the play and absorb its moral principles. The play is set at the time of the Spanish Armada, but it is thoroughly contemporary in tone. The prosperous, kindly merchant, Thorowgood, represents the virtues admired by the commercial classes. George Barnwell, a simple apprentice from the country, is led astray by the heartless glitter of the metropolis. Thorowgood's daughter, Maria, whose love offers George Barnwell all he could possibly want, is the embodiment of true and selfless love. Millwood, the seductive femme fatale, hates the male-dominated society that has violated and rejected her. She gets money and revenge by luring men to her voluptuous nest, where she robs and destroys them.

As the play unfolds, Millwood persuades Barnwell, who is ensnared by her beauty and charm, to rob his master and kill his uncle. The play is filled with melodramatic speeches, as Barnwell's anxiety and remorse mount. At the end Barnwell realizes, too late, that his folly has deprived him of the opportunity to marry Maria, inherit Thorowgood's fortune, and lead the life of a respected merchant. Millwood meets her end as bitterly as she has lived. Despite the bombast, The London Merchant is a penetrating study of the destructive nature of evil.

Although Walpole could accept the light-hearted innuendos of The Beggar's Opera, the increasing use of the theatre for political criticism was more than annoying. The managers of the patent theatres found it prudent to stay on good terms with the government, but Henry Fielding shared the views of the political Opposition. He drew audiences to his unlicensed little theatre in the Haymarket by presenting political satires. Fielding's plays pushed the Walpole ministry to the point where firm action appeared to be essential.

Equally important in the demand for regulation of the theatres were complaints of its moral and aesthetic shortcomings. Traditionally the lord chamberlain, acting through the master of the revels, had the power to regulate the theatres. The patentees, however, claimed that their patents made them solely responsible for the content of their plays. Moreover, unlicensed theatres sprang up and prospered by presenting political and social satires. Local magistrates feared that un-licensed theatres would become centers of immorality and disorder. In 1735 Sir John Barnard, Member of Parliament for London and a critic of the Walpole regime, introduced a bill to regulate the number of playhouses.

Two years later, Walpole secured passage of the Licensing Act, which strengthened the monopoly of the patent theatres and gave the lord chamberlain power to censor plays prior to performance. The lord chamberlain restricted spoken plays to Covent Garden and Drury Lane and opera to the Royal Opera House. Consequently, the smaller, un-licensed theatres in Lincoln's Inn Fields and other places concentrated on plays with music and dancing. Actors performing in an unlicensed theatre were subject to arrest and confinement for vagrancy. In actual practice the law was enforced leniently, but it is likely that the Licens-ing Act cut off the greater imagination and vitality shown by entrepre-neurs such as Fielding. The most talented writers turned to the novel as the freest and most penetrating means to explore human nature and relationships.

Painting

The principal patrons of art were the Whig aristocracy, and they were convinced that great art was defined by the masterpieces of Re-naissance Italy. Their stately homes included galleries where their col-lections of Italian Renaissance paintings or ancient Greek sculptures could be displayed. The Grand Tour was an opportunity to study and buy such works and ship them home. Thousands of paintings and sculptures, many of them fakes, were imported from Italy to ornament the great country houses of the aristocracy. They were bought and sold by dealers at auction houses, and London became a great market for art.

With the decline of history painting, the portrait became the ma-jor form of painting. Jonathan Richardson, a painter of portraits and rival of Kneller in popularity, sought to elevate portraiture to the level of history painting. He argued that history painting displays the vir-tues of the great men of the past while portraiture does the same for the great men of the present. To reach the status of history painting, the portrait has to be more than an accurate likeness—the portrait must capture the character of the sitter. With the death of Kneller, Richardson became the premier English portrait painter. He painted a full-length portrait of Frederick, Prince of Wales and the portraits of a wide range of aristocrats, politicians, clergymen, and writers.

Richardson introduced a new informality to portraits by painting subjects in relaxed poses wearing informal dress. He also developed the "conversation piece," in which members of a family or some group of friends are seen engaged in some activity such as performing on instruments or playing cards. Richardson was an active writer on art in works that emphasize the moral qualities that art should promote. He introduced the public to critical principles that they should know as they entered the growing commercial art market. His principal work was <u>Two Discourses: I. An essay on the whole art of criticism as it relates to painting, and II. An argument in behalf of the science of a connoisseur</u> (1719).

Conversation pieces became a popular addition to the decoration of large houses, where they were hung among the family portraits. Arthur Davis, who was trained in topographical art, became the most popular painter of conversation pieces, producing more than 300 of them. Landscape painting, where the Dutch were recognized as the unquestioned masters, was popular to decorate the walls of the middle class, but was seen as a less prestigious genre than the conversation piece.

A distinctive landscape painter was Giovanni Antonio Canal, known as Canaletto. He discovered that views of Venice, his native city, sold briskly among English tourists and were a profitable way to make a living. Joseph Smith , a wealthy banker who was resident in Venice, married the beautiful singer, Catherine Tofts and became the English consul there. Smith assembled a great collection of early printed books (incunabula) as well as Renaissance paintings. He was an avid collector of Canalettos, and for several years he bought all of Canaletto's works. Smith commissioned Canaletto to paint the most important buildings of Palladio, whose architecture he greatly admired. In 1762 business reverses compelled Smith to sell his books to King George III for £10,000 and his pictures for another £10,000. Most of the books were donated to the British Museum and eventually became part of the

British library. The Canalettos and other paintings remain in the Royal Collection.

Since many of his customers were English, Canaletto moved to London in 1746 and remained there for ten years. His many paintings of London give a brilliant portrayal of London and the Thames in mid-century. He also painted country houses for aristocratic clients. Canaletto's paintings were replicated by engravers and widely distributed, and to this day are frequently used as illustrations in books about London.

William Hogarth

Hogarth's father was a London schoolmaster who wrote Latin and Greek textbooks that produced little return. For a time he operated a Latin-speaking coffee house. He died in poverty, and his son was deprived of an opportunity to receive a good education. Hogarth's ambition was to be a history painter, and for a time he attended an academy established by Sir John Thornhill. He also eloped with Thornhill's daughter. In the meantime, he had been apprenticed to a silversmith, where he learned engraving. In 1720 he set up his own shop as an engraver. He did routine printing jobs and more ambitious projects such as book illustrations. He went beyond routine engraving work with two satirical prints—The South Sea Bubble (1721) and Masquerades and Operas (1723) were criticisms of the materialism of society and were replete with caricatures of well-known figures.

Hogarth's connection with Thornhill enabled him to develop a successful practice as a painter of portraits and conversation pieces. He added a story-telling element to the conversation piece by including objects that indicate the occupation of the father and personal items of the rest of the family such as individual costumes, family recreations, and pets. He first came to public attention with a painting, The Beggar's Opera (1729), which depicts a dramatic moment in John Gay's popular play. Hogarth was intensely patriotic and resented the dominance of art in England by Italian and Dutch works. When Thornhill died he revived his father-in-law's academy on St. Martin's Lane to train English painters.

Unexpectedly, Hogarth achieved financial and popular success with engravings depicting the social life and problems of London. In so doing, he became the first English painter to achieve success in the commercial market and become independent of patronage. <u>A Harlot's Progress</u> (1732) was Hogarth's first great success. In six paintings, which he engraved and sold as prints, he tells the story of a simple girl from the north who comes to London, falls into prostitution, and meets a bad end. Hogarth's approach was not moralistic but rather realistic, pointing out the corrupting environment of a great city. Interest in the series is heightened by many characters, pertinent objects, discarded letters, and references to recent events. The progression of the episodes is literary—each episode could be the chapter of a novel or an act of a play. Imitations and send ups of the series flourished, much to Hogarth's dismay. He succeeded in passage of the Act for the Encouragement of the Arts of Designing, Engraving, Etching etc. (1735) which gave copyright protection to engravers.

Following up the success of <u>The Harlot's Progress</u>, Hogarth went on to <u>A Rake's Progress</u> (1735), a series of engravings that tell of a young man who inherits a fortune from his miser father but is destroyed by his own extravagance and the false standards of London society. Like its predecessor, <u>A Rake's Progress</u> gives a vivid picture of the low life of London, as the young heir is drawn into descending depths of depravity and eventually is consigned to Bedlam. His young wife takes up the life of a grand lady. When she is discovered by her angry husband in a love nest with the lawyer who negotiated their marriage, swords are drawn and the husband is killed. She dies in her father's house in London, in view of London Bridge. In <u>Marriage-a-la-Mode</u> (1745) Hogarth takes aim at marriages based on the vanities of rank and wealth instead of love and mutual support.

<u>Industry and Idleness</u>

On the surface, the series entitled <u>Industry and Idleness</u> (1747) appears to be a simple moral tale of two apprentices.

No 1. Tommy Idle has woven a small spool of cloth because he has wasted his time reading <u>Moll Flanders</u> while Frank Goodchild has woven a large spool.

No. 2. Frank Goodchild courts his master's daughter by sneaking into the family pew in church while the warden with her keys who is supposed to keep out intruders is distracted.

No. 3. Tommy Idle gets into trouble gambling in the churchyard.

No. 4. France Goodchild is made overseer of the factory.

No. 5. Tommy Idle is seized by the press gang and sent off to sea while his mother weeps.

No. 6. Frank Goodchild marries his master's daughter and on their wedding night they are roused out of bed to be serenaded by street musicians.

No. 7. While Frank Goodchild enjoys the wholesome bliss of marriage, Tommy Idle consorts with an ugly prostitute in a decrepit room.

No. 8. Frank Goodchild advances his political ambitions by serving as host of a banquet held in the Guild Hall for prominent citizens.

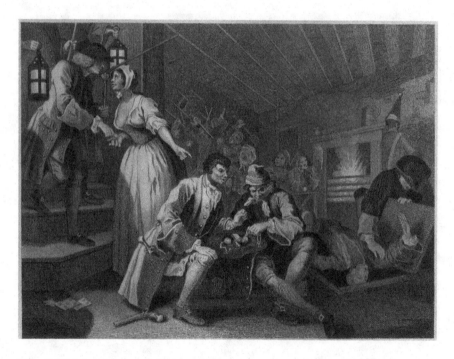

No. 9. When Tommy Idle brings some jewelry to a fence, the prostitute, who has informed the magistrate to get the reward points him out to an officer.

No. 10. Tommy Idle is brought before Frank Goodchild, now a magistrate, who shows his dismay as Tommy pleads for mercy.

No. 11. Tommy Idle is sent in a cart to Tyburn to be hanged while a clergyman offers him an opportunity to repent and save his soul.

No. 12. Frank Goodchild, Lord Mayor of London, is hailed by the people as he parades through the streets in the Lord Mayor's coach.

Hogarth built a second set of meanings into <u>Industry and Idle-</u><u>ness.</u>.Upon closer examination, it appears that Frank Goodchild is a shameless social climber who curries favor with his master, sneaks into his master's pew to court his daughter, and feasts the elite while the poor clamor at the doorway for justice. Tommy Idle is a victim of circumstances and a corrupt society. He falls in with evil companions in the churchyard because the packed doorway shows that there is no room in the church. Tommy is cast adrift by his master, who replaces the wholesome English system of apprenticeship with machines operated by cheap female labor. Tommy is a victim of the pressgang, which Hogarth realizes is an arbitrary and unjust means of manning the navy. Tommy consorts with an immoral woman because he has no opportunity to marry and settle down. Although he has been framed, he is convicted of a felony because Frank Goodchild, pretending dismay, looks away while he puts his right hand under the bar of justice to take a bribe. Tommy is hanged at Tyburn as a deterrent to crime, while pickpockets work the crowd.

Hogarth also turned his attention to public issues. <u>The March of the Guards to Finchley</u> (1750) satirizes the amateurishness of the local militia, which had been called out to fend off the uprising led by the Young Pretender in 1745. <u>O the Roast Beef of Old England: The Gate of Calais</u> (1748) shows his patriotic dislike for French culture. His <u>Beer Street</u> and <u>Gin Lane</u> (1751) were part of the campaign against gin-drinking. <u>Credulity, Superstition and Fanaticism</u> (1763) was an attack on Methodism and Catholicism, which offended Hogarth's easy-going religious views. <u>Four Prints of an Election</u> (1754-58) is a commentary on corruption in elections that was stimulated by the Oxfordshire election of 1754, which became a spending contest. Hogarth communicated the typical Londoner's point of view, which was critical of Whig courtiers, politicians, and rich men who abused their privileged positions for their own purposes. His good-natured print, <u>Midnight Modern Conversation</u> (1733) shows a rowdy drinking party. It was widely used throughout England and on the continent on drinking mugs and punchbowls.

Hogarth achieved fame and fortune through his engraved series, but he aspired to assume the role of Sir John Thornill as England's premier history painter. Some of his most important works in that genre were done for London philanthropic institutions. To demonstrate his ability as a history painter, he decorated free of charge the main staircase at St. Bartholemew's Hospital with The Pool at Bethesda and The Good Samaritan (1737). He persuaded prominent artists of the time to contribute pictures to the Foundling Hospital. He contributed his own Moses Brought before the Pharaoh's Daughter (1747) and a splendid portrait of Captain Coram (1740). He continued painting portraits, among them David Garrick as Richard III (1745) and a double portrait, Garrick and his Wife (1752). He also painted a portrait of himself, Hogarth Painting the Comic Muse (1758). His The Graham Children (1742), a conversation-piece about three happy children and an infant shows Hogarth in a joyous mood. Shrimp Girl (c. 1745) is a good-natured painting of a cheery working-class girl. In 1757 Hogarth's achievements were recognized when he was appointed sergeant-painter to King George II.

Hogarth was a feisty Londoner who refused to accept the secondary status assigned to English artists. He was passionately committed to the idea that English painters should develop their own native tradition instead of conceding primacy to long-dead foreigners. He was active in promoting exhibits of works by English artists in competition with exhibits sponsored by the Royal Academy of Arts. Hogarth's common touch and rejection of classicism made him an outsider in the world of the intellectual and cultural elite.

Francis Hayman, a contemporary and friend of Hogarth, also had a successful career as an artist. He was apprenticed to a decorative painter in London and gained his first employment as a painter of theatre sets at Drury Lane. He moved from there to painting portraits and conversation pieces for successful business and professional men. One of them was the proprietor of Vauxhall Gardens, who employed Hayman to decorate the supper boxes with pictures depicting scenes of family recreations and incidents from popular novels and plays. Hayman painted about fifty of these, which include Mayday, or, The Milkmaid's Garland and Sliding upon the Ice. Some of them were engraved and sold as prints. Hayman was active as a book illustrator and provided illustrations for Samuel Richardson's Pamela. He also painted an informal group portrait of Richardson and his family (1747). Influenced by Hogarth, Hayman donated The Finding of the Infant Moses in the

Bulrushes to the Foundling Hospital. His last major work was four history paintings for the rotunda at Vauxhall Gardens. Hayman was not a major artist; he was a workaday artist who demonstrated the opportunities available in the commercialized London market for art.

Music: Handel, Arne

The English have not been known as composers or performers of music, but eighteenth-century London had a great appetite for music and London continues to be a major musical center to this day. Prior to the eighteenth-century, music depended on the patronage of the Crown, the Church, or the aristocracy. In the eighteenth century music, like literature, theatre, and the arts, increasingly depended on a market economy. The demand for performances of professional quality led to a great influx of foreign-born musicians, who performed on the concert stage and in the opera, the theatre, the pleasure gardens, or the great houses of the aristocracy.

Italian opera seria (heroic or tragic opera) was firmly established in London by George Frideric Handel, Kappelmeister at the court of Hanover. Handel's musical talent became evident in Hamburg, one of the musical centers of north Germany. From 1706-10 Handel visited Italy, where he absorbed the style of Italian opera seria. He spent part of his time in Rome, where opera was not permitted, In Rome he wrote cantatas and oratorios. He adopted the dignified style of Corelli, who was the preeminent musical figure in Rome.

Handel first visited London in 1710 and was invited to compose an opera. He hastily patched together Rinaldo (1711), which was a great success. The renowned Italian castrato, Niccolini, sang the lead role, and lavish sets and stage machinery contributed to public acceptance. The next year Handel settled in London permanently. He composed and conducted more operas, and wrote a great Te Deum (1713) to celebrate the Peace of Utrecht, for which he received a pension from Queen Anne.

In 1714 the Elector George of Hanover turned up in England as King George I. Despite his irritation with Handel for leaving Hanover, he renewed Handel's pension and supported his work. George I loved opera seria, sung in Italian by Italian singers. He contributed £1000 per year to the Royal Academy of Music (1719-29), a joint-stock company organized by Handel to present operas that were performed in the large Haymarket theatre, commonly called the Royal or King's Theatre. Handel was appointed director, recruited singers from Italy, and composed operas for the company to perform

Italian opera was widely criticized as a foreign import and an empty spectacle. The recitative, in which ordinary communications are sung with a light accompaniment, was seen as ridiculous. The audience for Italian opera was small, and the Royal Academy of Music closed in 1729. Italian operas continued to be produced in London, but <u>pasticcios</u>, which used an English language libretto and Italian arias and choruses were more successful financially. Italian arias in English were published separately and used as songs, keyboard pieces, and instrumental solos. As such, Italian music lost its identification with opera and became part of popular music.

As the vogue for opera faded, Handel turned to oratorio. Oratorio resembles opera in that it has an overture, arias, small ensembles, recitatives, and choruses, but it is sung as a concert without acting. Handel's first oratorio, <u>Esther</u>, was a chamber oratorio that was performed privately in 1732 and sung by the singers of the Chapel Royal. Hiss first large-scale oratorio, <u>Saul</u> (1739), was highly operatic. Handel used a larger chorus than usual and called for an expanded orchestra, including a pair of deep-throated military kettledrums borrowed from the arsenal at the Tower of London. Handel followed with <u>Israel in Egypt</u> (1739). Handel's oratorios were dramas, not religious works that told a story in which the Israelites were confronted by neighboring people. Often the main story was accompanied by a romantic subplot. The public responded well to dramatic works that dealt with powerful leaders from the Old Testament..

In 1741 Handel accepted an invitation to go to Dublin and present an oratorio for Easter. The result was <u>The Messiah</u> (1741). When he presented it in London the next year, Handel was at first doubtful about its reception by the worldly London audience. The work is filled with deep religious feeling, and was rapturously received. <u>The Messiah</u> is a setting of Biblical texts, and as such gives a misleading impression of Handel's other oratorios. There is a myth that King George II stood up for the "Hallelujah Chorus" and the audience with him, establishing a tradition that has continued to the present. Actually, the precedent was established later by his son, Frederick, Prince of Wales.

After the success of The Messiah, Handel followed with Samson (1743), Judas Maccabeus (1747), Joshua (1748), and a militaristic oratorio about the conquest of Canaan with its dramatic chorus, "See the conquering hero comes." Solomon (1749) and Jeptha (1751) were Handel's last oratorios.

Handel's oratorios continued to be popular, even after baroque became passé. Judas Maccabeus was presented more then 40 times before the composer's death. In oratorio, Handel could appeal to the patriotic and Protestant sensibilities of his audience, whereas opera was foreign and associated with Catholic countries.

Handel began by using Italian singers, but soon he changed to English singers. His oratorios combined the solid melodies and harmonies of the Lutheran church music of Hamburg, the flair of Italian Opera, and the stateliness of French music, especially for dignified overtures and dances. He made the chorus the principal element in his oratorios. Handel was an energetic, confident man who understood power, and his oratorios communicated the sense of power that Englishmen were beginning to feel about their country. His choruses were highly variable in form and style, but always powerful and thrilling. Since plays were not performed during Lent, Handel could present oratorios on Biblical themes in theatres, which were vacant at that time. He was criticized by the Methodists for using sinful places for sacred music.

Throughout his life, Handel wrote ceremonial music for the court. Zadok, the Priest (1727), an anthem for the coronation of King George II, has been played at every coronation since. Other oft-played works are his touching music for the funeral of Queen Caroline (1737), the triumphant Te Deum (1743) for the victory of George II at the Battle of Dettingen, and Music for the Royal Fireworks (1749) to celebrate the Peace of Aix-la-Chapelle. A lighter piece was his ever-popular Water Music (1717) composed for a royal barge trip on the Thames. Among Handel's finest works of sacred music are the eleven Chandos Anthems (1717-18), which he composed for James Brydges, Duke of Chandos.

Handel was also important for the development of the concerto. His Twelve Grand Concertos (1739) exhibit great variations from the common concerto form as developed by Corelli and Vivaldi. Handel performed his concertos on the organ between the acts of his oratorios. His sonatas for violin or flute and other instruments accompanied by the harpsichord were easy enough for England's many amateur musicians to play.

Handel gave his audience a melody that his listeners could follow, a clear and steady rhythm, and a variety of forms, tempos, and emotions. Despite his German origins and sojourn in Italy, Handel was a fully assimilated Englishman. He was a flamboyant person and a great performer and showman as well as a shrewd businessman. He lost his eyesight in 1752, and the blind musician drew tears from his audience as he performed Samson from memory at the organ. When he died in 1759 Handel had £17,500 in the Bank of England—a small fortune in those days. In the cultural free market of London, Handel survived and prospered by his great energy and musical talent and by his ability to give the public what it wanted.

Although Handel had abandoned opera, Thomas Arne, a young English musician, attempted to present an opera in English. In 1723 Arne formed a group of young musicians who opened a season with Amelia, an English opera composed by Arne to a libretto written by Henry Carey, successor to Eccles as the main theatrical musician of his time. In the next fifteen months, the group performed seven newly-composed English operas. The English operas of Arne and others were not opera seria. They were plays with music. The music did not tell the story but intensified the story as it unfolded. The experiment failed because the middle-class was not interested in opera of any kind, and the small, upper-class audience for opera preferred the Italian style and singers.

In 1734 Arne's sister, Susannah, a splendid singer, married Theophilus Cibber, son of Colley, who succeeded his father as manager of Drury Lane theatre. Arne became the house composer at Drury Lane, where he wrote music for more than 80 staged works, including plays, pantomimes, masques, and other productions. Arne was one of the leaders of the London musical world in 1738, when he was invited to join with Pepusch, Handel, and others in forming the Royal Society of Musicians. He produced a patriotic hit with "God bless our noble king" (1745), which was sung daily in the theatres during "the '45" and became the national anthem.

Arne enjoyed success in the theatre with <u>Thomas and Sally</u> (1760) and <u>Love in a Village</u> (1762), for which he wrote the music. Eventually Arne succeeded in <u>opera seria</u> in English with <u>Artaxerxes: An English Opera</u> (1762), which was popular for the next fifty years. His oratorio, <u>Judith</u> (1761) was well received and frequently performed. In the 1750s Arne published many of his works. Among them were <u>Six Cantatas for Voice and Instruments</u> (1755), and <u>VII Sonatas for Two Violins with Thorough Bass</u> (1757). He composed harpsichord sonatas in baroque style. The best known are the harpsichord sonata No. 2 in e minor (1756) and the trio sonata No. 2 in G major (1757). Arne published separately many overtures and popular collections of his songs. Much of his voluminous production was published in imperfect editions or not at all.

Arne's orchestrations were rich and varied, and he was an innovator in his use of brass and woodwind instruments in the orchestra. His light-hearted melodies with simple harmonic accompaniments were typical of the transition from baroque to the style known as rococo or "galant."

Ch. 11. London

By mid-century, London had become the largest city in Europe and dominated English life and culture. London was not confined by its medieval walls and could spread along the Thames and into the countryside. The City of London, originally founded by the Romans, was a distinct political unit. Westminster to the west, the center of government and fashion, was not an incorporated town but part of the County of Middlesex, and was governed by the justices of the peace of that county. Parts of the urban area spread into the County of Surrey across the Thames. The name London, however, was applied generally to the City and Westminster collectively.

Eighteenth century culture was centered in London, where the wealth of a great metropolis and the interaction of talented people in all fields of activity stimulated creativity and provided opportunities for cultural achievements. Beneath the brilliant surface of London lay a mass of poverty, crime, and disorder with which the rudimentary institutions and best efforts of philanthropy could not cope.

The City

The nucleus of the City was London Bridge, which was built in the Middle Ages on the site of the former Roman bridge. In the course of time it became covered with houses and shops, which burned in the fire of 1666 but were rebuilt. By 1750 the bridge was so dilapidated that the houses were removed. At the center of the City were the Bank of England and the Royal Exchange, the twin bulwarks of London's financial and mercantile leadership. Chartered in 1694, the Bank of England was the core of the English financial system. It received deposits and made payments for the Crown, serviced the national debt, and issued banknotes that provided as a reliable medium of exchange. The Royal Exchange was a center for foreign and domestic merchants. It was built in the form of a quadrangle, with a portico around an inner court where merchants could meet and discuss business. Above the portico were specialty shops that sold goods from all over the world at retail.

The medieval walls were crumbling or had been torn down, although the gates remained as landmarks. One of them, Newgate, was converted into a prison. Dominating the scene was St. Paul's Cathedral. Its great dome, dignified west towers, impressive nave, and rich accoutrements proclaimed the wealth and dignity of London and the role of England as the leader of European Protestantism. Fleet Street ran parallel to the Thames from Ludgate (near St. Paul's) to the Strand. From there, the Strand flowed westward along the Thames to Charing Cross. Then as now, two churches, St. Mary le Strand and St. Clemens Danes, stood in the middle of the street with traffic passing on both sides. Formerly the Strand had been distinguished by the fine townhouses of the nobility, which were built between the street and the river. By the eighteenth century the Strand had become a major business and shopping street. North of the Strand was Covent Garden, built in the seventeenth-century as an elegant residential square. By the eighteenth century Covent Garden had become a vegetable market and a center of low-life entertainment.

Westminster

Charing Cross was an open place at the junction of the Strand and Whitehall, where the river turns southward. Charing Cross coffee houses and taverns were popular gathering places, and at night it collected a large population of roisterers, inebriates, and prostitutes. At Charing Cross one could turn south on Whitehall to the Banqueting Hall, the Horse Guards (offices of the army) and No. 10 Downing Street, home of the prime minister.

At the end of Whitehall stood Westminster Abbey, which was both a place of worship and a national shrine. The abbey church was an impressive Gothic structure, with two imposing towers on the west end that were added in the early eighteenth century. Westminster Abbey served as a place for coronations and other ceremonial events and as a burial place for distinguished persons. The king's judges held court in ancient Westminster Hall. The judges sat on a dais at one end, and both sides of the building were lined with booths where law reports and other legal materials were sold. Nearby was St. James's Palace, old and unimpressive, but still used as a convenient location for the king to meet with his ministers and for ceremonial occasions, such as the reception of foreign ambassadors and other social gatherings. St. James's Park was a lovely spot where "the quality" could gather to walk, take the air, and converse with their equals. Buckingham House, later Buckingham Palace, was purchase by George III as a residence for the queen and the children.

The Houses of Parliament were located along the Thames near Westminster Abbey. They would appear rather shabby to a modern visitor, bearing slight resemblance to the magnificent Victorian building one sees today. On ceremonial occasions the king would meet with the House of Lords, wearing his crown and robes and seated on the throne. The peers sat on one side with the archbishops and bishops on the other. In the center the lord chancellor and clerks sat on sacks of wool, emblematic of the importance of that product in the history and economy of England. The Members of the House of Commons stood at the back behind a wooden barrier.

The House of Commons was surprisingly small, with tiers of benches on either side of a center aisle and the speaker seated at one end. The ministers of the Crown sat on the front bench to the right of the speaker, with their supporters behind them. The leaders of the opposition sat on the opposite side with their supporters. On the higher benches and on the benches in back of the speaker's chair sat the "back-benchers"— members uncommitted to any political leader, many of them country gentlemen. In the gallery above sat visitors and sometimes newspaper reporters taking surreptitious notes, a practice prohibited by the rules of the House but not enforced.

The House of Commons did not provide seats for all its 558 Members, and it was a rare and exciting event when more than 400 were present and voting. On such occasions the principal speakers unleashed their best oratory, adorning their eloquence with classical quotations and flashes of wit. Their speeches were punctuated with shouts and laughter. Debates began in the late afternoon, and on a controversial topic might continue into the wee hours of the morning.

This part of London, known as the West End, was the fashionable part of town. Enterprising landlords like Lord Burlington built residential developments consisting of attractive streets and squares with up-scale homes and shops for an affluent population. The well-to-do inhabitants of the West End were attended by a host of domestic servants and hangers-on. The streets collected a large population of shop-keepers, apprentices, shop-girls, casual laborers, peddlers, adventurers, loose women, pickpockets, criminals and "rabble". Foreign visitors to the West End were amazed by the enormous variety of people and activities, the contrast between great wealth and abject poverty, the elegant shops filled with costly goods, and the conviviality of the coffee houses.

Vauxhall Gardens, originally called Spring Gardens, on the south bank of the Thames, was a place of public entertainment open to anyone who could pay the 1 s. entrance fee. It was reached by boat until the opening of Westminster Bridge in 1750 made it easy to reach by carriage or on foot. Jonathan Tyers, a bold entrepreneur, leased the property in 1728and rebuilt the facilities and replanted the gardens which had become rundown. Tyers held a grand opening in 1732 that was attended by Frederick, Prince of Wales. Soon Spring Gardens/Vauxhall became a popular place for evening entertainment. It opened in May as stayed open as long as pleasant weather continued.

In the center was a rotunda with a stage for musical performances. Later a saloon (tavern) was added where customers who did not have boxes would be protected from inclement weather. The gardens consisted of tree-lined walks with attractive pavilions built in a variety of architectural styles that provided places to sit, walk, converse, or meet people, some of them ladies of the night. At the end of some of the walks Tyers placed large paintings that gave the illusion of the ruins of Palmyra or a miller's house and water mill. In the main part, facing the stage, were tiers of boxes where people could see and be seen, converse, listen to the music, and enjoy refreshments. Tyers had cultural interests, and he called on prominent painters, among them Hogarth, to create works to add to his own collection or ornament the rotunda. The scene painter, Francis Hayman, was taken from Drury Lane and was employed to decorate the boxes with happy scenes of popular recreations. Among the musicians who performed there were Handel and the young Wolfgang Amadeus Mozart. Thomas Arne wrote songs for Vauxhall that were collected and published. As the gardens grew in popularity, Tyers installed an organ and a famous statue of Handel by Roubilia. In the evening Vauxhall was lighted by hundreds of lanterns. Its shadowed recesses offered discreet meeting places for private conversations, meetings of lovers, or those seeking professional ladies of pleasure. Foreign visitors were astonished at the brilliance of the place and the social democracy that flourished there. One foreign visitor noted that there was no rowdiness and the people conducted themselves with great decorum.

A more dignified place for entertainment was Ranelagh, a large, domed building open to the public, where gentlemen and ladies could meet, listen to music, and enjoy food and conversation. Ranelagh attracted people of wealth with an established position in society.

Fairs offered entertainment for humbler persons, and were often criticized for rowdiness or for encouraging the poor to spend money they could not afford. The 1740s were unusually cold, and "ice fairs" were held on the frozen Thames. Professional boxing matches drew large crowds. Dog-fights and cock-fights were also popular, as was bear-baiting. Gambling seemed to be a national passion.

Across the river from the Houses of Parliament was Lambeth with Lambeth Palace, residence off the Archbishop of Canterbury when he was in London. The opening of Westminster Bridge led to population growth on that side of the river.

Defoe's Tour

In his Tour Thro' the Whole Island of Great Britain Defoe devoted a large section to the metropolis in which he had been born and bred and where he spent most of his long and productive life. He was struck by the remarkable growth of the metropolitan area in his lifetime, which he describes in considerable detail. London's urban sprawl lacks planning and direction, he says, but it is the product of individual freedom, respect for private property, and the entrepreneurial spirit—

characteristics that Defoe admires. Equally remarkable to Defoe is the qualitative improvement of London, as seen in fine stone buildings and well-laid out streets and squares. He is proud of London's public buildings, and in the characteristic manner of tour guides he calls attention to them—Wren's Monument, the Royal Exchange, the many new parish churches, and Wren's masterpiece, St. Paul's.

When he turns to Westminster ("the Court end of town") Defoe finds a striking contrast between the power of the English government and the shabbiness of the buildings that house it. St. James's Palace, he complains, despite the elegant furnishings within, gives a poor impression of the English monarchy to the visitor. Defoe's national pride is offended by the ancient buildings in which Parliament and the public offices were housed. Westminster Hall, he comments, despite the veneration owed to its antiquity, "looks like a barn at a distance." When Defoe wrote his <u>Tour</u>, Westminster Abbey was in the process of restoration, which included adding the twin towers that give distinction to its west end. Other sights in Westminster that Defoe brings to the attention of the visitor are Westminster School, the Cock-Pit (a small auditorium), the Horse Guards building, and the Admiralty. Defoe gives special attention to the hospitals and other charitable institutions of London. He praises the civic spirit and humanitarian feeling that counter-balance the naked quest for power, wealth, and distinction characteristic of a great metropolis.

Social Problems of London

The growth of the metropolis brought with it social problems unprecedented in scope and character. London was a net consumer of people—deaths exceeded births, but still the population grew, fed by immigrants from the towns and villages of rural England. People flocked to London because London promised employment and excitement. A few found that talent, determination, and luck could pay off handsomely; most entered the maw of the monster and disappeared from view. The great houses of the aristocracy, the substantial homes of the middle class, and the many shops created an inexhaustible demand for domestic servants and shop assistants. Thousands of apprentices labored for their masters learning a trade with little likelihood of rising above modest day wages. Eighteenth-century London was like a glittering pagan god, giving generous rewards to some but consuming many of its votaries.

One problem was a mass of poverty, as the metropolis drew to it great numbers of people who had poor prospects in their native towns and villages and who found their hopes of employment in the great city disappointed. The struggle of the urban underclass for survival was compounded by squalor, disease, gin, and their unreadiness for urban living. The established attitude toward poverty was embodied in the Elizabethan Poor Law, which assumed a comparatively stable rural society in which each parish was responsible for its poor, either by providing employment for those who could work or by caring for those who could not. Urban parishes, swamped by the rootless poor, were unwilling or unable to assume such responsibilities. Cruelty and corruption characterized many of the parish overseers of the workhouses in which the destitute, orphans and the elderly were deposited.

That poverty was part of a deeper malaise was demonstrated by the epidemic of gin drinking that swept the London lower class from 1720 to 1751. Gin was first brought to England from Holland in the later seventeenth century, and the distilling of grain spirits (whether flavored with juniper or not) was a growing industry in England after 1720. At first Parliament encouraged the industry, for it was thought that distilled spirits would provide a new market for home-grown grain. Legislation was passed that removed most controls from the distilling and retailing of gin. The drinking of cheap gin spread like a plague.

By the 1730s the authorities of London and Westminster recognized that gin was ravaging the urban poor. The evils of gin were so appalling that the Gin Act (1736) increased the tax on distilled spirits and imposed a high license fee on the retailers of gin. Riots broke out and the London population made the Act unenforceable. The sale of gin continued, reaching a peak of eight million gallons in 1743. Since almost all gin was sold illegally, the business was even more disorderly than before. Urgent pressure by the London authorities and dramatic appeals to humanitarian feeling, including Hogarth's Gin Lane, persuaded Parliament to pass the Gin Act of 1751, which brought the curse of gin under some control.

Those who found in London an unsatisfying present and an uncertain future were easily diverted into crime or vice. Lack of street lighting and inadequate law enforcement permitted a large criminal class to flourish, undeterred by savage but sporadic punishment. The random crime found in small towns and villages was quite different from the crime of the metropolis, which for many was a way of life. The City of London maintained some degree of law enforcement through its long-established system of magistrates and constables. Crime flourished most in the urban sprawl of Westminster and the out-parishes, which did not have municipal institutions and depended on the justices of the peace of the county of Middlesex—the infamous "trading justices"—who obtained appointment through patronage or corruption and used their power for personal gain.

A new standard of law enforcement was set in 1749 when Henry Fielding, already famous as a playwright, novelist, and journalist, became a magistrate in the Bow Street criminal court. As a magistrate, Fielding went after the attorneys, constables, clerks and turnkeys who fleeced people accused of crime. He refused to take the usual cut from the fines imposed in his court. With his blind brother, Sir John Fielding, he established the "Bow Street Runners"—the first professional police force. They responded to the hue and cry when a crime was committed, and pursued the criminal to make an arrest. Later, Sir John established a horse patrol for the roads leading into London, which were infested with highwaymen.

In 1751 the government recognized the extent of the evil and proposed legislation to deal with crime in the metropolis. Fielding aroused public support for the measure with his An Enquiry into the Causes of the Late Increase of Robbers (1751) in which he attributes crime to the spread of luxury and vice to the lower classes. His solution was to destroy the attractions that led to crime. The Disorderly Houses Act (1752) adopted his views by requiring licenses for places of music or entertainment. Such legislation could not eliminate the economic and social bases of crime, but with vigorous enforcement it could reduce the number of professional criminals. Fielding's A Proposal for Making an Effective Provision for the Poor (1753) was an attempt to protect the poor from the abuses and exploitation of parish overseers by encouraging parishes to join together to establish well-managed poorhouses.

Newgate Prison was notorious, for persons accused of the most serious crimes were held there. Most of the cost of imprisonment was born by the prisoners themselves or their families. The jailers operated the prisons as private businesses, and could make the prisoner comfortable or miserable according to his ability to pay. Even if acquitted, the prisoner could not leave until the jailer's fees were paid. Debtors were imprisoned until their debt and the jailor's fees were paid. Some debtors remained in prison for the rest of their lives, even if the original debt was small.

Philanthropy

The ruling class of England sought to mitigate the problems of a growing metropolis through philanthropy. Religious piety and humanitarian feeling combined to develop sensitivity to human suffering and a desire to do something about it. The major philanthropy of the time was the establishment of hospitals to provide medical care for the indigent. Thomas Guy, a bachelor bookseller, accumulated a fortune by selling Bibles under contract with the two universities, which had a monopoly of printing them. He also profited by speculating in South Sea stock and getting out in time. He gave money to build and endow the hospital that still bears his name.

James Oglethorpe, an army officer and Member of the House of Commons, concerned himself with the plight of debtors in prison when a friend, who had been imprisoned for debt died of smallpox contracted in the prison. Oglethorpe investigated and was appalled by the squalor he found. He headed a parliamentary committee to investigate prisons in England. He formed a group of trustees who received a charter from the Crown to establish a colony in Georgia where debtors could make a fresh start in life. The colony was founded in 1732, and Oglethorpe spent ten years governing the colony with a firm military hand. His geometrical street plan for Savannah continues to this day. A variety of complaints arose, but the crucial question was the establishment of slavery in the colony, which Oglethorpe opposed. After Oglethorpe left in 1742 slavery was established in Georgia.

Thomas Coram, a retired sea-captain and merchant, dedicated himself to projects to alleviate the social problems of London. He became a trustee (1732) of James Oglethorpe's colony of Georgia, and founded a colony in Nova Scotia for unemployed craftsmen. Perhaps the most touching problem of the age was the vast number of orphans and abandoned children who were consigned to parish workhouses, where the death rate was close to 100 percent. Coram was a kindly bachelor who was appalled by the carnage. In 1739 he won the support of a group of influential aristocrats and ladies, and the Foundling Hospital was established to care for orphans and prepare them for employment. In 1741 the first children were admitted. Destitute mothers competed to get their small children admitted, which in most cases took place in their first year. As was customary among the London upper class, the children were sent to wet nurses in the country, which was healthier. The boys were trained to go to sea, and the girls to work as domestic servants.

The number of children cared for by the Foundling Hospital was small in proportion to the need, but it set a standard that was adopted elsewhere. Eventually, Parliament required parish authorities to apply the same standards of care as the Foundling Hospital to children in parish workhouses.

The First Modern Metropolis

By mid-century the great metropolitan agglomeration known as London was coming to terms with itself. London was beginning to deal with mushrooming population, urban sprawl, poverty, vice, crime, and misery. A Parliament dominated by the landed aristocracy and gentry began putting the force of law behind the efforts of local authorities, magistrates, corporate bodies, and philanthropic organizations. The towns of antiquity and medieval Europe had been small, compact, homogeneous and tightly governed. Eighteenth-century London was open-ended, without walls or natural limits, sprawling, varied, and unstructured.

London was the center of English culture in the eighteenth century, as it is today. People of rank, wealth, and leisure gathered in London for intellectual and cultural stimulation and persons of talent followed them, for it was in London that careers were made. Provincial towns emulated London with theatres and assembly rooms, but they could not challenge the primacy of the metropolis. The high culture of eighteenth-century England was concentrated in London, where writers, actors, artists, and musicians exercised their energy and talents in a market economy.

London exhibited the characteristics of modern metropolitan centers—extremes of wealth and poverty, magnificence and squalor; congestion, disease, crime, creativity, opportunity, and restless energy. "Why, Sir," declared Samuel Johnson, "you will find no man, at all intellectual, who is willing to leave London. No, Sir, when a man is tired of London he is tired of life; for there is in London all that life can afford."

Ch. 12. English Culture at Mid-Century

By mid-century a new dynamism had appeared in English life. The Seven Years War on the continent (1756-63) merged with a parallel struggle between Britain and France for colonies, in which Britain gained the upper hand. A small island country was transformed into a great imperial power.

Despite the war, English culture continued in its established paths. After the pioneering works of Defoe, Richardson, and Fielding, the novel flourished with a cluster of writers of both genders. The theatre received new inspiration from David Garrick. Samuel Johnson finally achieved the success for which he had struggled so long.

The Seven Years War (1756-63)

The Seven Years War (known in American History as the French and Indian War) began as a conflict between Britain and France for control of the interior of North America. In 1754 the colony of Virginia sent a young man named George Washington with 400 militiamen to destroy a fort that the French were building at the Forks of the Ohio River (modern Pittsburgh). Washington was attacked by the French and forced to withdraw. The Duke of Newcastle, prime minister, was determined to maintain British territorial claims in America, and the next year he sent Gen. Edward Braddock with a force of redcoats supported by colonials to drive out the French. Braddock was ambushed in the forest, dying bravely with many of his men, fighting an invisible foe that would not exchange volleys in the open like a European army. At the time, it appeared to be just another skirmish on the fringes of the empire.

In 1756 a "Diplomatic Revolution" took place when Maria Theresa of Austria allied with France, bringing an end to her long-standing alliance with Britain. George II was concerned to protect Hanover and maintain a continental ally. Despite previous tensions, Britain made an alliance with Frederick II, King of Prussia, In 1756 a major European war broke out when Spain attacked Minorca, Britain's principal Mediterranean naval base, and Frederick II of Prussia, facing an alliance of Austria, France, and Russia, got the jump on his enemies by attacking Saxony. War broke out in central Europe as Frederick fought with his back to the wall. George II established a British/Hanoverian army to guard the Hanover against attacks by France. In 1757 the Duke of Newcastle, the prime minister, made a political alliance with the fiery William Pitt, who directed the war as secretary of state. Pitt attacked the French empire in North America and the West Indies while protecting Hanover and providing financial support for the campaigns of Frederick II in Germany. Newcastle, as first lord of the treasury, raised the huge loans needed to meet the demands of Pitt's ambitious plans. Buoyed by British gold, Frederick II was able to hold his own. The British/Hanoverian army in the Rhineland drove the French back.

Pitt's main objective was to drive the French out of North America. In 1758 he sent one army to attack the French at the Forks of the Ohio, another to attack northward from Albany toward Quebec; and an amphibious force was sent to attack the French fortress of Louisbourg on Cape Breton Island, key to the St. Lawrence valley. Under a brilliant young leader, Gen. James Wolfe, the redcoats established a beachhead near the fort and attacked by land while British warships pounded the fort from the sea. When Louisbourg fell, the way to Quebec, the heart of French Canada, was open, but it was too late in the season to advance farther. In Britain the news of victories in distant lands aroused great enthusiasm and Parliament voted unprecedented sums for the campaigns of 1759.

Pitt responded with the greatest victory of all—the capture of Quebec. Having gained experience in the difficult art of combined operations, the army and navy reassembled at Louisbourg in the spring,

1759. The navy sailed its troop-laden vessels boldly up the St. Lawrence, piloted by James Cook, later the famous explorer.

The city and fortress of Quebec were located atop a craggy cliff overlooking the river. The French commander, the Marquis de Montcalm, had fortified the only likely landing spot, which was downstream from the city. His second in command, Louis Antoine de Bougainville (later an explorer), commanded a second force upstream. Wolfe landed his men across the river and attempted to bring Montcalm out of his fortifications by bombarding the city with naval artillery and siege guns. When Montcalm refused to budge Wolfe attempted a direct assault but his soldiers were repulsed.

Wolfe decided it was necessary to attack the city between Montcalm downstream and Bougainville upstream. He found a steep, rocky path up the cliffs to the Plains of Abraham, just outside the walls of the city. During the night his infantry overpowered the guards and silently scrambled up the slope; sailors came behind them dragging cannon from the ships. When dawn broke Montcalm was informed that the British were arrayed for battle outside the gates of the fortress. Impulsively he left his fortifications, hastily organized his men, and attacked the redcoats, who stood firmly in their ranks, firing the withering volleys that won Canada. When the smoke cleared Wolfe and Montcalm lay dying on the battlefield.

But the troubles of the victors were not yet over. The French rallied and the British troops were trapped in the fortress, where they held out under great hardships. In 1760 the conquest of Canada was completed with the taking of Montreal and the besieged garrison at Quebec was relieved. Britain was the master of North America from the Atlantic coast to the Mississippi.

The British navy swept the French navy from the seas, and the French colonies in Africa and the West Indies fell like ripe plums into British hands. When the Spanish belatedly entered the maritime war in support of France, they suffered the same fate. By 1761 Austria and France were exhausted, and the Empress of Russia, Frederick's mortal enemy died, and was succeeded by an admirer of Frederick. Fuelled by British gold, Frederick was able to turn the tables on his enemies. Newcastle grumbled about the enormous debt that had accrued, but

Pitt was the great national hero and imperial expansion had made Britain the dominant power of Europe and the colonial world.

The Accession of King George III

Suddenly Pitt's plans were disrupted by a political change at home. On October 25, 1760 King George II drank his morning cup of chocolate and fell over dead. George, Prince of Wales was now King George III, and his tutor and friend, the Earl of Bute, was the dominant figure at court. The first step for Parliament was to pass the Civil List Act, which provided the financial support for the king, queen, royal family, the royal household, the officers of the civil government, diplomats, palaces and parks, pensions, and a mysterious category called "secret service." The second was to find a wife for the young king. The year 1760 was not a vintage year for princesses in Germany, but the decision was made to marry the Princess Charlotte of Mecklenburg-Strelitz, a small principality in north Germany. Charlotte was plain and ordinary, but so was George, and the marriage was a success. The royal couple had fifteen children.

George III had been raised to exercise personally the constitutional powers of the monarchy. It was said that his mother admonished him with the words "George, be a king." He was influenced by "the patriot king" ideas of Lord Bolingbroke and his father, Frederick, Prince of Wales. The young king was determined to make "morality and virtue" the characteristics of his government. He viewed Newcastle as the embodiment of political partisanship and corruption, and he resented Pitt's personal popularity and overbearing ways.

With the accession of George III many considerations led toward peace. The King and Bute were convinced that England had gained all she could handle and should prepare to come to a settlement with her foes. Lord Bath (formerly William Pulteney) issued a pamphlet entitled Seasonable Hints from an Honest Man (1761) which declared that a new reign with a young king would bring changes that would end political partisanship and strengthen the personal role of the monarch. Another court writer, Israel Mauduit, heralded the move for peace with a pamphlet entititled, Considerations on the German War (1761), which expressed a widespread sense of weariness with the war and its heavy costs.

While Pitt insisted that nothing but total victory would secure Britain's gains, Newcastle inclined to peace, partially for financial reasons but also because war inflated the importance of Pitt. When the Cabinet showed its desire for peace, Pitt resigned angrily, declaring: "I will be responsible for nothing that I do not direct." The court contingent in the Cabinet was strengthened when Bute took office as secretary of state. Newcastle's main concern was to continue to support Frederick II of Prussia financially so that Britain would have a strong continental ally after the war. When the king and the Cabinet refused to finance Frederick II any longer, Newcastle resigned and Bute became prime minister. The new king and his mentor were now in charge, and a splendid embassy was sent to Paris to negotiate peace.

The Peace of Paris (1763) gave Britain great colonial gains, including Canada and the interior of North America to the Mississippi River. Britain got Florida and West Florida (the Gulf coast to the Mississippi River) from Spain. Under the assertive leadership of Robert Clive, the East India Company gained the great province of Bengal and became the dominant power in India. Francis Hayman drew crowds to Vauxhall Gardens with decorative paintings of The Surrender of Montreal to General Amherst, The Triumph of Britannia, Lord Clive Receiving the Homage of the Nawab, and Britannia Distributing Laurel to the Victorious Generals.

George III and Bute anticipated popularity for making a peace with such splendid acquisitions, but the expectations of the people were even higher and public opposition was aroused. Bute was disliked as a court favorite, a Scotsman, and the supposed lover of the king's mother. The City of London, center of Pitt's popularity and imperial ambitions, opposed the new ministry and the peace. A rabble-rouser named John Wilkes, supported by politicians connected with Pitt, published a hard-hitting periodical, The North Briton that criticized Bute (and by implication, the king) for extending the power of the Crown and threatening the rights and liberties of Englishmen.

Hogarth, who had received a pension from George III, came to the support of the government with John Bull's House Sett in Flames (1761), a cartoon that shows Europe ablaze, Pitt fanning the flames, London aldermen worshipping Pitt, the Duke of Newcastle stoking the fire with opposition newspapers, Frederick II (like Nero) playing the fiddle while Europe is reduced to ashes, and Bute valiantly trying to put out the fire. Other cartoonists attacked Bute (often represented by a boot), and the king's mother as Bute's paramour. Hogarth's defense of Bute made him an object of scurrilous attacks.

When the peace was approved, Bute announced that he had accomplished his purpose and resigned. His aloof and retiring personality did not fit into the turmoil of politics, and he welcomed a more private life. He worked with the king in developing Kew Gardens, a splendid arboretum west of London. Reluctantly the young George III accepted the resignation of his tutor and friend. George III had dropped the pilot and was now on his own.

The Writer and the Bookseller/Publisher

By the middle of the century, Robert Dodsley had replaced the Tonson firm as England's principal publisher of literary works. Dodsley, a lively, likeable young man, began life as a humble footman in several aristocratic houses. He fancied himself a poet, and his mistress, swayed by his charm, recruited 200 of her prominent friends, including Sir Robert Walpole, to subscribe to a collection of his poems. The book was published as A Muse in Livery, or, The Footman's Miscellany (1732), and was described on the title page as "By R. Dodsley, now a Footman to a Person of Quality at Whitehall." Dodsley caught the attention of Alexander Pope, who assisted him in 1735 to open a bookshop and arranged for him to have a share in the publication of the Works of Alexander Pope. Dodsley continued to publish works by Pope, and became acquainted with Pope's circle of friends. In 1738 he published London, a poem by Samuel Johnson, who had recently arrived in London. He became Johnson's principal publisher.

By the 1740s Dodsley was publishing important literary works, among them Edward Young's Night Thoughts, Gray's Elegy Written in a Country Churchyard, and Samuel Johnson's The Vanity of Human Wishes and Rasselas. He diversified his list with works on philosophy, religion, travel, and science, including William Cheselden's The Anatomy of the Human Body. In 1758 he introduced The Annual Register, an annual volume edited by Edmund Burke, an Irishman who had come to London to pursue a career as a writer. The Annual Register summarized the main events of the year (foreign and domestic), and included important state papers, a chronicle of unusual events, lists of marriages and births, books published, plays performed, and brief essays on a variety of topics. It was bound and indexed to occupy a gentleman's bookshelves as a permanent record. In collaboration with five other booksellers, Dodsley supported and published Samuel Johnson's <u>Dictionary of the English Language</u> (1755).

Dodsley also published large, important anthologies, especially Thomas Percy's <u>Reliques of Ancient English Poetry: Consisting of Old Heroic Ballads, Songs, and other Pieces of our Earlier Poets</u> (3 vols., 1765), which appealed to the growing interest in the English past and the development of the English language. Percy industriously collected ballads from a wide variety of sources and edited and revised them to suit contemporary tastes. The work was praised as a revelation of the "natural" foundations of English poetry, as opposed to artificial poetry based on classical authors. Dodsley had some personal success as a playwright, and his shop became a gathering place for London's literary figures.

Booksellers and professional writers found that well-written histories were highly marketable. Tobias Smollett, already famous as a novelist, capitalized on the patriotic feelings unleashed by the Seven Years War in his highly successful <u>Complete History of England</u> (1758) and <u>Continuation of the Complete History</u> (1760-65). Smollett's history was a fast-paced, highly readable work that presented a Tory view of English history. In 1776, as the War of American Independence was breaking out, John Wesley published a <u>History of England</u> that "put God back into history." He displayed his patriotism by supporting the policies of King George III.

The Novel at Mid-Century

By mid-century the novel had displaced poetry as the dominant form of literary expression, a position it would hold until the Romantic Movement brought poetry back to the forefront. In mid-century, the pattern of the novel established by Fielding was continued by Tobias Smollett, a Scot, who received a good Scottish education and was apprenticed to a surgeon. When war broke out with Spain in 1739, Smollett went to sea as a surgeon on an English warship and participated in the disastrous attempt to capture Cartagana (1741). In his novel, <u>Rod-</u>

erick Random, he describes life on an English warship and gives a harrowing picture of surgery as then practiced. He settled in London and supported himself as a surgeon while pursuing a career as a writer.

Smollett's novels exploit the diversity of people that constituted English society. He had his first success with The Adventures of Roderick Random (1748), a rambling tale of a young man who retains his high spirits despite the bizarre disasters and grotesque individuals that he encounters in a life filled with adventures. Roderick comes from a wealthy family that has fallen on evil days. He has to earn a living, so he becomes an apprentice to a surgeon. In that role he performs so well he goes to London to seek an appointment as a ship's surgeon in the navy. He is seized by the pressgang and put on a man-of-war, where he serves as a ship's surgeon at the bloody battle of Cartagena (1741). When Roderick returns to England he meets Narcissa, a young woman of marriageable age to whom he is attracted. She lets him know that she shares his love. Various new adventures, each vividly described, keep the couple apart until they arrive at the inevitable happy ending.

Smollett exhibits the genius of a born storyteller, as he relates in colorful detail one remarkable incident after another. He delights in depicting the coarseness, brutality, and ugliness of his time. He includes an interesting description of the Scottish game of golf ("goff"). He states his purpose as a novelist is to incite "that generous indignation, which ought to animate the reader against the sordidness and vicious disposition of the world."

A visit to Paris stimulated Smollett's next novel, The Adventures of Peregrine Pickle (1751) about, a stubborn and rebellious young gentleman whose passions and impulsiveness lead him into a series of incidents that trouble his parents. He is sent to Winchester School, where he meets Emilia, a pretty girl who is visiting in the town. He leaves school to be near her. He is called home and sent to Oxford to continue his studies. Emilia joins him there. To get him away from her, Peregrine is sent to France on the Grand Tour. Smollett uses Peregrine's visit to Paris to satirize the French. Returning to London, Peregrine becomes a reckless young man about town, involved with a great variety of people of low repute who are part of the corrupt life of the city. He meets Emilia again and tries to rape her. His affairs go from bad to worse, and eventually he is confined for debt in the Fleet Prison. He is freed when his father dies and leaves him his estate. Smollett's Toryism is evident as he laments the decline of traditional values in an age devoted to power and wealth.

By 1756 Smollett had become one of the most distinguished literary figures in London. He abandoned novels to edit The Critical Review (1756-63), a formative influence on the development of literary criticism. With a subsidy from the treasury, he published a weekly political journal entitled The Briton (1762-63) that supported the young King George III and the ministry of a fellow Scot, the Earl of Bute. The journal was savaged by John Wilkes in The North Briton, which capitalized on the public detestation of Scots in general and Lord Bute in particular.

Smollett's most polished novel, The Expedition of Humphrey Clinker (1771), published in the year of his death, is a comic depiction of England, Scotland, and Wales in the form of an epistolary novel. Sir Matthew Bramble, a Welsh landowner, is afflicted with gout, and goes to Bath for relief. He is accompanied by his middle-aged sister, who still has hopes of marriage, his manservant, his sister's maidservant, and their orphaned nephew and niece. The members of the party have comical experiences at Bath, but the squire is disgusted with Bath and disappointed by the failure of the waters to help his gout. They set off for London, where they have more comical experiences, after which they travel to Scotland. Eventually the hopes with which they set out are satisfactorily resolved, and the squire happily returns to his estate in Wales.

Humph Clinker is presented in the form of letters written by the travelers, who tell of their adventures and report on what they have seen and heard. Their observations confirm Smollett's humanitarian strictures against the luxury and pretentiousness of the wealthy and the widespread poverty, wretchedness, and injustice found in town and country alike. The material about Scotland is intended to inform English readers about the land and people to the north and dispel widespread anti-Scottish prejudices. Smollett's wide-ranging imagination, vivid detail, unrelenting honesty, fierce concern for justice, and comic sense exerted an important influence on Dickens.

Lawrence Sterne's novel, The Life and Opinions of Tristram Shandy, Gentleman (9 vols., 1759-67) is a remarkable example of imagination and mastery of the medium. Sterne was an Anglican clergyman who lived a quiet village life in his parish. When volumes I and II of Tristram Shandy were published in 1759, the novel was an immediate success due to its comical characters and unusual structure. Several printings were needed to meet the demand. Fans of Tristram Shandy waited impatiently for the next two volumes, which appeared in 1760. The flow of volumes was interrupted by a trip to France, but after that they came out steadily until Vol. XI was published in 1767, a year before Sterne's death. The novel is like a serial that never actually ends.

Tristram Shandy sets out to tell the story of his life, beginning with his conception, which is interrupted when his mother asks his father if he had remembered to wind the clocks, an irregularity that Tristram blames for the problems of his life. Tristram also attributes many of his problems to the fact that the attending doctor at his birth flattened his nose with a forceps. He suffered another disfigurement as a three-year old boy when he was urinating through an open window, which fell and injured an important and sensitive part of his anatomy.

While waiting for Tristram to be born, Tristram's father engages in a long conversation with his brother, Uncle Toby, about the nature and idiosyncrasies of women and the observable fact that everything in the world has two handles. Uncle Toby, who had been wounded at the siege of Namur in 1695, analyzes the battle and tells tedious anecdotes about it. Uncle Toby has built an elaborate layout of the fortifications and military emplacements at Namur where he can relive the events of that memorable day. And so the novel proceeds from one colorful incident or conversation or digression to another as long as Sterne lived to continue writing it.

Sterne was impressed by the unexpected ways in which ideas are associated in the mind, and he built his novel on that principle. Episodes come and go with no apparent relationship to each other. Memory and the present are inextricably mingled. Tristram Shandy has no beginning or end; to the extent that it has a plot it is soon forgotten.

Sterne defies the conventional concept of a well-constructed novel to wander wherever his fancy takes him. The story is interrupted by so many explanations and digressions that Tristram is not born until vol. IV, and in the later volumes he disappears from sight. The novel is a complex assemblage of episodes and conversations, seemingly casually linked and getting no place, but skillfully permitting its many characters to reveal their thoughts and idiosyncrasies in bits and pieces. Tristram Shandy is a learned book, filled with references to the major writers of the previous century. It includes disquisitions on such arcane subjects as obstetrics and fortifications. Some of the attraction of the novel is its colorful and racy language. Sterne was rebuked by some clergymen and critics for his bawdy humor, which did not fit comfortably with his responsibilities as a minister of the Gospel.

Sterne's last novel, A Sentimental Journey through France and Italy (1768) was an example of the trend toward "sentimentality"—awareness of one's own feelings and the feelings of others. Parson Yorick tells of his travels, which are based on trips taken by Sterne in his later years. The parson is more interested in the feeling of the people he meets than the details of great cities or striking landscapes. The book is comprised of a series of episodes, many of them romantic encounters. This good-natured, self-indulgent book was Sterne's swan song, and was published a month before his death in 1768.

The vogue for sentimentality is seen in the novels of Henry Mackenzie, a prominent Edinburgh lawyer who also dabbled in literature. In his novels, "sentiment" means a capacity to imagine the feeling of others when confronted with calamity. Mackenzie's novel, The Man of Feeling (1771), relates the experiences of a good man who discovers the evils of the world and sympathizes with other people's problems.

Very little is told about the main character, Harley, a country gentleman of modest means whose memoirs are found by the fictional editor on scraps of paper. Harley lives an isolated life, and is a simple, good-hearted gentleman unacquainted with the world. He goes to London to obtain a loan to buy some Crown lands. Instead, the lease he wants to buy goes to a revenue officer who prostitutes his sister to get it. While he is in London, Harley hears a series of lurid tales of misfortune, corruption, and betrayal. Since he is naïve, he is easily taken advantage of. These episodes are, to some extent, a catalog of the typical disasters found in the popular novels of the day. Indirectly, Mackenzie condemns the authors of such novels for exploiting the reader's capacity for sympathy while failing to point out the importance of benevolence to help those who suffer.

Mackenzie also wrote a reverse novel, The Man of the World

(1773), which exhibit the evils wrought by a heartless man who seeks satisfaction of his personal desires without concern for other people or moral principles. Modern critics regard Julia de Roubigné (1777), an epistolary novel about love gone wrong, as his best novel.

Women Writers

Charlotte Lennox was born in Albany, New York, where her father was an army officer. After his death, Charlotte traveled to England to take up a post as companion to a wealthy widow, which proved to be a disappointment to the spirited teenager. She had no resources of her own, and at the age of sixteen she impulsively married Alexander Lennox, improvident member of the Scottish aristocracy. She failed as an actress and had to write to help support the family. Her first novel, The Life of Harriot Stuart (1750), was a success. Samuel Johnson reviewed it favorably and threw a big party to celebrate her triumph. Johnson continued to be her friend and wrote a variety of prefaces, dedications etc. for her publications. She also enjoyed the friendship of Samuel Richardson, Henry Fielding, and David Garrick. Her play, Old City Manners (1775) ran for seven nights.

Lennox's most successful novel, The Female Quixote, Or, The Adventures of Arabella (1752) concerns a young woman whose life is guided by romantic novels. Arabella makes bad choices in love, but the disastrous outcomes of her conduct eventually bring her to her senses. The work had lasting appeal, was reprinted several times, and was translated into French, German, and Spanish. A later novel, Henrietta (1757) was critically praised but did not sell well, and after that Lennox turned to translations. She also established an essay journal, The Lady's Museum.

Frances Sheridan was the wife of Thomas, who was an actor and theatre manager in Dublin, and a teacher of elocution. She was the mother of Richard Brinsley Sheridan, playwright and politician. Out of sheer necessity, she became an important novelist. Her married life was plagued by poverty and insecurity, and, like many women writers, she wrote to keep the wolf from the door. Encouraged by Samuel Richardson, she wrote The Memoirs of Miss Sidney Biddulph (1761), a novel inspired by Richardson's Clarissa Harlowe. Sidney Biddulph is a naïve young woman who is abused by her husband and confronted with difficult moral and economic choices that lead eventually to disgrace, poverty, and isolation. The novel has a cynical streak and rejects the notion that virtue will eventually be rewarded. The Memoirs of Miss Sidney Biddulph was a commercial success and was translated into French. It became popular among European devotees of Richardson. A sequel, Continuation of the Memoirs of Miss Sidney Biddulph was published in 1767.

As one of a theatrical family, Frances Sheridan also wrote for the theatre. Her most successful play was The Discovery (1763), which ran for seventeen nights in the first season and was frequently revived. The play centers on the efforts of a mercenary father to marry off his children for his own gain. A secondary plot deals with a dysfunctional family who are guests in a household. It is a "sentimental comedy" in that there are many powerful scenes dealing with moral issues, but in the context of family bitterness characteristic of Sheridan's work. The Dupe (1764), another play dealing with family intrigue and betrayal, was not a success on the stage but enjoyed good sales when published. An uncompleted play, A Journey to Bath, provided material for The Rivals by her son, Richard Brinsley,, including the prototype of Mrs. Malaprop.

Oliver Goldsmith

One of the most versatile writers of mid-century was Oliver Goldsmith, another of the talented Irishmen who made literary careers in London. Goldsmith, the son of an Anglo-Irish clergyman, was educated at Trinity College, Dublin, where he came in contact with the theatre and other cultural activities of that flourishing city. He studied medicine at the University of Edinburgh, and enjoyed the cultural activities of another regional capital. After additional medical studies at Leyden, he vagabonded through France, Switzerland, Germany, and Italy. Goldsmith was an impulsive, feckless individual, who had to struggle against poverty and other problems, many of his own making. He never developed the manners and polish of a gentleman, but his lively conversation and graceful writing won him the friendship of the prominent writers of the day, including Samuel Johnson.

In 1756 Goldsmith opened a medical practice in Southwark, an impoverished part of London on the south bank of the river. He had plenty of patients but they could not afford to pay the fees. At heart, Goldsmith was a writer, and like many of the best writers of the eighteenth century, he honed his skills writing for magazines and newspapers, including Smollett's Critical Review. His first book was An Enquiry into the Present State of Polite Learning in Europe (1759), which displayed a wide knowledge of thought and letters but was not a critical or commercial success. In The Citizen of the World (1762), based on letters published originally in the Public Ledger, a financial newspaper, Goldsmith adopts the persona of a disingenuous Chinese traveler who writes letters to his friends expressing his bewilderment at London life and customs.

Goldsmith could be described as a Grub Street hack, grinding out pages to earn a living, except that he was a man of enormous talent and understanding of people. He was a quick compiler of information on a great variety of subjects, which he packaged as attractive books. In his role as a professional writer, he wrote a successful History of England (6 vols., 1764, 1771), a history of Rome (2 vols.,1769), a history of Greece (2 vols., 1774), and An History of the Earth and Animated Nature (8 vol., 1774).

Goldsmith achieved literary success as a novelist. When he faced imprisonment for debt, his friend Samuel Johnson found the manuscript of a novel, The Vicar of Wakefield (1766) in his lodgings. Johnson took it to a publisher and was paid £60 for it. The novel was enormously popular. The vicar, Dr. Primrose, is a good-hearted scholar lacking a realistic grasp of worldly affairs. The life of his family is an idyllic vision of the virtues of rural life. The family has many adversities, most of which are the result of the deceitfulness of others and their own gullibility. Nevertheless, they remain mutually supportive until the wheel of fortune turns in their favor.

The Vicar of Wakefield is a classic example of the sentimental novel. It drew tears from the distresses of a virtuous family, whose misfortunes were suddenly reversed by a happy ending. By that time Goldsmith was recognized as an important writer and was a member of the famous Literary Club founded by Sir Joshua Reynolds, the painter, and dominated by Samuel Johnson.

In the meantime, Goldsmith was also writing for the theatre. His play, The Good Natur'd Man (1768) was a success at Covent Garden and made him temporarily solvent. She Stoops to Conquer, or the Mistakes of a Night (1773) was an instant hit and one of the most frequently performed eighteenth-century comedies. The handsome hero, Charles Marlow, has a problem—he is bashful when speaking to genteel women but a lecherous rogue with attractive servants. He is sent by his parents to visit a potential bride whom he has never met. Accompanied by a friend, he arrives at the house of his intended bride, but mistakenly the young gentlemen think it is an inn. Consequently, Marlow orders his prospective father-in-law around as if he were the proprietor and his future bride as if she were a barmaid. Shrewdly, the intended bride disguises herself as a servant (she stoops to conquer) to win the heart of her intended husband and cure him of his affliction.

Goldsmith's lasting fame rests upon his poem, The Deserted Village (1770)—a tribute to the simple joys of village life and a touching depiction of the ravages of commercialized agriculture. "Ill fares the land, to hastening ills a prey,/Where wealth accumulates, and men decay;/Princes and lords may flourish, or may fade;/A breath can make them, as a breath has made./But a bold peasantry, their country's pride,/When once destroyed, can never be supplied."

George Crabbe responded to Goldsmith's idealized vision of country life. He was typical of the many ambitious writers who could not make a living in the London literary world and needed some other source of financial support. After trying a variety of occupations and applying to various politicians for assistance, he found a patron who helped him find a career in the Church. Crabbe served several rural parishes, where he saw an England quite different from the idealized visions of poets, ancient and modern. In his long poem, The Village (1783), he finds instead "a bold, artful, surly savage race."

"Where Plenty smiles," he continues, "alas, she smiles for few,/And those who taste not, yet behold her store,/Are as the slaves that dig the golden ore./The wealth around them makes them doubly poor."

The Age of Garrick

By mid-century, the theatre had settled into the role established by Colley Cibber at Covent Garden—a venue for middle-class entertainment. The most successful playwright of mid-century was Isaac Bickerstaff, an Irish ex-Marine, who was a successful writer of librettos for musical shows. His first success was Thomas and Sally (1760), a ballad opera with melodious songs by Thomas Arne. The simple plot tells the story of a village girl who resists seduction by an evil squire until rescued by the return of her sailor boyfriend. This popular ballad opera was followed by a more ambitious work, Love in a Village (1762), which included 41 songs, including five by Arne. Most of the songs were adaptation of songs from French or Italian comic operas, an innovation that supplanted the English songs of the Beggar's Opera . The show ranked with The Beggar's Opera as one of the most popular of its kind in the eighteenth century.

Bickerstaff followed these successes with The Maid of the Mill (1765), a comic opera with romantic themes based on Richardson's Pamela. The Romp (1769), was an urban companion piece to Love in a Village. Most successful of all was The Padlock (1768), produced by Garrick at Drury Lane. The plot was conventional—young man rescues his sweetheart from an old man who keeps her under lock and key intending to marry her. The show features a West Indian servant played by a comedian in blackface who sings in West Indian dialect "Dear Heart, What a Terrible Life am I Led." The song was a huge hit and the play with it.

Bickerstaff's career had an unfortunate end. He was an active homosexual at a time when sodomy was a felony. His sexual orientation was revealed and he fled to the continent. While incognito, he wrote The Spoil'd Child (1775), a play that was popular in England and the colonies. The date and circumstances of his death are unknown.

Although comedies and ballad operas continued to be popular, a shake-up was needed to bring to the theatre a more challenging repertoire and better acting. The theatre gained renewed vitality from David Garrick, who in 1737 had accompanied his teacher, Samuel Johnson, to London in search of a career. Although Johnson had a long struggle to achieve success, the lively and talented Garrick soon made a name for himself as the most creative and versatile actor of his time. In 1740 he played the lead in a production of Fielding's The Mock Doctor, which took place at the offices of The Gentleman's Magazine, where Johnson was employed.

Garrick first came to public attention in 1741 at Goodman's Fields, a small, unlicensed theatre in the unfashionable East End of London.

His performance of the title role in Shakespeare's Richard III (Cibber's version) stunned audiences with its power and individuality. His characterization of King Lear brought the audience to tears. One of his most popular characters was as Lothario in Nicholas Rowe's, The Fair Penitent. He was equally talented in comedy. Huge audiences packed the small, virtually unknown theatre. At a time when acting consisted of dignified declamation, Garrick depicted his characters in a way that seemed "natural," although today we probably would regard his style as melodramatic. After viewing Garrick's performances, one of the leading actors of the day commented, "We are all wrong, if this is right."

In 1742 Garrick had a triumphant season in Dublin. When he returned to London later in the year, he was a star at Drury Lane. He thrilled audiences in Shakespeare and also in comedy, notably Farquhar's The Beaux' Stratagem. One of Garrick's favorite roles was as Sir John Brute in Vanbrugh's The Provok'd Wife. His lightweight farce, Miss in her Teens (1747), was a hit that ran for 42 performances. Hogarth painted a dramatic portrait of Garrick as Richard III that was widely circulated as an engraved print.

In 1747 Garrick bought a half share in Drury Lane theatre, where he became the manager as well as the leading actor. He introduced into acting a degree of discipline, technique, and polish that previously was unknown. His insistence on high standards of professionalism and thorough rehearsals generated quarrels with actors. He also attempted to educate the audience to give thoughtful attention to the play instead of the coming and going and general disorder that prevailed in theatres. Riots among the patrons of Drury Lane caused difficulties that led Garrick to travel abroad for a time.

Part of Garrick's effort to dignify the theatre with serious drama was his revival of Shakespeare's plays. His King Lear was considered his finest role. As Lear, he imitated the madness he had seen in a friend who had become insane when he accidentally killed his daughter. In 1775 Garrick brought out his revised and simplified version of Hamlet, which made Hamlet a better role for an actor at the expense of authenticity. During his career, Garrick played Lear 85 times, Hamlet 90 times, Richard III 88 times, and Benedick in Much Ado about Nothing 113 times. His Catherine and Petruchio (1756), a rewriting of Shakespeare's Taming of the Shrew, was so popular it replaced Shakespeare's play in theatres. He presented Samuel Johnson's ponderous tragedy, Irene, and maintained it for nine nights despite declining audiences so Johnson would have three benefit nights.

In 1769 Garrick organized a Shakespeare Jubilee at Stratford-upon-Avon to celebrate the two-hundredth anniversary of the Bard's birth. Despite constant rain, which discouraged attendance and destroyed sets, the Jubilee drew people from all over England and the continent. Garrick was a likeable, gregarious man and a superb showman, who made himself a well-known public figure. He was a welcome guest at the great country houses of the aristocracy and a member of the Literary Club of authors and journalists that gathered around Samuel Johnson.

Garrick's success as an actor and theatre manager owed much to a cluster of great actresses. Margaret ("Peg") Woffington, a charming Irish actress, met Garrick in Dublin in 1742. Her performance later that year as Cordelia in Garrick's production of King Lear established a close romantic and professional relationship. Nevertheless, she pursued her career independently and performed important roles at both Covent Garden and Drury Lane. Her strengths were comedy and "breeches roles" that showed off her trim figure. In 1740 she appeared in a breeches role at Covent Garden in Farquhar's, The Recruiting Officer.

Kitty Clive, another Irish actress, began her career under Colley Cibber as a singer and dancer. In 1732 she starred as Polly in The Beggar's Opera. Her career settled down when Garrick became manager of Drury Lane, where she played a variety of comic roles. When she retired, she established her main residence at Twickenham and became a friend and neighbor of Horace Walpole.

Susannah Cibber was the sister of Thomas Arne. Her career began as a singer in opera and oratorio. After she married Theophilus Cibber, son of Colley, she turned to acting, where she adopted the new "natural" style of Garrick. In 1744 she joined Garrick's company at Drury Lane. Garrick and Cibber performed beautifully together; she received the highest salary (apart from Garrick) of the company. At Drury Lane, Cibber played the top female roles, including Polly in The Beggar's Opera and Cordelia in King Lear. One of their most popular performances was playing opposite each other in Rowe's The Fair Penitent.

Samuel Johnson

In the meantime, Samuel Johnson was establishing a reputation as a thoughtful writer. He had long pondered the need for a comprehensive, reliable dictionary of the English language, and in 1747 he published a prospectus entitled The Plan of the English Dictionary, which he dedicated to the Earl of Chesterfield, whom he hoped would be the patron of the project. Chesterfield turned him down, but five booksellers, led by Dodsley, agreed to fund the project and share the copyright. In France and Italy dictionaries had been compiled by learned academies using the labor of many scholars over long periods of time. Johnson undertook the task single-handed, with the assistance of a few copyists. His dictionary was built on historical principles. He went through important works of English writing, noting words and their context, which were copied on slips of paper. From these slips he prepared definitions based on usage. Johnson's Dictionary gives not only the definition or definitions of each word, but includes the citations upon which the definition is based, thus providing a history of the English language and a stockpile of apt quotations. He took his citations from works that met his approval, and in this way he helped define the masterpieces of English literature. He would not take citations from the works of irreligious writers, such as Bolingbroke or Hume. The work took nine years to complete and required a capital investment by the booksellers of almost £5,000. It was a profitable investment that produced good returns for many years, but it could not have been undertaken if a large commercial market for works of literary and cultural merit had not existed..

Johnson's Dictionary was an outstanding example of those who turned to the distinctive roots of English culture for an alternative to the rationalism and universalism of the Enlightenment. Johnson loved language and appreciated its richness and variety. He took the English language as he found it, without attempting rigid systematization, and brought order into the language while preserving its character and complexity. Johnson carried out an extensive revision in the edition of 1773.

In addition to his Dictionary, Johnson maintained his literary productivity. In The Vanity of Human Wishes (1749) he explores one of his favorite themes—the disappointments that are part of human existence. He includes the lives of those who attempt to live by the pen: "There mark what ills the scholar's life assail,/Toil, envy, want, the garret, and the gaol." Some of Johnson's best writing appears in his essay journal, the Rambler (1750-52), in which he deals with moral questions as they relate to everyday life. Johnson roots his ethics in an honest assessment of human experience, avoiding undue optimism or fatalism. He relies upon the common sense of his readers to recognize the ways in which his ideas may apply to them. He gives special attention to the illusions by which people give a false meaning and purpose to their lives, while conceding with good-natured indulgence that these self-deceptions are often necessary to make life tolerable. He also contributed more than 100 essays of a lighter sort to a weekly, the Universal Chronicle (1758-60), which were published under the name "the Idler." The Rambler and The Idler mark the effective end of the essay journal in England, as a new readership and new forms of expression in print replaced it.

One of Johnson's most attractive works is his short novel, Rasselas, The Prince of Abyssinia (1759), which tells of three young people who search for a philosophy by which they can guide their lives. Rasselas is an African prince who lives with his brothers and sisters in the Happy Valley, a place with all the requirements of a good life. Nevertheless, Rasselas is restless and wants to see how other people live. In the palace, Rasselas meets Imlac, a poet, who has traveled widely and seen much of the world. Imlac agrees to leave the Happy Valley with Rasselas. Nekayah, sister of Rasselas, and her maid, Pekuah go with them. Guided by Imlac, they go to Egypt, where the glories and corruptions of a complex and ancient culture are laid before them. There they meet people of all kinds and degrees, and have a variety of experiences. They find that most people do not choose their way of life, they stumble into it. They find no one who is happy; everyone thinks that others are more fortunate than they are. They found one happy man, a philosopher, who stated that he was happy because he used Reason to control the normal passions of life. When they go back to see him the next day, he is in despair. His daughter has died during the night, and his Reason is useless in dealing with such a personal catastrophe.

They learn that much of the brilliance and gaiety of Cairo is false and empty. Rural life, idealized by poets, proves a disappointment too.

Efforts to live by the laws of Nature prove fruitless, since there is no agreement on what they are. They discover that marriage and family life are often far from happy, but the single life is worse. Youth is restless, middle-age burdened, and old age a matter of holding on.

Despite these dismal findings, the young people maintain the resilience of youth and do not despair. They learn the importance of trade-offs—if you want to enjoy one thing you cannot have another. They learn that they will not be disappointed if their expectations of life are modest. They eventually choose careers that seem reasonably satisfying and settle for them. Pekuah decides that she wishes to live in a convent; Nekaya decides to found a school where she can continue her quest for knowledge. Rasselas decides he wishes to rule a small kingdom. Imlac decides to wander through life because no career is satisfying anyway. They look forward to returning, someday, to the Happy Valley. They gain (as does the thoughtful reader) wisdom that usually takes a lifetime to acquire.

By 1760 Johnson had become recognized as a major literary figure. In 1762 he achieved financial security when a pension of £300 per year was settled on him by King George III.

Ch. 13. The Culture of Knowledge in Georgian England

Eighteenth-century England was notable for the organization and advancement of knowledge in subjects that were seen as interesting and useful. The professions set standards for practioners of specific bodies of knowledge. The Royal Society served as a clearing house for new knowledge and occasionally sponsored projects that it thought important. The great theoretical works that are the foundation of modern science had appeared in the later seventeenth century. Eighteenth-century knowledge was generated by and for gentlemen, who adopted the principle of Sir Francis Bacon—"knowledge is power,—and applied it to investigation of practical matters that concerned them. One of the most striking examples of the increase of knowledge was the exploration of the Pacific Ocean. The development of cartography made the growing knowledge of the world available to the gentlemen and ladies of England.

The Professions

One of the distinctive features of the modern world is the role and importance of organized professions, a development that made important strides in eighteenth-century England. A profession is identified by advanced education and is regulated by its members. The professions originated in the medieval universities, which offered preparation for careers in theology, the law (civil and canon), and medicine. In the eighteenth century the clergy of the Church of England were the largest profession, with approximately 10,000 beneficed clergymen, most of whom were university graduates.

The eighteenth century was not a notable age in the history of the universities, for the curriculum was stereotyped in the mould of the past, teaching was indifferent, and standards for degrees were low. Yet the university faculties contained many fine scholars and produced distinguished graduates. The aristocracy and gentry sent their sons to the university for a year or two of genteel learning, usually without an interest in receiving a degree. All too often the young man's time was spent more in amusement than study. A major benefit of attendance at a university was establishment of contacts with other young men of the same social class. The universities offered scholarships for poor boys, and in this way they provided opportunities for able and ambitious young men to pursue careers in the Church, medicine, or public office.

Some prestigious secondary schools, such as Eton, Winchester, and Westminster gave a good classical education to the sons of gentlemen. Town grammar schools, many founded in the Tudor period, provided an education in the classics for local boys, some of whom went on to a university. A variety of private and village schools provided elementary education for those children whose parents had the desire and the modest means to send them. Dissenters' academies were noted for their practical education. Dissenters who wanted advanced education went to the Scottish universities or to the University of Leyden.

The Law

The legal profession possessed high prestige, for the eighteenth century was a legalistic age that placed great emphasis upon the rule of law. The lord chancellor was the highest judicial officer and also presided over the House of Lords. He was usually a member of the Cabinet, and the greatest lord chancellors were also active politicians. The court of chancery was a court of equity, giving decisions based on reason and fair play in cases where the Common Law did not cover the problem or would result in injustice. Lord Hardwicke, lord chancellor and confidante of the Duke of Newcastle, made his court responsive to the new needs of a commercial society. The court of chancery increasingly assumed jurisdiction over commercial transactions and developed the law of contract.

There were three courts of Common Law going back to the Middle Ages—king's bench, common pleas, and exchequer. Presumably they dealt respectively with crimes, civil suits, and the royal revenue, but in reality they overlapped, for each had invented ways to extend its reach into the jurisdiction of the others. The Common Law courts met in Westminster Hall for regular terms, and each summer the judges, followed by an entourage of barristers seeking clients, went on circuit to "the assizes" (county courts) where they heard and decided criminal and civil cases. The Common Law judges had security of tenure and could be removed only for cause.

The English universities did not teach the Common Law. Young men who wished to be barristers had to find their own sources of instruction, which was usually accomplished by reading legal textbooks, receiving private instruction from an established barrister, and visiting the courts to observe cases being tried. In the later Middle Ages, places for instruction in the law had grown up in the Inns of Court. By the eighteenth century the Inns had lost almost entirely the instructional role that they once filled and had become the location of barristers' offices or residences for young gentlemen enjoying the pleasures of the town. The principal function of the Inns of Court was admission to the bar, for only those accepted by the Inns could plead cases in the courts of Common Law. The law was a career that gave great rewards to talent and good connections, but a few distinguished barristers dominated the profession and the "briefless barrister" was a common figure in eighteenth-century society and literature.

In the meantime other workers in the law—the attorneys—were becoming organized as a profession. Attorneys could not plead cases in the courts, for which a barrister was required, but they prepared briefs for the barristers and performed many other legal services such as preparing marriage contracts and wills, handling transfers of property, and managing estates. In 1729 Parliament took an important step when legislation was passed that required a prospective attorney to spend five years as an articled clerk (apprentice) in a law office and be examined by a judge before being permitted to transact legal business. Shortly thereafter the attorneys of London organized themselves into a professional body known as the Law Society, and similar organizations developed later in major provincial towns. In comparison with barristers, who were recognized as gentlemen, the social status of attorneys was low. Nevertheless, by the second half of the century many attorneys had become successful and prosperous, and their status as professional persons was becoming accepted.

Medicine

The medical profession was regulated by the Royal College of Physicians, established by Henry VIII in 1523, which admitted only persons with medical degrees from Oxford, Cambridge, and Trinity College, Dublin. Medical instruction at the universities was poor and most physicians who took their profession seriously did additional study on the continent at such noted medical schools as Leyden, Padua, Montpelier, or Paris.

The eighteenth century was a period of dynamic change in medicine. The major developments took place through the application of scientific knowledge and clinical experience to medical practice. The Dutch physician, Hermann Boerhaave, had an enormous influence on English medicine through the students whom he trained at the University of Leyden. Boerhaave made the study of anatomy an important part of the medical curriculum. He supplemented the established method of lecture and disputation with teaching through clinical observation of patients. His The Institutes of Medicine (1705) was a widely used summary of medical knowledge. Boerhaave also was a distinguished chemist. His Elements of Chemistry (1732) was extensively used in the eighteenth century.

A pupil of Boerhaave, Sir John Pringle, an army physician, worked to improve the health and sanitation of soldiers. Pringle received his MD degree from the University of Leyden and became a professor at the University of Edinburgh. During the War of the Austrian Succession he was physician-general to the British army in the Netherlands, where the treatment of wounded soldiers was appalling. Pringle worked to improve sanitation in hospitals (military and civil) and thus reduce the transmission of infectious diseases. His most important publication was Observations on the Nature and Cure of Hospital and Jayl Fevers (1750). He was admitted to the Royal Society and became an active and highly-respected member. He was honored by the Society with its gold Copley Medal, an award comparable in prestige to the Nobel Prize today.

With medical advances came development of the medical profession. The members of the Royal College of Physicians were the elite. They possessed medical degrees and practiced in high social circles, where they commanded high fees. Given the cost and small number of physicians, most of the population had to get medical attention elsewhere, mainly from apothecaries (pharmacists), who were trained through apprenticeship. Apothecaries were shop keepers who sold medicines, filled prescriptions for physicians, and also sold nostrums to people who could not afford a physician's care. In 1703, after a struggle with the physicians, the apothecaries gained the legal right to attend patients and prescribe remedies. In 1738 Henry Pemberton, a physician who had studied with Boerhaave, was commissioned by the Royal College of Physicians to revise their book of prescriptions. In 1746 he published <u>Translation and Improvement of the London Dispensary</u>, a collection of prescriptions that was much used by apothecaries. Throughout the century the apothecaries made efforts to improve their training and status. They did not gain a professional organization until 1815, but long before that they were the chief providers of medical attention to the general public.

An important development in eighteenth-century medical practice was the rise in standing of the surgeons, who were previously linked with the barbers. In 1745 the surgeons broke away from the barbers and formed the separate Royal Company of Surgeons, which enabled them to set their own standards for admission and improve the level of training in the profession. William Cheselden, a surgeon famous for the speed and deftness of his operations, urged surgeons to study anatomy. His <u>Anatomy of the Human Body</u> (1713) went through many editions, partially because the text was in English instead of Latin. He was a prominent figure in London. He was active in founding the Company of Surgeons (1745) and one of the founders of the Foundling Hospital.

Surgery was not taught in the universities and most surgeons were trained through apprenticeship, often in the military services. Before the discovery of anesthesia and antiseptics, surgery was an ugly and bloody business. Lacking a university education, surgeons were not regarded as gentlemen. Tobias Smollett, the novelist, was a naval surgeon. In n his novel, <u>Roderick Random</u>, he gives a vivid description of surgery as practiced in his time.

In 1740 William Hunter, a Scot with a university education, and hence a gentleman, came to London to study surgery and anatomy. After additional study in Paris, where anatomy lectures included dissection of cadavers, Hunter began teaching anatomy in London. Hunter was an outstanding lecturer and anatomical demonstrator, and he soon attracted students from England, Europe, and North America.

Childbirth, usually assisted by a midwife, an older woman with hands-on experience, was dangerous for both the mother and the child. Hunter specialized in studies of the female reproductive organs. Concern for the problems of childbirth led to the establishment of the Lying-In Hospital in London in 1750, where wives of poor tradesman could give birth. Hunter was appointed manmidwife (obstetrician) in charge of delivering babies. A new facility was opened in 1773 that was built by a public subscription. Initially infant mortality was higher in the hospital than elsewhere, due to the presence of puerperal fever, a highly infections disease, but improved sanitation eventually made childbirth safer for both mother and child.

Hunter was a man of pleasing personality and social ambitions. He became a friend of many of the leading political and cultural figures of the day. His professional and social status was enhanced in 1761 when he was engaged to supervise the pregnancy of Queen Charlotte, and in subsequent years he served as manmidwife for all her pregnancies. His publications on anatomy led to membership in the Royal Society. Hunter's insistence that anatomical publications be illustrated accurately and in detail secured his appointment to the Royal Academy of Art.

William Smellie, a Scottish apothecary and pupil of Hunter, began assisting midwives who ran into complications they could not handle. He gave up his apothecary shop to specialize as a manmidwife. He established himself in London as a teacher of midwifery to male and female students. He attended poor women in their homes without charge, using them as subjects for clinical observations. His comprehensive three-volume work, <u>A Treatise of the Theory and Practice of</u>

Midwifery (1752, 1764) was accompanied by illustrations that were published as A Set of Anatomical Tables, with Explanations (1754). These became standard reference works for midwives for many years.

An important medical advance was inoculation for smallpox, a highly contagious disease (now eradicated) that often brought death, blindness, or disfigurement. Inoculation was brought to England by Lady Mary Wortley Montagu, who learned of it in Turkey when her husband was British ambassador at Constantinople. The procedure consisted of scratching the skin to introduce a mild form of the disease. Inoculation was widely accepted after 1722 when the noted physician, Sir Hans Sloane, inoculated the two royal princesses. Later in the century inoculation was improved by Edward Jenner, a rural medical practitioner who had studied for two years in London with Hunter. Jenner called his new approach vaccination. He noticed that milkmaids rarely got smallpox. He conjectured that they were immune because they picked up cowpox, a mild form of smallpox. He vaccinated patients with the dried fluid from cowpox pustules and had a high success rate. In 1798 Jenner published Inquiry into the Cause and Effect of the Variola Vaccinae and because famous throughout England and Europe.

Advances in medicine were accompanied by medical fads, such as the taking of mercury as a general nostrum for all sorts of ailments. One user of mercury was embarrassed when this heavy mineral slipped down his alimentary canal and on to the floor at a social event. This was also an age of famous "empiricks"—self-taught purveyors of medical services. Joshua Ward became famous for his "pill and drop," a violent medicine that included sulfuric acid and mercury among its components. Ward was a colorful figure in London. He was praised by some and criticized by others, among the Alexander Pope, as a shameless quack. He was patronized by King George II and other eminent persons, including Sir Robert Walpole and Lord Chesterfield. One of the most famous "empiricks" was Mrs. Mapp, the bone-setter, who had exceptional skill in setting dislocations and fractures.

The Inquiring Gentleman

One of the salient features of the age was its enormous appetite for knowledge, which reached the court itself. Queen Caroline was a patron of learning and was much praised for her grotto at Richmond

Park, with its sculptured busts honoring English scholars, among then Locke, Newton, and Francis Bacon. Queen Caroline's grotto was also good political propaganda, for it linked the Hanoverian dynasty with English dignitaries.

Despite symbolic actions such as Queen Caroline's grotto, the pursuit of knowledge owed little to the Hanoverian monarchy and even less to the Walpole government. The age of patronage was passing, and those institutions that had been so important in the past—the Crown, the Church, the universities—no longer played the principal role in the development of English culture. Many of the advances of the Georgian age resulted from the efforts of gentleman-scholars pursuing their special interests.

The Royal Society, comprised of aristocrats, gentlemen of leisure, barristers, physicians, clergymen, merchants, and other dedicated amateurs, was the center of scientific activity, holding meetings, reading papers, and publishing the results in the <u>Philosophical Transactions</u>. The Society was imitated on a smaller scale by local societies in provincial towns such as Birmingham and Nottingham. In London the spread of literacy and intellectual interests among shop-keepers and artisans was seen in the Society of Free and Candid Inquiry, commonly known as the Robin Hood Society, where interested persons gathered to express their views and gain experience in public speaking. For 6 d., which also included beer and lemonade, anyone could attend and speak for five minutes on the topic of the evening. The authorities were concerned that such gatherings might become centers of sedition, and the Church complained that the speakers discussed matters of religion.

One of the distinctive features of the Georgian age was a strong sense of the importance of the English past. The achievement of constitutional government, personal liberty, a prosperous society, and an important role in the European balance of power led Englishmen to seek in their ancestors the precedents and national traits that had led to their present felicity. The gentleman-scholars of the Society of Antiquaries of London, founded in 1707 and chartered ten years later, were intrigued by the remains of the Celtic and Roman past, especially such venerable structures as Stonehenge and Hadrian's Wall. The Buck brothers did engravings for them and in 1779 the Society began publishing a periodical, <u>Archaeologica</u>. Literature, painting, and architecture showed the influence of the revived interest in medieval and Tudor England. The Academy of Ancient Music was founded in 1710 to perform folk songs and early Church music. Johann Christophe Pepusch, one of the founders, was its director until his death in 1752.

William Kent designed "Gothic" villas and gardens ornamented with picturesque hermitages, grottos, thatched houses, and fake ruins covered with ivy. As roads improved and travel became a favorite recreation, visits to historic sites became fashionable and numerous guidebooks and itineraries were published. The Gentleman's Magazine, that touchstone of public taste, published articles by contributors on items of local historical interest. The magazine published many articles about the remarkable discoveries at Herculaneum and Pompeii.

Eighteenth-century science was not speculative, but in the tradition of Bacon and Locke it was empirical and devoted to practical solutions to everyday problems. One example of the practical nature of eighteenth-century science was the attention given to the study of weather. The weather is a likely subject for scientific study—it is one of the most conspicuous of natural phenomena; it is of great economic importance; and it daily affects the personal health and comfort of everyone. The study of weather suited the eighteenth-century propensity for collecting and recording empiric data, and in a country with weather as diverse and variable as in England it is not surprising that the subject attracted widespread interest. Weather was especially suitable for the amateur scientist, for it was an object of investigation that anyone could conveniently observe and record. Tne necessary equipment (thermometer, barometer, rain gauge, and weathercock) was not expensive.

In 1723 James Jurin, secretary of the Royal Society and compiler of statistics on London mortality, noted the influence of the weather on health. He invited members to make daily observations and submit annual reports of temperature, barometric pressure, wind direction and velocity, precipitation, appearance of the sky, and storms. Originally the thermometer was clumsy and inaccurate, but by mid-century the thermometer had been made convenient and reliable and any gentleman could afford to own one. In England the Fahrenheit scale was most commonly used, although each maker might have his own scale.

The study of electricity was another example of the kind of empirical science that could be done by gentlemen. The apparatus was simple and easily obtainable; a technical language had not yet been developed; and electricity displayed uniformities of behavior that confirmed the concept of a world of consistent natural laws. Electrical experiments first became feasible in the 1740s, when machines were developed to generate static electricity by whirling a glass globe or tube while it was being rubbed by the hand or a pad. The electrical charge was collected in a suspended gun barrel with a silk cord touching the rotating globe. In 1745 electrical experimentation was further advanced by the invention of the Leyden Jar, a corked glass container filled with water, which was attached by a wire to the gun barrel. A series of Leyden Jars linked together could give a powerful electrical discharge.

With this simple equipment, electricity became a popular subject for scientific study, and electrical demonstrations provided entertainment at social gatherings. People at a party would join hands, laughing and screaming with amazement when the gun barrel was touched and everyone jumped simultaneously. The King of Prussia made an even more dramatic display, performing the experiment with a regiment of guardsmen, all of whom rose as one when the electrical connection was made.

Benjamin Franklin, a Philadelphia printer, took electricity out of the realm of party games by demonstrating that lightning was an electrical discharge. Like many others, Franklin had long been interested in weather, tides, winds, and storms. He identified the Gulf Stream as a river of warm water in the chilly Atlantic. Franklin's stroke of genius was to link his interest in weather with the new ideas about electricity. Franklin offered a theory of precipitation based on the assumption that rainfall was caused by changes in the electrical charges of clouds. To demonstrate that clouds were electrified, Franklin made the famous experiment in which he flew a kite into a thunderstorm. The practical outlook of eighteenth-century science was seen when Franklin showed that the damage of lightning—long feared as the thunderbolt of Zeus—could be avoided by the simple device of a lightning rod fastened to the top of a house or barn or to the mast of a ship with a wire leading the electrical charge harmlessly to the ground or the sea. His Experiments and Observations (1751) was comprised of letters originally published in The Gentleman's Magazine. He complained that Cave did not pay him any "copy money."

Franklin's achievement was accepted almost immediately. It had the simplicity and universality that the eighteenth-century admired. Part of Franklin's success was his literary skill. His reports were presented in the form of letters to a friend; his style was warm, frank, and engaging as he revealed the procedures he had followed and the conclusions he had reached. When the Royal Society conferred its Copley Medal on Franklin in 1753 the chairman praised, not only his scientific work, but "the public spirit, the modesty, the goodness and benevolence" which Franklin displayed. Franklin was in every respect an eighteenth-century gentleman, and his scientific achievements were a vindication of the breed.

The Vision of the World

While England was rising to world power and gaining a great empire of trade, sea power, and colonies, the concept of the world was being changed by the restless desire of mankind to understand and utilize the great globe itself. Building on the achievements of previous generations, it was in the eighteenth-century that the modern vision of the world was established. Improvements in navigation made it possible to sail throughout the world, wherever oceans, seas, and rivers made water transportation feasible. Larger, faster, and stronger ships were built; instruments for navigation became more accurate; maps and charts were more reliable; and the winds and ocean currents were identified. Improvements in the health of seamen made it possible to remain at sea for long periods of time.

One notable advance was an improved method for finding longitude. Latitude could be determined fairly accurately by the altitude of the sun above the horizon at noon, but determination of longitude depended upon rough estimates of speed and direction made by the ship's captain. Spurred by a prize offered by the Crown, a London clock-maker built a clock (chronometer) strong and accurate enough to keep correct time on a moving ship for months. The navigator could determine noon at sea by observing the sun and comparing it with the time at Greenwich as shown by the chronometer. Since each degree of longitude equals four-minutes on the clock, he could determine his longitude east or west of Greenwich from the difference in time.

Although the outlines of the continents were clear enough by mid-eighteenth century, there were still great unknown areas of land. In 1725 Peter the Great of Russia sent Vitus Bering, a Danish explorer, across the trackless wastes of Siberia to the Pacific shore. Bering built a ship to explore the Pacific and sailed through the straits that bear his name. He did not realize that he had reached North America at the point where it approaches Asia. In 1741 Bering commanded an expedition that left from Siberia, crossed the northern Pacific, and reached the west coast of North America. Then disaster struck. Bering died; the ship hastily returned to Siberia; and the Russian government abandoned for a time its explorations in the North Pacific.

In the meantime the interior of North America was becoming better known. In the seventeenth century, French fur traders and missionaries had explored the Great Lakes and the Mississippi Valley, and later they crossed the Great Plains and penetrated into the Rockies. In the 1740s English traders and land speculators began exploring the Trans-Appalachian West. English acquisition of this area in 1763 encouraged exploration. Daniel Boone explored Kentucky in the 1760s and 1770s. Not until the expedition of Lewis and Clark, however, was a systematic effort made to explore North America from the Mississippi to the West Coast. As to South America, the Spanish kept their knowledge to themselves to keep European competitors out of their empire.

Marco Polo's fourteenth-century account of his travels in China made Europeans aware of the marvels of that great civilization, and in the sixteenth century Jesuit missionaries established a foothold there. The Chinese emperors, however, closed their country to European travelers and permitted a limited trade only at certain specified ports. The most reliable account of China was provided by a French Jesuit, Pierre Du Halde, who's <u>Description of the Empire of China</u>, including a magnificent series of maps, was translated and published by <u>The Gentleman's Magazine</u> in 1738. Little was known about Africa, since most European contacts were made by slave traders, who dealt only with coastal peoples.

The most important new area of exploration was the Pacific Ocean, which covers almost one-third of the area of the earth, a larger area than all the dry land put together. At the beginning of the eighteenth century the Pacific was virtually unknown. The voyages of Magellan and Drake were isolated instances of heroic effort, which confirmed the existence and size of that great ocean but revealed little else. The Spanish had learned to sail a galleon annually along a fixed degree of latitude from Acapulco to Manila, but beyond that they did little in the way of exploration and did their best to keep other nations out.

In the seventeenth century Abel Tasman, a Dutch explorer seeking the unknown continent, sailed from the Dutch East Indies to Mauritius and followed a course set at 44 degrees south latitude eastward. He discovered Tasmania and New Zealand and returned via the Fiji Islands and the north coast of New Guinea. He had sailed completely around Australia without seeing it.

The exploration of the Pacific was a result of the imperial rivalry of Britain and France. It was believed that the South Pacific must contain an undiscovered continent (Terra Australis Incognita) to balance the landmass of the northern hemisphere. This unknown continent might contain great civilizations, ripe for trade or conquest, and the discoverer might reap a bonanza similar to that of Cortez in Mexico or Pizarro in Peru. In 1642-1643

A spate of travel books appeared dealing with the prospects in the Pacific Ocean. The most influential were William Dampier's A Voyage Around the World (1697) and Voyages and Descriptions (1699), in which he tells of his voyages in the western Pacific and gives a valuable account of the trade winds. In 1699-1701 Dampier was sent by the admiralty to explore the coasts of Australia and New Guinea using Tasman's charts, but he was forced to return early due to the deteriorating condition of his ship.

In 1768 the admiralty sent Capt. James Cook on the first of his three voyages to explore the Pacific. For the first time that great body of water was explored and mapped with a degree of thoroughness and accuracy that opened it to the trade and navigation of the world. Cook was a great sea-captain—he was an expert navigator and map-maker; he was able to maintain the health and discipline of his crew for long periods at sea; and he was utterly determined to complete his missions.

Capt. Cook learned seamanship sailing the sturdy ships that transported coal along the stormy and dangerous east coast of England to

London. In 1755 he joined the royal navy and served as navigator at the capture of Louisbourg. He explored and mapped the St. Lawrence estuary and piloted the ships that captured Quebec in 1759. In 1767 the Royal Society planned an expedition to the South Pacific to observe the transit of Venus across the face of the sun, which would make it possible to calculate the distance of the earth from the sun. Cook was put in command of the expedition.

In his first voyage (1768-71) Cook sailed to Tahiti, where the transit of Venus was observed and recorded. After that, Cook charted the coasts of New Zealand and the eastern coast of Australia, which he claimed in the name of King George III and named New South Wales. In his second voyage (1772-75) he exploded the idea of a valuable southern continent by sweeping the seas as far south as possible to the coasts of Antarctica. In the winter he sailed northward into warmer climes, charting numerous Pacific islands. When he returned, he was elected to the Royal Society and received the Copley medal.

On his third voyage (1776-80) Cook explored the North Pacific. He sailed through the Bering Straits into the Arctic Ocean until stopped by ice, thus demolishing the long-held English dream of a Northwest Passage from the Atlantic to the Pacific. He also discovered the Hawaiian Islands, where he was killed in a scuffle with the natives.

Cook was more than a great sea captain. As an explorer and member of the Royal Society, he recorded the great variety of strange plants and animals that he encountered. He reported on the religious practices and social customs of the native populations and their reactions to the incursion of Englishmen into their tropical island culture. In the meantime the French were also interested in the Pacific. In 1767 a Frenchman, Louis Antoine de Bougainville, visited the islands of the southern Pacific. He established a French claim to Tahiti, and reported on the Polynesian peoples and their seemingly idyllic way of life.

Cartography

In early modern Europe three factors came together that changed the vision of the world—the explorations, mathematics and science, and printing. The culmination of these was the atlas. The explorations brought a mass of new information to be added to existing world maps, which were based on the maps of the Greek geographer/astronomer,

Ptolemy. Mathematics and science offered the idea of a geometrical grid to be imposed on the image of the world to make it measurable and usable. And printing made it possible to disseminate the new knowledge to a wider public.

Perhaps the most influential cartographer of the early modern period was a Fleming named Gerardus Mercator. He published a world map in 1569 that was made for navigators who wanted to plan a route that was a straight line. To accomplish this purpose, Mercator made the lines of longitude parallel rather than converging at the poles. The Mercator projection is accurate at the equator but distorts the continents by increasing the size of land in higher northern or southern latitudes. Mercator prepared an atlas of 170 maps that was published in 1595, the year after his death. The Mercator projection is still extensively used.

In the seventeenth century the Dutch were the leading mapmakers, producing magnificently decorated atlases that were used throughout Europe. In the eighteenth century leadership in cartography passed to the French. The most famous French mapmaker was Guillaume De L'Isle, who held the post of royal cartographer. De L'Isle's most important maps deal with the interior of North America, where the French were extending their trade and empire. Jean B. D'Anville prepared atlases and special maps as royal cartographer and an official of the French navy. These maps eschewed the colorful decorations of the earlier Dutch maps and were typically French in their classically pure lines and words. They were especially prepared for the naval and colonial conflict with Britain.

As in so many other aspects of their culture, the English drew upon the work of others but used it in their own way. Herman Moll, a German who settled in London c. 1675, found employment as an engraver working for map publishers. He opened his own shop in 1688 and began publishing maps and atlases. His reputation was established when he published A System of Geography (1701), geography of the world with maps, which was followed in 1708 by Fifty-Six New and Accurate Maps of Great Britain. Moll published Atlas Geographus, a periodical with maps of parts of the world that ran for six years (1711-1717). When the series was complete, the maps were published in five volumes that provided the reader with a comprehensive geography/atlas of the world. He also published pocket-sized atlases that were very popular. His <u>A View of the Coasts, Countries, and Islands within the Limits of the South-Sea-Company</u> with maps (1711) may have contributed to the hysteria that led to the Bubble. His most important atlas, <u>The World Described</u> (1715), was comprised of thirty large double-folio sheets with geographical commentaries. <u>A New and Exact Map of the Dominions of the King of Great Britain on the Continent of North America</u> was a ringing endorsement of imperial expansion in that area. Moll also provided maps for other publications, among them William Dampier's <u>A New Voyage Round the World</u> (1698) and Defoe's <u>Tour Thro' the Whole Island of Great Britain</u> (1724).

The atlases of the early eighteenth century were intended for the libraries of powerful, high-born, and wealthy men, and were magnificently printed, colored, ornamented, and bound. With the growth of publication and printing, inexpensive atlases became available. Maps were used to illustrate modestly priced books. <u>The Gentleman's Magazine</u> responded to the interests of its readers by including maps.

The War of the Austrian Succession and the Seven Years War aroused popular interest in the geography of central Europe. The imperial conflicts that continued through the Seven Years War brought new parts of the world to the attention of the English public. One of the most prolific English mapmakers was Thomas Jefferys, an engraver, who opened his shop in 1744. His first publication was <u>The Small English Atlas</u> (1748-49). In 1753 he published the survey of Virginia by Joshua Fry and Peter Jefferson, and in 1761 a map of New Hampshire. His work on North America was completed with <u>A General Topography of North America</u> (1768).

Jefferys also published important geographical books relating to the origins of the Seven Years war in America—<u>The Conduct of the French with Regard to Nova Scotia</u> (1754) and <u>The Journal of Major George Washington</u> (1755), which tells of Washington's expedition to the Forks of the Ohio in 1754. When Spain came to the support of France in the Seven Years War, Jefferys published <u>A Description of the Spanish Islands . . . of the West Indies</u> (1762), which were regarded as ripe for conquest. He also imported foreign maps to sell in his shop. As England became a major power with trade and an empire that were global in scope—her leaders and people had no choice but to widen their horizons accordingly. And their vision of the world began with a map.

Ch. 14. Revolution in the Empire and in the Mind

Twenty years after the great victories of the Seven Years War, England tasted defeat in the War of American Independence. In the Mother Country, radicalism challenged political privileges that went back to "the Glorious Revolution." Despite failure in America and fiscal breakdown at home, the English people rallied behind their established institutions, .and radical reform was postponed to another day.

At the same time the Enlightenment—a revolution of the mind—put established institutions and ideas to the test of Reason. The center of the Enlightenment was France. In England and Scotland, the Enlightenment stimulated brilliant writers on history, government, and society, but mainstream culture continued to develop along familiar paths.

George III and the Politicians

King George III came to the throne in the midst of the great victories of the Seven Years War, but after the war England hit a bad patch. The first ten years of George III's reign were filled with partisan bitterness, shifting ministries, divisive issues, popular tumults, crisis in the colonies, depressed trade, poor crops, and business setbacks. George III's notions about a government of "virtue and morality" were cast aside. "We must use bad men to govern bad men," the young king wrote to Bute.

George III realized that it was necessary to adopt the usual techniques of parliamentary management. The efforts of George III to exert the powers and "influence" of the Crown were opposed by a revived Whig Partly led by the Marquis of Rockingham. Edmund Burke, who had abandoned his literary aspirations for a career in politics, served as Lord Rockingham's spokesman in the House of Commons. Burke's Thoughts on the Causes of the Present Discontents (1770) accused the "friends" of the king, beginning with Lord Bute, of misusing "the influence of the Crown" to enhance the powers of the Crown at the expense of Parliament.

Finally, in 1770, George III found the prime minister he wanted. Frederick, Lord North, chancellor of the exchequer and leader of the House of Commons, was a loyal servant of the Crown, a capable manager of the finances, personally very likeable, and a good debater. Lord North became prime minister in 1770, and the king supported him with all the political "influence" at his disposal, including distribution of honors, patronage, and pensions in places where they would do the most good. North was a successful prime minister who emphasized economy in government and debt reduction until confronted with a war in the American colonies.

In the meantime, another factor had appeared in the political mix—radicalism. The roots of radicalism were the long-established "Country" fear of a strong executive power in the Crown. Londoners had always had a strong anti-court attitude. English radicals were in close touch with the American colonists, whose resistance to royal authority encouraged radicalism in the Mother Country.

Radicalism was a movement for reform of the House of Commons, including such features as reduction of royal "influence," exclusion of office-holders from the House of Commons, measures to reduce corruption in elections, and redistribution of seats to recognize changes in population that had taken place over the years. Some radicals went so far as to demand the right to vote for all adult males.

Radical ideas were strongest among middle-class business and professional men, shopkeepers, skilled artisans and craftsmen, and Dissenters. In London wealthy bankers and merchants were inclined to support the government, but the dominant factor in London politics was "the middling sort," who frequently opposed the government and parliamentary politicians. Radical ideas were strong in London and

Westminster and in the urban sprawl in the adjacent counties of Middlesex and Surrey.

Many of the concerns of radicals were brought to a head by the career of the charming demagogue, John Wilkes. In 1763 Wilkes, editor of The North Briton, an anti-Bute newspaper, attacked the peace treaty and the policies of the government as stated in the king's speech to Parliament. Agents of the secretary of state ransacked the office where The North Briton was published to obtain evidence against Wilkes, who was charged with seditious libel. When the case came to trial Wilkes successfully pleaded that as a Member of the House of Commons he was exempt from arrest. The printers were let off on the grounds that their arrest was based on an illegal warrant. The decision was hailed by the Londoners as a defense of civil liberties against an oppressive regime. They vented their feelings with parades, mass meetings, and riots. Wilkes was expelled from the House of Commons and fled to France.

In 1768 Wilkes came back to England and became a candidate for the House of Commons for the county of Middlesex. He won the poll, but he was rejected by the House of Commons as ineligible. He returned to the hustings and was elected three more times by overwhelming majorities. After the fourth election, his opponent was declared elected and riots again took place. Wilkes was imprisoned and troops were called in to restore order. The ministry and implicitly the king were charged with threatening the rights of the voters to express their views in elections.

John Horne Tooke, an articulate, combative clergyman, actively supported Wilkes in the Middlesex election and became one of the mainstays of English radicalism. In 1769 he founded the Society of Gentleman Supporters of the Bill of Rights to support Wilkes financially. When complaints were made that Wilkes was using the money to live in luxury in prison, the Society disbanded. As conflict arose in the American colonies, Horne Tooke came to the support of the colonists. "When the people of America are enslaved," he wrote, Englishmen "cannot be free." He was delegated to bring money to Benjamin Franklin to support the American cause, but before he could leave he was convicted of seditious libel and imprisoned.

The King and the Colonies

In 1770 a flare-up occurred in Boston when English troops fired on a mob that was harassing them. Angry colonists called this event "the Boston Massacre," but cooler heads prevailed in England and America and tensions subsided. It seemed that the storm had blown over. In 1773, the Bostonians, disguised as Indians, showed their defiance by boarding an East India Company ship disguised as Indians and casting its cargo of tea into the harbor. "The Boston Tea Party," as it was called, further inflamed tensions.

A decade of controversy had left a bitter legacy in the American colonies, but it had also left its mark in England. The king and those who supported a strong monarchy feared that further concessions would encourage disorders in the colonies and also in England. In his magnificent Speech on American Conciliation (1775), Edmund Burke supported the American colonists in their defense of "the rights of Englishmen." English radicals claimed that the policies of the Crown in America demonstrated the danger of tyranny at home and the need to reform the House of Commons to check the aggrandizement of royal power.

Samuel Johnson supported the Crown with a powerful pamphlet entitled Taxation No Tyranny (1775). Reminding the Americans of their own shortcomings Johnson asked, "How is it that we hear the loudest yelps for liberty from the drivers of negroes?" John Wesley was politically conservative. He supported the power of the Crown as essential to public order. At first Wesley believed that the American colonists had grievances that needed to be addressed, and he expressed his views in Calm Address to our American Colonies (1775). When hostilities broke out, Wesley published Some Thoughts on Liberty (1776), which condemned the American actions and equated them with English radicals.

As war clouds gathered, American opinion was crystallized by one of the most influential political pamphlets ever written—Tom Paine's, Common Sense (1776). Paine, an English radical from a Quaker family, emigrated to America in 1774 and settled in Philadelphia. He became editor of a political periodical and was acquainted with Benjamin Franklin and other prominent figures in that city. Common Sense was identified as "written by an Englishman." The argument that Paine presents is not limited to Americans but is a message to all humanity. Actually Paine was not an American patriot but an international revolutionary.

Paine rejects the idea of kingship and calls upon the Americans to set an example for the world by establishing a republic based on the will of the people. He rejects the notion of reconciliation with England. His pamphlet was of enormous importance in convincing waverers that independence was not only necessary but achievable. He saw America as the hope of a world seeking freedom and personal dignity. He foresaw a great future as the new republic expanded to continental size. The Declaration of Independence echoed some of the themes sounded by Paine.

In July 1776 the Second Continental Congress took the final step when it adopted the Declaration of Independence, which cut the last link with England by denying the authority of the Crown. In eloquent words the Declaration presented to the world the "self-evident truths" that justified the American claim to "the separate and equal station to which the laws of Nature and of Nature's God entitle them." King George III was condemned as the source of "repeated injuries and usurpations, all having in direct object the establishment of an absolute Tyranny over these States." The Declaration was an appeal to world opinion, to public opinion in England, and to Americans, who were called upon to commit to the fight for freedom "our lives, our fortunes, and our sacred honor."

Whether George III deserved the harsh condemnation of the Declaration of Independence was by that time immaterial. The American colonists were prepared to fight for independence, and American delegates led by Benjamin Franklin were sent to France to seek aid from the French Crown. In Britain, powerful forces were assembled to assert the supreme authority of Crown and Parliament and maintain the unity of the empire. George III, most of the Cabinet, and the overwhelming majority of the Parliament and the English public agreed that it was time to settle the matter for once and for all. Lord North found himself the leader of a country at war

When the opening stages of the war went badly for Gen. George Washington and the Continental Army, Paine rushed into print with The American Crisis (1776) to encourage Americans to persist. "These are times that try men's souls," Paine wrote. "The summer soldier and the sunshine patriot will, in this crisis, shrink from the service of his country. . . . We have this consolation with us, that the harder the conflict, the more glorious the triumph." Paine was as good as his word, and served Washington and the Continental Congress in a variety of capacities.

English radicals rallied behind the Americans, who, in their opinion, were fighting the same battle that they were. The conflict in America convinced Major John Cartwright, a retired naval officer, that Parliament itself was corrupt and needed to be reformed. He called the radicals to the cause with Take Your Choice! (1776). In the edition of 1780 Cartwright came out for universal manhood suffrage, annual elections for Parliament, equal electoral districts, a secret ballot, abolition of property qualifications for Parliament, and payment of Members of Parliament. Cartwright's book set the agenda of English radicalism for the next 100 years, and, with the exception of annual elections for Parliament, all his other points were eventually adopted. Cartwright founded the Society for Constitutional Information to unify British radicals in the attack on "the influence of the Crown" and the unrepresentative structure of the House of Commons. He continued to crusade for his principles until his death in 1824.

War in the Colonies and Crisis at Home

As an island country, Britain's security, finances, and trade depended on her colonies and sea power. England was the world's greatest power, and the English expected that a blockade and a brief land campaign in New England would settle the matter quickly. They were mistaken. When France came to the aid of the colonists in 1778 and Spain declared war in 1779, Britain faced powerful enemies that had built up their navies to challenge the royal navy in a war for control of the seas.

When the war began, the navy was widely dispersed and unable to bring the enemy fleets to a decisive battle. Furthermore, England had lost the American ships, seamen, and naval stores that in previous wars had been an important addition to her sea power. The army was embroiled in war with a scattered population that could form into an armed militia in a few days, fight a battle, and then dissolve. Gen.

George Washington, commander of the Continental Army, skillfully kept the American cause alive by avoiding pitched battles against the well-trained, well-supplied redcoats.

When France came to the aid of the colonists in 1778 and Spain declared war in 1779, Britain faced powerful enemies that had built up their navies to challenge the royal navy in a war for control of the seas. When the war began, the navy was widely dispersed and unable to bring the enemy fleets to a decisive battle. Furthermore, England had lost the American ships, seamen, and naval stores that in previous wars had been an important addition to her sea power. The army was embroiled in war with a scattered population that could form into an armed militia in a few days, fight a battle, and then dissolve. Gen. George Washington, commander of the Continental Army, skillfully kept the American cause alive by avoiding pitched battles against the well-trained, well-supplied redcoats.

In 1781 the French landed in New England ground forces of 5,500 men with ample artillery under the command of the Comte de Rochambeau, a distinguished general. Washington and Rochambeau planned to cooperate in an attack on New York City, when unexpectedly favorable circumstances arose farther south. Lord Cornwallis, commander of British forces in the southern colonies, had been sent to subdue Virginia and the Carolinas. After suffering heavy losses that he could not replace, Cornwallis retreated to the coast, where he dug in at Yorktown and waited to be relieved by the navy. Instead, a splendid French fleet came northward from the Caribbean and cut off Yorktown by sea. Washington and Rochambeau saw their opportunity and rapidly moved their forces southward. Too late, the British realized that Washington was not attacking New York City but was on his way to Yorktown. Washington and the Continental Army, joined by local militia and supported by French gold, siege guns and troops, reached Yorktown in September. Cornwallis was besieged by land while the French fleet had him trapped by sea. In October 1781 Cornwallis surrendered and the British cause in America had suffered a fatal blow.

As the war in America came to a close, England was swept by a powerful movement of public protest. In December 1779, the Rev. Christopher Wyvill, a Yorkshire clergyman, called a meeting of the gentlemen of Yorkshire to present a petition to the House of Commons that complained about the corrupt and wasteful use of "the influence of the Crown" to support the damaging policies of the government. The next year county meetings were held throughout England that prepared similar petitions. Lord Rockingham saw an opportunity to overthrow the North ministry. His parliamentary spokesman, Edmund Burke, presented a Bill for "economical reform" that concentrated on reducing "the influence of the Crown" by abolishing costly and useless offices and restricting pensions. It appeared that Lord North's government might fall.

The London radicals were dubious—only parliamentary reform would accomplish the purpose, they said. Wyvill's country gentlemen did not want to be linked to urban radicals, and the two branches of English radicalism failed to cooperate. In any case, Lord North survived the crisis, but he established a Commission for the Public Accounts that revealed gross mismanagement of expenditures in America and abuses in the exchequer and other government offices.

"Economical Reform" and "The Influence of the Crown"

When the news of Yorktown arrived in London, the independent gentlemen in the House of Commons turned against the war in America. Lord North knew it was time to resign. George III was determined to continue the war in some form, but North explained the realities of the situation to the king:

"The torrent is too strong to be resisted; Your Majesty is well apprized that, in this country, the Prince on the throne, cannot with prudence, oppose the deliberate resolution of the House of Commons; Your Royal Predecessors (particularly King William the Third and his late Majesty) were obliged to yield to it much against their wish in more instances than one: They consented to changes in their Ministry which they disapproved because they found it necessary to sacrifice their private wishes, and even their opinions to the preservation of public order, and the prevention of these terrible mischiefs, which are the natural consequence of the clashing of two branches of the Sovereign Power in the State."

George III claimed the right to choose his own ministers, but under the circumstances he had no choice but to accept the decision of the House of Commons. Lord Rockingham became prime minister and

American independence was assured. The Whigs took steps to reduce "the influence of the Crown" by passing Burke's Bill for "economical reform." After that, the reports of the Commission for the Public Accounts turned "economical reform" into a movement for administrative efficiency and economy. When the Rockingham government refused to support parliamentary reform, Major Cartwright weighed in with <u>Give us our Rights</u> (1782). A rising star, William Pitt the Younger, son of the great leader in the Seven Years War, pledged his support for reform of the House of Commons and elections.

William Pitt the Younger

In December, 1783 George III appointed Pitt as first lord of the treasury and prime minister. Pitt was supported by a landslide victory in an election in 1784 in which the king played an active part. He satisfied the radicals with a modest proposal for parliamentary reform that was rejected by the House of Commons. He restored financial stability, carried out some of the reforms of fiscal management that had been proposed by the Commission for the Public Accounts, and established a sinking fund to begin paying off the national debt. With the revival of trade and the finances, Britain could again play a role in the European balance of power. By 1793 Britain was ready to face the challenge of revolutionary France.

Pitt realized the importance of the empire to Britain's trade and sea power. At the end of the American Revolution, the population of Canada was changed by a large influx of Loyalists. It seemed evident that the English and French populations—divided as they were by language, religion, and culture—could not be unified politically. The problem was resolved by Pitt's Canada Act of 1791, which divided Canada into two provinces. The French part spoke French and had French land tenure and law. The English part spoke English and had English law and land tenures. The Church of England was established in both parts, but Catholicism continued as the religion of the majority of the population in the French part. The Canada Act worked well for the next fifty years. Pitt's India Act (1784, 1786) brought the British East India Company under public control, and Lord Cornwallis atoned for his defeat in America by bringing order to the affairs of the Company and its agents in India.

The Pitt government took another important step in the development of the empire when it established a prison colony in Australia. In the eighteenth century the most common punishment for felony was transportation to the colonies, and until the American Revolution transportation was usually to America. With American independence, however, that outlet was gone, and large numbers of convicts were kept in derelict ships ("hulks") anchored in the Thames, which technically met the requirement. In 1788 a fleet of eleven ships commanded by Capt. Arthur Philip was sent with 1,030 convicts and marines to Botany Bay, which proved to be unsatisfactory. The colony was moved to the present site of Sidney, which has a spectacular harbor.

At first the colony depended almost entirely on supplies from Britain and starvation was widespread. The adjustment to agriculture was difficult for convicts from London, and the marines were unhappy with their remote location. Philip left in 1792 due to illness, and eventually the colony became largely self-supporting. Sidney became the capital and principal city of New South Wales.

The Enlightenment

In the second half of the eighteenth century, English culture received stimulating new influences from "the Enlightenment," a term applied to an intellectual movement that was centered in France and spread to Germany, Austria, Italy, Spain, and the court of Catherine the Great of Russia. The essential feature of the Enlightenment was its confidence in Reason. The main purpose of the movement was to apply rational analysis to existing institutions of government, law, and religion, which invariably were found wanting.

The leading thinkers of the Enlightenment, known as philosophes, were French. Many of them admired England, the country of Locke, Newton, and Hume, for its limited government, religious toleration, and freedom of speech and the press. One of the leading philosophes was François-Marie Arouet, who called himself Voltaire. He first came to public attention as a witty playwright whose plays became vehicles for his enlightened ideas. Voltaire visited England and describes the free society he found there in his Letters on the English (1733). He was most impressed by the scientific revolution wrought by Sir Isaac Newton. He disseminated Newton's ideas throughout Europe in his

Élements de la Philosophie de Newton (c.1750). His novel, Candide (1759), tells the story of an idealistic young man whose adventures expose him to the many man-made evils of the world but do not shake his belief in human goodness.

In France, the enlightenment critique was directed primarily at the Catholic Church, whose doctrines and rituals were dismissed as irrational relics of earlier ages and its persecutions of people who disagreed with its teachings as barbarism. "Ecrasez l'infame" (wipe out the infamous), was Voltaire's cry. His anti-clericalism eventually forced him to live in French-speaking Switzerland.

The principles of the philosophes were embodied in the great Encyclopédie, ou Dictionnaire raisonné des Sciences, des arts, et de métiers (17 vols.,1746-72). The Encyclopédie was an effort to cover all aspects of knowledge and put them in the rational context of the Enlightenment. It included articles on subjects as varied as history, geography, literature, theatre, music, art, crafts, inventions etc. The principal editor was Denis Diderot, with considerable assistance from Jean Le Rond d'Alembert. Many of the philosophes, including Voltaire, contributed articles. Its critique of established institutions and traditional ideas had an enormous influence on public opinion in France and throughout Europe. The Enlightenment led to wide-ranging proposals for reform in government and society and the relation of church and state. In some places, as in France in 1789, enlightened ideas contributed to revolution.

The Enlightenment in Scotland

Scotland was the center of enlightenment influences in Britain. English schools and universities were tied down by the humanist concentration on classical studies. The Scottish universities, unlike Oxford and Cambridge, taught modern subjects and attracted learned faculty and ambitious students. The University of Edinburgh was pre-eminent, but Glasgow and St. Andrews were not far behind.

William Robertson, the distinguished historian, was principal of Edinburgh University. Adam Smith, who graced the faculties of Glasgow University and later Edinburgh, laid the foundation of economics. Adam Ferguson, a professor at the University of Edinburgh published Essay on the History of Civil Society (1767), which was an early effort at establishing social science. He denied the existence of a "state of nature" and an original contract. He traced the growth of civilization through a series of stages, from primitive to advanced. John Millar, a distinguished professor of civil law at Glasgow, published The Origin of the Distribution of Ranks (1771), a pioneering study of social stratification and mobility, which he attributed to the economic organization of society. His Historical View of the English Constitution (1787) was a pioneering study of English constitutional development, which he attributed to economic and social change. These scholars based their work on careful examination of available sources that would lead to persuasive conclusions. The Encyclopedia Britannica (1768), which followed the example of the great Encyclopédie of the French Enlightenment, originated in Edinburgh as a source of reliable information on a wide variety of topics.

The Enlightenment and History

In the eighteenth-century, history separated itself from chronicles and memoirs and became a third person narrative about individuals and events of the past based on reliable sources. White Kennett, Bishop of Peterborough and a prominent Whig, was active in historical and antiquarian studies. In 1706, thirteen booksellers collaborated to publish his three-volume Compleat History of England. The first two volumes were a compilation of medieval and Tudor chronicles with brief historical comments. The third was a narrative with supporting documents that covered English history from the reign of Charles I to the reign of William III. The work presented the first continuous history of the English past. It was reprinted four times, and a new edition was issued in 1719.

To thrive in the world of commercialized publication, history had to be interesting to the general public, and, as such, history took on some of the characteristics and popularity of the novel. David Hume, philosopher, needed to write works that would earn money if he were to be an independent intellectual who did not need the support of patrons. The popularity of Kennett's history suggested that historical writing could be financially successful in a way that philosophy never could. Hume's History of England from the Invasion of Julius Caesar to the Revolution of 1688 (1754-62) shocked many readers by upsetting the Whig pieties of Kennett and others. The reading public was ready for new ideas, and the work made Hume wealthy.

Hume's strength as an historian was his insight into character and motivation joined to a smooth and ingratiating style. He explained the actions of historical characters in human terms based on his understanding of their ideas and passions. As a Scot, Hume brought to English history an air of detachment that both intrigued and infuriated Englishmen. He gained popularity as a "debunker" who disturbed almost everyone's received opinions.

Hume is sometimes called a "Tory" because he undermined the Whig interpretation of English history, which had been carefully crafted to damn the Stuarts, praise the role of Parliament in the Puritan Revolution, and justify the Revolution of 1688-89. Hume was on the side of strong, effective government, while the characteristic eighteenth-century Whig view was to praise liberty and fear tyranny. Hume expresses negative feelings about the theological formulations and controversies of the Reformation—Protestant or Catholic—and as such his history was regarded by many as impious. The Church of England, which was praised by Englishmen for the purity of its doctrine and dignity of its worship, Hume presents as another attempt to impose clerical power on the people. As a Scot, he defends the Stuarts rather more than Englishmen of the eighteenth-century were willing to accept. He dislikes the religious fanaticism of the Puritans, and he is appalled at the execution of King Charles I, whom he depicts as a good but inept man faced with a situation with which he could not cope. From the experience of the Civil Wars, Hume draws the lesson that the power of the people could be as dangerous as that of kings. He despises the vicious dogmatism and partisanship of the later seventeenth century, especially as seen in the controversies of "the Popish Plot." He reserves his highest praise for William III, who rejected partisanship and dogmatism and brought to England a settlement of government and religion based on a pragmatic adaptation to the realities of the situation. He writes of William "it will be difficult to find any person, whose actions and conduct have contributed more eminently to the general interest of society and mankind." He extends his praises to "the Glorious Revolution"—"we, in this island, have ever since enjoyed, if not the best system of government, at least the most entire system of liberty that ever was known among mankind."

In his political thought Hume was the advocate of pragmatic solutions rather than grand general principles. In his Essays Historical and Political (1742) he ridicules divine right theory, which could be used to justify the most violent despot as well as the best ruler. On the other hand, he also rejects the contract theory of Locke, arguing that there was no historical evidence that a contract had been made to establish the English state or any other. He demonstrates historically that most governments were founded "either upon usurpation or conquest, or both, without any pretence of a fair consent." He concludes that the "influence of the Crown" was growing and would in time overpower the rest of the constitution, and the eventual end of the English constitution would be despotism.

In 1763 the Earl of Hertford was appointed ambassador to France, and Hume was invited to accompany the embassy to Paris. He was given a salaried position as secretary to the embassy. He was already well-known among French intellectuals as a philosopher, and they were eager to meet him. By 1769 Hume was rich and famous, and ready to settle down. He returned to Edinburgh, where he was reprobated by the Kirk as an infidel awaiting hellfire but was admired by other leading Scottish intellectuals for his keen mind and sociability.

While Hume was gaily destroying the established ideas of his time, his own life was far from radical. Personally, he was very much a likeable man of the world, which he sought to enjoy because he expected nothing beyond the grave. His purpose was to replace dogmatic pronouncements and universal principles with moderation and a pragmatic sense of human limitations. He encouraged men to trust their own judgment and instincts, which had been formed empirically, rather than relying on the proclamations of politicians and preachers. His friend, Adam Smith wrote of Hume that he approached "as near to the idea of a perfectly wise and virtuous man, as perhaps the nature of human frailty will permit."

Hume was refuted by one of the most influential radical intellectuals of the time, Mrs. Catherine Macaulay, daughter of Alderman Sawbridge, a leading London radical. Macaulay was privately educated and read extensively in her father's well-stocked library. Socially, she was connected with John Horne Tooke and the radicals who supported Wilkes. She attacked Edmund Burke and the Whigs in <u>Observations on a Pamphlet, Entitled, Thoughts on the Causes of the Present Discontents</u> (1770). She regarded the Whig aristocracy as obstacles to the full achievement of the rights of Englishmen. As tensions arose in the American colonies, she published <u>Address to the People of England, Scotland, and Ireland on the Present Important Crisis of Affairs</u> (1775).

In 1763 Macaulay published the first volume of her eight-volume <u>History of England from the Accession of James I to the Elevation of the House of Hanover</u> (8 vols, 1763-83). The work was critically and financially successful in England and the American colonies. In contrast to Hume, who had praised the rise of monarchy as the basis for creation of a strong state, Macaulay depicts the Crown as hostile to freedom. Her heroes are Englishmen who had contributed to the growth of Parliament and civil liberties. Her radical views are revealed in Vol. IV, where she praises the republicanism of the Puritans who deposed and executed King Charles I. She criticizes "the Glorious Revolution of 1688-89," the lynch-pin of the Whig view of English history, as the work of aristocratic opponents of liberty who blocked the radical intentions of the people. In a later volume she shows her support for the American colonists. In 1784 she visited America, where she met many dignitaries, including George Washington, who honored her for the influence of her history on the intellectual background of American independence.

William Robertson, principal of the University of Edinburgh, brought history out of its subordination to political and religious disputation, and undertook to provide a broad, fair-minded account of the past. Robertson attended Edinburgh University, and as a young clergyman, he became a leader of the moderate wing in the Church of Scotland. His historical inclinations became evident when he wrote a preface to <u>Ruins of the Palace of the Emperor Diocletian at Spalatro</u> (1757), a lavishly illustrated work on architecture in late antiquity by his cousin, Robert Adam, who later became a distinguished architect.

Robertson's first major historical work was <u>A History of Scotland during the Reigns of Queen Mary and King James VI</u> (2 vols.,1759). Robertson presents Scottish history as a story of progress toward participation in the modern world, including a sympathetic presentation of the tragic career of Mary, Queen of Scots. Until Robertson's book appeared, the history of Scotland was virtually unknown and the book was a huge success. Supported by the Earl of Bute, prime minister and mentor of King George III, Robertson was appointed to the prestigious posts of principal of Edinburgh University and historiographer royal in Scotland. He was important in transforming the university into a major academic institution, especially in science and medicine.

Robertson established his position as the leading historian of his time with his <u>History of the Reign of King Charles V</u> (3 vols., 1769), which deals with the powerful king of Spain and ruler of the diverse Hapsburg Empire at the time of the Reformation. The publishers paid a record price of £3,500 for the first edition and £500 for the second. A French translation appeared in 1771. The work traced the establishment of the European state system and the emergence of balance of power politics in the conflicts of the Hapsburg and Valois (French) dynasties. Robertson rooted his subject in a broader theme—the progress of European civilization from the fall of the Roman Empire to the sixteenth century.

Robertson's work on the Emperor Charles V familiarized him with Spanish and Portuguese colonization. <u>The History of the Discovery and Settlement of America</u> (2 vols., 1777) was commercially successful and gave English readers a comprehensive view of the role of sixteenth-century Spain in Europe and the New World. The importance of imperial issues in the run-up to the American Revolution gave the book immediate relevance. The work was even more successful on the continent, where it went through nine editions in translation between 1770 and 1780. Robertson interwove information about the culture of the native Americans with the story of the Spanish conquests. He presents the Spanish conquest as a clash between two distinct stages of civilization. Initially he intended to include English colonization as well, but the outbreak of the American Revolution introduced a new element into the story that had to be resolved before the history of the British Empire could be dealt with. As an historian, Robertson had given dignity and drama to subjects that had been known largely through dry chronicles or polemical argumentation.

Adam Smith and the Foundation of Classical Economics

In addition to the American <u>Declaration of Independence</u>, the year 1776 saw the publication of Adam Smith's classic argument for economic freedom—<u>An Inquiry into the Nature and Causes of the Wealth of Nations</u>. Smith's masterpiece overturned the conventional wisdom concerning economic and imperial policy. Smith was born in Scotland, received a thorough Scottish education, and spent six years at Oxford, where he read extensively in ancient philosophy and English and continental literature. In 1751 Smith became professor of moral philosophy at Glasgow University. His first major publication, <u>The Theory of Moral Sentiments</u> (1759), builds on Hume's view that moral principles are acquired by growing up in a family and a community and a natural desire for the approval of others. Like Hume, Smith believes that experience is the foundation of emotions as well as ideas, and normal human desires and feelings can be expected to produce results beneficial to the larger community. He bases this principle on the loyalty and responsibility that people feel toward their family, friends, neighbors, and country. He regards moral conduct as more a matter of feeling ("moral sentiments") than rational calculation. Individuals want to be respected by their fellows. For that reason, they stay within the limits established by the common morality. He rejects the narrow, Puritanical morality of the Church of Scotland, because he believes that self-interest and moral sentiments will establish sufficient moral guidelines for most people.

In 1764 Smith accepted an invitation from Charles Townshend, who would soon become chancellor of the exchequer, to accompany his stepson on the Grand Tour as tutor. The tour lasted almost three years, and was a great opportunity for Smith to meet Voltaire and other French leaders of the Enlightenment, including the <u>physiocrats</u>—economists who advocated economic freedom and held that agriculture was the basis of national wealth. When the tour ended, Smith returned to Scotland to work on his masterpiece, <u>An Inquiry into the Nature and Causes of the Wealth of Nations</u> (1776). The book was an immediate success, and for two years Smith enjoyed the plaudits of London and association with its intellectual leaders. The rest of his life he spent quietly in Edinburgh.

In the <u>The Wealth of Nations</u>, Smith argues that the desire to work and be rewarded for it leads individuals to do things for which there is a demand and that they can do best. The result is that individual initiative and effort produce economic outcomes that are beneficial to all. The key economic principle for Smith is the division of labor, which leads individuals and nations to engage in those economic activities in which they have an advantage. The best manager of economic activity, he says, is a free, competitive market, which will direct economic activities into those areas where a demand for the product or service is most needed, and thus bring about the maximum production of wealth. Division of labor also applies to nations, which is the foundation of international trade.

Smith's practical purpose is to attack the complex web of restrictions and privileges that constituted the economic policies called mercantilism. He argues that attempts to regulate or block international trade are harmful if enforced, and if not enforced have the evil effect of discouraging respect for law through smuggling and other evasions. Smith points out the evils that had arisen in the North American colonies and in the affairs of the East India Company by the attempt to maintain monopoly controls over trade that should be free.

Smith does not oppose all activities of government. He recognizes the importance of a supreme authority to be responsible for national defense, law and order, public works, security of property, and education. He defends the Navigation Acts, although they interfere with economic laws, because the need for sea power might over-ride the maximum production of wealth. It is his opinion that, in general, the expenditures of government are wasteful, since they are devoted to grandeur, patronage, wars, and other burdens on the people. Political leaders, he says, are the least qualified of all to meddle in economic matters, which they do constantly in response to political pressure from powerful individuals or businesses. He is equally severe with businessmen, whose instinct, he believes, is always to restrain competition for their own personal advantage.

Smith comments extensively on British policy toward the American colonies. He argues that the grievances of the colonists were not great. They had almost complete freedom in managing their domestic affairs; they had the protection of the British navy against foreigners; the tax burdens imposed on them by Parliament were light; and the existing restrictions on trade were minor and mainly evaded anyway. He concludes that the basis of the quarrel between Britain and her North American colonies lay in the policies and stubbornness of Parliament, which responded to the demands of special interests rather than considering the welfare of the entire empire. Smith thought the best policy was to give the colonies their independence, and then trade with them as before. In 1778 Smith was appointed to the board of customs in Edinburgh with a comfortable salary, and there he spent the rest of his life.

Edward Gibbon and the Decline of the Roman Empire

Edward Gibbon was very much a man of the Enlightenment. One of the common themes of the Enlightenment was the political pathology of the corrupted state, which Gibbon found fully displayed in the fate of the Roman Empire. His The History of the Decline and Fall of the Roman Empire (1776-87) appeared too many of his countrymen as relevant to their own time. As the volumes appeared, beginning in the magical year, 1776, the reading public was entranced by its narrative power, well-defined characters, and application of rational explanations to a long historical process with fateful consequences.

During his sickly boyhood, Gibbon read extensively in English, French, and Latin works of literature and history. He spent a year at Oxford, where he dabbled in Catholicism. In 1753 he was sent to Lausanne, in French-speaking Switzerland, and placed in the care of a Protestant clergyman. There he returned to Protestantism, freed from commitments to dogmatic religion and ecclesiastical authority of any kind. He lived in Lausanne for five years, during which time he read extensively in ancient and medieval literature and met Voltaire. He returned to England and lived as a gentleman scholar on an annuity provided by his father. During the Seven Year War, Gibbon served as a captain in the Hampshire militia, which had been mobilized to resist a possible French invasion.

Early in life Gibbon decided to write a great history. When the war ended he visited Paris and Rome. His reading in the classics had made him an admirer of the power and magnificence of the early Roman Empire and the rationality and humanity of its culture. As he viewed the monuments of Rome's past greatness, he saw about him a

Rome that was poor and unattractive—dominated by a corrupt papal court and the dead hand of organized religion. He was saddened by the decline of a once great civilization. He decided to write a history that would tell the story of the Roman Empire from its prime in the second century AD to the fall of the Western Empire during and after the barbarian invasions. As a man of the Enlightenment who was much influenced by the philosophes, Gibbon undertook to offer a rational analysis of the corruption of Roman political and social institutions and the process by which they broke down.

In the 1770s, Gibbon's life flourished. He settled in a comfortable house in London, was elected to the House of Commons by the influence of a relative, and steadily supported the North government. He was appointed to the board of trade with a salary of £1000 per year. He associated with leading intellectuals and scholars and was a member of several prestigious clubs, including Samuel Johnson's Literary Club.

The first volume of The History of the Decline and Fall of the Roman Empire (1776) was immediately recognized as a masterpiece. Englishmen eagerly awaited each new volume, anxiously reading about the decline of the Roman Empire as their own empire seemed to be coming apart at the seams. Gibbon contrasts the freedom and rationality of the early Roman Empire with the corruption, violence, and religious fanaticism that followed. After the death of the Emperor Marcus Aurelius (180 A D), the Empire falls into civil wars, as generals and their armies struggle for power while the Senate sinks into dependence. Gibbon sees Roman decline partially as a result of the growth of comfort and self-satisfaction among the upper and middle classes, who leave government and security to the emperors and the legions. Eventually this power becomes corrupted and abused, and the decline of the empire has begun. One of the reasons Gibbon gives for Rome's decline is "the domestic quarrels of the Romans," which may be seen as a reference to the intense partisanship of his own time.

In 1782 Lord North resigned and the Whigs came to power. Burke's Economical Reform Act abolished the board of trade including Gibbon's sinecure position. Without sufficient income to support his London lifestyle, Gibbon returned to Lausanne. He finished the last three volumes in 1787, for which his publisher paid £4,000, a generous price. He continued living in Lausanne until the French Revolution and the outbreak of war in 1792 compelled him to return to England.

The most controversial part of Gibbon' history was Chapters 15 and 16, where he presents the spread of Christianity as one of the reasons for the decline of the empire. Christianity, he writes, with its promise of eternal life, spread first among the common people, who sought in religion the satisfactions denied them in their everyday lives. Gibbon's account of the rise of the Christian Church, which he attributes to human factors, not the will and purposes of God, and his scornful treatment of many Christian beliefs and practices, brought down upon him the wrath of those who were devoted to the Church of England and its teachings. He was masterful in depicting the energy and devotion of the Christians while detailing the bitterness of their interminable theological disputes and the savagery with which they attacked their enemies, including fellow Christians with whom they disagreed. Gibbon argues that the emperors who persecuted the Christians were not villains but rulers who suffered serious provocations by the Christians before they cracked down on them. Eventually the emperors gave into the Christians, who proceeded to abuse their new-found powers more viciously than the emperors ever had.

Weakened by corruption, militarism, civil strife, and the stubborn separateness of the Christians, who were loyal to their heavenly king, the empire fell victim to the German barbarians, who further debased the level of government and society. Gibbon summarizes his explanation of the fall of the Roman Empire in the phrase—"the triumph of barbarism and religion."

With the fall of the Roman Empire in the West, Gibbon had completed his project, but he decided to continue his work by telling the story of the Roman Empire in the East, where Constantinople (Byzantium) was the center of the Greek-speaking Byzantine civilization. He is, in general, out of sympathy with the Byzantine Empire, which was characterized by religious formalism, exploitation of its subjects, and dependence on Italian merchants. He covers Byzantine history briefly in one chapter and describes it as a "uniform tale of weakness and misery." Gibbon brings the story down to the fall of Constantinople to the Ottoman Turks in 1453.

In the process, Gibbon gives the first extended account in any Western language of the history of Muslim civilization. Nine of the thirty-three chapters in the later part of the work are devoted to Islam. Gibbon covers the life of Muhammed, the spread of Islam, the administration of the Muslim Empire by the caliphs, and the rise of the Seljuk and Ottoman Turks. The sources available to him in English, Latin, Greek, or modern foreign languages were few, but he used them to create a fascinating account of what was known about Islam in his own time. He praises Lady Mary Wortley Montagu's <u>Letters Written during her Travels</u> (1762) for Lady Mary's shrew observations of Muslim society, particularly Muslim women.

Gibbon's language is magisterial and sonorous and his tapestry is Miltonic as he traces the decline of a great and noble institution into ugliness and misery. The <u>Decline and Fall</u> is a work of enormous learning, dignified style, gripping narrative, astute and believable characterizations, and magnificent pageantry. Gibbon is often sarcastic as he unfolds what he considers to be the crimes and follies of mankind. In that respect, Gibbon is quintessentially a man of the Enlightenment.

Gibbon was not just an Englishman seeking to draw lessons suitable for his countrymen. His perspective was cosmopolitan. Although he began with praise for the Roman Empire, he was an opponent of imperialism and an advocate for the independence of nations. He may have been thinking of the American Revolution when he wrote "There is nothing perhaps more adverse to nature and reason than to hold in obedience remote countries and foreign nations, in opposition to their inclinations and interest."

In respect of the barbarian invaders of the Roman Empire, he cites their brutality and destructiveness and rejects the widespread concept of the noble savage. He recognizes that the Germans laid the foundations of the languages and states of Europe. Although Gibbon shows no respect for religious belief, he concedes that the Church had held civil society together for centuries and had transmitted the heritage of Greece and Rome to the modern age.

He urges respect for the high civilization of his own time, and calls for a vigorous defense of that civilization against the ignorance of those who would destroy what they cannot understand. He ends his account of decline into barbarism and superstition on an optimistic note. He is confident that a similar collapse will not recur, and that the civilization of his own time will increase "the real wealth, the happiness, the knowledge, and perhaps the virtue, of the human race."

The Dissemination of Enlightened Ideas

The ideas of the Enlightenment would have been confined to a small number of cognoscenti without enlightened publishers who could recognize the importance of the new ideas and the merits of the Enlightenment writers. Andrew Millar, a Scot, set up as a bookseller in London and became a member of the Stationers' Company in 1728. In his early years in the business, he sold many books published in Scotland, and published the works of a fellow Scott, James Thomson. He paid his authors well, including £250 for Thomson's Liberty, £600 for Tom Jones, and £4000 for Hume's History of England. He was one of the booksellers, along with Dodsley, who contracted for Johnson's Dictionary. Samuel Johnson remarked that Millar "had raised the price of Literature."

When Millar died in 1768, Thomas Cadell, who began with Millar as an apprentice, took over the firm and made it one of the most distinguished in London. Cadell had a great success with Gibbon's Decline and Fall of the Roman Empire. He also published works by Hume, Robertson, Adam Smith, Catharine Macaulay, Hannah More, and Fanny Burney. He was one of the booksellers who contracted with Samuel Johnson to write the prefaces to The Works of the English Poets. He paid his authors generously. He remarked: "I had rather risk my fortune with a few such Authors as Mr. Gibbon, Dr. Robertson, D. Hume . . . than be the publisher of a hundred insipid publications."

One of the most remarkable publishers of the late eighteenth century was Joseph Johnson, who published works of the growing radical movement. He published many works of Dissenters and Unitarians, who challenged the restrictions of the Test and Corporation Acts. He published works supporting Wilkes and the American Revolution, the political works of Benjamin Franklin, and Laws Respecting Women as they Regard their Natural Rights (1777), a valuable handbook for early feminists. He published books on science and medicine, and children's books. Johnson welcomed new and stimulating ideas in all fields of interest, and collected around him a circle of friends that met for dinner in his house. His greatest period of publishing was during the controversy over the French Revolution, which led him eventually to a stay in prison.

Ch. 15. English Institutions and Culture in an Age of Change, 1784-92

Despite the political and colonial crises of the first three decades of the reign of King George III, there was general satisfaction that England had achieved liberty under law, prosperity, and freedom of expression within the framework of the "mixed and balanced constitution." The pace of economic growth, referred to by historians as the "Industrial Revolution," and advances in agriculture seemed to justify the political changes that had taken place in the previous century. There were disturbing counter-currents to the dominant outlook. Hogarth had depicted vividly the evils that underlay the glittering world of London. Fielding's works on crime and social disorder pointed to ill-understood problems that threatened polite society and aroused concern among humanitarians.

By the later eighteenth century, a more fundamental sense of restlessness and dissatisfaction with the existing order was evident. The radical movement for parliamentary reform grew out of a sense that the House of Commons was structurally flawed, which permitted government by small partisan cliques rather than representing the people. Economic growth developed a new class of business and professional men who were not satisfied with the political and social domination of the aristocracy and gentry.

Religion was supported for its social utility, but it was expected that the doctrines of the Church would be based on general principles that reasonable people could accept. Despite the efforts of dedicated evangelical reformers, the Church of England fell short of its ideals. Other denominations continued to exist under the limitations of the Toleration Act. Reformers complained that the Common Law, the guardian of English liberty and property, included gross injustices, and prisons were disgraceful. Slavery and the slave trade, the foundation of the imperial system, were portrayed as moral atrocities that cried to Heaven for remedy.

Some contemporary observers sensed that they lived in an age of change that held out the possibility of "improvement." They were no longer satisfied with the status quo. The notion arose that the powers of the state and the privileges of those who controlled it should be tested by appeals to universal principles of justice and individual rights.

Economic Growth

The increasing momentum of change was clearly noticeable in the economy. England experienced rapid economic growth, beginning in the 1740s and gaining momentum in the 1780's. This development was marked by a growing population, flourishing foreign trade, a thriving internal market, rising productivity in agriculture, important developments in manufactures, and improvements in transportation, notably the building of canals, turnpike roads, and larger ships. Economic growth was made possible by a stable government that maintained order, protected property, preserved freedom under law, and encouraged capital formation by its own extensive fiscal operations. The wars that punctuated the period slowed, but did not stop the process.

The term "Industrial Revolution" refers broadly to many aspects of economic growth, but it applies more directly to the increased use of machinery and the factory system in manufacturing, beginning with cotton textiles. Richard Arkwright revolutionized the industry by developing the water-frame, a spinning machine with many spindles driven by waterpower. Arkwright, who began his career as a barber, was a confident, entrepreneurial man who recovered from various failures and false starts and eventually achieved success. He built his factories in isolated valleys with a river to turn his waterwheel, and brought in pauper children to tend his machines. He was one of the first to use a steam engine to power his factories. The cotton textile industry was aided by Eli Whitney, an American, who invented the cotton gin, which increased the supply of raw cotton by removing the seeds that were part of the boll. The woolen cloth industry was still dominated by hand spinners and weavers working in their homes or small shops and subject to a wide range of regulations inherited from the past.

A similar transformation took place in the potteries of the west of England. The industry was based on a system of small potters, each making dishes and pots in his own shop. Quality was highly variable and often low. Josiah Wedgwood, a gentleman potter, saw the potential to increase production and improve quality by establishing a factory system. He employed skilled potters and decorators in one place, which enabled him to control costs and standardize quality at a high level.

Wedgwood pottery gained fame due to its elegant design and the specialized skills of the workers and artists who hand-decorated each piece. His basic, creamy-white design ("queen's ware") could be afforded by the middle class, and he used the same product to produce magnificently decorated sets of dishes for the crowned heads and aristocrats of Europe and George and Martha Washington.

The power of the new industrialists was seen in 1785, when Pitt attempted to equalize duties between England and Ireland to reduce smuggling and improve the revenue. The textile manufacturers feared competition from cheap Irish labor, and organized the Great Chamber of Manufacturers to oppose the proposal in Parliament. Josiah Wedgwood, who feared similar competition in the pottery industry, was chosen as their leader. Pitt's proposal was defeated by factious opposition in the House of Commons and public clamor, assisted by Irish objections to some parts of the plan.

The manufacture of iron was brought under the factory system by Abraham Darby and the Darby family, ironmasters in the west of England. For centuries, iron had been smelted in small lots by using charcoal, which meant that most ironworks were located in remote forests where wood was plentiful. The Darbys found they could smelt iron by using coke derived from coal. They built a large ironworks along the Severn River, which provided water for the smelting process and water transport for coal and other requirements. They built an iron bridge over the river. John Wilkinson, another ironmaster, invented a cannon-boring machine that greatly improved the range and accuracy of cannon. It also made it possible to bore a true cylinder for steam engines. Wilkinson installed an iron pulpit in the local church and was buried in an iron coffin.

Since waterpower was seasonally variable, factories needed a source of power that would be constant throughout the year. Development of an efficient steam engine went through many stages during the eighteenth century, but the key figures in the process were James Watt, an instrument maker from Glasgow who improved the engine, and Matthew Boulton, a Birmingham businessman who manufactured and marketed it. Boulton exhibited the boldness and insights into the needs of industry that characterized the successful entrepreneurs of the Industrial Revolution. Birmingham was famous for the metal trades, which were conducted in small family shops with a few employees and apprentices. Boulton was a man of expansive views, who not only manufactured well-made products but engaged in the export of Birmingham metal goods to France and the Baltic.

Like his friend, Josiah Wedgwood, Boulton recognized the advantages, both in quantity and quality, of large-scale factory production as opposed to the small shops typical of Birmingham, Sheffield, and other metal-working towns. He built a large factory and commodious house with central heating at Soho, a Birmingham neighborhood. Boulton was personable and sociable, and his Soho factory and house were visited by nobility and prominent businessmen from England, France, Germany and North America. He was a member of the Lunar Society, a group of business and professional men who met monthly to discuss science and industry. Josiah Wedgwood was a member, and they were visited on occasion by Benjamin Franklin and Thomas Jefferson. He was an active citizen of Birmingham and participated in the construction of a hospital and the Theatre Royal.

Boulton discussed with Franklin and others the possibility of developing a more efficient steam engine. In 1768 James Watt, who held a patent on an improved steam engine, visited Boulton, who was fascinated by the possibility of manufacturing and marketing it. Boulton's parliamentary connections enabled him to obtain a twenty-five year extension of Watt's patent, and in 1775 he went into partnership with Watt to manufacture steam engines. Their first major market was pumping water out of copper mines in Cornwall. Boulton recognized the potential of using steam engines to power cotton mills, and Watt developed a device to change the reciprocating motion of the steam engine to a rotary motion. Watt also developed a unit of measurement for steam engines called "horsepower," which is still used today. Boulton was a talented organizer of production and marketing, and the firm of Boulton & Watt manufactured and sold several hundred steam engines in the next two decades.

The Industrial Revolution could not have taken place without improvements in transportation. After 1740 great activity began in building smooth-surfaced turnpike roads, primarily for use by carriages and mail coaches. England has many rivers that flow gently from west to east, and they provided water transportation for heavy goods. Coastal shipping between ports was important for inland transportation. In the 1760s canal building began in earnest, usually to Link Rivers but sometimes to carry heavy goods, like coal, from the mines to an industrial town.

One of the leaders was the Duke of Bridgewater, whose estates contained large quantities of coal. He employed James Brindley, a millwright, to design the Bridgewater Canal to carry coal from his mine to Manchester. The Bridgewater canal used tunnels and an aqueduct over the Irwell River to avoid using locks, and became a great tourist attraction. It made the Duke a wealthier man (he was already wealthy) and Bridley went on to design many other canals.

Since much of the new industry was located in the north of England, the population and prosperity of those underdeveloped parts of the country increased remarkably. Much of the wealth generated by economic growth flowed upward to the aristocracy in the form of increased rents and charges for mineral rights, but a more widely distributed prosperity was evident to well-informed observers. Factories provided a new kind of employment for people from decaying villages. The workday was long, the factories were dangerous, wages were low, and housing for the workers was miserable. One must remember, however, that the rural villages or congested towns from which the workers were drawn provided a meager standard of living too.

Advances in agriculture were among the most notable economic developments of the period. These had begun in the later seventeenth century, but were more widely extended as knowledge spread and stability encouraged long-term investment in landed property. The new agriculture utilized turnips and clover in crop rotations that improved the fertility of the land and provided fodder for cattle, which made it possible to keep more animals through the winter. The new methods could not be introduced without enclosing the wastelands and large open fields of medieval England, a process that usually was done by Act of Parliament. When the open fields were enclosed they were commonly divided into fields of 15-20 acres separated by hedges of whitethorn or other tough, prickly shrubs. In areas of heavy soils, drainage ditches and tiles were laid to remove excess water. All of these changes required investment with a view to long-term results, and this could happen only in a society with political stability and good economic prospects. In the Midlands, which had heavier soils, low farm prices led to a shift from agriculture to sheep-raising, which produced wool for the growing industries of Norfolk and Yorkshire. In the process, many of the agricultural workers were left to shift for themselves and the small villages decayed.

The key figure in this period of agricultural advance was the tenant farmer. The landlord was seldom interested in the details of agriculture, and the holders of small plots lacked the knowledge, capital, and perhaps the ambition to adopt new methods. The tenant farmer, possibly leasing several hundred acres, was an entrepreneur. He paid rent to the landlord and wages to the agricultural workers who lived in the villages. The profits of the farm, if there were some, went to him. He directed the work of the laborers, and often shared in the work himself. His wife and children worked too—the women and girls exercised responsibility for the dairy, chickens, vegetable garden, and housekeeping. One son might be sent to the local grammar school to prepare for a profession. Landlords eagerly sought such tenants. Successful farmers were literate, followed public affairs, probably qualified to vote, might own some good furniture, a picture or two to hang on the wall, and a harpsichord for their daughters. They occupied a respected place in their communities.

An important factor in economic growth was the improvement of roads. An Act of Parliament was usually required to obtain the right of way and build a turnpike. The main roads between major towns were turnpikes, which required formation of a turnpike trust and selling shares to raise capital that was amortized by charging tolls. Turnpike roads spread from London to the north, northwest, and west, connecting with Bristol, Birmingham, Manchester, Norwich, Newcastle, York and Edinburgh. Turnpikes were established by prominent gentry and businessmen who wanted fast and comfortable travel. Some wagon drivers resented losing a road that was bad but free, and tore down toll-gates. Turnpike riots broke out, to which Parliament reacted with severe punitive legislation. By 1780 Britain had a system of arterial roads that made possible comfortable travel in scheduled coaches, faster delivery of mail, and greater interweaving of regional economies. Most travelers were delighted by fast coaches on smooth, well-maintained roads, and travel by coach increased remarkably. A trip by coach, with a diversity of passengers, became a cliché of eighteenth-century novels.

The Church of England

As the institution that was responsible for the religious life of the nation, the Church of England continued to play an important role in the national life, but new currents of thought and feeling began to challenge the complacency that the Church had exhibited under the first two Georges. At the beginning of his reign, King George III stated that he would encourage "religion and morality," and he did his best to live up to that promise. He took seriously his role as supreme governor of the Church, and endeavored to appoint men of ability and dedication to the archepiscopal bench. He attended divine service regularly and conducted himself with a degree of probity that provided a good example to his people.

Despite the king's support, there was a growing awareness of the shortcomings of the Church. Complaints were made that the bishops devoted too much of their time and energy to politics and good living in London while their responsibilities toward the parish clergy were neglected. Many of the clergy came from the influential classes and owed their appointments to private patronage and the right connections rather than zeal for their duties. In the growing industrial towns there were not enough parish churches and clergy, and in the thinly populated north of England parishes were often sprawling and churches widely scattered. These problems were not new, but a spirit of criticism was growing within the Church and without, and there was less willingness to accept abuses that had been tolerated earlier.

The dominant theological view in the Church of England was still the latitudinarianism of the past, expressed most effectively by William Paley in The Principles of Morals and Political Philosophy (1785). Paley first considers the existence of God. He points out that the existence of a watch implies the existence of a watchmaker and the complexity of the universe implies the existence of God. He presents God as the divine Creator, Christ as the Son of God who revealed the moral order that God had created, and Christianity as a system of belief and worship in harmony with God's natural order. He regards the Church as a governing institution that does not respond to the people but gives them what they need.

Thomas Secker, Archbishop of Canterbury, was responsible for leadership of the Church in facing the challenges of the new era. Secker, a man of extensive learning and impressive personal presence, came from a modest Dissenting family. He explored a variety of theological and career alternatives before accepting the Thirty-Nine Articles, which was required for admission to Oxford. Secker's talent for preaching and his industriousness in carrying out his pastoral responsibilities brought him to the attention of King George II and Queen Caroline. His Whig politics meant that court favor, as exercised by his patron, the Duke of Newcastle, brought him steady advancement, first as rector of St. James's, Piccadilly, then as Bishop of Bristol, Bishop of Oxford, Dean of St. Paul's, and finally in 1758 to the leadership of the Church as Archbishop of Canterbury. Politically, Secker supported the Whigs, but on some measures that concerned moral principles, such as lowering the tax on gin to improve the revenue, he dissented. In 1761, Secker presided at the coronation and marriage of King George III, with whom he continued to be on good terms.

Secker made his archiepiscopal palace in London, Lambeth Palace, an active center for administration of the affairs of the Church. His main concern as Archbishop of Canterbury was to improve the training and discipline of the clergy, who were often criticized for non-residence and lack of attention to their duties. Secker was an authoritarian type, who expected every clergyman to be as conscientious and industrious as he was. Much of the growing appeal of Methodism was attributable to the shortcomings of the parish clergy. Coming from a Dissenting background, Secker felt considerable sympathy with the zeal of the Methodists, and he urged his clergy to "go and do thou likewise." Theologically, Secker adopted latitudinarian views early in his life. As archbishop, he drew the line at clergy who rejected the established doctrines of the Church, such as justification by faith. He opposed efforts of liberal clergymen to obtain exemption from some of the Thirty-Nine Articles that they found theologically offensive.

He supported the attempt to establish an Anglican bishop in the American colonies, which was advocated by the Society for the Propagation of the Gospel in Foreign Parts. Anglicanism, however, was weak in the colonies, and the idea was opposed by the non-Anglican majority as another example of the determination of the Crown to bring the colonies under imperial control.

Within the Church a small group of clergy called "Evangelicals" sought a religious life that was more personal and spiritual. They emphasized religious experience, Bible-reading, prayer, church-going, strict observance of the Sabbath, and Puritanical morality. As clergy or active laymen in the Church of England, the Evangelicals sought to preserve the influence of the established Church by increasing its concern for the general public. Their devotion to the salvation of souls was accompanied by strenuous efforts in educational and humanitarian activities. Although few in number, the Evangelicals exercised a powerful influence within the Church, especially early in the next century.

The patriarch and inspiration of the Evangelicals was John Newton, son of a London ship-captain. His mother was a pious Dissenter and taught him the catechism and the hymns of Isaac Watt. He was enrolled in grammar school for two years, but at the age of eleven he went to sea with his father. He was seized by the pressgang in 1744 and shipped out on an English warship, but he managed to be transferred to a ship engaged in the African slave trade. He made three trips as master of a slave ship. He began reading the Bible, and in 1748 he committed himself to the Christian faith, although he still continued his career as a slaver. In 1754, back in London, he began attending religious meetings led by George Whitefield. He left seafaring and became a customs officer at Liverpool, which gave him time to study Latin and Greek in preparation for the ministry.

Newton was a powerful preacher and conducted large revival meetings as a layman. He became acquainted with "awakened" clergymen throughout the country, including Whitefield and the Wesleys. When he applied to several bishops for ordination as a clergyman of the Church of England, he was rejected as a "Methodist," which at that time was a derogatory term for Evangelicals. In 1764, after seven years of frustration, Lord Dartmouth, an evangelical nobleman and major political figure, persuaded a bishop to ordain him. Dartmouth placed him in the poverty-stricken parish of Olney, north of London. John Thornton, a wealthy evangelical London banker, subsidized the parish. Thornton also contributed financially to Dartmouth College. At that time, Newton published An Authentic Narrative of some Remarkable and Interesting Particulars of the Life of --- (1764), a fascinating story of the adventures, love life, and conversion of a hardened sinner. The book went through numerous editions in England and America, and established Newton as one of the leading Evangelicals in the Church of England.

While at Olney, Newton became known for his assiduous attention to his parishioners as well as for his preaching. He collaborated with the poet, William Cowper, in writing and publishing the Olney Hymns (1779). Cowper contributed "God moves in a mysterious way/ His wonders to perform." Among the hymns that Newton wrote are "Glorious Things of Thee are spoken," "How Sweet the Name of Jesus Sounds," and "Amazing Grace."

In 1780 John Thornton obtained for him a parish in the City that was primarily a pulpit for preaching. Newton drew visitors from far and wide for his sermons, and many of his spiritual letters were published. He deeply regretted his participation in the slave trade. His Thoughts upon the African Slave Trade (1787), written from his own experience, was an important contribution to the movement for abolition.

Dissent, Methodism, Catholicism

The older Dissenting denominations responded to new currents of thought. The Presbyterians were divided by disputes concerning the Trinity and predestination. Some Presbyterians, who were much influenced by rationalism and science, gave up Calvinism and drifted toward Unitarianism. Others clung to their traditional Calvinist doctrines. The Independents (Congregationalists) and Baptists, like the

Evangelicals and Methodists, continued to preach Gospel Christianity emphasizing sin, salvation, and the experience of conversion.

In 1787 the Dissenting denominations joined in a political movement for repeal of the Test and Corporation Acts. Despite the Toleration Act and annual acts of indemnity, Dissenters were still treated as second-class citizens. Dissenting clergymen, for example, objected to the requirement that they agree to most of the Thirty-Nine Articles, and their formal compliance with this requirement was generally regarded as an unavoidable hypocrisy. When the bishops declared their opposition to repeal of the requirement, Pitt had no choice but to back them up, although his own personal views were broad-minded and tolerant.

By that time, Methodism was entering the ranks of Dissent. As an ordained clergyman of the Church of England, John Wesley had hoped that Methodism would revitalize the Church. When he and the movement he led were rejected, Wesley began developing a separate organization outside the Church. Wesley's Methodist societies ordained their own clergymen, built chapels for worship, and offered leadership and participation to committed laymen. In 1744 a Methodist conference was held that drew up a statement of beliefs. Annual conferences maintained unity within Methodism, and in 1784 Wesley issue a Deed of Declaration that gave legal status to Methodist conferences. Many Methodists wanted to remain nominally part of the Church of England, since they did not want to suffer the social stigma attached to Dissent. When Wesley died in 1791, however, it was apparent that Methodism was on the way to becoming another Dissenting denomination under the terms of the Toleration Act.

Methodism appealed primarily to small shopkeepers and working people, who felt out of place in the Church of England or who lived in the many under-churched areas of the West and North. A traveler in the Midlands in 1780 wrote that "at most places the curates never attend regularly, or to any effect, or comfort, so no wonder the people are gone to the Methodists." Methodism gave its adherents a sense of purpose and self-respect, and Wesley's rather strict rules for living brought order to lives that previously had been without guidance or direction. In time Methodists began to prosper and joined the lower middle class. One industrialist wrote in 1787 "I have left most of my works in Lancashire under the management of Methodists, and they serve me exceedingly well."

Roman Catholicism continued, despite legal disabilities, mainly in the remote areas of the North. Irish immigrants added a significant Catholic element to London and seaports in the west of England. The growing sense of religious tolerance led to a movement to relax the laws against Catholics, most of which were sporadically enforced, if at all. The Catholic Relief Act of 1778 permitted priests to serve their flocks and removed restrictions on Catholics' owning land. A powerful anti-Catholic backlash took place among the underclass of London, led by an eccentric nobleman, Lord George Gordon. "The Gordon Riots" were a four day orgy of vandalism, plundering, release of prisoners, and drunken rioting. The army was called out and King George III became personally involved in restoring order. In 1791 Catholics received full religious toleration. The crucial restrictions on Catholics, however, were the Test and Corporation Acts, and all efforts to end the exclusion of Catholics from the political process were staunchly resisted.

The Slave Trade

The Atlantic slave trade was an important part of the English imperial system. Nevertheless, a powerful movement that combined both religious piety and humanitarian feelings arose to challenge the existence of slavery. In 1774 John Wesley published his Thoughts on Slavery, in which he denounced the practice. In 1783 the Quakers presented a petition to Parliament for abolition of the slave trade. Lord North expressed sympathy with their purpose, but he declared that the slave trade had become necessary to almost every nation in Europe and that it would be impossible to renounce it.

The anti-slave trade movement was strengthened by an especially atrocious incident that took place in 1783. When a contagious illness spread through a slave ship, the master ordered 132 Africans flung into the sea. A trial took place between the owners and the insurers to determine who should bear the loss. The court accepted the argument that the question was entirely one of property, which would have been no different if it applied to horses or dogs instead of human beings.

Leadership of the movement to abolish the slave trade and eventually slavery itself fell to William Wilberforce, Member of Parliament for

Yorkshire, who was closely linked with leading Evangelicals. Wilberforce was born in Hull, a thriving seaport on the east coast of England, where his father was a merchant. He graduated from Cambridge and at the age of twenty, his inherited wealth enabled him to win election to the House of Commons. There he adopted an independent stance in the political crisis that led to the fall of the North government. He was a close friend of his Cambridge contemporary, William Pitt, who stayed with him at his house in Wimbledon when Parliament was in session. When Pitt became prime minister, Wilberforce supported him strongly in Yorkshire in the decisive election of 1784, and was himself elected Member of Parliament for Yorkshire at the age of twenty-five.

Wilberforce did not have ambitions to hold public office and devoted his parliamentary career to reform movements. In 1785 he experienced a spiritual crisis and was converted to evangelical views with the assistance of John Newton. He decided to devote his wealth and political position to the service of God. Wilberforce was a cheerful, gregarious, charming man with an unflinching determination to continue, despite discouragements, to work for the causes he believed in.

In 1787 Wilberforce's growing opposition to the slave trade was confirmed in a conversation with Pitt, who urged Wilberforce to devote himself to the cause. The anti-slavery movement gained another powerful advocate in Thomas Clarkson, a young Cambridge graduate of evangelical views, who abandoned his plans to enter the Church to promote the anti-slavery cause. His <u>Essay on the Slavery and Commerce of the Human Species</u> (1786) was widely circulated. Clarkson traveled to seaports, collecting information from sailors and others involved in the trade, and published the results of his interviews in <u>A Summary View of the Slave Trade and the Possible Consequences of its Abolition</u> (1787). Granville Sharp was active in many reform movements, including establishment of Sierra Leone in West Africa (1787) as a place for freed slaves. He had been active in prosecuting Somerset's case (1772), in which James Somerset, whose American master had brought him to England, was given his freedom by Lord Mansfield, chief justice of the Court of King's Bench, on the grounds that slavery was "odious" and unknown in the English Common Law. He collected a mass of evidence of the evils of the voyage from West Africa to the West Indies. Clarkson and Sharp joined with other activists to form the

Society for the Abolition of the Slave Trade. In 1788 Wilberforce took their case to the House of Commons, where he was able to state that no more than half the Africans who were initially sent into slavery lived to become effective workers.

The opponents of slavery adopted the view that slavery would gradually die out if the slave trade were abolished, for they believed slavery could not exist without a continuing supply of fresh slaves. In 1788 more than one hundred petitions were presented to Parliament opposing the slave trade, and Pitt agreed that the petitions would be considered and debated. William Dolben, an independent Member of the House of Commons, succeeded in passing a temporary regulation of the worst abuses of the slave ships. The Evangelicals and Methodists were active in supporting abolition, as were the Quakers.

In 1790 Wilberforce led in establishing a parliamentary committee that took voluminous testimony, and Dolben's Act was extended for another year. In 1791 Wilberforce moved for legislation to abolish the slave trade, and the opponents of the trade made their strongest effort to arouse public opinion in support. The slave trade interests were powerful, however, and there was a strong aversion in Parliament to interfering with an important and long-established part of imperial trade. King George III, who opposed almost all changes, opposed abolition and made his views known. The proposal was defeated, 163-88 and Dolben's Act was not renewed.

Opposition to the slave trade continued until 1807, when it was abolished. Wilberforce continued to campaign for the abolition of slavery within the Empire, and lived to know that abolition, which took place in 1833, was assured.

The Spirit of "Improvement"

Wilberforce was also committed to moral reform of English society, which he believed would have to come from the top down. In his book, A Practical View of the Prevailing Religious System of Professed Christians in the Higher and Middle Classes of this Country (1797) Wilberforce criticized luxury and irresponsibility. He urged the upper classes to improve the moral tone of the nation by providing a good example to their social inferiors. He was active in the British and Foreign Bible Society and the Church Missionary Society.

Wilberforce was supported in his endeavors by Hannah More, the evangelical daughter of a Bristol schoolmaster. Hannah and her four sisters were educated to earn a living, and they began by operating a boarding school for girls. Hannah early began writing. A play dealing with female education, The Search after Happiness (1773) was published and sold 10,000 copies. More was disturbed by the irreligion and immorality of the leaders of society, and wrote numerous tracts on that topic from an evangelical point of view. Her Thoughts on the Importance of the Manners of the Great to General Society (1788) was a surprisingly successful critique of the lives of the well-to-do and the bad example they gave to ordinary people. Her An Estimate of the Religion of the Fashionable World (1790) also sold well, but she began to receive criticism as a killjoy and common scold. By that time, she had given up on her efforts to improve the morality of the rich and powerful, and had interested herself in education.

Hannah More was especially interested in the education of women, who, she believed, determined the moral condition of the nation. She accepted the existing hierarchical and deferential society and women's place in it. Her concern was to improve the lives of women within the existing system. She urged women to accept gender differences and not attempt to emulate men. As an Evangelical, she advocated education for women that focused on Christian principles and the development of moral character. Essays on Various Subjects, Principally Designed for Young Women (1777) offered advice on various aspects of conduct and morality. Her Strictures on the Modern System of Female Education (2 vols. 1799) was a popular exposition of evangelical principles and went through seven editions in the first year.

In the 1790s More turned her attention to the education of poor children. In 1789, when Wilberforce was visiting her, they went to a nearby village, where they were appalled by the poverty, ignorance, and disorderly lives of the common people. More and her sisters left their school for girls and established a school in the village where children would be taught to read the Bible and the catechism. They were not taught to write—the More sisters did not want them writing pamphlets criticizing the social system in which they were trapped. The school was praised by the Evangelicals, and within a decade the More sisters had established a dozen schools in the area. The schools began offering evening classes for adults, where the participants were taught to be prudent and industrious, and women learned to sew and knit. They organized societies where women learned the benefits of cleanliness, proper conduct, and Godly living, which led to accusations that the More sisters were Methodists.

In the process, Hannah More noticed the neglect of the area by the Church. There was no resident curate in any of the thirteen parishes of the area. To counter the lack of formal religious influences, More included religious materials in her schools, which aroused opposition from the Church. They complained that she was undermining the authority of ordained clergy among the parishioners whom they so blatantly neglected. Her complaints brought her the title: "Bishop in Petticoats."

More's political and social conservatism made her an articulate opponent of English radicals who had been energized by the French Revolution. She published <u>Village Politics: Addressed to all the Mechanics, Journey, and day Labourers, in Great Britain</u> (1792) in opposition to the works of Tom Paine, which were widely read in cheap editions, possibly by some of her former pupils.

Robert Raikes, a Gloucester printer and newspaper publisher, also became interested in the education of poor children. He noticed that Dissenters in the area had begun setting up Sunday schools to teach children the three Rs and decided to do the same for the Church of England. In 1780 he established a Sunday school in his parish, which he supported with his own money. Four years later, a notice praising the school appeared in the <u>Gentleman's Magazine</u> and Raikes began receiving inquiries about it. Partially as a result of this publicity, Sunday schools began springing up throughout the area. The bishops of Gloucester and Salisbury encouraged Sunday schools, and in 1786 the Church of England established the Sunday School Society to promote the movement. The next year Raikes was granted an audience with Queen Charlotte. By the end of the century, Sunday schools were common throughout the country, and were especially important in bringing the rudiments of an education to the children who worked in the factories that were part of the Industrial Revolution.

The Law, Prisons

The English Common Law was frequently praised for its protection of personal liberty and property, but it became apparent to thoughtful persons that its system of punishment for crime was grossly irrational. There were many laws, some of great antiquity, imposing different punishments for the same crime. The savage punishments of felony were imposed for theft of amounts of money that at one time were considerable but which by the later eighteenth century had become trifling.

In 1786 Samuel Romilly, who had visited France and met the leading figures of the Enlightenment, undertook a crusade for reform of the criminal law. His <u>Thoughts on Executive Justice</u> (1786) lists 220 capital punishments, many of them for minor crimes. He argues that certainty of punishment was more important than severity of punishments. He points out some of the anomalies of the criminal law—it was a capital offence to cut down trees in a garden or orchard or to break a fishpond so that the fish escaped. On the other hand, it was not a capital offence for a man to attempt to murder his father or to commit perjury that led to the execution of an innocent man. To steal fruit which had been gathered was a felony; to enter an orchard and steal fruit off the tree was only a trespass. To break a pane of glass in a shop-window and steal something was punishable by death; to enter a house in the summer through an open window and steal something was only a misdemeanor.

Where punishments were out of all proportion to the offence juries often refused to convict, in which case no punishment was imposed at all. Professional criminals preferred to take their chances with a capital charge, for it was easier to get off than if they were charged with a misdemeanor. Romilly devoted his life to reduction of the number and inconsistencies of capital punishments, for which he was hated and derided by judges, lawyers, and men of property, who were convinced that such severe punishments stood between them and anarchy. Over the next twenty years, Romilly was able to secure passage of some useful legislation in the House of Commons, but it was always rejected by the House of Lords. In 1818, at the age of 61, he committed suicide.

The methods used in executions were as barbarous as the legal code. The convict was taken through the streets of London in a cart to Tyburn, where he was publicly hanged for the amusement of the crowd.

In 1783 the trip through the streets, which often led to disorders, was abolished. Executions remained public but took place in front of Newgate prison. A humanitarian gallows was adopted, by which the convict dropped suddenly, broke his neck, and died instantly instead of strangling, as had often been the case before.

John Howard was to prisons what Romilly was to the criminal law. Howard was a prosperous gentleman of good education who was appointed High Sheriff of Bedfordshire, normally an honorary office. When he inspected the jails of his county he was appalled at the filth, disease, and abuses he found, and from that time he became England's greatest prison reformer. That reform was necessary had been seen in 1752 when the judges, jurors, and some 40 visitors holding court in Newgate Prison contracted jail fever and died. As a result, a ventilator fan was installed on the roof.

Howard traveled through England examining prisons, with special attention to the great prisons of London. His findings were published in The State of Prisons in England and Wales (1776). He reported that most prisons contained large numbers of people who had not committed any crime—some were debtors, some were awaiting trial, others had been found innocent but could not leave until they paid the jailer's fees. The prisoners had insufficient food and water and were crowded together in dark, damp dungeons. They had no bedding and many prisons were unheated in winter. Heavy chains and iron collars were commonly used. Persons of all ages, sexes, and severity of crime were lumped together. Disease was rampant and the odor unbearable. Most prisons were operated by the jailers for their personal profit. Convicts who could pay lived in comfort, often supported by friends who engaged in crime to pay the cost.

Howard's book made its mark, although reform was slow to come. In 1774 Howard testified to a parliamentary committee, and that year legislation was passed that established requirements for cleanliness and fresh air in prisons. The shire was required to pay the jailer's fees of persons who had been found innocent. In 1779 legislation was passed to relieve overcrowding by building new prisons. Howard also pointed out the injustices resulting from imprisonment for debt, which prevented the debtor from earning the money to pay what he owed and often burdened him with legal costs greater than the debt itself. In

1785 Howard began investigating hospitals and prisons in Europe. He died of jail fever in Russia in 1790.

James Neild, a wealthy Quaker, became interested in prison conditions when his apprentice was imprisoned in Kings Bench Prison for debt and died of jail fever. Neild founded the Society for the Relief and Discharge of Persons Imprisoned for Small Debts (1773). He continued to inspect prisons and found that Howard's legislation had not been enforced by the magistrates. He reported on his visits in letters to a friend. From 1803-1813 the Gentleman's Magazine published 77 of Neild's letters.

Another object of reformers was dueling. Although the law did not distinguish between killing a man in a duel and any other murder, dueling was supported by public opinion, including the judges. A great many public men engaged in duels, including William Pitt. When William Wilberforce tried to bring dueling before the House of Commons, he found that no more than five or six others would support him. Humanitarians also criticized the cruelty characteristic of the age—flogging in the schools, blood sports, cruelty to animals, and abuse of children. In 1788 legislation was passed to restrain the abuse of the children used as chimney sweeps.

While many evils were left unchanged, they were to some extent mitigated by a great increase in philanthropy. There was a long tradition in England that the well-to-do should look after the unfortunate, a tradition embodied in the Elizabethan Poor Law. However, this tradition broke down in the impersonal environment of London or the growing industrial towns. London was already notable for its variety of hospitals and charitable institutions, and new ones continued to be founded. The enthusiasm for charitable works became so great that some Evangelicals complained that "benevolence" had become a substitute for Christianity.

Mrs. Elizabeth Montagu and the Bluestockings

The intellectual and cultural elite of London gathered from time to time at evening assemblies held at the London townhouse of Mrs. Elizabeth Montagu. Mrs. Montagu was born into a wealthy and well-connected family in Yorkshire. As a child, she spent part of the year in Cambridge with her grandfather, a distinguished classical scholar. She studied Latin, French, and Italian, and was introduced to ancient and English history and literature. She grew up with people of wealth and position who engaged in intellectual conversations that included men and women equally, and this became the model for her assemblies. At age twenty-four she married Edward Montagu, a Member of Parliament and owner of landed estates and coal mines in the north of England. As was typical of people of their status, they lived in London during the winter social season and at their country estate in the summer.

In the 1760s Mrs. Montagu began holding large assemblies, sometimes including 120 people. Her husband was often absent supervising his properties in the north. She provided a large room and refreshments, and the guests were expected to engage in conversation on intellectual and cultural topics. Attire was informal, which included blue stockings for the women. The people who attended at one time or another were a Who's Who of London cultural life—Samuel Johnson, Sir Joshua Reynolds, Edmund Burke, David Garrick, Horace Walpole, Hannah More, Frances Burney, Sarah Fielding, and Elizabeth Carter. These assemblies included both genders, although women predominated.

Mrs. Montagu took a serious interest in English literature. In 1769 she published An Essay on the Writings and Genius of Shakespeare, in which she patriotically identifies the qualities that made Shakespeare superior to other dramatists. She defends the Bard against criticism by Voltaire and others who held to the neoclassical ideals of French drama. After her husband's death she became interested in architecture, and employed Robert Adam to redecorate the large room in which her assemblies were held. In the 1770s she built Montagu House, a large mansion on Portman Square. Her country home was rebuilt in a Gothic style. The grounds were landscaped by "Capability" Brown, his last project before his death.

Scotland

The age of improvement also extended to Scotland and Ireland. Economically, Scotland began to enjoy the promise of the Act of Union. Glasgow's trade with America and the West Indies increased remarkably. Agriculture was improved by the introduction of potatoes for human consumption and turnips for cattle feed. Iron and coal production increased dramatically, and the inventions that were transforming textile production in England were introduced into Scotland also. Distilling of whisky and gin, much of it illegal, was a large-scale industry, supplemented by small stills in remote places where the excise surveyors did not reach. Military roads and forts opened up the Highlands, which were denuded of their villages and crofters by landlords who found that raising sheep was more profitable. Edinburgh was the legal and social center of Scotland and boasted a distinguished university and an important publishing industry.

Ireland

Dublin, the second largest city in the British Isles, became a beautiful city. In the later seventeenth century four bridges had been built across the Liffey. The Corporation (city government) laid out St. Stephen's Green and required that houses be built of brick or stone with tiled or slate roofs. Dublin developed an attractive center along Sackville St. (now O'Connell St.), which was extended across the river. New housing developments were laid out with straight streets and beautiful squares surrounded by elegant townhouses. The Castle, where the viceroy held court, was old and undistinguished but the interior was splendidly appointed.

The Parliament House (now the Bank of Ireland), the Royal Exchange, the Custom House, the Four Courts, and Trinity College were distinguished examples of Palladian architecture. In 1757 a Wide Streets Commission was established with extensive authority to widen and beautify streets. Dublin attracted the Anglo-Irish ruling class. In 1786 a patent was issued to establish the Theatre Royal with a monopoly of producing plays, and the theatre at Smock Alley was closed. Ireland produced many talented young men like Edmund Burke and Richard Brinsley Sheridan, but the most ambitious were drawn to London, where careers could be made.

The Irish countryside was dotted with Palladian mansions with fine furniture and pictures, and set in formal gardens. Country gentry and prosperous farmers continued to live in well-built thatched houses. Thatched cabins were usually for small farmers, and tenants lived in mud-walled cottages.

Ch. 16. A Conservative Culture at a Time of Change

From the perspective of today, the late eighteenth century is notable for the French Revolution, Industrialism, and the origins of Romanticism. From the perspective of contemporaries, it was a time when long-established institutions continued to provide an attractive way of life for the genteel classes and adequate opportunities for the growing middle class. Leaders in government, the Church, the law and society came together to resist radical movements for reform and the challenge of the French Revolution.

Early indicators of the rise of Romanticism did not shake the literary tradition established by Addison and Steele, Fielding, Smollett, and Samuel Johnson. In the theatre the plays of Richard Brinsley Sheridan did not break new ground. In the arts, the classicism of Reynolds and the success of history painting looked to the past. "Sensibility" in portraits and landscapes was a natural outgrowth of long-existing trends. Architecture and sculpture maintained continuity with the earlier part of the century. Music received powerful new influences from the continent that were attractive but not native to England and not readily absorbed.

Most of the people of all social classes were not advocates of change. They had inherited a political system, an economy, a social structure, religious institutions, and cultural values of which they were proud. Burke, Johnson, Sheridan, the Burneys, Reynolds, and Horace Walpole accepted a world that was good to them. If they were satisfied with the culture they knew, who can blame them?

The Debate over the French Revolution

In 1789 the French Crown was bankrupt. In desperation, King Louis XVI called the Estates General, the medieval representative body that had not met since 1614. When the Estates General assembled, the Third Estate, which represented the people, rose up against the Crown and demanded a constitution. They were joined by the clergy and aristocracy, and the Estates General was transformed into the National Constituent Assembly with the Marquis de Lafayette as its leader. The Declaration of the Rights of Man and the Citizen (1789) was promulgated, and sweeping changes were made in local government and in the Church. The National Assembly drew up a constitution for France with a limited monarchy and a Legislative Assembly to represent the people. France seemed to be following the trail blazed by Britain.

In November 1789, the Rev. Richard Price, a Dissenting clergyman with radical views, preached a sermon to the Revolution Society, an organization established to commemorate the "Glorious Revolution of 1688-89." Price identified three key features of the Revolution—liberty of conscience, the right to resist arbitrary power, and the right of the people to form their own government. Edmund Burke came forward to defend the constitution from radicals like Price. In the past, Burke had been a leader in movements for reforms that he felt would make the English constitution better without changing it fundamentally—"economical reform," greater self-government for Ireland, equal political rights for Dissenters and Catholics, and abolition of the slave trade. He was a conservative reformer who believed that timely reform was the best way to save the constitution from radical movements that would destroy it. He opposed parliamentary reform and other steps toward democracy as violations of the ancient constitution.

Burke replied to Price with Reflections on the Revolution in France (1790), in which he attacks the radicalism of the French revolutionaries. He praises English government as an organic growth based on the accumulated experience of generations and fitted to the national character. He notes the dangers created by changing long established institutions. He rejects the Lockean concept of universal human rights by which all governments should be judged and, if necessary, overthrown. Destruction of a long-existing government with the idea of forming a better one, he argues, is an act of arrogance by ambitious and ignorant men that will lead to chaos and eventually despotism. Burke's conservatism was in step with the prevailing attitudes of the time, and he finally found himself on the popular side, honored by King George III and the political and religious leaders of England.

Tom Paine, sensing the next field of action, had gone from America to France in 1787. He was present in the early phases of the French Revolution, which he saw as the next stage in the world revolution that had begun in America. Paine responded to Burke with The Rights of Man (1790, 1792), a ringing defense of republicanism and democracy. He ridicules Burke's contention that "the Glorious Revolution of 1688-89" was a permanent constitutional settlement that could not be changed. "Every age and generation," he writes, "must be free to act for itself." He rejects Burke's veneration for the English constitution, which he declares was based on conquest (the Norman Conquest) and a long history of royal usurpations and attacks on Liberty. The Rights of Man was dedicated to Gen. George Washington and the Marquis de Lafayette.

The book was enormously popular in England and sold an estimated 1.5 million copies. The Rights of Man was printed in cheap editions that were widely disseminated, and it established the intellectual foundations of working-class radicalism. Paine returned to France and became actively involved as the Revolution entered its violent phases.

While in prison in France, Paine dropped his next bombshell. The Age of Reason (1793, 1795) was first published in France in a French translation, and then published in England. It was an all-out attack on organized religions, which Paine describes as "human inventions, set up to terrify and enslave mankind, and monopolize power and profit." Paine was a deist—"I believe in one God," he writes, "and no more, and I hope for happiness beyond this life." He launches into an extensive criticism of the doctrines and practices of Christianity. The work was roundly criticized as "atheistic" and subversive of all public order. More than any other of his works, The Age of Reason damned Paine in public opinion. He returned to America in 1802, where his friend, Thomas Jefferson was president.

Other radical leaders joined the fray. Mary Wollstonecraft, an intellectually ambitious your woman, came from a modest background. She was largely self-educated. She developed her ideas and writing skills by working as an editor for Joseph Johnson, a publisher of radical works, who took her under his wing and encouraged her ambitions to be a writer. She supported herself as a writer of fiction until her outrage at Burke's Reflections on the Revolution in France led her to publish A Vindication of the Rights of Man (1790). She followed that with her most famous work, A Vindication of the Rights of Woman (1792), in which she argues for equal rights for women in marriage, the law, and especially in education.

The indefatigable Catherine Macaulay weighed in with Letters on Education (1790), which includes a plea for the education of women. She chides women for passively accepting the subordinate role that society had designated for them. Until women were better educated, she concludes, there was no hope of gaining political, legal, and social equality. Her Observations on the Reflections of the Rt. Hon. Edmund Burke, on the Revolution in France (1790) contributed to a vigorous pamphlet war that continued for years.

The poetry and novels of Charlotte Smith contributed to the spirit of reform. Smith's father was a prosperous landowner and she received a genteel education. Despite the ups and downs of her life, Smith always maintained the image of a gentlewoman. She married the son of a wealthy businessman and owner of plantations in Barbados. When her husband proved to be utterly reckless with his money, she was left to provide for herself and her children by writing. Her first success was as a poet, an appropriate role for a gentlewoman. Her Elegiac Sonnets and other Essays by Charlotte Smith of Bignor Park, Sussex (1784) was a surprising success. Her poetry reveals the feelings of a gentlewoman suffering from unfortunate circumstances and appealed to readers of the age of "sensibility."

Smith's first novel, Emmeline, the Orphan of the Castle (1788) was a success, and was followed by more. Her novels are in the sentimental mode, and often deal with the social problems faced by women, especially their inferior status in the English legal system. She often uses the figure of the wanderer. In The Old Manor House (1793), the novel considered her best, the protagonist goes to America, where he sympathizes with the Indians and criticizes imperialism and slavery. Initially she sympathized with the French Revolution as a movement for political and social equality. In her novel, Desmond (1792), the hero travels to France and writes letters that favor radical reforms in Britain. When revolutionary France became a threat to its neighbors, she modified her views but held firmly to the general principles that the Revolution proclaimed. Her popularity waned due to her radical political ideas, but was regained with The Letters of a Solitary Wanderer (5 vols., 1801-02).

In the meantime, radical activists carried the ideas of Paine and others into the public arena. John Horne Tooke emerged as a leading figure in radical agitation. In 1789 the Society for Constitutional Information, in which Horne Tooke was active, sent a message of congratulation to the French National Assembly. He organized the Society's efforts to distribute cheap copies of Paine's The Rights of Man. He was active in the London Corresponding Society, which was organized to create a network of radical organizations throughout the country.

William Pitt, prime minister, did not immediately join the ideological battle. From his perspective, the French Revolution meant that France was no longer a military threat. In 1792, as he reviewed the success of his economic policies, Pitt made an ill-fated prophecy. "There was never a time in the history of this country," he declared, "when, from the situation of Europe, we might more reasonably expect fifteen years of peace, than we may at the present moment."

Later that year the revolutionaries seized control of the government of France and imprisoned King Louis XVI and Queen Marie Antoinette. Prussian and Austrian forces advanced toward France to rescue the king and queen, and the revolutionaries raised a large army that repulsed them at the border. The execution of Louis XVI in 1793 and Marie Antoinette later set all the crowned heads of Europe against the Revolution. The next year England declared war—a war that lasted with one brief interlude until the defeat of Napoleon in 1815.

A powerful reaction took place, and many of the Whigs, including Burke, supported the Tory government of Pitt. In 1794 habeas corpus was suspended and radicals like Horne Tooke were imprisoned on suspicion of treasonous activities. The next year the Pitt government cracked down with the Treasonable Practices Act and the Seditious Meetings Act. The period of public agitation and mass meetings came to an end, and radicalism was driven underground.

The New Toryism

The word "Tory" has had many meanings, but in the eighteenth-century it meant respect for established institutions such as the Crown, the Church, the courts of Common Law, and the constitution of Parliament. The political conflicts of the reign of George III—Whig challenges to "the influence of the Crown," the disturbances created by Wilkes and the American colonists, and the agitation for parliamentary and "economical" reform— created a sense of uneasiness that led the country to rally behind the king and William Pitt the Younger in the election of 1784. When the French Revolution broke out and threatened England, George III became a national symbol and for the first time enjoyed popularity. George III suffered from mental problems that may have been inherited, and as time passed his mental breakdowns increased in number and duration. When he died in 1820 his mind had left him completely.

As prime minister, Pitt was sympathetic to reform, but he had to limit his policies to suit the prejudices of the king and Parliament. His personal commitments to parliamentary reform, relaxation of the laws against Catholics, establishment of closer economic relationships with Ireland, and abolition of the slave trade foundered on the reluctance of the House of Commons to support change that might be unsettling. Pitt was a nonpartisan leader, but the word "Tory" became attached to his supporters, and in this sense he is sometimes deemed to be the founder of a new Tory Party. The consolidation of the Tory Party came with the French Revolution, when Englishmen rallied behind the Crown and Church.

Sir William Blackstone

While reformers like Romilly, Howard, and Wilberforce evaluated existing institutions and found them deficient in some respects, a body of vigorous advocates defended English institutions and culture as the result of the accumulated experience of the nation. They identified tradition and custom as crucial in shaping political and moral values. Lawyers were important in this respect, for the Common Law was deeply rooted in the past and was revered by Englishmen as the basis for the security of their lives and property.

Chief among legal writers was Sir William Blackstone, who combined a university education at Oxford with study of the Common Law. The Common Law was not taught at the universities, but in 1758 a Mr. Jacob Viner endowed a Professorship of English Common Law at Oxford. Blackstone was appointed as the first Vinerian professor, and his lectures became the basis of his <u>Commentaries on the Laws of England</u> (4 vols. 1765-a69), which remained the basis of legal education in England and America for the next century.

Blackstone's <u>Commentaries</u> was the first complete, well-ordered presentation of the English Common Law. His style was smooth and graceful, and his book was written for lawyers and educated gentlemen. His conservatism in matters of government and law made his work welcome to judges and the country gentry. He hailed the balance and harmony of the constitution, praised the English criminal law, with its ancient procedures and vast array of punishments, and even found reasons to defend prosecutions for witchcraft, which had been decriminalized in 1736. Blackstone was a man of his time in that he sought to bring order to the confused and sometimes contradictory principles of the Common Law. He defended the law as a body of accumulated wisdom superior to that of any individual and not to be judged by abstract principles based on Reason.

In his political theory Blackstone rejects the doctrines of Locke. Conceding the existence of laws of Nature in the abstract, he directs the attention of his readers to the realities of English government, which was not the result of a contract between the people and their rulers but a system that had grown up over a long period of time. Blackstone defends the traditional concept of a "mixed and balanced constitution," in which the rights of the monarchy, the aristocracy and the people checked and balanced each other. "Thus every branch of our civil polity supports and is supported, regulates and is regulated, by the rest," he writes, "(impelling government in a direction) which constitutes the true line of the liberty and happiness of the community." He concedes that the "influence of the Crown" had increased as its legal powers had declined. He concludes that "the crown has, gradually and imperceptibly, gained almost as much in influence as it has apparently lost in prerogative."

Like Locke, Blackstone is concerned to define the area of freedom, but he sees it as exercised within the limits established by the laws of England and not based on abstract natural rights. The conflict between natural rights and legal rights was shown in his ambiguous position on slavery. "The spirit of liberty," he writes, "is so deeply implanted in our constitution . . . that a slave or Negro the moment he lands in England falls under the protection of the laws and so far becomes a free man." But the laws protecting property, Blackstone notes, protect the right of a master to the services of his former slave, a principle that applied mainly to slave owners who returned to England and brought one or more slaves with them as domestic servants. Blackstone declared that the former slave was still obligated to serve his former master as before. Blackstone was over-ruled in Somerset's Case (1772), which dealt with an escaped slave who was aided by an anti-slavery group to claim his freedom under English law. Chief Justice Mansfield ruled that slavery "is so odious that nothing can be suffered to support it but positive law." Since such a law did not exist, he ruled that slavery was illegal in England.

Samuel Johnson

Samuel Johnson was a powerful spokesman for the Christian humanist traditions of the past. His brilliant intellect, wide learning, and sound judgment raised him from the ranks of hack writers to the dominant literary figure of Georgian England. He developed a sonorous, dignified style that communicated a sense of authority and dignity. His use of polysyllabic Latinate words and rolling periods harked back to the ancient classics and the beauties of the King James Bible and the Book of Common Prayer. It was a prose style quite different from the simplicity and directness of Addison and Steele or Swift.

In politics Johnson is often called a "Tory", but that term had lost much of its meaning by mid-century. Basic to Johnson's political thought was the typical Londoner's suspicion of courtiers, politicians, and all who sought to use government to promote their personal power and wealth. He easily saw through the phony arguments, wishful thinking, and special pleading of political debates. His reaction to politics was that of the honest, independent citizen, prepared to cock a skeptical eye at politicians and their minions. Johnson was a Tory in that he looked to the king to rise above party politics and popular demagogues and give the nation leadership based on concern for the general welfare. For this reason he supported King George III, with whom he once had a long conversation that he regarded as one of the great experiences of his life.

One of Johnson's political principles was dutiful subordination to properly constituted authorities in a society of ranks. He was conservative in his desire to preserve an ordered society, which, like Blackstone and Burke, he regarded as best for most of the people. He rejected the rationalist ideas of the Enlightenment. He regarded radicals in Britain and America as presumptuous nobodies making trouble to inflate their own sense of self-importance. He suspected that calls for "Liberty" grew out of personal ambition or unreasonable expectations, neither of which was likely to contribute to the public good.

In The False Alarm (1770) Johnson attacked the rabble-rousing demagogue, John Wilkes, whom he later discovered to be a fine fellow despite his politics. Johnson wrote several pamphlets supporting the policies of the Crown against the American colonists who, in his view, were stiff-necked malcontents resisting an imperial system that was beneficial to all concerned. With his shrewd realism and practical good sense, Johnson opposed political or religious movements that depended upon shallow rhetoric and emotional arguments. In these respects, Johnson was a "Tory" in the tradition of Dryden, Pope, and Swift.

Samuel Johnson was a deeply religious man, committed to historic Christianity in an age when the dominant trend of thought was toward Deism or Skepticism. He saw mankind as terribly flawed, and he was acutely conscious of his own failings. For Samuel Johnson, religion stepped in where morality failed—it was a source of divine strength when one could not make it on his own; it was a source of divine wisdom where one could not understand for himself; it was a source of forgiveness for those shortcomings that one could not overcome. Johnson clung to his Christian faith because he needed it.

Literary criticism was one of Johnson's strengths. Sometimes a distinction is made between the creative literary figure whose works open the mind to new experiences, and the critic, who explains and judges that which he cannot achieve himself. But literary criticism can be creative in its own way, and such outstanding writers as Dryden, Addison,

Pope, and Johnson made literary criticism an important activity of the mind. Johnson wrote extensively for The Literary Magazine: or Universal Review (1756-58) and The Critical Review (1758 ff.), which were among the earliest periodicals devoted to literary criticism.

In 1765 Johnson brought out a magnificent edition of Shakespeare with introduction and notes. Shakespeare was much admired in the eighteenth century, but his plays had been edited and "improved" to bring them in line with eighteenth-century ideas of form and propriety. Johnson restored the correct text of Shakespeare and explained the greatness and meaning of his works. He argues that Shakespeare's imagination and grasp of human nature were more important than his violations of the neoclassical rules of drama.

A decade later, when Johnson was already feeling the effects of age, a group of publishers came to him with a proposal for an edition of the English poets since 1660. Johnson agreed to write biographical introductions to each poet and to supervise the provision of correct texts. He loved biography, for he believed it provided a stock of personal experience from which moral principles could be derived. He also believed that the life and works of an author were inextricably entwined—the one could not be understood without understanding the other.

Johnson wrote long prefaces for the works of Milton, Dryden, Pope and Swift, and briefer prefaces for those poets whom he considered minor. The prefaces are occasionally are marked by striking passages that make Johnson's judgments memorable. He begins each essay with information about the poet's family, the main events of his life, and the reasons for writing his most important works. He brings his own firmly-rooted moral principles to bear upon the life and works of each poet. His admiration for Paradise Lost was great, but he points out that all the characters were supernatural (even Adam and Eve in the garden were not like people in the fallen world), and for that reason the poem does not deal with realities of life that readers could relate to. He comments on Pope's touchiness about petty things that he felt were insulting, his unwillingness to heed criticism, and his long-held grudges. Often he examines individual lines to point out their beauties or their faults. He criticizes the haste and carelessness of Dryden, who neglects to polish and refine lines that should have been better than they are. In his evaluation of poets and works he looks for an understanding of life and the variety of human beings.

The biographical and critical prefaces that Johnson wrote were so admired they were published separately as his Lives of the Most Eminent English Poets (1779, 1781). The book had a formative influence on the development of literary criticism by considering and evaluating the characteristics of good literature in general, and by applying them to each author. By this time Johnson had achieved fame. In 1775 he received a doctorate from Oxford.

Johnson's appetite for experience and his sense of humanity are seen in his Journey to the Western Islands of Scotland (1775), which superficially appears to be one of the numerous travel accounts published at that time. The book tells of a trip that Johnson made with his young Scottish friend, James Boswell. Johnson analyzes with keen perception the pre-literate culture of the Highlands in all its many aspects. He also challenges the authenticity of Macpherson's poems of Ossian and calls upon him to produce the original manuscripts, which, of course, Macpherson could not do. A planned trip to Italy, which would have been the capstone of Johnson's travels, did not take place.

Johnson was the center of an informal Literary Club that included some of the most distinguished men of the day—Burke, Goldsmith, Garrick, Gibbon, Reynolds, Richard Brinsley Sheridan, and Charles Burney. With his friends Johnson displayed another of his talents—his powers as a conversationalist. Johnson was a marvelous talker; he could talk intelligently and forcefully on almost any subject. It was through conversation that his ideas were clarified and eventually found permanence in his works.

James Boswell

James Boswell was the son and heir of a Scottish judge from a prominent family. He was intended by his father for the law and was educated at the universities of Edinburgh and Glasgow. He made his living as a Scottish barrister, but he loved literary people and the brilliant social life of London, which he visited as often as he could. In 1763 he left for the continent, where he studied law at Utrecht, traveled extensively, and met Voltaire, Rousseau, and other celebrities of the Enlightenment. Boswell was a compulsive writer, and his journals are a mine of information about the age.

Boswell's close association with Johnson began on his trip to London in 1763. He was confined to Scotland by his law practice for most of the year, but he visited London regularly to see Johnson and the literary lions of Johnson's Club. He began collecting information for a biography, including accounts of Johnson's conversations. His tour of the Scottish Highlands with Johnson gave him an extended opportunity to observe Johnson and listen to his reminiscences. In 1791 Boswell's The Life of Samuel Johnson, LL.D (2 vols,1791) was published and instantly recognized as a masterpiece. He published two other important works— An Account of Corsica: The Journal of a Tour to That Island and Memoirs of Pascal Paoli (1768) and The Journal of a Tour to the Hebrides with Samuel Johnson, LL.D (1785).

Boswell had a marvelous ability to use details to build up a picture of an individual—warts and all. In his Life of Johnson we meet other members of a great generation, but Samuel Johnson—especially his brilliant conversation—is always center stage. Boswell's Life of Johnson is still the source to which we go to find the Samuel Johnson who, through his works and conversation, influenced one of the most brilliant generations in English literary history.

The Theatre of Richard Brinsley Sheridan

Richard Brinsley Sheridan was another of the talented Irishmen who came to London to pursue careers. His father was active in Dublin theatre and a teacher of elocution, neither of which paid much money. His mother was Frances Sheridan, the novelist. In 1759 the family moved to London and eventually settled in Bath. Richard was handsome and personable. When he was twenty-one he eloped with the young and beautiful Elizabeth Linley, who was a member of a musical family and a splendid singer. Thomas Gainsborough painted a famous portrait of Elizabeth and her sister (1772). Elizabeth's brother, Thomas Linley Jr. was a talented violinist, who studied violin in Italy, performed in public concerts, and wrote many violin sonatas and concertos. He was music director at Drury Lane and a prolific composer of music for the stage. His death at age twenty-three in a boating accident was a great loss to English music.

Faced with the need to support a wife, Sheridan looked to the theatre. He achieved a rousing success at Covent Garden with his first play, The Rivals (1775), which harked back to the Restoration comedy and as such was a refreshing change from the moralizing gentility of the sentimental comedy. The Rivals is set in Bath and centers on Captain Jack Absolute, a handsome young military officer who is in love with Lydia Languish, a devotee of romance novels. Jack wants to win Lydia as himself and not as an officer and a gentleman. He pretends to be a lowly soldier, and Lydia is thrilled with the romantic idea of casting prudence aside and eloping with a man without a fortune. Jack's overbearing father, Sir Anthony Absolute, who is tyrannical but considers himself indulgent, has arranged a marriage for Jack, who rebels against Sir Anthony's authoritarian ways and peremptorily rejects the marriage due to his love for Lydia. A parallel romance between Jack's friend, Faulkland and Julia depicts another dimension to the travails of young love. Broad comedy is added by Bob Acres, the uncouth country squire and Sir Lucius O'Trigger, a hot-tempered Irishman. A delightful feature of the play is the misuse of words by Lydia's aunt, Mrs. Malaprop (ex. "an allegory on the banks of the Nile").

Eventually Jack learns that Lydia is the woman his father has chosen for his bride. He is disappointed to discover that Sir Anthony gets what he wants, as usual. Lydia is disappointed to learn that her romantic elopement with a humble soldier will be replaced by a conventional marriage with a well-financed captain. However, Jack and Lydia love each other, and the play ends happily.

The Rivals was followed in the same year by another hit at Covent Garden, The Duenna, or, The Double Elopement (1775). The Duenna is a ballad opera with music written by Thomas Linley Jr, Sheridan's brother-in-law. Sheridan worked carefully with Linley to integrate the libretto and the songs. Donna Luisa, a young Spanish woman who loves Antonio, flees to escape her father's insistence that she marry a disagreeable older man. She disguises herself as her duenna, an older woman assigned to chaperone her. In turn, the duenna disguises herself as Donna Luisa, and serves as a go-between with Antonio. After various mix-ups in which Donna Luisa and the duenna are involved, Donna Luisa marries her true love and the wealthy older man is tricked into marrying the duenna.

In 1776 Sheridan, supported by a group of investors, bought out Garrick's share of Drury Lane theatre, where he became manager. He bought the other share in 1778. His play, The School for Scandal (1777), is a comedy of manners set in Lady Sneerwell's salon, which is a hotbed of gossip. The principal retailers of gossip are Sir Charles Surface, a blunt-spoken man, and his brother Joseph, a schemer who pretends to dislike gossip but is a cunning promoter of it.

The Critic, Or, A Tragedy Rehearsed (1779) is a satire of the theatre similar to Buckingham's The Rehearsal. The play begins at the home of Mr. Dangle, a devotee of the theatre, who is visited by three friends— Sir Fretful Plagiary, who has written a play and stubbornly refuses to accept any criticism of it; Mr. Puff, who has a play in rehearsal about the defeat of the Spanish Armada; and Mr. Sneer, a self-appointed critic who is quick to offer negative comments. As they discuss the theatre, they reveal their shallowness and pretentiousness. The central event of The Critic takes place when Dangle and Sneer watch the rehearsal of Mr. Puff's ridiculous play with its stale characters and stilted, hackneyed dialogue. Puff constantly interrupts the actors with complaints about their performance and utters exclamations at the beauties of his lines. In The Critic, Sheridan communicates his sense of the qualities that make a good play by ridiculing a truly bad one.

Sheridan's top star at Drury Lane was Sarah Siddons, the talented daughter of a theatrical family. She was tall, beautiful, and exuded a powerful stage presence. Success came slowly to Sarah Siddons. After several years of performing in provincial theatres, she was cast by Garrick in a play that flopped. She returned to the provinces and acted all the great female roles. In 1782 her performance at Drury Lane in Isabella, or, the Fatal Marriage, a reworking of Southerne's The Fatal Marriage, made her a star. From that point on, Sarah Siddons was recognized as England's premier actress in dramatic roles. She was famous for her portrayal of Lady Macbeth. Her brother, John Philip Kemble, a distinguished actor noted for his portrayal of Hamlet, played various roles with her. In 1788 Kemble became manager of Drury Lane. Siddons was also admired for her exemplary personal life, which lived up to all the conventional expectations of a wife and mother. After her husband died, she retired at age 56, the unchallenged queen of the English stage.

In 1780, Sheridan was elected to the House of Commons and became an eloquent advocate of parliamentary reform, Irish rights, religious toleration, and abolition of slavery. His speeches in the House of Commons supporting the impeachment of Warren Hastings for abuses while governor of the British territories in India were legendary. Tickets were sold for seats in the gallery when it was known he would speak. His wife, Elizabeth, sang at private concerts, although she would not sing in public. They were a popular couple in high society, and Sheridan became a respected member of Johnson's Literary Club.

Sheridan enjoyed personal successes in both the theatre and politics, but he left no permanent mark on either. His influence in politics was minimal, and as a theatre manager he continued the plays and dramatic techniques of the age of Garrick. His reputation rests upon three excellent plays that looked not to the future, but to the past.

Hannah Parkhouse Cowley continued the tradition of Aphra Behn, Susannah Centlivre, and Eliza Haywood into the late eighteenth century. She was the daughter of a prominent bookseller in the west of England. Her husband had a position with the East India Company. When she and her husband attended a dull play, she announced that she could do better, and she did. Cowley sent her play, The Runaway (1776) to Garrick, who produced it successfully in his last year as manager of Drury Lane. The play deals with the injustice of arranged marriages, and created a public controversy when the heroine complains about the word "obey" in the marriage ceremony. Cowley's plays were not strident. She used good-natured comedy to get her points across. In Who's the Dupe? (1779), a hilarious farce, the heroine complains that women's education is too limited to enable them to participate in refined conversation.

Her most admired play was The Belle's Stratagem (1780), which was frequently performed into the nineteenth century. The play deals with arranged marriages in a clever way. Letitia's promised husband, Doricourt, has a higher level of education than she has. When Doricourt returns from the Grand Tour, he looks down on Letitia for her lack of knowledge of the world. Through a series of disguises, capped by the revelation of her natural charm and beauty at a masked ball, Letitia brings him to see her as a person and they are wed. The play was enormously popular with audiences, and the best actors and actresses competed to perform in it. Thereafter, Cowley wrote a series of plays that were popular successes. She came a cropper in <u>A Day in Turkey, or, The Russian Slave</u> (1791). A minor character, an excitable French servant, makes comical remarks in favor of the French Revolution. They were misinterpreted as Cowley's own views and her reputation was severely damaged.

Hannah Cowley's career demonstrated that women were beginning to be accepted as playwrights. In his <u>Essay on the Theatre</u>, Oliver Goldsmith anticipated this change. "There are many situations of the female mind," he wrote, "which have not yet been described, and they never can be until the ladies themselves write honestly about Love."

Classicism and "Sensibility" in Painting

The conservatism of Blackstone, Burke, Johnson and Sheridan also dominated art, although new currents appeared that introduced elements of "sensibility" into the established standards of classicism. Sir Joshua Reynolds was the dominant force in late eighteenth-century painting. Unlike most painters, Reynolds was a gentleman. He came from a family of clergymen and scholars, and his father was a schoolmaster. He received a good grammar school education, which enabled him throughout his life to associate easily with learned or literary individuals. His talents inclined to painting, and his father apprenticed him for four years to an established London artist. By the age of twenty he was supporting himself by painting portraits. With the assistance of an aristocratic friend, Reynolds was able to spend three years (1749-52) in Italy studying the works of antiquity and the great painters, sculptors, and architects of the Renaissance.

Reynolds returned to England in 1752, thoroughly prepared to begin a career as an artist. He was an immediate success as a portrait painter. He was exceptionally industrious, and soon was painting over 100 portraits a year, including most of the major figures of the day. He employed assistants to do draperies and backgrounds for, as he astutely remarked, "no man ever made a fortune with his own hands." He was actively involved in exhibitions, where he showed his own work and his collection of Old Masters. He was a friend of Burke, Johnson, Goldsmith, and Garrick, and in 1764 Reynolds established the famous Literary Club where Johnson held forth.

In 1768 Reynolds accepted the presidency of the newly-established Royal Academy of Art, and in 1784 he became principal painter to the king, a post of honor rather than profit. He expounded his principles in the lectures he delivered at the annual meetings of the Academy. They were published shortly after they were delivered and later collected as Discourses Delivered at the Royal Academy (1797). Reynolds' discourses were the manifesto of those who admired the Grand Style of the Renaissance. He held that the objective of the artist should be to communicate the idea of a person, place, or thing in its perfection, rather than show it in the imperfect form in which it appears in the real world. He disliked the overly dramatic character of baroque art and the commonplace landscapes and still-life paintings of the Dutch, both of which failed to show mankind in its noblest aspects. He regarded history painting as exemplified by the Italian masters of the Renaissance as the pinnacle of the Grand Style. His most famous work in that genre is The Infant Hercules Strangling the Serpent (1785), painted for Catherine the Great of Russia.

Reynolds adopted Richardson's goal—to raise portraiture to the level of high art. One step in that direction was to paint portraits of great men. His portraits included naval and military heroes and distinguished men in government, the law, and the Church. Among his finest works are portraits of men of talent whom he knew personally, such as Samuel Johnson, Oliver Goldsmith and Edmund Burke. To communicate a sense of high art, he often uses poses from antiquity and the great works of Renaissance Italy. To confirm the sense of greatness in the subject, the background of the portrait usually includes references to the manner in which the person had gained distinction.

As a high-society painter, Reynolds painted a series of full-length grand-manner portraits of aristocratic women that were intended to give them the dignity of Roman matrons. His portraits of women often include references to classical mythology, as in Sarah Siddons as the Tragic Muse (1784). Reynolds had a tender side. The growing sense of humanity characteristic of the age is seen in his many portraits of women and children, among them a series about little girls with their pets. Paintings of an entire family (conversation pieces) were popular, and Reynolds' painting of The Marlborough Family is one of the finest.

Pride of place is given to the Duchess, who observes the five younger children, while the Duke looks at his young heir.

As the acknowledged leader of the art community in England, Reynolds was active with Sir William Chambers, the premier architect of the time, in establishing the Royal Academy of Art. Chambers provided attractive premises for the Academy in Somerset House, an office building in classical style that he was building for the Crown. The Academy sponsored instruction in the arts and provided space where members could display their works. Reynolds intended the Academy to promote history painting, but in actuality most of its exhibits were portraits and landscapes, which were the most marketable forms of art.

Hogarth opposed an academy, like those of Europe, which would promote works that met the official standards of taste. Most English artists lacked the education or training to be history painters, nor could they make a living doing it. Hogarth, who was a vigorous defender of English art, wanted a simple exhibition gallery where artists could display their works in all their variety and submit them to the judgment of the public. The growing art market showed that Hogarth was in tune with public taste, but the purpose of the Royal Academy was to "elevate" public taste, not respond to it.

Allan Ramsay was the son of Allan Ramsay Sr., the Scottish poet. Ramsay received a good Scottish education, and in the 1730s he began a successful career as a portrait painter in Edinburgh. In 1736 he went to Italy to study painting. When he returned he settled in London as a portrait painter. Ramsay was an immediate success, not only due to his artistic talent, but also due to his Scottish connections. He worked hard at his craft and 300 portraits survive from his first decade.

Ramsay's career took on a new dimension in 1757 when his Scottish friends brought him to the attention of Lord Bute, at that time the adviser and "friend" of George, Prince of Wales. He painted a portrait of the Prince, who was so pleased that he commissioned a full-length portrait of Bute. When the Prince became King George III, Ramsay painted his coronation portrait and the next year the portrait of Queen Charlotte. As painter to the king, Ramsay's studio became a factory, where he and his assistants painted at least 150 pairs of portraits (or replicas of portraits) of the king and queen for distribution to the royal family or for embassies and colonial authorities abroad. He developed a flourishing practice outside the royal family. His elegant portraits were relaxed and graceful with delicate shades of color.

Ramsay came to the defense of the Crown in the disturbances raised by Wilkes and the American colonists. He published <u>An Essay on the Constitution of England</u> (1765), <u>Thoughts on the Origin and Nature of Government</u> (1766), and <u>A Succinct Review of the American Contest</u> (1778). He was a delightful conversationalist and associated with the Johnson, Reynolds, Boswell circle.

History painting was invigorated by American artists, who dramatically changed the genre by using subjects from modern history. Benjamin West was a Pennsylvanian who displayed artistic talent at an early age, but he lacked formal instruction. He began his career painting portraits in Philadelphia and tried his hand at history painting with <u>The Death of Socrates</u> (1756), painted from an engraving in a history book. West's work impressed a local clergyman, who enabled him to study at the College of Philadelphia (antecedent of the University of Pennsylvania). In 1760 a group of wealthy Philadelphians supported him for three years of study in Italy, where he developed his talent by copying Old Masters.

In Rome, West associated with English artists studying there. He settled in England in 1763 and remained there for the rest of his life. He was tall, handsome, and personable, and his Quaker dress made him instantly recognizable. He was welcomed by Burke, Reynolds, Johnson, and others of that group. At first he was regarded as an artistic Benjamin Franklin, who brought to painting the vitality of the New World. Like other artists, West earned his daily bread by painting portraits, but he made his reputation with a stunning history painting—<u>Agrippina Landing at Brindisium with the Ashes of Germanicus</u> (1766). George III was so struck by the painting that he ordered a similar history painting for himself—<u>The Departure of Regulus from Rome</u> (1769).

In 1770 West abandoned events of antiquity with his masterpiece, <u>The Death of General Wolfe</u>, which he painted in contemporary instead of Roman dress. The picture was recognized as within the Grand Style of history painting, and as such was applauded by Reynolds. When exhibited, the picture drew vast crowds. At a time when the empire was sliding into deep trouble, the English public liked to be reminded of the glorious victories of their recent past. An engraved print based on the picture cleared £15,000, a princely sum. Reynolds commented: "West has conquered. This picture will occasion a revolution in art."

West's work was much admired by George III, who supported him with numerous commissions and a position as history painter to the king and later as surveyor of royal pictures. For the next twenty years West was busy painting history and Biblical pictures for Windsor Castle, which George III established as the main royal residence. He painted eighteen large religious pictures for the Royal Chapel and eight large pictures depicting events in English history for the audience chamber. His <u>Death of Lord Nelson</u> (1806) was a worthy counterpart to his <u>Death of General Wolfe</u>. When Reynolds died in 1792, West was elected president of the Royal Academy and served in that capacity for many years, a distinction that confirmed his prestige in the world of English art. West planned a series of history paintings about the American Revolution, but respect for the feelings of King George III caused him to drop the idea.

Another American who won acclaim in England for history painting was John Singleton Copley, a Bostonian, who distinguished himself in America before settling in London in 1776. Copley began as a printmaker and developed his portrait style by copying prints. He became the premier portrait painter in America, painting portraits of many of the leaders of colonial society. However, he realized that to be something more than a provincial painter he had to study in Europe. In 1774, as political tensions rose, Copley moved to London with his wife and children, leaving behind the reputation and property that he had accumulated in Boston. After a study tour of art in France and Italy, Copley settled in London and established a new career.

Copley's objective was to be a successful history painter, and he began with paintings of incidents from the Bible. Like West, Copley won fame and fortune with works depicting modern events. His first great success was <u>The Death of Chatham</u> (1781), which dramatically depicted Lord Chatham's collapse in the House of Lords while delivering his last speech, an oration opposing full independence to America. The picture includes portraits of fifty-five members of the House of Lords who observe the scene. Twenty thousand people paid admission fees to view the picture and 2,500 subscribed to the engraving of it. Copley's

The Death of Major Pierson (1783) depicts the death of a heroic Englishman leading his troops in battle against the French. Copley's most ambitious work, which was commissioned by the Corporation of the City of London, was The Defeat of the Floating Batteries at Gibraltar (1783-91), a heroic victory over the combined French and Spanish forces that brought the War of American Independence to a close. Bruised egos were satisfied by depicting one of the few English victories in an otherwise unsuccessful war. Copley showed the English forces rescuing Spanish survivors from exploding siege vessels. He exhibited the picture in a tent, and sold 60,000 tickets at 1s. per ticket as crowds flocked to see it. In so doing, he introduced the concept of the one-man show. King George III was so impressed that he commissioned Copley to go to Germany and paint the portraits of four Hanoverians who were present at the siege.

In the aftermath of the American Revolution, Copley painted another large and dramatic work—Charles I Demanding the Surrender of the Five Impeached MPs (1785), which had a political tinge as an expression of support for the heroes of the struggle for limited monarchy. Copley also painted portraits, and his The Children of George III (1785) is one of the finest examples of the family conversation piece.

The success of West and Copley in painting large, theatrical history paintings of individuals and events of modern times indicated that the English public had lost interest in the Greeks and the Romans, and sensed that they were living in a new age that deserved its own artistic expression.

Despite Reynolds' emphasis on dignity and decorum, the trend in portrait painting was toward informality and individual personality. George Romney became London's most popular painter of high-society portraits. He was born in Lancashire and became a successful regional painter. In 1762 Romney moved to London, where he failed to achieve success as a history painter. The Leigh Children (1768), a large group portrait followed by The Warren Family (1769), established his reputation as a painter of portraits. He visited Italy for two years (1773-75) and found much that interested him, but his style and methods were already established and did not change very much.

In contrast to Reynolds' attempt to raise portraits to the level of historia by painting eminent men, Romney's approach to portraits was sentimental. His portraits of men focus on their humanity. His portraits of women emphasize grace and femininity, in which he was aided by the light, flowing dresses and large hats that were fashionable at that time. His portraits of schoolboys, among them <u>Charles Grey, later Second Earl Grey</u> (1784), brought out the confidence of high birth and the freshness and charms of youth.

Romney was an intense, nervous man, who painted quickly and fluently, often skipping the usual preparatory stages of a portrait and painting the sitter directly from his palette to the canvas. This method gave an air of spontaneity and intimacy to his portraits, but it also led to carelessness with details. He was somewhat reclusive and did not employ assistants. He became infatuated with his model, the beautiful, charming Emma Hart, who later became the famous Lady Hamilton, lover of Lord Nelson. He painted her in many poses.

Romney held radical political views. He did not exhibit at the Royal Academy, which he saw as a tool of the monarchy, Reynolds, and elite painters. He was a close friend of John Howard, the prison reformer, with whom he visited Paris in 1790 to see the French Revolution first hand. He painted a portrait of Tom Paine (1792).

The principal rival of Reynolds and Romney as portrait painters was Thomas Gainsborough. About 1740 Gainsborough left his home in East Anglia for London. He began his career as a silversmith and studied drawing at Hogarth's academy on St. Martin's Lane. Possibly he worked with Francis Hayman in decorating the supper boxes at Vauxhall Gardens. He participated with Hogarth and other artists in providing art for the Foundling Hospital. He seems to have earned additional income by copying and restoring Dutch paintings, from which he learned the art of landscape.

Gainsborough soon established himself as a painter of small portraits and conversation pieces set in an attractive landscape. He settled in Bath and spent twenty-five years there as a portrait painter. The informality of his poses and his delightful landscape backgrounds appealed to an age which was turning away from the stiffer, more formal approach of Reynolds. Although he was a regional painter and not part of the London-based world of English art, in 1768 Gainsborough was invited to join the Royal Academy. His contribution to the Academy's first exhibition in 1770 was a stunning success. In 1774 Gainsborough moved to London, where prices were higher and the pool of commissions was much greater.

Gainsborough's special talent in portraiture was to relate his subject to the natural environment. His first important work was Mr. and Mrs. Andrews (1750), a refreshingly simple and natural portrait of a young married couple set in a topographical view of the area in which they lived. Gainsborough's portrait of Thomas Coke of Holkham Hall shows Coke wearing the hat, jacket, and boots of a Knight of the Shire as he loads his shotgun. The Hon. Mrs. Graham, a stunning portrait of a beautiful aristocratic woman, was a great success at the Academy's exhibition in 1777. Gainsborough's work was greatly admired by the king, and in 1781 he exhibited twin portraits—King George and Queen Charlotte—which became their official portraits, replacing those painted by Ramsay for their coronation. He also did portraits of the royal children.

Gainsborough responded to the spirit of the age by introducing more "sensibility" into his pictures. His Mr. and Mrs. William Hallett, or The Morning Walk (1785) is a tender evocation of young love. His paintings of children and animals, among them The Painter's Daughters Chasing a Butterfly (1750), have wonderful charm. His Blue Boy, exhibited at the Royal Academy in 1770, responds to the growing awareness of the special characteristics of adolescence.

While history painting held its place as the premier form of art, scenes of humble people and everyday life gained esteem. In The Cottage Door with Children Playing (1778), The Cottage Girl with Dog and Pitcher (1785), and The Woodman (1787) Gainsborough displays a sympathetic view of humble people reminiscent of Gray's Elegy Written in a Country Churchyard. The Cottage Door (1780) conveys the vulnerability of the small figures of a woman and her brood of children in front of a humble cottage overshadowed by frightening trees and threatening clouds. Gainsborough ignored slight imperfections of craftsmanship, which, at a distance, blended into a pleasing overall effect. "All those odd scratches and marks," Reynolds commented, "which, on close examination, are so observable in Gainsborough's pictures, by a kind of magick, at a certain distance assume form."

Richard Wilson, who gained fame as a landscape painter, came from a respectable Welsh family and grew up among the mountains, forests, and streams of Wales. After the usual six-year apprenticeship, he set up shop as a portrait painter. He found clients through family connections in the West of England. He met the tutor to the children of Frederick, Prince of Wales, and that connection enabled him to paint the children, one of whom was the future George III. He moved to London and became acquainted with Hogarth, Gainsborough, and other artists. In 1751 he went to Italy, where he abandoned portraiture for landscape. Rome from the Villa Madama (1753) and St. Peter's and the Vatican (1753) established his reputation as a painter of idealized landscapes in the classical mode.

In 1757 Wilson returned to London and immediately received commissions for Italian landscapes or country house views. His masterpiece, The Destruction of the Children of Niobe (1760), based on a story from Ovid's Metamorphoses, features a dramatic landscape where trees, mountains, and clouds overwhelm the small tragic figures in the foreground. The painting was a critical and popular success, and the engraved print of the picture was hugely profitable. Some of Wilson's landscapes were commissioned by publishers to be marketed as prints. He pioneered painting the rugged landscape of his native Wales, notably in Snowdon from Llyn Nantille and Caernarvon Castle. In the 1760s Wilson was one of London's most successful artists, and he became one of the founding members of the Royal Academy. In his later years his health and painting declined, but he is recognized as one of the founders of the English landscape tradition.

The growing diversity of English art was seen in the work of two provincial painters who painted in an unusual genre. George Stubbs, son of a harness maker, received brief instruction as a painter but essentially he taught himself. He began his career in Liverpool in 1744 by doing portraits. He studied human anatomy to make etchings for a book on midwifery, and in the process he dissected a female cadaver secretly in a garret. He decided to be a painter of horses—a subject popular with the aristocracy. To prepare himself he made many dissections of horses that culminated in a book of engravings entitled The Anatomy of the Horse. Including a Particular Description of the Bones, Cartilages, Muscles, Fascias, Ligaments, Nerves, Arteries, Veins, and Glands. In Eighteen Tables, all Done from Nature. (1766).

In 1754 Stubbs left for Italy, but he was not impressed by the

Grand Style of the Renaissance and soon returned home. He settled in London where he gained the attention of the aristocracy as a painter of horses and horse-races and rural scenes that featured horses, carriages, country gentry, and bucolic surroundings. He was commissioned by the Duke of Richmond to paint <u>The Third Duke of Richmond and the Charlton Hunt</u>, <u>Henry Fox and the Earl of Albemarle Shooting at Goodwood</u>, and <u>The Duchess of Richmond and Lady Louisa Lennox watching the Duke's Racehorses at Exercise</u> (1759). Many commissions followed, including twelve pictures for the Marquis of Rockingham. Stubbs' ability to combine people, landscapes, and horses was remarkable. His portraits of dogs were popular among country gentlemen. He also painted wild animals, usually in bloody encounters with horses or other wild animals. Many of his works were engraved and sold well as prints. He went beyond his specialty in two of his best genre pictures, <u>Haymakers</u> and <u>Reapers</u> (1786), which depict farm workers as a part of the natural order of the seasons. Surprisingly, George III, an avid horseman and hunter, showed no interest in Stubbs' pictures.

While Stubbs' works glorified rural England, Joseph Wright of Derby developed a different genre as the first important painter of the rising age of industry and science. Growing up in the industrializing Midlands, Wright early showed interest in drawing machinery. After studying painting for two years in London, he returned to his home town, Derby, in 1753, where he became a painter of portraits and developed skill in the use of light and shadow. While contemporaries looked to London to establish a reputation, Wright was satisfied to remain in Derby with his family and friends. Members of the Lunar Society of Birmingham, which included Boulton and Watt, stimulated him to make science a subject for art. Wright used scenes lit by candles or fire to lend drama and mystery to science. <u>A Philosopher Giving a Lecture on the Orrery, in which a Lamp is put in the Place of the Sun</u> (1766) shows people listening intently as a scholar uses a device to demonstrate the movements of the solar system. The best known of Wright's paintings is <u>An Experiment on a Bird in the Air Pump</u> (1768), which shows a scientist demonstrating the dependence of living creatures on a gas later identified as oxygen. The dramatically-lighted people of all ages and both genders who observe the demonstration are as important as the demonstration itself. In <u>A Blacksmith's Shop</u> (1771) and <u>An Iron</u>

Forge (1772) Wright gives high drama to the industrial processes that were so important in the Midlands. In 1775-76 he traveled to Italy, where he was enthralled by the ruins of Rome and produced several works about the eruption of Mt. Vesuvius that had taken place ten years before.

Wright painted portraits of early industrialists such as Richard Arkwright and Josiah Wedgwood. His Arkwright's Cotton Mill by Night (1782) gives mystery and drama to the hulking mill shrouded in darkness with points of light at every window. Wright's paintings defied the usual classifications of art both in subject and manner, and for that reason they were not highly regarded by the aristocratic, classically-oriented leaders of the Royal Academy.

Many artists painted conversation pieces, but the outstanding exemplar of the genre was Johann Zoffany, a German who settled in England about 1761. His talents were discovered by David Garrick, who commissioned several informal scenes set at his villa. Zoffany also painted scenes of Garrick onstage, among them Garrick and Susannah Cibber in Venice Preserv'd (1763) and The Provok'd Wife (1765). His painting of a performance of Love in a Village (1767) was an outstanding example of a popular genre. These conversation pieces stimulated a rash of commissions from actors for similar paintings that showed themselves on the stage.

Through Garrick, Zoffany met the Earl of Bute and his circle of Scottish friends, for whom he painted conversation pieces and full-length portraits. Bute put Zoffany in touch with the royal family, and he became a protégé of Queen Charlotte, who appreciated his ability to converse in German as he painted. He did a number of conversation pieces and informal portraits of the royal family. His portrait of George III in his everyday dress shows the king as a strong leader at the height of his powers. George III personally nominated Zoffany for membership in the Royal Academy. The Royal Academicians in the Life Class (1772) was a conversation piece comprised of the members.

Queen Charlotte was Zoffany's patron in 1772 when he traveled to Italy, the homeland of great art. The king and queen commissioned a painting of the great works of art in the Tributa of the Uffizi Gallery in Florence—the culmination of the Grand Tour—which they could never visit personally. Zoffany's The Tributa of the Uffizi (1777) was a spectacular achievement. Unfortunately, he humanized the picture by including English travelers on the Grand Tour visiting the Tributa, which the king and queen thought spoiled the picture. That ended his association with the royal family.

In 1783 Zoffany visited the English territories in India, where he painted colorful conversation pieces of Indian princes and English families with their Indian attendants. His conversation piece, Colonel Mordaunt's Cock Fight (1786), shows English and Indian onlookers at the climactic moment of the fight. One of his most spectacular Indian pictures is the colorful Embassy to Calcutta from the Vizier of Oude. When he returned to England, Europe was in the throes of the French Revolution, his previous contacts had vanished, and his career fell on hard times.

Tradition and Innovation in Architecture

In architecture, the term neoclassicism is normally applied to the period after 1750, in which classical values and themes were dominant in a reaction against the excesses of baroque and rococo. An important distinction arose between public and domestic architecture. Public architecture was strongly influenced by French neoclassicism, which emphasized Roman grandeur, classical regularity, and Renaissance ornamentation. Palladianism continued to dominate the country house or villa, but designs were less formal and tasteful ornamentation and furnishings added life and color to interiors. Growing wealth enabled prosperous professional and businessmen to build country houses or villas. They were more concerned with comfort than the display of power and status characteristic of the aristocratic stately home.

Sir William Chambers was the dominant public architect of the second half of the eighteenth century. In his person, he was dignified and confident. He was born in Sweden to Scottish parents, was educated in England, and returned to his family in Sweden. He took a position with the Swedish East India Company, which sent him on voyages to China where he developed an interest in Chinese architecture and decorative arts. He studied architecture in Paris and imbibed the principles of French neoclassicism. Throughout his career he remained in touch with French architects and architecture. He also studied in Rome and met many influential English noblemen on the Grand Tour.

He consistently opposed the nascent Greek revival that was stimulated by archaeological discovers in southern Italy. In 1755 Chambers decided to settle in London with his English wife. His <u>Designs of Chinese Buildings, Furniture, Dresses, Machines, and Utensils</u> (1757) made him an authority on chinoiserie, which had become a popular style of interior decoration.

Chambers' career as a public architect was established in 1757, when he was appointed architect to the Princess of Wales, mother of George, Prince of Wales. He instructed the young prince in the principles of architecture. At Kew Gardens he worked with the Princess and Lord Bute to carry out an ambitious project that included a Chinese pagoda, an Alhambra, a Mosque, mock temples, a ruined arch, and other picturesque structures. His <u>A Treatise on Civil Architecture</u> (1759) established his reputation as a major figure in the field. In this work Chambers praises the dignity and strength of Roman architecture, which he holds up as the ideal for public buildings. In his private practice, Chambers designed villas and townhouses, but his attention was devoted mainly to public architecture.

At the accession of George III, Chambers was appointed to the office of works and from there he eventually rose to be the dominant figure as comptroller and surveyor-general. When the board of works was abolished in 1782 by Burke's economical reforms, Chambers continued to manage all government buildings under the supervision of the lord chamberlain. He was criticized for his reliance on the architectural styles of the past, but he won the friendship and respect of cultural conservatives such as Johnson, Burke, and Reynolds. In 1768 he presented to King George III a proposal for a Royal Academy of Arts, which the king approved and named Chambers as treasurer. At the first meeting of the Academy, Sir Joshua Reynolds was elected president.

Chambers spent the rest of his life carrying out the construction of the central block of Somerset House, an office building between the Strand and the Thames (the two wings were added later). The building features a massive Palladian façade dignified by sculpture and softened by ornamentation derived from Chambers' experience of French neoclassicism. The visitor enters an imposing fountain court from the Strand and moves through a columned vestibule that divides the building into two parts. The vestibule leads to a broad terrace that overlooks the Thames and runs the length of the building. Somerset House is now separated from the river by a major roadway, but originally there were three river gates below the terrace to admit barges and river men.

Somerset House, the Strand

Somerset House was built to house the admiralty, navy board, and the revenue departments—the pillars of eighteenth-century English greatness. To display England's achievements in the finer things of life, space was provided for the Royal Academy of Art, the Society of Antiquaries, and the Royal Society. Extensive statuary personifies trade, sea power, Liberty, Justice, Valor, and other presumed national virtues. Somerset House was intended to be a showpiece of English architecture and craftsmanship, and it did not disappoint.

Defoe and others had complained that England lacked an impressive public building to equal other capital cities of Europe. Somerset House was intended to correct that deficiency. Referring to the origins of Somerset House, the secretary of the Royal Academy wrote, "Mr. Burke and various other Men of Taste (suggested) the propriety of making so vast and expensive a Design at once an object of national splendour as well as convenience." Ironically, construction began in 1776, the fatal year when the Empire began falling apart.

Robert Adam

While Sir William Chambers gained his reputation as the designer of a grandiose public building, Robert Adam became the premier designer of graceful stately homes and urban townhouses. He strengthened the movement toward neoclassicism in architecture, although considerably softened by his lively imagination. Adam was the son of a prominent Scottish architect who was devoted to Palladian principles. Adam studied at Edinburgh University and served an apprenticeship in his father's office. He toured Italy from 1754-57, where he studied the remains of ancient Rome. One result was Ruins of the Palace of the Emperor Diocletian at Spalatro in Dalmatia (1764) with a text written by his cousin, William Robertson. Adam's engravings of the ruins revealed a style of architecture that was less dominated by the classical rules than the earlier Roman architecture so admired by Chambers.

Adam settled in London and went into private practice with his brother James, although Robert was always the dominant figure. He worked quickly and was aided by a staff of draftsmen and craftsmen. The brothers began by remodeling stately homes and London townhouses. Adam was confined to conventional concepts at Kedleston Hall in Derbyshire, where he took over an unfinished Palladian house. He gave Roman dignity to the exterior and designed a lively interior. At Syon House near London he began with the remains of a medieval convent. He gave it a plain Palladian façade and designed a dazzling interior with rooms of varying sizes and shapes and decorations derived from ancient Rome. He drastically remodeled Osterley Park (1765-80), a Tudor house near London. He added a double-columned portico and gave the rooms his distinctive neo-classical decoration using Roman and Etruscan designs. He designed chairs for the dining room, carpet for the drawing room, and a bed for the state bedroom. Kenwood House (1767-69), built for another Scot, William Murray, Lord Mansfield, a distinguished judge, is perhaps the most perfect Adam House. Adam's Scottish connections enabled him to build a great house, Luton Hoo (1766-74) for the Earl of Bute. The initial plan (including a large portico) was abandoned and an existing house became part of the structure. Luton Hoo was the largest and most magnificent house that Robert Adam ever built. The grounds were spectacularly landscaped by "Capability" Brown.

Adam's greatest talent was as a designer and decorator of interiors, where he did the complete job—doors and windows, furniture, fireplaces, bookcases, mirrors, doorknobs, candelabra, inkwells, china, and silverware. He uses doors, windows, arches, and fireplaces to break up large areas of wall space. In so doing, he creates many small spaces that he fills with delicate paintings of people or landscapes, leaving no space on the walls for large history paintings or sober rows of ancestral portraits. His Works of Architecture of Robert and James Adam (1773, 1786) was a publishing success and indicated public acceptance of the graceful touch that was his trademark.

Adam was interested in the design of fine townhouses, where the Palladian stately home with its extensive park could not serve as a model. Townhouses were small and compact and required a clever imagination to make them usable and attractive. Derby House on Grosvenor Square (1773-74) had been built in 1728. It was a deep, narrow house that Adam transformed into a small but charming personal residence with a series of delightful reception rooms for entertaining. He also remodeled Lansdowne House on Berkeley Square (1761-68), the residence of Lord Shelburne. The house originally was built for Lord Bute and was considerably more spacious than most townhouses.

Together with his brother James, Robert Adam undertook an ambitious venture called the Adelphi (1768-72), a row of twenty-two townhouses along the Strand with wharves and warehouses underneath fronting the Thames. The houses were an architectural success, but the national credit crunch of 1772 led to abandonment of the project and financial ruin for the Adam brothers. Robert Adam was disappointed in his aspirations to design a grand public building or a church, and his ambitious plan to rebuild the Royal Opera House was never used.

The architecture of Robert Adam had a widespread influence in England due to the publication of his designs, many for buildings that were never built. A popular guide for local builders, William Pain's Practical Builder (1774) was strongly influence by the architecture of Robert Adam, as was the neoclassical furniture of the later years of Thomas Chippendale.

In 1775 Adam returned to Scotland, where he designed townhouses in Glasgow and Edinburgh and several country homes. Edinburgh was a capital without a king or parliament, although it continued to be important as the center of the courts of law, the Church of Scotland, and a distinguished university. The city was long, thin, dark, dreary, and congested. It was built along a ridge running from Edinburgh Castle at the top to Holyrood Palace at the bottom. To the north was a shallow loch (lake) that seemingly blocked expansion.

By 1750 the economy of Scotland was improving and Edinburgh began to grow as a social and cultural center frequented by people of rank and wealth. Supported by a group of wealthy people, in 1747 an unlicensed theatre was opened in Edinburgh, in defiance of Walpole' Licensing Act, which prohibited theatres outside of London and Westminster. The theatre was called The Canongate Concert Hall, and offered musical performances as well as plays. In 1767 the theatre received a patent permitting it to present plays.

In 1752 the Corporation proposed to make the city more attractive by draining and bridging the loch to build a New Town on the other side. In so doing, Edinburgh was transformed from a gloomy, ancient castle town to one of the finest small cities in Europe. The first step was to tear down some dilapidated buildings in the Old Town and build a Royal Exchange, which was finished in 1760. By 1772 the loch had been drained and a causeway built across it, which is known as the North Bridge. The Register House, a depository for government documents, was designed by Robert Adam to be built at the end of the North Bridge. Building began in 1774 but the money ran out due to the War of American Independence. For six years the shell was "the most magnificent pigeon roost in Europe." After the war the Register House was finished and building in the New Town proceeded.

The New Town was laid out in rectangular streets and squares, with fine townhouses, churches, and an Assembly Room for social occasions. Construction of the Theatre Royal symbolized the increasing sophistication and the changing attitude toward pleasure in austere, Presbyterian Scotland. A consistent architectural style was maintained. In 1789 Adam prepared plans for a new building in the Old Town for Edinburgh University. Construction began, but completion was delayed by the wars with revolutionary and Napoleonic France and much of his original design was not used. The unused Parliament House was rebuilt to serve as the Courts of Law. The rebuilding of Edinburgh took fifty years, but when it was completed the Old Town was much improved and the New Town was a showpiece of classical architecture.

Sculpture

Sculpture continued in the classical mode, but a greater sense of personality was added to portrait sculptures and memorial tombs. Joseph Colleens, an English sculptor, made a good living by producing portrait busts of the aristocracy of birth, money, and talent. As a young man, he won a series of prizes for sculpture, and in 1762 he went to Rome to study. He learned the elements of classical styles by making copies of ancient and Renaissance sculptures and by sketching important works of art. He made his reputation by sculpting portrait busts of Englishmen on the Grand Tour, including David Garrick and Laurence Sterne.

Colleens returned to England in 1770 and specialized in portrait busts. He had a remarkable ability to capture and animate a likeness. One of his best pieces was the sculptured portrait of his friend, Samuel Johnson. Some of his male busts are in contemporary dress, but most are in Roman style with cloak and cropped hair. He did busts of Whig statesmen—the Marquis of Rockingham, Sir George Seville, and Charles James Fox. As demand grew, his prices rose from 50 guineas (a guinea is a £ and a shilling) to 150 guineas, but clients kept coming. He also sculpted more than 100 funeral monuments. Creatively, Colleens was a sculptor of the second rank, but he achieved a good likeness in his portrait busts which are often used to illustrate the political and cultural history of the reign of George III.

From Baroque to Classicism in Music

By the 1740s baroque music had become stale, and a light-hearted spirit known as rococo or galant entered into music. Rococo music was characterized by a monophonic melodic line, simple harmony, and light accompaniment. The melody was embellished with many small figures, written out or improvised. The music was performed in a re-

343

laxed, graceful manner with subtle dynamic shadings, in contrast to the formality and dignity of baroque music.

Jean-Philippe Rameau took French music beyond rococo to a mature French classicism. Rameau composed a series of operas that were notable for their brilliant choruses and ballets and the prominent role given to the orchestra. His harpsichord sonatas took the instrument beyond its usual role in providing accompaniments. In his <u>Treatise on Harmony Reduced to its Natural Principles</u> (1722), Rameau shows that chords developed naturally out of the overtones of a vibrating string. As a man of the Age of Reason, Rameau declares that the true foundation of music is harmony, which is based on nature. This work was widely influential in that it gave theoretical validity to the ongoing transition from polyphony to music based on melody and chords.

The sonata was refined by Domenico Scarlatti, son of Alessandro, who composed more than 500 keyboard sonatas, many of them unpublished in his lifetime. A collection of 30 of Scarlatti's sonatas was published in 1738, and this collection was rapidly disseminated throughout Europe. Scarlatti's sonatas have two parts—the first sets out the main themes, and the second offers variations on the themes before returning to the home key. Scarlatti' sonatas displayed an intensity of composition that contrasted with the shallow melodies of the galant style.

By 1760 a reaction was taking place in favor of a more serious, ambitious, and structured kind of music. The sonata took on a new character as it changed from a modest form of chamber music to a concert sonata that provided an extended vehicle for public display of virtuosity. One aspect of the change was "sonata form," which refers to one movement, usually the first, of a sonata. Sonata form begins with the "exposition," which includes the main theme and a secondary theme (usually in a related key), followed by the "development," in which the main and secondary themes or parts of them appear as variations, often in different keys. By 1760 the sonata was changed by the use the use of a new keyboard instrument, the piano-forte (soft-loud) with strings that are struck by hammers instead of plucked.

Classical sonatas usually have three movements—the first is in sonata form and moderately fast (allegro), the second usually is a slow, lyrical movement (adagio), and the last movement is high-spirited and fast. Sometimes a dance such as a minuet is inserted between the second and last movement to make a four-movement sonata.

Strictly speaking, classical music begins with the works of Franz Josef Haydn, a prolific Austrian composer, who composed his first symphony in 1754 mad by 1764 his style was fully formed. In a long series of symphonies, Haydn solidified the structure of the symphony into four contrasting movements—the first movement is in sonata form, the second is slow and lyrical, the third is a dance, often a minuet, and the fourth is a free-flowing fast movement. Haydn composed a wide variety of music in all genres—symphonies, string quartets, piano sonatas and trios, concertos, operas, and oratorios. His music quickly became popular throughout Europe due to its high spirits, skillful interweaving of parts, and emotional sensitivity. The contrast with the homophonic simplicity of gallant was immediately evident. .

The classical style was solidified by the works of Wolfgan Amadeus Mozart, a prodigy from Salzburg and Vienna, who fitted seamlessly into the classical idiom and genres developed by Havdn. In 1763, when the Seven Years War came to an end, his father, Leopold Mozart, a violinist and composer took the seven-year old Wolfgang and his sister Nannerl, also a talented musician, on a three-year tour of London, Paris, and other musical centers, where they played for royalty and were a sensation. After three years in Italy studying opera, Mozart settled in Salzburg and later Vienna. His major works were operas, symphonies fifteen piano concertos that he played in public, concerts, concertos for violin and piano, piano sonatas, and string quartets.

London's active musical scene made it an attractive destination for foreign musicians. In 1764, Leopold Mozart brought his precocious son, Wolfgang Amadeus and his sister Nannerl to London. The eight-year old Wolfgang Amadeus astonished his hearers at concerts and played three times for the royal family, who were entranced by him. In 1791 and 1794 Franz Josef Haydn, by that time famous throughout Europe, visited London, where he was lionized. Haydn loved the stimulating atmosphere of the great city and the generous commissions that he received. During each of his two visits he composed a set of six symphonies, plus songs with English words and much chamber music. He received a Doctor of Music degree from Oxford University.

Johann Christian Bach, the youngest son of Johann Sebastian.had established his reputation as a composer of <u>opera seria</u> in Italy. He arrived in London in 1762 with a commission to write two operas for the Royal Opera House. His opera, <u>Orione</u> (1763), was a moderate success with the public, and it created a sensation when King George III and Queen Charlotte came to see it on two successive performances. Bach settled in London and became a major figure in the musical scene. Since he spoke German, he was a favorite of the king and queen. He accompanied George III when the king wished to play the flute, gave music lessons to Queen Charlotte and the royal children, and was acquainted with Charles Burney, the historian of music.

Bach's major contributions to music are his symphonies and piano concertos, which have some resemblance to the classical style of Haydn and Mozart. In 1765 he published a set of six symphonies in the three-movement Italian style. The first movement was in sonata form, followed by slow and fast movements. He published another set of symphonies in 1781, three of which were for two orchestras that played contrasting segments. His <u>symphonies concertantes</u> featured an orchestra and soloist. Bach actively promoted the new keyboard instrument, the piano, and in 1768 he performed the first piano concert in London. His piano concertos were important in establishing the piano in England and on the continent.

Bach cooperated with Karl Friedrich Abel, another German musician, who had arrived in London a few years earlier. They presented a series of concerts that were a major addition to London's musical life. Abel was a true impresario—gregarious and outgoing and with a keen instinct for the music business. Subscribers paid a fee to attend a series of Bach-Abel concerts, conducted alternately by one of the partners. Some of Bach's symphonies and piano concertos were written for these concerts, but works of other composers were heard as well. The program was not announced in advance—their high-toned subscribers simply came, confident that they would hear music that they would enjoy.

Charles Burney maintained continuity in English music. His musical talent appeared early in his life. In 1744 he became an apprentice of Thomas Arne and served as a keyboard player and violinist at Drury Lane theatre. He wrote some music for Arne's masque, <u>Alfred</u>. After two years, he left Arne and became the organist at a London church.

He collected pupils and began offering organ concerts. By that time he was married, and eventually Burney had seven children by two wives. His first published composition was <u>Six Sonatas for Two Violins, With a Bass for the Violoncello or Harpsichord</u> (1748). He wrote theatre music for Garrick, and his ballad opera, <u>The Cunning Man</u> (1766) was performed at Drury Lane. In 1769 Burney received a doctorate in music from Oxford. He was elected a member of the Royal Society and became a member of Johnson's Literary Club. The Burneys led an active social life as part of the literary and cultural elite of London. Samuel Johnson became a familiar figure in the life of the large Burney household.

Burney's compositions were enjoyable but they are not of importance in the history of music. He turned his attention to writing about music. He loved travel, and in 1770 he made an extensive tour in Europe. He visited important musical centers and met eminent musicians. The next year he published <u>The Present State of Music in France and Italy</u> (1771), a popular work that included interesting social and cultural commentary. A second tour led to <u>The Present State of Music in Germany</u> (1773). In 1776 Burney published the first volume of his <u>History of Music from the Earliest Ages to the Present Day</u> (4 vols. 1776-89) with a preface by Samuel Johnson. The work was well received and is still an interesting and useful source for the subject.

Frances Burney

Frances (Fanny) Burney was a modest, quiet child who early in life became an avid writer. She was shy and withdrawn in society, although lively and witty with her family and friends. Through her father, Charles Burney, she knew Johnson, Sheridan, and other prominent figures of the day. As a member of a large family, she was able to maintain a low profile and her writing did not attract attention. Since writing novels was not a proper activity for one of her social class, she wrote her first novel in secret. When she approached publishers she employed clever schemes to preserve her anonymity.

After several disappointments, Frances found a publisher. <u>Evelina, or, a Young Lady's Entrance into the World</u> (3 vols. 1779) was an immediate success and became the talk of the town as reviewers attempted to identify the name of the author. The novel tells of a young girl's feelings as she enters into polite society, and includes vivid, often humorous descriptions of London, Bath, and the social life of the genteel class. It is in the form of letters that reveal the heroine's intimate feelings. Evelina is the illegitimate offspring of Sir John Belmont. She has been brought up in isolation by a virtuous clergyman and knows nothing about the real world of London. A neighboring family takes her to London to introduce her to polite society. She goes through a series of personal and moral challenges but comes out of them with her virtue intact.

Johnson, Burke, Reynolds and others of that circle read and praised the novel, not knowing that "little Fanny" was the author. Eventually the name of the author was revealed and blushing Frances Burney became a celebrity in literary circles. A full and fascinating account of these events is preserved in her diaries.

Her second novel, <u>Cecilia, or, Memoirs of an Heiress</u> (5 vols. 1782), tells the story of a wealthy and virtuous young woman who decides to devote her wealth and privileged social position to philanthropy. She discovers to her dismay that her good intentions are frustrated by a variety of cheats, liars, and other social predators, who endeavor to lay hands on her wealth and lead her to self-destructive behaviors that nearly ruin her. The novel was a financial success and was popular in lending libraries, although its cynical tone was not well received by critics.

In 1786 Burney accepted a position in the household of Queen Charlotte, which was regarded as an excellent provision for a woman in her thirties apparently destined for spinsterhood. In 1793, at the age of forty, she married a French military officer who was a refugee from the French Revolution. They were often short of money, and from time to time they lived in Bath, where they could maintain their style of living less expensively than in London. Burney spent her last years editing her father's <u>Memoirs</u>.

The novels of Frances Burney were in the long-established tradition of novels by women about women. The novel was already established as a literary genre, and Burney broke no new ground. Her novels are of interest today for their insights into the thoughts and feelings of gentlemen and ladies at the end of an era.

Horace Walpole

Horace Walpole's position as the youngest son of Sir Robert Walpole enabled him to engage in many of the activities characteristic of the gentlemen of his time. He grew up under the care of his mother, who was separated from Sir Robert. Most contemporaries regarded Horace as somewhat effeminate. He became knowledgeable about art by studying the great collection of paintings that his father had accumulated at Houghton. After Sir Robert's death, he published a catalogue of the paintings in Aedes Walpoliana (1747).

He attended Eton and Cambridge, where his record as a student was undistinguished, although eventually he became a knowledgeable and cultivated individual. He was a school friend of Thomas Gray, the poet, and from 1739-41 the two toured France and Italy. Sir Robert provided his son with a good income by conferring on him the sinecure office of usher of the exchequer and several other offices. In 1741 Horace was elected to Parliament, where he observed the titanic struggle that led to the downfall of the great prime minister. He spoke once in 1741 and again in 1742, but he was too gentle and refined to assert himself in the rough-and-tumble debates of the House of Commons. He left the Commons in 1768, but he continued to give close attention to politics and conducted intrigues behind the scenes. His Memoirs of the Last Ten Years of the Reign of George II, Memoirs of the Reign of King George III, and The Last Journals of Horace Walpole are important historical sources, although marred by his bitter antagonism toward George III, Lord Bute, and almost anyone who was willing to work with them.

Walpole was a gentleman of the type described by Lord Shaftesbury or Lord Chesterfield. He did not marry, but he collected a large number of female friends with whom he corresponded and interacted socially. He conducted an extensive correspondence that includes a wide range of serious ideas as well as delightful gossip. He maintained an active social and cultural life during the London season. He set up his own private press, which published fine books. He was an avid connoisseur of books and art, as shown in his A Catalogue of the Royal and Noble Authors of England, with Lists of their Works (1758). His Anecdotes of Painting in England (1762-71) and A Catalogue of Engravers (1762-71) were based on the notes of George Vertue. His Historic Doubts on the Life and Reign of King Richard the Third (1768) defends Richard against charges that he did away with the two young princes in the Tower.

In most of his activities Horace Walpole, like Sheridan and the Burneys, maintained the interests and values of the earlier years of the century. In architecture, however, he started a new vogue. In 1741 he bought a Georgian house in Twickenham with 40 acres along the Thames. He enjoyed his lively neighbor, Kitty Clive, the actress. He named the house Strawberry Hill and remodeled it in the style of a medieval castle/abbey, thus inaugurating the "Gothic Revival." He stated that Strawberry Hill was not a serious work of architecture subject to the rules of Taste, but merely an "amusement" that followed no rules. With its round tower, great cloister, gallery with papier maché fan-vaulting, armory, castellated battlements, arched stained-glass windows, and remarkable library, Strawberry Hill captured the imagination of contemporaries. Walpole was an avid collector, and filled the house with paintings, sculptures, china, armor, Queen Mary's comb, Cardinal Wolsey's red hat, and King William's spur. His prized possession was a Roman eagle. People came in such large numbers to see Strawberry Hill that Walpole had to issue tickets. He published A Description of the Villa of Mr. Horace Walpole (1774) with engravings of the house and an inventory of his collections.

By the 1740s English architecture was in a state of flux. Palladianism was too stern and baroque was passé. People were tired of Greeks and Romans and were looking for something fresh. Gothic was an alternative that spoke of Magna Charta, the origins of Parliament and the Common Law, and "the ancient constitution." Medievalism tied in with the castles, cathedrals, and ruined abbeys that dotted England. "I give myself a Burlington-air," Walpole wrote in 1753, "and say, that as Chiswick is a model of Grecian architecture; Strawberry Hill is to be so of Gothic." He was right.

The Gothic Revival, to which Horace Walpole was an important contributor, drew upon an aspect of eighteenth-century culture that had been overwhelmed by classicism but had never completely disappeared. By mid-century, the rationality and calm of classicism were challenged by increasingly emotional and irregular elements in the concept of Beauty. Dramatic scenes, such as the Alps Mountains, were felt to be awesome, magnificent, and beautiful, although they certainly did not meet the classical standards of harmony and symmetry. The plays of Shakespeare were far from regular and did not adhere to the classical unities of time, place, and action, but they stirred the emotions. The beauties of Nature proved, on examination, to be a pleasing combination of irregularities. The Middle Ages became interesting again, as seen in the fake grottos, ruins, and thatched cottages of Stowe and Stourhead Gardens. Horace Walpole's little house, with its playful medieval features, was a harbinger of a style of architecture that would sweep away Palladianism and dominate the Romantic era.

Walpole's fantasy novel, The Castle of Otranto, a Story. Translated by William Marshal, Gent. From the Original Italian of Onuphrio Muralio, Canon of the Church of St. Nicholas at Otranto (1764) set a new trend in fiction. The novel was presented to the public under the fictional pretext that it had been published in Naples in 1529 but was based on a manuscript that went back to the Crusades. The novel is set in a castle in medieval Naples that lies under a curse. Manfred, Prince of Otranto and guests attend the marriage of Conrad, son of Manfred, to Isabella, daughter of the Count of Vicenza. They find, to their horror, that Conrad has been crushed by a gigantic helmet with black plumes. That evening, Manfred informs Isabella that he intends to divorce his wife and marry her, to beget another son and heir. Isabella runs away and seeks refuge in the underground passageway below the castle.

As the plot unfolds, the novel is filled with fantastic images—frightening underground groans, a gloomy subterranean passageway, a gigantic foot, a bleeding statue, an enormous sword, a hermit whose austerities have reduced him to an animated skeleton, a portrait that steps out of its frame. The destruction of the castle is accompanied by a powerful clap of thunder. The book immediately became popular and set a trend that led eventually to Mary Shelley's Frankenstein.

Summation

<u>Eighteenth Century England—A Cultural Approach</u> deals with English culture within its historical context. Many factors contributed to the achievements of the period. The cultural development of eighteenth-century England would have been impossible without political unity. In 1660, the English people restored King Charles II and their historic institutions, with changes that dealt with some of the problems that had led to conflict between the Crown and Parliament (1642-1658). Political unity was strengthened by "the Glorious Revolution of 1688-89" and its sequel, which established a "mixed and balanced" constitution that most Englishmen found satisfactory for a century. Another important development of the revolutionary period was the decline of the religious disputes that had distracted England in the seventeenth century. The Toleration Act (1689) preserved the Church of England as the official expression of the religious life of England, but extended toleration to Protestant Dissenters. Freedom of the press and periodic elections fostered a luxuriant growth of political thought and journalism.

Economic growth in industry, agriculture, and trade provided the necessary material resources. Writers, dramatists, artists, and musicians competed with each other for attention and income in the cultural marketplace. Publication of reference works, sermons, and travel books flourished. Journalism and periodicals poured from the presses. The novel was a new literary form with wide public appeal. The small, intimate theatres of the Restoration era were replaced by large theatres to provide seats for greatly increased audiences. Plays of genuine merit mingled with mediocre works. Artists responded to a growing demand for pictures, sculptures, and engravings to ornament the homes of well-to-do landed or moneyed gentlemen. The increase of wealth made possible notable works of architecture for individuals and the Church. Eighteenth-century England was responsive to foreign influences as expressed in the contrasting styles of baroque and classicism, while preserving an English moderation and eclecticism. Foreign virtuosos and composers (like Handel and Haydn) performed for large ticket-buying audiences in concert halls and opera houses. A culture based on the vagaries of the market produced much that was trivial and ephemeral. Amazingly, it produced much that was good, and these works are the substance of this book.

England played an important role in European philosophy with the works of Newton, Locke, and Hume. Ordinary gentlemen made important contribution in the application of science to practical uses. One of the most important achievements of eighteenth-century England was an enlarged vision of the world and England's place in it. The English people expanded their power and trade to global scope. They explored the continents and the oceans. They engaged in scientific and poetic explorations of nature.

In other countries, the king, the aristocracy, and the Church were the principal patrons of literature, theatre, architecture, and the arts. The Stuart monarchs attempted to follow the continental model of patronage, but they were hampered by political and religious dissensions and lack of money. In the later seventeenth century the landed aristocracy became important patrons of the arts. Their cultural contributions arose mainly from building and decorating magnificent stately homes, which required the services of architects, painters, sculptors, and landscapers. After the fire of 1666, Londoners rebuilt their city, adorning it with beautiful parish churches and Christopher Wren's ultimate achievement, St. Paul's cathedral. The universities commissioned Wren and other architects to add buildings of distinction. Eighteenth-century England made an investment in beauty and refinement, and received value for the money, as any visitor to England today will attest.

But the crucial factor in the development of eighteenth-century culture was the emergence of a middle class of gentlemen and ladies with enough education, income, and leisure to afford and appreciate the finer things of life. The life-style of a gentleman or lady was expected to include "politeness"—an ideal combining morality and good manners with personal refinement. An important value of the genteel class was "taste," which meant informed judgment and sound instincts regarding conduct and art. Of course, many fell short of the standards that they espoused, but these were the ideals (if not the realities) of the people who shaped the culture of the age.

No effort has been made to present a "balanced" view of the period. This book is about "culture." The eighteenth-century, like any period of human history, including our own, had many contradictions. The English people developed a powerful state, but its principal energies were devoted to war. The wealth of a growing economy went primarily to the powerful and wealthy, while the bulk of the population lived at a poverty level or below. Like most great metropolitan centers, London boasted a brilliant social and cultural life, which co-existed with an urban underclass demoralized by poverty, crime, promiscuity, infant mortality, and gin. The unity of the British Isles involved suppression of the Highland clans and the native Irish. The British Empire in North America was built at the expense of Native Americans. The core of imperial trade—so important to Britain's economic growth—was sugar, produced by the labor of African slaves. The manifest evils of the time should not detract from an appreciation of its accomplishments, among them a growing awareness of these problems and the emergence of movements for reform.

SUGGESTIONS FOR FURTHER READING

The New Columbia Encyclopedia (6th ed., 2001-05) is the single most useful reference work for students of the Humanities. It is a good place to check names, dates, places, and events. The Oxford Dictionary of National Biography (61 vols. 2004) provides authoritative articles on persons prominent in English history from earliest times to the present. Lives of the Stuart Age, 1603-1714 (1976) and Lives of the Georgian Age, 1714-1837 (1978) offer brief, interesting biographies of prominent people. Who's Who in History, Vol. III: England, 1603 to 1714, ed. C. P. Hill (1965) and Who's Who in History: Vol. IV: England 1714-1789, ed. Geoffrey Treasure (1969) are similar biographical dictionaries that are well-written and interesting, and organized to provide a continuous history of the period. For modern interpretations of social and cultural history see Culture and Society in Britain, 1660-1800, ed. Jeremy Black (1997). Black's introduction is a brilliant synthesis of cultural history and Roy Porter's "The New Eighteenth-Century Social History" does the same for social history.

History

A two-volume sequence that provides a good general survey of the period is Geoffrey Holmes, The Making of a Great Power, 1660-1722 (1993) and Geoffrey Holmes and Daniel Szechi, The Age of Oligarchy, 1722-1783 (1993). Paul Langford, A Polite and Commercial People: England, 1717-1783 (1992) is a broad survey with considerable attention to social history. For the later Stuart period, see Craig Rose, England in the 1690s: Revolution, Religion, and War (1999) and W. A. Speck, The Birth of Britain: A New Nation (1994). H. T. Dickinson provides a good introduction to Georgian politics in Walpole and the Whig Supremacy (1973) and The Politics of the People in Eighteenth-Century Britain (1994). Dickinson's Bolingbroke (1970) is a good biography of Walpole's great antagonist. See also Brian W. Hill, Sir Robert Walpole (1989). An important aspect of English politics is covered in Jeremy Black, The English Press, 1621-1861 (2001).

For the Church and Dissent see A History of Religion in Britain: Practice & Belief From Pre-Roman Times to the Present, ed. Sheridan Gilley & W. J. Shiels (1994). Norman Sykes, From Seldon to Secker, 1660-1768 (1959) is an authoritative work on the Church of England. For English society see Roy Porter, English Society in the Eighteenth Century (1994). Pleasure in the Eighteenth Century, ed. Roy Porter and Marie Rodzent (1999) deals with an important aspect of eighteenth-century culture. Jeremy Black describes The British and the Grand Tour (1985). Histories of London are Roy Porter, London: A Social History (1998) and Francis Sheppard, London: A History (1998). See also Tim Hitchcock Down and Out in Eighteenth-Century London (2004).

On science, good general books are Herbert Butterfield, The Origins of Modern Science (1950) and Thomas Hankins, Science and the Enlightenment (1985). See also Colin A. Ronan, Edmond Halley: Genius in Eclipse (1969) and Stephen Inwood, The Man who Knew too Much: The Forgotten Genius: A Biography of Robert Hooke (2003). Richard Westfall has written a good account of The Life of Isaac Newton (1993). Roy Porter covers a crucial period in the history of medicine in Disease, Medicine and Society in England, 1550-1860 (1995). William Hunter and the Eighteenth-Century Medical World, ed. W. F. Bynum and Roy Porter (1985) has interesting material on a wide range of medical practices.

The economy is surveyed by John Rule, The Vital Century: England's Developing Economy, 1714-1815 (1992). Fundamental works in the history of the family are Lawrence Stone, The Family, Sex and Marriage in England, 1500-1800 (1977) and Randolph Trumbach, The Rise of the Egalitarian Family: Aristocratic Kinship and Domestic Relations in Eighteenth-Century England (1978). See also John R. Gillis, For Better, For Worse: British Marriages, 1600 to the Present (1988). An interesting insight into English life is provided by Mary Abbott, Life Cycles in England, 1560-1720 (1996).

A good introduction to the history of women is Mary Prior, Women in English Society, 1500-1800 (1985). See also Margaret Hunt, The Middling Sort: Commerce, Gender, and the Family in England, 1688-1780 (1996). The Gentleman's Daughter: Women's Lives in Georgian England (1998) by Amanda Vickery explores the varied activities of genteel women. Bridget Hill has studied Women, Work, & Sexual Politics in Eighteenth-Century England (1994). She also covers Women Alone: Spinsters in England, 1660-1856 (2001). For Lady Mary Wortley Montagu see Embassy to Constantinople: The Travels of Lady Wortley Montagu, ed. Deryla Murphy and Christopher Pick (1988).

T. M. Devine, The Scottish Nation: A History, 1700-2000 (2000) is a good introduction. Another good survey is Gordon Donaldson, Scotland: The Shaping of a Nation (1980). For the development of a sense of Britishness see Linda Colley, Britons: Forging the Nation, 1707-1737 (1992). J. C. Beckett, The Making of Modern Ireland (1966) is an excellent starting-place book. More detail is provided in T. W. Moody, ed., A New History of Ireland, Vol. IV: Eighteenth-Century Ireland, 1691-1800 (1986). See also Thomas Hachey, The Irish Experience: A Concise History (1996).

For the expansion of the empire see Earl A. Reitan, Politics, War, and Empire: The Rise of Britain to a World Power, 1688-1793 (1994). Much attention has been given recently to the development of an Atlantic community involving Britain, France, Spain, North America, the West Indies, and the Atlantic slave trade. One of the first works on this topic is Peggy Liss, Atlantic Empires: The Network of Trade and Revolution, 1713-1828 (1983). Bernard Bailyn summarizes the topic in Atlantic History: Concept and Controversies (2005). Other important studies of this topic are David Armitage and Michael Braddick, The British Atlantic World, 1500-1800 (2002) and Kathleen Wilson, ed., New Imperial History: Culture, Identity and Modernity in Britain and the Empire, 1660-1840 (2004). See also Felicity Nussbaum, ed., The Global Eighteenth Century (2003). James A. Williamson provides an interesting account of Capt. Cook's explorations in Cook and the Opening of the Pacific (1948). See also Glyndwr Williams, <u>Great South Sea: English Voyages and Encounters, 1570-1750</u> (1997). Hugh Thomas summarizes recent research in <u>The Slave Trade: The History of the Atlantic Slave Trade, 1440-1870</u> (1998). See also Edward Reynolds, <u>Stand the Storm: A History of the Atlantic Slave Trade</u> (1985). John A. Richardson, <u>Slavery and Augustan Literature: Swift, Pope, Gay</u> (2004) makes a valuable contribution to the topic.

Intellectual and Cultural History

Intellectual and cultural matters are well covered in <u>The Cambridge Cultural History of Britain: Vol. V, Eighteenth-Century Britain</u>, ed. Boris Ford (1992). See also Joseph Levine, <u>Between the Ancients and the Moderns: Baroque Culture in Restoration England</u> (1999). Biographies of leading thinkers are Maurice Cranston, <u>John Locke: A Biography</u> (1957), Roger S. Woolhouse, <u>Locke: A Biography</u> (2006), and E. C. Mosner, <u>The Life of David Hume</u> (2nd ed., 1980).

For the Enlightenment see <u>British Philosophy and the Age of Enlightenment</u>, ed. Stuart Brown (1996) and Roy Porter, <u>The Creators of the Modern World: The Untold Story of the British Enlightenment</u> (2000). In the same vein are Armand Chitnis, <u>The Scottish Enlightenment</u> (1976). See also <u>The Cambridge Companion to the Scottish Enlightenment</u>, ed. Alexander Brodie (2003). For the influence of the Enlightenment on historical writing, see Karen O'Brien, <u>Cosmopolitan History from Voltaire to Gibbon: Narratives of Enlightenment</u> (1997), and Laird Okie, <u>Augustan Historical Writing: Histories of the England in the English Enlightenment</u> (1991). Roy Porter analyzes <u>Gibbon: Making History</u> (1989).

Historical Biographies

The Stuart rulers are discussed in J. P. Kenyon, <u>The Stuarts</u> (1958), Good biographies are Reginald Hutton, <u>Charles the Second: King of England, Scotland, and Ireland</u> (1991), Tony Claydon, <u>William III</u> (2002), Hester Chapman, <u>Mary, Queen of England</u> (1953), and Edward Gregg, <u>Queen Anne</u> (1980). An interesting book about the Royal Court is Robert Bucholz, <u>The Augustan Court: Queen Anne and the Decline of Court Culture</u> (1993). See also Maureen Waller,

Ungrateful Daughters: The Stuart Princesses Who Stole their Father's Crown (2002). Biographies of major political figures include Brian W. Hill, Robert Harley: Speaker, Secretary of State and Premier Minister (1988) and J. R. Jones, Marlborough (1993). The Augustan Court: Queen Anne and the Decline of Court Culture (1993) is an important study of the structure and role of the Court in the later Stuart period.

J. H. Plumb, The First Four Georges (rev. ed., 1974) consists of a chapter on each Hanoverian king. For George II and his queen see John Van de Kiste, King George II and Queen Caroline (1997). Peter Quennel has written an interesting biography of Caroline of England: An Augustan Portrait (1940). For Frederick, Prince of Wales, see The King that Never Was (1996) by Michael De-la-Noy. King George III has two good biographies, Christopher Hibbert, George III: A Personal History (1998) and Jeremy Black, George III: America's Last King (2006). Good biographies of William Pitt the Elder are by J. H. Plumb (1953), Stanley Ayling (1976), and Marie Peters (1998). Peter D. G. Thomas has written good biographies of Lord North (1976), the much misunderstood prime minister at the time of the American Revolution (1776) and John Wilkes: A Friend to Liberty (1996). Michael Duffy, The Younger Pitt (2000) is among several good biographies. For Pitt's persistent antagonist see L. G. Mitchell, Charles James Fox (1992). Frank O'Gorman, Edmund Burke: His Political Philosophy (1973), explains the views of Edmund Burke, the most philosophical of politicians.

English Literature

The Cambridge History of English Literature, 1660-1780, ed. John Richetti (2005) offers interpretative essays by established scholars on topics, themes, and individuals. For a broad, interpretive view see Donald Greene, The Age of Exuberance: Background to Eighteenth Century English Literature (1970). The relevant chapters in A Literary History of England, ed. Albert Baugh (2nd ed., 1967) still have value. See also Bonamy Dobree, The Oxford History of English Literature, Vol II, English in the Early Eighteenth Century, 1660-1749 (1959) and John Butt, The Oxford History of English Literature, Vol. III, The Mid-Eighteenth Century, 1740-1789, (1970). See also Butt, The Augustan Age (1950) and A. R. Humphreys, The Augustan World: Life and Letters in Eighteenth Century England (1954). James Sambrook in The Eighteenth Century: The Context of English Literature (1986) and W. A. Speck, Society and Literature in England, 1700-1760 (1984) provide useful background. An interesting cross-disciplinary study is H. T. Dickinson, Politics and Literature in the 18th Century (1974). The Context of English Literature: The Eighteenth Century, ed. Pat Rogers (1979) is a collection of essays by Rogers, W. A. Speck , George Rousseau and others. Another collection of essays is The Widening Circle: Essays on the Circulation of Literature, ed. Paul Korshin (1976). See also Literature and Social Organization in Eighteenth Century England, ed. Stephen Copley (1984). J. H. Plumb, "The Public, Literature, and the Arts in the 18th Century," in The Triumph of Culture, ed. Paul Fritz and David Williams (1982) is a stimulating synthesis. See also Pat Rogers, Literature and Popular Culture (1984). Eighteenth-Century English Literature (1969), ed. Geoffrey Tillotson, Paul Fussell, Jr., and Marshall Waingrow is a comprehensive, well-edited anthology. The Oxford Anthology of English Literature: Vol. I. The Middle Ages through the Eighteenth Century, ed. Frank Kermode and John Hollander (1773) offers an assortment of important works.

Works on women writers are Mary R. Mahl and Helene Koon, Female Spectators: English Women Writers before 1800 (1977), Patricia Spacks, The Female Imagination (1975), and Susan Staves, A Literary History of Women's Writings in Britain, 1660-1789 (2006).

John Richetti, The English Novel in History, 1700-1780 (1999) is a critical summary and assessment of the landmark novelists and novels of eighteenth-century England. The Columbia History of the British Novel (1994) ed. John Richetti offers an overview of the novel from a variety of perspectives. See also Jerry C. Beasley, Novels of the 1740s (1981) The Best of the Gentleman's Magazine, 1731-1754, ed. Earl A. Reitan (1987) includes an introduction and a variety of articles from eighteenth-century periodicals as abridged in that popular magazine.

Literary Biographies

For John Dryden see James A. Winn, John Dryden and His World (1987) and David Hopkins, John Dryden (1987). R. L. Greaves tells a fascinating story in Glimpse of Glory: John Bunyan and English Dissent (2001). See also Greaves' John Bunyan (1969) a topical study of his beliefs. Maureen Duffy, <u>The Passionate Shepherdess</u> (1977), a straightforward biography of Aphra Behn. Janet Todd, <u>The Secret Life of Aphra Behn</u> (1996) by a prominent feminist scholar is an account of her life and works. Resistance to stereotyped roles for women is seen in <u>The Celebrated Mary Astell: An Early English Feminist</u> (1986) and Patricia Springborg, <u>Mary Astell: Theorist of Freedom</u> (2005). Paula Backscheider and John Richetti edited <u>Popular Fiction by Women, 1660-1730: An</u> Anthology (1996), which is supplemented by Backscheider, <u>Selected Fiction and Drama of Eliza Haywood</u> (1999).

The standard biography of Richard Steele is Calhoun Winton, <u>Captain Steele: The Early Career of Richard Steele</u> (1964) and <u>Sir Richard Steele, M. P.: the Later Career</u> (1970). Richard H. Dammers, <u>Richard Steele</u> (1982), is a readable study of the life and major works of Steele, especially his play, <u>The Conscious Lovers</u>. For Joseph Addison see Peter Smithers, <u>Life of Joseph Addison</u> (2 vols. 1958) and Robert Otten, <u>Joseph Addison</u> (1982). <u>Addison and Steele: The Critical Heritage</u> (1980), ed. Edwin A. and Lillian D. Bloom puts their work in perspective. Peter Earle, <u>The World of Defoe</u> (1976) is readable. An important biography is Maximilian Novak, <u>Daniel Defoe, Master of Fiction: His Life and Ideas</u> (2001). John Richetti, <u>Daniel Defoe</u> (2000) and Paula R. Backscheider, <u>Daniel Defoe: His Life</u> (1989) are important studies of that seminal novelist. See also Backscheider, <u>Being More Intense: A Study of the Prose Works of Bunyan, Swift, and Defoe</u> (1780). Backscheider offers a study of Defoe's <u>Moll Flanders: The Making of a Criminal Mind</u> (1990). Richard I. Cook, <u>Bernard Mandeville</u> (1974) is a good summary of his works. See also M. M. Goldsmith, <u>Private Vices, Public Benefits: Bernard Mandeville's Social and Political Thought</u> (1985) and Hector Monroe, <u>The Ambivalence of Bernard Mandeville</u> (1975).

A brief introduction to Alexander Pope is Pat Rogers, <u>An Introduction to Pope</u> (1975). Important biographies of Pope are Donald B. Clark, <u>Alexander Pope</u> (1967), Maynard Mack, <u>Alexander Pope: A Life</u> (1985). See also Peter Quennell, <u>Alexander Pope: The Education of a Genius, 1688-1728</u> (1969) Mack, <u>The Garden and the City: Retirement and Politics in the Later Poetry of Pope, 171-1743</u> (1969) and Robert Rogers, <u>The Major Satires of Alexander Pope</u> (1955). Morris R. Brownell writes about <u>Alexander Pope and the Arts of Georgian</u>

England (1978). An important guide to the world of Pope is Pope and his Contemporaries, ed. James Clifford and Louis Landa (1949) and Peter Dixon, The World of Pope's Satires (1969). For the context of Jonathan Swift see The World of Jonathan Swift, ed. B. Vickers (1968). Important biographies are John M. Murray, Swift: A Critical Biography (1956) and Irving Ehrenpreis, Swift: The Man, his Works, and the Age (3 vols. 1962-83). B. S. Goldgar, The Curse of Party: Swift's Relationships with Addison and Steele (1961) and F. P. Locke covers Swift's Tory Politics (1983) cover Swift as a political writer. See also Martin Kallich, The Other End of the Egg: Religious Satire in Gulliver's Travels (1970). Stimulating comparisons of Swift and the Duke of Marlborough are drawn in Michael Foot, The Pen and the Sword (1962). See also John F. Ross, Swift and Defoe: A Study in Relationships (1941).

David Nokes, John Gay: A Profession of Friendship (1995) and Sven Armens, John Gay, Social Critic (1954, repr. 1966) discuss the life and works of the author of the Beggar's Opera. Isaac Kramnick, Bolingbroke and his Circle: The Politics of Nostalgia in the Age of Walpole (1968) is a perceptive study of Bolingbroke's ideas and his relationship to Defoe, Mandeville, Swift, Pope, Gay, and the Commonwealthmen.

Other important authors of the Georgian age are dealt with in Harold Forster, Edward Young: The Poet of the Night Thoughts, 1683-1765 (1986), Robert Halsband, The Life of Lady Mary Wortley Montagu (1967), Isobel Grundy, Lady Mary Wortley Montagu (1999), James Sambrook, James Thomson, 1700-1748: A Life (1991), Robert Mack, Thomas Gray: A Life (2000) and Howard Gaskill, Ossian Revisited (1991). Paul J. deGategno, James Macpherson (1989) is a readable summary of his life and the influence of the Ossian poems.

Reliable biographies of Samuel Richardson are Jocelyn Harris, Samuel Richardson (1986) and T. C. D. Eaves and B. D. Kimpel, Samuel Richardson: A Biography (1971). See also Ira Konigsberg, Samuel Richardson and the Dramatic Novel (1968). Margaret Anne Doody considers, A Natural Passion: A Study of the Novels of Samuel Richardson (1974). For an introduction to the life and works of Henry Fielding see Pat Rogers: Henry Fielding, A Biography (1979). See also Martin C. Battestin and Ruth R. Battestin contribute Henry Fielding:

A Life (rev. ed., 1993). Brian McCrea covers Henry Fielding and the Politics of Mid-Eighteenth Century England (1981). See also David Nokes, Henry Fielding, Joseph Andrews (1989 and Martin Battestin, The Moral Basis of Fielding's Art: A Study of Joseph Andrews (1959). For Smollett see Louis M. Knapp, Tobias Smollett, Doctor of Men and Manners (1949) and Robert D. Spector, Tobias George Smollett (1968). George M. Kahrl, Tobias Smollett, Traveler-Novelist (1945), covers an important aspect of the novelist's life.. Arthur H. Cash, Lawrence Sterne (2 vols. 1975, 1984) is a comprehensive study. Arthur Cash considers Sterne's Comedy of Moral Sentiment: The Ethical Dimension of the Story (1966). Marion R. Small, Charlotte Ramsay Lennox, an Eighteenth-Century Lady of Letters (1960) considers an important mid-century woman novelist. A good introduction to a popular but puzzling novelist is Gerard A. Barker, Henry Mackenzie (1975). Laura Rosen considers an important topic in Infamous Commerce: Prostitution in Eighteenth-Century British Literature and Culture (2006).

Among the mass of scholarship and literary criticism on Samuel Johnson, the best place to begin is Boswell's Life, followed by Donald Greene, Samuel Johnson, Updated Edition (1989), Walter Jackson Bate, Samuel Johnson (1977), John Wain, Samuel Johnson (1974). Much new light has been shed on The Early Career of Samuel Johnson (1987) by Thomas Kaminski. Readable books for the general public are Margaret Lane, Samuel Johnson and his World (1975) and Christopher Hibbert, The Personal History of Samuel Johnson (1984). A more recent biography is Lawrence Lipking, Samuel Johnson: the Life of an Author (1998). Specialized studies are John Cannon, Samuel Johnson and the Politics of Hanoverian England (1994), Donald Greene, The Politics of Samuel Johnson (1960), and Charles E. Pierce, The Religious Life of Samuel Johnson (1983).

For the later eighteenth century, see Claire Harman, Fanny Burney: A Life (2000) and Margaret Anne Doody, Frances Burney: The Life in the Works (1985), which is primarily a literary study. Wilmarth S. Lewis, Horace Walpole (1961), is the definitive biography.

Theatre

The Cambridge History of British Theatre, Vol. 2: 1660-1895, ed. Joseph Donohue (2004) and The Cambridge Companion to British

Theatre, ed. Janet Moody and Daniel O'Quinn (2007) are good places to begin. The Cambridge Illustrated History of British Theatre (1994) ed. Simon Trussler is very enjoyable. See also Shirley Strum Kenney, British Theatre and the Other Arts, 1660-1800 (1984). Allardyce Nicholl offers a broad survey in A History of English Drama, 1660-1900 (6 vols. 1955-59). More specialized works are John Loftis, The Politics of Drama in Augustan England (1963) and Comedy and Society from Congreve to Fielding (1959). Misty Anderson, Female Playwrights and Eighteenth-Century Comedy: Negotiating Marriage on the English Stage (2002) and Lisa Freeman, Characters Theatre: Genre and Identity on the Eighteenth-Century English Stage (2002). See also J. E. Gagen, The New Woman: Her Emergence in English Drama, 1660-1730 (1954). Important aspects of the theatre are treated in Richard Altick, The Shows of London (1978) and R. Fiske, English Theatre Music in the Eighteenth Century (1973). John O'Brien deals with an important aspect of eighteenth-century theatre in Harlequin Britain: Pantomime and Entertainments, 1660-1760 (2004), as does Christopher Baugh, Theatre, Performance , and Technology (2005).

For the Restoration period see Derek Hughes, English Drama, 1660-1700 (1996) and Robert Hume, The Development of English Drama in the Later Seventeenth Century (1976). Derek Hughes, The Theatre of Aphra Behn (2001) is quite comprehensive..

Helen Koon, Colley Cibber: A Biography (1986) and Leonard R. N. Ashley, Colley Cibber (1989) are good biographies of a key figure in the English theatre in the early eighteenth century. The Provok'd Wife: The Life and Times of Susannah Cibber (1977) by Mary Nash is interesting. See also James Lynch, Box, Pit, and Gallery (1953). F. P. Locke, Susanna Centlivre (1979) is a critical study of her plays with a biographical introduction. Calhoun Winton's John Gay and the London Theatre (1993) is authoritative. Fielding's career as a playwright is examined in Robert D. Hume, Henry Fielding and the London Theatre, 1728-1737 (1988). For David Garrick, see George Winchester Stone and George M. Kahrl, David Garrick: A Critical Biography (1979) and Jean Benedetti, David Garrick and the Birth of Modern Theatre (2001). Carola Oman, David Garrick (1958) is an interesting biography. See also Cecil Price, Theatre in the Age of Garrick (1973). Jack D. Durant, Richard Brinsley Sheridan (1975) is a readable summary of his life and works. See also L. Kelly, Richard Brinsley Sheridan: A Life (1997) and John Loftis, Sheridan and the Drama of Georgian England (1977). Mark Auburn, Sheridan's Comedies: Their Context and Achievements (2001) is an important study of the man and his plays. Jane Moody examines an important outlet for imaginative playwrights in Illegitimate Theatre in London, 1770-1840 (2000). See also Daniel O'Quinn, Staging Governance: Theatrical Imperialism in London, 1770-1800 (2005).

Painting, Architecture, Sculpture

The New Grove Dictionary of Art Online (2001) and The Oxford Companion to Western Art online provide comprehensive coverage of movements and individuals. See also The Oxford History of Western Art, ed. Martin Kemp (2000), which is profusely illustrated. Arnold Hauser, The Social History of Art (4 vols. 1958) connects art with its context. An introduction to baroque architecture and art is J. Martin, Baroque (1977). A definitive work is Rudolph Wittkower, Art and Architecture in Italy, 1600-1750 1965). See also Anthony Blunt, The Painting of Nicholas Poussin: A Critical Catalog (1966).Robert Tavernor, Palladio and Palladianism (1991) is a good introduction t to the subject. A brilliant synthesis of the arts and the business of the arts in England is John Brewer, The Pleasures of the Imagination: English Culture in the 18th Century (1997).

The Tudor, Stuart, and Early Georgian Portraits in the Collection of Her Majesty the Queen (1966) and Later Georgian Portraits in the Collection of her Majesty, the Queen, ed. Oliver Millar, (2 vols., 1969) provide a good introduction to the period. The standard work on painting is Ellis K. Waterhouse, Painting Britain, 1530-1790, first published in 1953 and republished with color illustrations in 1994. Waterhouse also wrote Three Decades of British Art, 1740-1770 (1965). Margaret Whinney and Oliver Millar, English Art, 1625-1714 (1957) and Joseph Burke, English Art, 1714-1800 (1976) are solid volumes in The Oxford History of English Art. They contain many illustrative plates, although they are black and white. Richard Humphrey, Tate Britain Companion to British Art (2001) is useful.

An interesting guide to an exhibit is Oliver Millar, Sir Peter Lely, 1618-80 (1978). For an overview of English art, see Michael Foss, The

Age of Patronage: The Arts in England, 1660-1750 (1971), and Luke Hermann, British Landscape Painting of the 18th Century (1974). Judith Hook interprets the period in The Baroque Age in England (1976). See also David Irwin, English Neoclassical Art (1966) and Laurence Lipking, The Ordering of the Arts in Eighteenth Century England (1970). Mary Ede discusses Arts and Society in England under William and Mary (1979). Ronald Paulson, Hogarth (3 vols. 1991-) is the definitive work. See also Paulson's Emblem and Expression: Meaning in English Art of the Eighteenth Century (1975). For the background see Derek Jarrett, England in the Age of Hogarth (1974) and The Ingenious Mr. Hogarth (1976). Ellis Waterhouse, Reynolds (1973) covers the dominant artist of the later eighteenth century. Ann Uhry, Benjamin West and Grand Style History Painting (1985) examines an important genre of English art. See also Robert C. Alberts, Benjamin West: A Biography (1978) is a competent, readable account of his life. Grose Evans, Benjamin West and the Taste of His Times (1959) puts West in context. Profusely illustrated books on West are Helmet von Erffand and Alan Staley, The Paintings of Benjamin West (1986) and Benjamin West: American Painter at the English Court (1989), a catalog of an exhibition held at the Baltimore Museum of Arts. A biography of the other great American history painter is Emily Neff, John Singleton Copley in England (1995). Biographies of prominent painters are Ellis Waterhouse, Gainsborough (1966), Basil Taylor, Stubbs (1971), and Judy Edgerton, Wright of Derby (1990), a beautiful catalog of an exhibition at the Metropolitan Museum of Art. Benedict Nicholson, Joseph Wright of Derby: Painter of Light (2 vols. 1968) is a comprehensive study of Wright with detailed catalogs. Robert Rosenblum traces Transformations in Later Eighteenth-Century Art (1967). John Barrell, The Dark Side of the Landscape (1979) discusses Gainsborough's depictions of the poor. Margaret D. Whinney, Sculpture in Britain, 1530-1830, rev. John Physick (1988) is fundamental.

A good introduction to English architecture is Sir John Summerson, Architecture in Britain, 1530-1830 (1993). Nicholas Pevsner, The Best Buildings of England: An Anthology by Bridget Cherry and John Newman (1986) is a reworking of a classic with excellent illustrations. Sir John Summerson, Georgian London (1988) is an extensive revision of a classic by Barrie Jenkins. See also Marianne Butler, London

Architecture (2004). For the Stuart period, an important book is Kerry Downes, English Baroque Architecture (1966). There are many good books on Christopher Wren, among them Kerry Downs The Architecture of Wren (2nd ed., 1988), Margaret Whinney, Christopher Wren (1971), and The Works of Christopher Wren by Geoffrey Beard, a superb collection of illustrations. Downs has also written biographies of Sir John Vanbrugh (1987) and Hawksmoor (3rd. ed., 1996). Other biographies are Sir John Summerson, Inigo Jones (2000) and Terry Friedman, James Gibbs (1984). John Harris, The Palladians (1981) is a well-illustrated survey of prominent and less-prominent architects.

Michael Nicholson surveys Great Houses of Britain (1968). John Harris covers a broader scope than suggested by the title of The Palladian Revival: Lord Burlington, his Villa and Garden at Chiswick (1994). Michael I. Wilson examines the various talents of William Kent: Architect, Designer, Painter, Gardener, 1685-1748 (1984). See also Christopher Hussey, English Gardens and Landscapes, 1700-1750 (1967) and Edward Hyams, Capability Brown and Humphrey Repton (1971).

D. Stillman, English Neo-classical Architecture (2 vols. 1988) and John Harris, Sir William Chambers: Knight of the Polar Star (1970) cover the neoclassical dimension of eighteenth-century architecture. See also Sir William Chambers: Architect to George III (1991) ed. John Harris and Michael Snodin. J. Lees-Milne, The Age of Adam (1947) is a good survey of the life and work of Robert Adam. Good biographies are Doreen Yarwood, Robert Adam (1970) and J. Bryant, Robert Adam, 1728-1792: Architect of Genius (1992). G. Beard, The Works of Robert Adam (1978) and J. Rykwerst and A. Rykwert, Robert and James Adam: The Men and the Style (1985), are excellent. See also G. Beard, Craftsmen and Interior Decorators in England, 1660-1820 (1981).

Two influential books are John Dixon Hunt, The Figure in the Landscape (1976) and The Genius of the Place: The English Landscape Garden, 1620-1820 (1992). See also Olive Cook, The English Country House (1974) and Mark Girouard, Life in the English Country House: A Social and Architectural History (1978).

A History of Scottish Architecture from the Renaissance to the Present Day (1996) by Miles Glendenning, Ronald MacInnes, and Angus MacKechnie is a well-illustrated survey with a strong chapter on the work of the Adam brothers in Scotland and the eighteenth-century architecture of Edinburgh. Walter Ison, <u>The Georgian Buildings of Bath from 1700 to 1830</u> (1980) is a well-illustrated survey.

For a survey of English sculpture see Margaret Whinney, <u>Sculpture in Britain, 1550-1830</u> (1964). See M. I. Webb, <u>Michael Rysbrack</u> (1954)

Music

The standard reference work for music is <u>Groves Dictionary of Music and Musicians</u> (many editions), which is now available in the much improved <u>New Groves Dictionary of Music and Musicians</u> (2nd ed., 29 vols. 2001). A companion work is <u>The New Groves Dictionary of Opera</u> (1992). John Caldwell, <u>The Oxford History of English Music</u> is a good reference work. <u>Vol. I: From the Beginnings to 1715</u> (19991) has a chapter on the later Stuart period. <u>Vol II: From c. 1715 to the Present Day</u> (1999) has a chapter on Handel and his contemporaries and a chapter on music after 1760. There are many good histories of Western music. <u>The New Oxford History of Music</u> (10 vols.) includes VI: <u>Concert Music, 1630-1750</u>, ed. Gerald Abraham (1986) and VII: The <u>Age of Enlightenment</u>, ed Egon Wellesz and Frederick Sternfeld (1973). Another reliable survey is <u>The Blackwell History of Music in Britain: The Seventeenth Century</u>, ed. Ian Spink (1992) and <u>The Eighteenth Century</u>, ed. H. Diak Johnstone and Roger Fiske (1990). Good general histories are Percy M. Young, <u>A History of British Music</u> (1967) and <u>A History of Western Music</u> (6th ed., 2001) by Donald Jay Grout and Claude V. Palisco.

<u>Late Renaissance and Baroque Music</u> by Alex Harman (1959) is an important work. M. Anderson, <u>Baroque Music from Monteverdi to Handel</u> (1994) is a comprehensive study. John Harley has written <u>Music in Purcell's London: The Social Background</u> (1968). A valuable biography is Maureen Duffy, <u>Henry Purcell</u> (1995). See also Paul Palisco, <u>Baroque Music</u> (2nd ed., 1981), a musicological study of selected works, and William S. Newman, <u>The Sonata in the Classic Era</u> (1963). "The Composer," by Paul Henry Lang in <u>Man versus Society in Eighteenth Century Britain</u>, ed. James Clifford (1968) is a stimulating synthesis. Music at the end of the century is discussed in Asa Briggs,

English Musical Culture, 1776-1876 (1977). Michael Burden is preparing a book on the staging of opera in London, 1660-1860.

Music in the later part of the eighteenth century is described in Percy A. Scholes, The Great Dr. Burney: His Life, His Travels, His Works, His Family, and his Friends (2 vols., 1948). Other interesting biographies are Donald Brown, Handel (1993), Christopher Hogwood, Handel (2007), and H. C. Robbins Landon, Handel and his World (1984). Paul Henry Lang, George Frideric Handel (1966) is a profound study of Handel's place in the history of music, which has much of value concerning the period. On the violin, see David Boyden, History of Violin Playing From its Origins to 1761 (1965). See also Marc Pincherle, Corelli: His Life, His Works (19799) and E. Careri, Francesco Geminiani (1687-1762 (1993) a biography of the violinist.

INDEX OF INDIVIDUALS

Abel, Karl Friedrich (1723-1787), composer, musical impresario

Adam, James (1732-1794), architect with Robert Adam

Adam, Robert (1728-1792), architect

Addison, Joseph (1672-1719), journalist, playwright

Anne (1665-1714), Queen who ruled 1702-1714

Arkwright, Richard (1732-1792), early industrialist

Arne, Thomas (1710-1778), composer of theatre music

Astell, Mary (1666-1731), feminist writer

Avison, Charles (1710-1770), composer; writer on music

Bach, Johann Christian (1735-1782), composer

Bach, Johann Sebastic (1685-1750), composer

Baker, Thomas (1681-?), minor playwright, founded The Female Tatler (1709)

Barry, Elizabeth (1658-1713), greatest tragic actress of her time

Bacon, Sir Francis (1561-1626), advocate of empiricism

Behn, Aphra (1640-1689), playwright, novelist

Bering, Vitus (1681-1741), explored N. Pacific; discovered Bering Strait

Bernini, Gianlorenzo (1598-1680), baroque architect and sculptor.

Betterton, Thomas (d. 1710), actor of the Restoration era.

Bickerstaff, Isaac (1733-?), writer of musical comedies.

Boerhaave, Herman (1668-1738), Dutch physician

Blackstone, Sir William (1723-1780), summarized the Common Law

Boileau-Despreaux, Nicholas (1636-1711), French critic and advocate of classicism

Bolingbroke, Henry St. John, Viscount (1678-1751), Tory politician and writer

Bononcini, Giovanni (1642-78), compose of sonatas

Boswell, James (1740-1795), biographer of Samuel Johnson

Boucher, François (1703-1770), French rococo painter

Bougainville, Louis Antoine (1729-1811), French explorer of S. Pacific

Boulton, Matthew (1728-1809), Birmingham manufacturer

Boyce, William (1711-1779), organist, composer

Boyle, Robert (1627-1694), founder of scientific Chemistry

Bracegirdle, Anne (1671-1748), actress

Braddock, Gen. Edward (1695-1755), British commander ambushed by French and Indians

Bray, Thomas (1658-1730), founder of SPCK and SPG

Bridgewater, Francis Edgerton, Third Duke of (1736-1803), canal builder.

Brindley, James (1716-1772), canal designer

Brown, Lancelot "Capability" (1716-1783), landscape gardener

Brydges, James, Duke of Chandos (1674-1741), patron of the arts

Buck, Samuel ((1696-1779), topographical engraver

Buckingham, George Villiers, Duke of (1628-1687), politician, author of The Rehearsal

Bunyan, John (1628-1688), Dissenting writer

Burke, Edmund (1729-1797), politician, reformer, Conservative

Burlington, Dorothy Boyle, Countess of (1690-1758), wife of Richard

Burlington, Richard Boyle, Earl of (1694-1752), advocate of Palladianism

Burnet, Gilbert (1643-1715), political bishop, historian

Burney, Charles (1726-1814), musician

Burney, Frances (1752-1840), novelist

Bute, John Stuart, Earl of (1713-1792), adviser of George III; prime minister, 1762-1763

Cabot, John (1450-1498), Italian sailor; explored northern coasts of North America

Cadell, Thomas (1742-1802), publisher

Calvin, John (1500-1564), French leader of the Reformation

Campbell, Colen (1676-1729), Palladian architect

Carey, Henry (1687-1743), composer of theatre music

"Canaletto", Giovanni Canal (1696-1762), painter of scenes of London

Caroline of Ansbach (1683-1737), Queen to George II

Carter, Elizabeth (1717-1806), poet, scholar

Carteret, John, Earl Granville (1690-1763), opponent of Walpole

Cartwright, Major John (1740-1824), advocate of parliamentary reform

Catherine of Braganza (1638-1705), Queen of Charles II

Cato the Younger (d. 46 b. c.), Roman politician; opponent of Caesar

Cave, Edward (1691-1754), founder of the Gentleman's Magazine

Cavendish, Lady Margaret (1623-1673), aristocratic writer

Centlivre, Susannah (169?-1723), actress, playwright

Chambers, Sir William (1722-1797), architect

Charles I (1600-1647), King 1625-1647

Charles II (1630-1685), King, 1660-1685

Charlotte of Mecklenburg-Strelitz (1744-1818), Queen to George III

Cherbury, Lord Edward Herbert (1582-1648), Latitudinarian writer

Cheselden, William (1688-1752), anatomist, surgeon

Chesterfield, Philip Dormer Stanhope, Earl of (1694-1773), politician, writer

Cheselden, William (1688-1752), anatomist, surgeon

Chippendale, Thomas (1718-1779), furniture designer

Cibber, Colley (1671-1757), comedian, playwright, theatre manager

Cibber, Susannah (1714-1766), singer, actress

Clarendon, Sir Edward Hyde, Earl of (1609-1674), adviser to Charles II

Clarkson, Thomas (1760-1846), anti-slavery campaigner

Clayton, Thomas (1666-1720), composer of English opera

Clive, Kitty (1711-1785), actress

Cobham, Sir Richard Temple, Viscount (1675-1749), opponent of Walpole; developed Stowe

Coke, Sir Edward (1552-1634), Chief Justice; opposed royal interference with the Common Law courts

Colbert, Jean-Baptiste (1619-1683), economic minister of Louis XIV

Collier, Jeremy (1650-1726), critic of the immorality of the stage

Columbus, Christopher (1451-1506), Italian explorer; sailed the Atlantic to the New World

Congreve, William (1670-1729), playwright

Cook, James (1728-1779), sea-captain; explored Pacific Ocean

Copernicus, Nicholas (1473-1543), heliocentric theory of the solar system

Copley, John Singleton (1738-1815), history painter

Coram, Capt. Thomas (1668-1751), led in establishment of Foundling Hospital

Corelli, Arcangelo (1653-1713), violinist, composer of violin music

Cornwallis, Charles (1738-1805), British general trapped at Yorktown

Cortez, Hernando (1485-1547), Spanish conqueror of Mexico

Couperin, François (1688-1733), composer of keyboard music

Cowley, Hannah Parkhouse (1748-1809), playwright

Crabbe, George (1754-1832), clergyman, poet

Cranmer, Thomas (1489-1553), Archbishop of Canterbury; promoted the Reformation

Da Gama, Vasco (1460-1524), Portuguese explorer; sailed around Africa to India

D'Alembert, Jean le Ronde (1717-1783), French mathematician and scientist; edited articles on math and science for the Encyclopédie

Dampier, William (1652-1715), explorer of the Pacific Ocean

D'Anville, Jean B. (1697-1782), French cartographer

Darby, Abraham (1677-1717), ironmaster; smelted iron with coke

Davenant, Sir William (1606-1688), theatre manager

Defoe, Daniel (1660-1731), journalist, novelist

DeLisle, Guillaume (1675-1726), French cartographer

Devis, Arthur (1712-1787), painter of conversation pieces

Diderot, Denis (1713-1784), editor of the Encyclopédie

Dodsley, Robert (1704-64), bookseller, publisher

Dolben, Sir William (1727-1814), proposed reform of slave ships

Dryden, John (1631-1700), poet, dramatist, translator

Duhalde, Pierre, published accounts of Jesuit missionaries in China

Eccles, John (1668-1735), theatre composer

Edward VI (1537-1553), boy king, 1547-1553; promoted the Reformation

Elizabeth I (1533-1603), Queen of England, 1558-1603; restored Protestantism

Erasmus, Desiderius (1466-1536), Dutch Christian humanist scholar

Farquhar, George (1678-1707), playwright

Ferguson, Adam (1723-1816), Scottish social scientist

Fielding, Henry (1707-1754), playwright, journalist, novelist, magistrate

Fielding, Sarah (1710-1768), novelist

Fiennes, Celia (1662-1741), traveler

Flamsteed, John (1646-1719), astronomer

Franklin, Benjamin (1706-1790), demonstrated that lightning is electricity

Frederick II (1712-1786), King of Prussia, 1774-1786

Gainsborough, Thomas (1727-1788), painter of portraits, landscapes

Galen (second century a. d.), Greek physician; wrote on medicine.

Galileo Galilei (1564-1642), showed that celestial and terrestrial matter are the same

Garrick, David (1717-1779), actor, theatre manager

Gay, John (1685-1732), poet, The Beggar's Opera

Geminiani, Francesco (1687-1762), violinist

George I (1660-1727), ruled, 1714-1727

George II (1683-1760), ruled 1727-1760

George III (1738-1820), ruled, 1760-1820

Gibbon, Edward 1737-1794), historian

Gibbons, Grinling (1648-1721), woodcarver

Gibbs, James (1682-1754), architect

Gibbs, Joseph (1699-1788), organist, composer for the violin

Gibson, Edmund (1669-1748), Bishop of London, supported Hanoverian monarchy

Gideon, Samson (1699-1762), Jewish financier

Goldsmith, Oliver (1728-1774), poet, novelist, playwright

Gordon, Lord George (1751-1793), led anti-Catholic riots in London

Grasse, François, Comte de (1723-1788), French admiral.

Gray, Thomas (1716-1771), poet, scholar

Guy, Thomas (1645-1724), founder of Guy's Hospital

Gwyn, Nell (1650-1687), actress; mistress of Charles II

Handel, George Frideric (1685-1759), composer

Hart, Emma, Lady Hamilton (1761-1815), famous beauty; model for Romney; m. Lord Hamilton; mistress of Adm. Nelson

Harvey, William (1578-1657), demonstrated the circulation of the blood

Hawksmoor, Nicholas (1661-1736), architect

Haydn, Franz Joseph (1732-1809), classical composer

Hayman, Francis (1708-1776), painter

Haywood, Eliza (1693-1756), playwright, novelist, journalist

Henrietta Maria (1609-1669), Charles I's Queen; fled to France

Henry VI (1457-1509), first Tudor king, 1485-1509; stabilized England

Henry VIII (1491-1547), King, 1509-47; ended papal authority over the Church in England

Herschel, William (1738-1822), musician, astronomer

Hoadly, Benjamin (1676-1761), controversial bishop

Hogarth, William (1697-1764), engraver, painter

Hooke, Robert (1635-1703), development of the microscope

Howard, John (1726-1790), prison reformer

Hume, David (1711-1776), philosopher, historian

Hunter, William (1718-83), anatomist, man-midwife

James I (1566-1625), King of Scotland; first Stuart king of England, 1603-1625

James II (1633-1701), King, 1685-1688

James Francis Edward Stuart (1688-1766)), son of James II; known as "the Old Pretender"

Jefferys, Thomas (1719-1771), cartographer

Jenner, Edward (1749-1823), physician; developed vaccination for smallpox.

Johnson, Joseph (1738-1809), radical publisher

Johnson, Samuel (1709-1784), writer, critic

Jones, Inigo (1572-1652), architect; advocated classicism

Jonson, Ben (1572-1637), poet, playwright

Jurin, James (1684-1750), physician; urged study of weather

Kemble, John Philip (1757-1823), actor, brother of Sarah Siddons

Kennett, White (1660-1728), historian

Kent, William (1686-1748), artist, landscape architect

Kepler, Johannes (1571-1630), astronomer

Killegrew, Thomas (1612-1683), theatre manager, playwright

Kneller, Sir Godfrey (1664-1723), portrait painter

Laud, William (1573-1645), Archbishop of Canterbury; opposed Puritanism

Le Brun, Charles (1619-1690), neoclassical French painter

Lely, Peter (1618-1689), portrait painter

Lennox, Charlotte (1731-1804), writer

Le Vau, Louis (1612-1670), French architect

Linley, Elizabeth (1754-1792), singer.

Linley, Thomas Jr. (1756-1778)), violinist, composer

Locke, John (1632-1704), philosopher

Louis XIV (1643-1715), King of France

Lully, Jean-Baptiste (1662-1687), led music at Court of Louis XIV

Luther, Martin (1483-1546), German monk; began the Reformation

Macaulay, Catherine Sawbridge (1731-1791), historian, radical writer

Mackenzie, Henry (1745-1831), novelist

Macpherson, James (1736-1796), published poems of Ossian

Magellan, Ferdinand (1480-1546), Portuguese explorer; his expedition circumnavigates the world.

Mandeville, Bernard (1670-1733), philosopher of self-interest

Manley, Delarivier (c 1670-1724), journalist, playwright, novelist

Mansart, Jules Hardouin (1646-1708), French architect

Mansfield, William Murray (1705-1793), Chief Justice of Court of King's Bench.

Marlborough, John Churchill, Duke of (1650-1722), commander of allied forces in the War of the Spanish Succession

Marie Antoinette (1755-1793), Queen of Louis XVI, executed 1793

Marlborough, Sarah, Duchess of (1660-1744), wife of the Duke; mistress of Blenheim Palace

Mary I (1516-1558), Queen, 1553-1558; restored Catholicism

Mary II (1662-1694), Queen; ruled 1689-1694

Mary Beatrice of Modena (1658-1718), Queen of James II

Matteis, Nichola (fl. 1670-1698), Italian violinist and violin teacher

Mercator, Gerardus (1512-1594), Flemish cartographer

Millar, Andrew (1705-1768), Scottish publisher

Millar, John (1735-1801), Scottish sociologist

Moll, Herman (1654-1732), cartographer

Monck, George (1608-1670), Puritan general; initiated the Restoration

Montagu, Elizabeth (1718-1800), bluestocking hostess

Montcalm, Louis Joseph, Marquis de (1712-1759), French commander at Quebec

More, Hannah (1745-1833), evangelical reformer

Mozart, Leopold (1719-1787), teacher of the violin

Mozart, Wolfgang Amadeus (1756-1791), classical composer

Nash, Richard Beau (1674-1761), master of ceremonies at Bath

Neild, James (1744-1814), advocate of prison reform

Newcastle, Thomas Pelham-Hollis, Duke of (1693-1768), Whig politician, first lord of the treasury in the Seven Years War

Newton, Sir Isaac (1642-1727), mathematician, physicist

Newton, John (1725-1807), clergyman; anti-slavery activist

Nollekens, Joseph (1737-1823), portrait sculptor

North, Frederick Lord (1732-1793), prime minister during American Revolution

James Oglethorpe (1696-1785), philanthropist; founder of Georgia

Otway, Thomas (1652-1685), playwright

Oxford, Robert Harley, Earl of (1661-1724), politician

Paine, Thomas (1737-1809), revolutionary writer

Paley, William (1743-1805), Anglican theologian

Palestrina, Giovanni Pierluigi da (1526-1594), Renaissance composer

Palladio, Andreas (1508-1580), Italian architect; noted for classicism

Pemberton, Henry (1694-1771), prepared book of prescriptions

Pepusch, Johann Christophe (1667-1752), German immigrant musician

Pepys, Samuel (1633-1703), naval administrator, diarist

Percy, Thomas (1729-1811), published old English poems and ballads

Perrault, Charles (1628-1703), provoked "the quarrel of the ancients and the moderns"

Perrault, Claude (1613-1685), French architect

Philip V (1683-1746), grandson of Louis XIV; became King of Spain

Philip, Arthur (1738-1814), naval officer; first governor of Australia

Pitt, William, the Elder (1708-1781), leader in Seven Years War

Pitt, William, the Younger (1759-1806), prime minister under George III

Pizarro, Francisco (1471-1541), Spanish conqueror of Peru

Pope, Alexander (1688-1744), poet

Poussin, Nicholas (1594-1665), French neoclassical painter

Pringle, Sir John (1707-82), army physician

Pulteney, William, Earl of Bath (1684-1764), opponent of Walpole

Purcell, Henry (1659-1695), musician, composer

Raikes, Robert (1735-1811), Sunday schools for poor children

Rameau, Jean-Philippe (1683-1764), French composer, theory of harmony

Ramsay, Allan (1684-1758), Scottish poet

Ramsay, Allan (1713-1784), portrait painter, son of the above

Rembrandt (1606-1669), Dutch painter

Reynolds, Sir Joshua (1723-1792), portrait painter

Richardson, Jonathan (1667-1745), portrait painter

Richardson, Samuel (1689-1761), printer, novelist

Robertson, William (1721-1793), Scottish historian

Rochambeau, Compte de (1725-1807), commander of French troops at Yorktown

Rockingham, Charles Watson-Wentworth, Marquis of (1730-1782), Whig leader in opposition to George III

Romilly, Sir Samuel (1757-1818), worked for reform of criminal law

Romney, George (1734-1802), painter of high-society portraits

Roubiliac, Louis François (1702-1762), sculptor

Rowe, Nicholas (1674-1718), playwright, Shakespeare editor

Rubens, Peter Paul (1577-1640), Flemish baroque painter

Rysbrack, Michael (1694-1770), sculptor

Sancroft, William (1617-1693), Archbishop of Canterbury; defied James II

Scarlatti, Alessandro (1660-1725), composer of operas.

Scarlatti, Domenico (1685-1757), composer of keyboard sonatas

Secker, Thomas (1693-1768), Archbishop of Canterbury, 1758-68

Shadwell, Thomas (1640-1692), playwright, poet laureate

Shaftesbury, Anthony Ashley Cooper, First Earl of (1621-1683), Whig opponent of Charles II

Shaftesbury, Anthony Ashley Cooper, Third Earl of (1671-1713), moral philosopher

Shakespeare, William (1564-1616), Elizabethan/Jacobean dramatist

Sharp, Granville (1735-1813), anti-slavery campaigner

Sheridan, Frances (1724-1766), novelist, dramatist

Sheridan, Richard Brinsley (1751-1816), playwright, politician

Shirley, William (1694-1771), Governor of Massachusetts who led in the capture of Louisbour in 1745.

Siddons, Sarah (1755-1831), actress

Smellie, William (1697-1763), man-midwife

Smith, Adam (1723-1790), moral philosopher, economist

Smith, Charlotte (1749-1806), poet, novelist

Smith, Joseph (1673-1770), English consul in Venice and art collector

Smollett, Tobias (1721-1771), novelist, journalist, historian

Southerne, Thomas (1660-1746), playwright

Sprat, Thomas (1635-1713), historian of the Royal Society

Steele, Richard (1672-1729), journalist, playwright

Sterne, Laurence (1712-1768), novelist

Stubbs, George (1724-1806), painter of horses, rural landscapes

Swift, Jonathan (1667-1745), journalist, writer of satires

Sydenham, Thomas (1624-1689, physician

Tasman, Abel (1603-1659), Dutch explorer; discovered Tasmania

Temple, Sir William (1628-1699), diplomat; defended the ancients in "the quarrel between the ancients and the moderns"

Theobald, Lewis (1688-1744), editor of plays of Shakespeare

Thornton, John (720-1790), evangelical philanthropist

Tillotson, John, (1639-1694), latitudinarian bishop

Thomson, James (1700-1748), poet

Thornhill, Sir James (1675-1734), history painter

Tofts, Catherine (d. 1756), opera singer

Tonson, Jacob (1655-1730), bookseller, publisher

Tooke, John Horne (1736-1812), radical agitator

Tyers, Jonathan (1702-1767), proprietor of Spring/Vauxhall Gardens

Valentine, Robert (1674-1731?), violinist

Vanbrugh, Sir John (1664-1726), playwright, architect

Van Dyck, Sir Anthony (1599-1641), portrait painter

Vertue, George (1684-1756), engraver

Villiers, George, Duke of Buckingham (1628-1687), courtier, politician, author of The Rehearsal (1671)

Vivaldi, Antonio (1678-1741), violinist, composer

Voltaire, François-Marie Arouet (1694-1778), French philosophe.

Wales, Frederick Lewis, Prince of (1707-1751), son of George II and Queen Charlotte; father of George III

Walpole, Sir Robert (1676-1745), Whig prime minister

Walpole, Horace (1717-1797), Gothic novel; architecture

Ward, Joshua (1684-1761), quack doctor

Washington, George (1732-1799), commander of Continental Army

Watt, James (1736-1819), developed improved steam engine

Watteau, Jean-Antoine (1684-1721), French rococo painter

Watts, Isaac (1674-1748), hymn writer

Wedgwood, Josiah (1730-1795), pottery manufacturer

Wesley, Charles (1707-1788), brother of John Wesley; hymn writer

Wesley, John (1703-1791), founder, leader of Methodism

West, Benjamin (1738-1820), history painter

White, Kennnett (1660-1728), historian

Whitefield, George (1714-1770), evangelist

Whitney, Eli (1765-1825), invented cotton gin

Wilberforce, William (1759-1833), evangelical; anti-slavery leader

Wilkes, John (1727-1797), radical agitator

Wilkinson, John (1728-1808), ironmaster

William III (1650-1702), King of England, Scotland, Ireland, 1689-1702

Wilson, Richard (1713-1782), landscape painter

Woffington, Margaret (1720-1760), actress

Wolfe, James (1727-1729), captured Quebec, killed on battlefield

Wood, John (1704-1754), Bath architect

Wollstonecraft, Mary (1759-1797), radical writer

Wortley Montagu, Lay Mary (1689-1762), travel writer

Wotton, William (1666-1727), defended the moderns in "the quarrel between the ancients and the moderns"

Wren, Sir Christopher (1632-1723), architect

Wright, Joseph (1734-1797), painter of industrial scenes

Wycherley, William (1641-1716), playwright

Wyvill, Christopher (1740-1822), economical reform leader

Young, Edward (1683-1765), poet

Zoffany, Johan (1733-1810), painter

ABOUT THE AUTHOR

Prof. Earl A. Reitan was born in Grove City, Minnesota in 1925, and graduated in 1942 from Alberta High School, Alberta MN..He served in World War II as a combat rifleman in France, where he was wounded. After the war he received the Bachelor of Arts degree from Concordia College, Moorhead Minnesota (1948) and the Masters Degree and Ph. D. from the University of Illinois, Urbana (1954). In that year, he joined the History Department at Illinois State University, Normal. He is now Prof. Emeritus of History. He is married, and has two children and two grandchildren.

Prof. Reitan is the author of George III: Tyrant or Constitutional Monarch? (1964), Politics, War, and Empire: The Rise of Britain to a World Power (1994), and co-author of The English Heritage (2 vols. 3rd. edition, 1999). His other books include The Thatcher Revolution: Margaret Thatcher, John Major, Tony Blair and the Transformation of Modern Britain, 1979-2001 (2003) and Liberalism: Time-Tested Principles for the Twenty-First Century (2004). His most recent book is Politics, Finance and the People: Economical Reform in England in the Age of the American Revolution, 1770-92 (2007).